Studies in Rhetorics and Feminisms

Series Editors, Cheryl Glenn and Shirley Wilson Logan

Rethinking Ethos

A Feminist Ecological Approach to Rhetoric

Edited by Kathleen J. Ryan, Nancy Myers, and Rebecca Jones

Southern Illinois University Press
Carbondale

Southern Illinois University Press
www.siupress.com

Copyright © 2016 by the Board of Trustees,
Southern Illinois University

Cover illustration: photograph by Jennifer Rains Jones

Library of Congress Cataloging-in-Publication Data
Names: Ryan, Kathleen J., 1968– editor. | Myers, Nancy, 1955–
editor. | Jones, Rebecca, 1973– editor.
Title: Rethinking ethos : a feminist ecological approach to rhetoric
/ edited by Kathleen J. Ryan, Nancy Myers, and Rebecca Jones.
Description: Carbondale : Southern Illinois University Press,
2016. | Series: Studies in Rhetorics and Feminisms | Includes
bibliographical references and index.
Identifiers: LCCN 2015036755| ISBN 9780809334940 (paperback)
| ISBN 9780809334957 (e-book)
Subjects: LCSH: Rhetoric—Social aspects. | Women—Language.
| Ecocriticism. | Feminism and literature. | Women's studies. |
Rhetorical criticism. | BISAC: LANGUAGE ARTS & DISCIPLINES /
Rhetoric. | SOCIAL SCIENCE / Women's Studies.
Classification: LCC P301.5.S63 R45 2016 | DDC 808—dc23 LC
record available at http://lccn.loc.gov/2015036755

Printed on recycled paper. ♻

Contents

Contents

Preface

This collection represents our effort to disrupt everyday definitions of *ethos* as "credibility" or "character." Ethos has been a fundamental term in rhetorical studies for centuries, and this collection rethinks it to create more ways for women to enter and shift dominant public discourse. It is a commonplace among feminist rhetoricians to acknowledge that women—particularly those who are not white, middle class, and heterosexual—face countless challenges in constructing an authoritative Aristotelian ethos "outside their home community" (Pittman 47). Krista Ratcliffe's observation in *Rhetorical Listening* is also suggestive of the difficulties women face in constructing ethos. She contends, "reducing *ethos* to individual ethical appeal is metonymically linked to a rugged-individualist ideology" (124). By extension, "the reduced *ethos* of the rugged individualist in rhetorical theory translates as the reduced *ethos* of the rugged white male individualist" (124). In other words, women are often being asked to adopt a troublesome ethos, whether they try to use an Aristotelian ethos or a common, contemporary rendering of ethos. Even as privileged white women, we find this observation consistent with our experiences, and we feel a responsibility to interrogate it. We are compelled, then, to ask how else have, do, and might women compose their ethos? By focusing on ethos, we highlight a complex issue: the cultural, historical, and social positions that restrain and invigorate women's rhetorical prospects as agentive rhetors. Ultimately, we offer a description of women's ethos construction as an ecological habit of mind that rethinks scholarship on ethos to advocate for new theories that start with feminist philosophical and rhetorical interpretations of women's rhetorical experiences.

In assembling past research and examining submissions to the collection, the three of us recognized that women often enact ecological thinking as a matter of course, as a way of negotiating the world as a historically margin-alized yet diverse group. Ecological thinking, of course, is not new, nor is it restricted to women. As we explain in the introduction, ecological thinking is a habit of mind that takes into consideration the entire ecology of a given rhetorical situation. The rhetor accounts for her subject position relative to others, as well as the shifting material, cultural, and historical situations cir-culating around rhetorical acts. This approach is an ethical stance we observe women rhetors embracing or enacting repeatedly across time and in different situations when they enter public discourses. As such, our concerns about ethos evolved into the following questions for a contemporary feminist dis-cussion of women's ethos: what does it mean to act in the world as a woman, a feminist, an ecological thinker? How are these positions or mindsets related? What are their rhetorical, ethical, and material consequences?

The collection's title, *Rethinking Ethos: A Feminist Ecological Approach to Rhetoric*, captures these lines of inquiry, focusing on women's public speech (whether they consider themselves feminist or not) as they grapple with living in the world. By women, we always mean to imply a diversity of women (i.e., women of diverse race, ethnicity, religion, class, sex, and age) who nonethe-less share a history of oppression under patriarchy. The subtitle points to our methodology and observations. *Feminist* highlights a diversity of theoretical practices that work toward equality for women and other marginalized peo-ples. As we have suggested, *ecological* describes a model of thinking and acting in the world. Particularly, we have observed that women value this thinking as they act to connect the relations, locations, and dynamism that compose their ethos. Rather than referring to our *approach* as a new paradigm, we think of it as an imaginary, "a loosely integrated system of images, metaphors, tacit assumptions, ways of thinking" (Code 29). Imaginaries are more flexible and open systems than paradigms and better account for the artful nature of this work. By naming women's ethos practices as feminist ecological ethē, we shift away from an Aristotelian framework toward a conceptualization of women's ethos that accounts in new ways for interrelationality, materiality, and agency. The introduction, "Identifying Feminist Ecological Ethē," de-scribes and defines feminist ecological ethē.

Evidence of this approach in the collection ranges from historical to con-temporary women, from the writing classroom to case studies, from scientists to political activists, and extends to queer theory, transnational feminism, radical feminism, indigenous perspectives, and Chicana feminism. This range requires us to talk about ethos in the plural, as ethē. While there is no singular women's ethos, we observe that rhetorical strategies of feminist ecological ethē fall into a few descriptive categories: interruption, advocacy, and relation. The borders between these categories blur, and this collection highlights those distinctions. Each section opens with a discussion of the key concept. This brief discussion is followed by a chapter by an established scholar and then chapters by newer scholars taking up a range of innovative subjects. Hopefully, each section provokes thought and conversation across chapters and between sections for the different ways they take up interruption, advocacy, and relation, in conjunction with other ways the chapters may be understood and organized. Given that we are three professional women who identify as white, these chapters have asked us to consider our own rhetorical strategies and our attendant privileges in negotiating ethos in public conversations. The chapters' insights necessitate that we shift our daily communications, reconsider our teaching practices, and more clearly articulate our positions, relations, and commitments.

The chapters in the first section, "Ethē as Interruption-Interrupting," explore women rhetors' efforts to use rhetorical maneuvers to interrupt historical and contemporary normative discourses about women's bodies and minds and change discursive habits. In "A Reformer Rides: Radical Photographic Ethos in Frances E. Willard's *A Wheel within a Wheel*," Kristie S. Fleckenstein studies the six halftone illustrations in Willard's fin-de-siècle cycling memoir to construct a radical photographic ethos that promotes authority and emancipation as desirable virtues for women. Fleckenstein reveals how the first image of Willard as True Woman is disrupted by the five additional images that reconstruct Willard as a New Woman. Fleckenstein resituates two distinct patriarchal practices of ethos formation, Isocratean reputation and Aristotelian situation, to establish women's authority in the polis through spatial emancipation. Valerie Palmer-Mehta's "Andrea Dworkin's Radical Ethos" discusses the ways Dworkin defies most conventions of the public speech genre, especially finding common ground or avoiding angering audiences. Palmer-Mehta argues that Dworkin adopts a "politics of confrontation" as an ethos to force audiences, both men and women, to confront their complicity in women's oppression. In "The Unavailable Means of Persuasion: A Queer Ethos for Feminist Writers and Teachers," Stacey Waite queers the common acceptance of Aristotle's claim that rhetoric is discovering "the available means of persuasion." Waite imagines the possibilities for teaching a queer ethos that disrupts normative ways of looking and static notions of time and place. The final chapter in this section, "Changing Audience, Changing Ethos," by

Beth Daniell and Letizia Guglielmo, briefly outlines historical challenges to women's political speech and observes how digital spaces facilitate contemporary women rhetors' opportunities to disrupt normative political discourses. Daniell and Guglielmo argue that contemporary women use Web 2.0 technologies to circumvent normative discourses attempting to silence them and respond to such efforts with diverse, dispersed, and sometimes temporary ethē.

The chapter authors in the second section, "Ethē as Advocacy-Advocating," use writing (from letters to memoirs) and public performance as avenues for their analyses, and they also highlight unusual rhetorical maneuvers such as sharing a meal or reclaiming stereotypes as ways that women advocate for themselves and others. In "Ethos as a Social Act: The 'Unauthorized' Susanna Wesley," Lynée Lewis Gaillet examines how Wesley negotiates an ethos of advocacy within the patriarchal religious system and social domains of seventeenth-century Britain to subtly shape the roles of Methodist women. Wesley challenges prevailing notions about women preaching and defends her right to speak using both forceful and conciliatory letters, even as she influences her local Christian community through personal prayer and guidance as a mother and community leader. In "Hospitality as Kenosis: Dorothy Day's Voluntary Poverty," Sean Barnette argues that Day's material practice of hospitality allows her to deploy an ethos of kenosis, a giving up or sharing of power through the Christian practice of "self-emptying," to advocate alongside others. Barnette reclaims hospitality as a complex ethotic act through a study of Day's material practices. In "Powerlessness Repurposed: The Feminist Ethos of Judy Bonds," Mary Beth Pennington studies Bonds's construction of her "Hillbilly Moses" ethos to fight mountaintop removal in Appalachia. Pennington argues that Bonds's campaign to protect the land and the people of Appalachia operates as a "rhetorical blueprint" for helping environmental activists use feminist ethos-building strategies to negotiate the relationships between a disadvantaged rhetor and diverse, often more powerful, audiences. Paige A. Conley, in "Strategically Negotiating Essence: Zitkala-Ša's Ethos as Activist," describes the ways Zitkala-Ša constructs a multiple, shifting ethos. Conley emphasizes how Zitkala-Ša uses stereotypes of Native Americans, particularly "playing Indian," to cater to white audience expectations as a rhetorical maneuver to advocate for her home community. These women rhetors take seriously their roles as advocates and, consistent with a feminist ecological imaginary, consider the ethical consequences of their choices.

The chapters in the third section, "Ethē as Relation-Relating," explore all manner of relations, from transnational women's alliances to the quiet of a woman's breath in a yoga studio and from scientific collaborations between women to contested borderlands. In "Ethos Righted: Transnational Feminist Analytics," Wendy S. Hesford argues that transnational feminist alliances compel a more robust theory of ethos that dislodges ethos from its moorings in liberal notions of the public sphere and attends to the asymmetrical terrain of international politics. Risa Applegarth looks at the collaborative challenges between two women anthropologists with different understandings of power, professional voice, and intellectual property that call up ethical distinctions between "working *with*" and "working *for*." "Working With and Working For: Ethos and Power in Women's Writing" articulates ethos as a product of a writer's positioning within material, social, and symbolic locations. In "Creating Contemplative Spaces: Ethos as Presence and the Rhetorics of Yoga," Christy I. Wenger challenges the limitations of tying feminist definitions of ethos to Western conceptions of space and instead reframes ethos through Eastern contemplative rhetorics, which value integrative and embodied spatial relationships. She argues for a feminist-contemplative version of ethos as "presence" predicated on the fullness of bodies as they self-consciously negotiate language and material space without being reduced to either. This section concludes with Kendall Leon and Stacey Pigg's reading of Gloria Anzaldúa's conocimiento, a seven-stage nonlinear movement across multiple rhetorical stances, as a path to ethos. In "Conocimiento as a Path to Ethos: Gloria Anzaldúa's Networked Rhetoric," Leon and Pigg address how Chicana theory challenges "hyperlocation" in favor of dynamism and multiplicity. Interrupting, advocating, and relating become broad terms describing the artful negotiations of ethics, relations, and communications of women in public discourses.

The afterword explicitly extends our hope that readers put these chapters, concepts, and issues into conversation. By invoking *Reclaiming Rhetorica's* afterword through chapter writers' speculations about the collection's contributions, "Afterwords" imagines the possibilities that may be set in motion for future scholarship and teaching related to a feminist ecological ethē. Because ecologies and imaginaries shift in response to different pressures, this collection of gathering, observing, and theorizing is only a beginning. As teachers and scholars, we realize the importance of collecting new ideas about such a vital term as ethos and retheorizing it, both for our students and for the field. Moreover, we hope that *Rethinking Ethos* advances scholarship in rhetoric and composition studies, feminist rhetorical theory and historiography, rhetorical theory more generally, communication and women's studies, and especially in the teaching of ethos in the classroom.

The creation of *Rethinking Ethos: A Feminist Ecological Approach to Rhetoric* is collaborative at every turn. We wish to thank the participants who attended our panel presentation at the Feminism(s) and Rhetoric(s) conference in Mankato and who encouraged us to pursue this project, especially Heather Brook Adams, Tarez Samra Graban, and Barbara L'Eplattenier. We also wish to thank Laura Duncan, an English major at the University of Tennessee at Chattanooga, who helped us edit the initial chapters, and Dr. Hugh Parker, department head of classical studies at the University of North Carolina at Greensboro, who helped us with Greek terms. The series editors of Studies in Rhetorics and Feminisms at Southern Illinois University Press, Cheryl Glenn and Shirley Wilson Logan, as well as our outside reviewer, provided us with valuable encouragement and focus. We thank Kristine Priddy, acquisitions editor for theatre, rhetoric, and composition at SIU Press for her gracious editorial guidance. We are thankful to each of our chapter authors for their compelling research and analyses on ethos and for their provocative contributions to the afterword. Last, but by no means least, we offer appreciation to friends and family for supporting our work on this project. Kate appreciates the encouragement of John, Cima, and Eva, each in his or her own way. Nancy thanks Bob and Kris for their sage advice throughout this process. Rebecca thanks Will and Cameron for their patience and for being a joyous diversion from the work.

Works Cited

Code, Lorraine. *Ecological Thinking: The Politics of Epistemic Location.* Oxford: Oxford UP, 2006. Print.

Lunsford, Andrea A., ed. *Reclaiming Rhetorica: Women in the Rhetorical Tradition.* Pittsburgh: U of Pittsburgh P, 1995. Print.

Pittman, Coretta. "Black Women Writers and the Trouble with *Ethos*: Harriet Jacobs, Billie Holiday, and Sister Souljah." *Rhetoric Society Quarterly* 37.1 (2007): 43–70. Print.

Ratcliffe, Krista. *Rhetorical Listening: Identification, Gender, Whiteness.* Carbondale: Southern Illinois UP, 2005. Print.

Rethinking Ethos

Introduction

Identifying Feminist Ecological Ethē

Kathleen J. Ryan, Nancy Myers, and Rebecca Jones

A s a young woman, Terry Tempest Williams was taught to not "make waves" or "rock the boat." Fortunately, she did not heed this advice. In "The Clan of One-Breasted Women," Williams weaves dream and nightmare, Cold War politics, and Shoshone song to recount an act of embodied protest to reclaim land and lives lost to the effects of nuclear testing near her Utah home. Williams and nine other women were arrested for trespassing on "military lands." On the way to jail, the officials stopped the vehicle and dropped the women off just outside of town:

> The officials thought it was a cruel joke to leave us stranded in the desert with no way to get home. What they didn't realize was that we were home, soul-centered and strong, women who recognized the sweet smell of sage as fuel for our spirits. (407)

This essay, part poetry, part protest, part ecological philosophy, is rooted in a particular place and responsive to the web of connections between religion, history, family, a woman's agency, a geographic place, international politics, and collective action. Williams's ethos emerges from this ecology of forces. She draws from the multiple threads of her experiences and interactions with others to create a relational and situated ethos, one responsive to and

1

reflective of her evolving, multiple roles as a daughter, naturalist, Mormon woman, and desert dweller. From contending with a matrilineal legacy of breast cancer due to atomic testing in the Nevada desert, Williams learns:

> What I do know, however, is that as a Mormon woman of the fifth generation of Latter-day Saints, I must question everything, even if it means losing my faith, even if it means becoming a member of a border tribe among my own people. (405)

Williams's activism in the desert and her public ruminations on it exemplify the complexities of women creating and negotiating ethē explored in this collection.[1]

Like Williams, many women rhetors find that there is no comfortable ethos to employ if they want to shift the dominant discourse on a particular topic. Common, normalizing ethē (i.e., Mormon woman, mother, angel of the house, whore, bitch) ascribed to women do not lend themselves readily to public speaking. As such, new ethē must be created and defined to push against these socially determined ethē. Our feminist rhetorical perspective challenges us to examine women's ethos with the acknowledgment that it is culturally and socially restrictive for women to develop authoritative ethē, yet acknowledges that space can be made for new ways of thinking and artful maneuvering. This collection accounts for the complexities of Williams's ethos negotiation by arguing for an alternative theory of ethos at the confluence of ecological thinking and feminist rhetorical theory: feminist ecological ethē.[2] This term both describes women's public ethos construction relative to time, contexts, and different relationships *and* attempts to collect, name, and observe patterns in the dispersed work of feminist rhetorical scholars focusing on ethos. In this sense, women's ethos construction can be read as ecological thinking. Ecological thinking moves beyond the narrow understanding of ecology tied to environmentalism as a movement or the study and preservation of Nature even as it is rooted in these rich traditions. Rather, an ecological model of knowledge regards more broadly "place, embodied locatedness, and discursive interdependence" as "conditions for the very possibility of knowledge and action" (Code, *Ecological* 20). Lorraine Code specifically argues for ecological thinking as an instituting imaginary having the same kind of revolutionary promise as "Kant's Copernican revolution," which moved man to the center of the "philosophical-conceptual universe" (1).[3] In Code's feminist, ecological model, men and women engage purposefully with each other and all aspects (animal, plant, human, and technological) of the local and global environment. Active engagement toward living together becomes the goal, guided by an ecological epistemology that "locates inquiry 'down on the ground' where knowledge is made, negotiated, circulated" (5). A feminist ecological imaginary is a creative and social way of thinking, a living philosophy that better accounts for contemporary theorizing of inter-subjectivity in ethos construction. We offer the concept feminist ecological ethē because, like Nan Johnson, we recognize that, "variations in definitions of ethos correspond to different views of the relationship between rhetorical practice, philosophy, and ethics" (98). Simply put, adding ecological thinking to feminist rhetorical theory widens the scope of feminist considerations of ethos, and ethos more generally.

Feminist ecological ethē open up new ways of envisioning ethos to acknowledge the multiple, nonlinear relations operating among rhetors, audiences, things, and contexts (i.e., ideological, metaphorical, geographical). This theorizing recognizes all elements of any rhetorical situation as shifting and morphing in response to others (persons, places, things), generating a variety and plurality of ethos, or ethē. In particular, this collection focuses on interruption-interrupting, advocacy-advocating, and relation-relating as patterns we have observed across the chapters that enact this way of thinking and constructing ethos.[4] As Williams's narrative illustrates, women can seek agency individually and collectively to *interrupt* dominant representations of women's ethos, to *advocate* for themselves and others in transformative ways, and to *relate* to others, both powerful and powerless. These three terms, *interrupt*, *advocate*, and *relate*, offer broad descriptive categories for the kinds of ethē women adopt and the rhetorical strategies they employ, often in resistance to more static constructions of ethos privileged by normalizing expectations. Williams ultimately rejects the traditional ethos of a "good" Mormon woman who does not challenge authority because she decides the risks of silence are too high. Williams does not reject her Mormon heritage, but learns the more complex dance of negotiating between normative expectations and her evolving beliefs by examining her relations with others and reflecting on her values to create a new ethos as a Mormon woman and environmental activist.

Many feminist writers and other scholars of public deliberation acknowledge that marginalized rhetors have a keen sense of the burdens of ethos negotiation. This collection explores particular rhetorical maneuvers women use to try to construct new ethē that bring their arguments into wider circulation and to alter ecosystems. As members of border tribes, women rhetors have, more often than not, found themselves members of "counterpublics" rather than participating members of what Michael Warner names the "dominant public."[5] More important for this collection is his acknowledgement that

> a counterpublic maintains at some level, conscious or not, an awareness of its subordinate status . . . [Where] dominant publics are by definition those that can take their discourse pragmatics and their lifeworlds for granted, misrecognizing the indefinite scope of their expansive address as universality or normalcy. (86)

What we observe in our own research and the chapters in this collection is that women rhetors take this understanding of "subordinate status," relative to knowledge of the entire communicative landscape, and use it to craft a viable ethos for participation in a dominant public. Ecological thinking, while not a cure-all for a marginal or conflicted status in a discourse community, is a mindset that makes possible the development of methods for "infiltrating gaps in the discourses of mastery" (Code, *Ecological* 7). While we maintain that any marginalized rhetor can employ ecological ethē, women's rhetorical practices provide an instructive site for analysis and theorizing for at least three reasons: (1) women have traditionally operated outside normative publics; (2) women have often recognized, due to their marginalized cultural positions, connections, bridges, and borders between culture and nature, different races and groups, and even genders; and (3) women have historically and actively appropriated, adapted, and generated new ethē to speak to and within patriarchal publics. Moreover, where both essentialist and unmoored postmodern accounts of discourse fail to capture women's rhetorical negotiations, ecological thinking places a feminist, rhetorical subjectivity in relationship with others, in and between places.

This introduction begins by examining trajectories of historical scholarship on ethos that provide a preexisting ecological framework. Following this etymological discussion, we trace ecological workings found in contemporary feminist rhetorical theory and feminist philosophy. After tracing this scholarship and defining feminist ecological thinking more fully, the introduction describes three specific rhetorical concepts and strategies to enact feminist ecological ethē: ethē as interruption-interrupting, ethē as advocacy-advocating, and ethē as relation-relating. These paired nouns and verbs (concepts and actions) name and describe contemporary and historical rhetorical practices of women's ethē gathered in this collection. These terms represent both the creative force and risk of adopting feminist ecological ethē, the types of moves Williams uses to "make waves" and "rock the boat."

Disrupting Habitual Definitions of Ethos

Everyday definitions of ethos tend to assume the composing subject is a solitary individual crafting his or her character to firm up reputation and persuasive power. Ethos is often "discussed under such varied stylistic headings as 'tone,' 'writer's voice,' 'personal appeal,' 'attitude,' 'persona,' and 'credibility'" (Johnson 112). Much of the scholarship on ethos centers on Aristotelian ethos, where a rhetor's constructed ethos is comprised of his intelligence, good will, and good character as a persuasive aid in the courts, at ceremonial venues, or in the polis.[6] This classical concept of ethos was created and used, primarily, in a homogenous community among male orators in positions of power, whether in the context of law, politics, or public events and then taken up again by men over time in ways that continued to hinder if not halt women's abilities to speak and be heard.[7] The powerful influence of this historical legacy remains in circulation. People still act on cultural beliefs that men are better speakers, that character derives from social standing, and that humans are born into particular characters from which they cannot escape. These ways of understanding ethos layer outmoded modernist notions of the isolated subject onto a vital, ancient concept and ignore postmodern and feminist critiques of selfhood and discussions about ethics. Moreover, they do not account for feminist rhetoricians' efforts to move "rhetorical studies from traditional paradigms based largely on Western cultural expectations and values to paradigms that make considerably more room" for women (Royster and Kirsch 29). In other words, typical definitions of ethos do not presume difference, the shared yet diverse oppression of women, or contemporary theorizing about the subject as starting points for constructing ethos. To adopt a feminist ecological ethē we acknowledge, following American pragmatists, that we live in one world and need to contend with critical concepts that others believe even as we push for alternatives.

Over the last thirty years, feminist scholars have confronted cultural, physical, historical, and religious rationales that have diminished and discredited women as authoritative speakers. This rich body of scholarship demonstrates women constructing ethos despite significant barriers.[8] Due to this feminist rhetorical scholarship that models ways and means of "pushing the boundaries" (Royster and Kirsch), *Rethinking Ethos* reconsiders ethos to offer a feminist ecological imaginary that better accounts for the diverse concerns and experiences of women rhetors and feminist rhetoricians. In doing so, the collection honors the resilience women rhetors have demonstrated throughout time and across place, where resilience refers to a "process of rhetorically engaging with material circumstances and situational exigencies" that is relational, responsive, and potentially transformative (Flynn, Sotirin, and Brady 7).

In the spirit of "building on previous scholarship, demonstrating ideological flexibility, and connecting the local to larger conversations" (Gold 26), we link our argument for ecological ethē to revisionist etymological scholarship on ethos that recuperates its social, ethical, and spatial dimensions (Halloran; Hyde; A. Miller; Reynolds, "Ethos"; Smith). This collection is a feminist extension of projects that "revise a theoretically important sense of the concept of ethos as a central feature of rhetoric, moving ethos beyond 'credibility' to take in its role as central to place, community, identity, and social action" (Benson ix). These discussions often center on two Greek terms: ēthos (ἦθος) (pl. ēthē) and ethos (ἔθος) (pl. ethē). The etymology of ethos, according to the *Greek-English Lexicon* compiled by Henry George Liddell and Robert Scott, is simply "custom" and "habit," while the denotations of ēthos and its plural, ēthē, entail social, ethical, and located dimensions. Arthur Miller's description of the etymology of ēthos, also reliant on the *Lexicon*, expands the familiar definition of ethos as character or credibility in important ways.

> Significantly, the basic denotation is *not* character, but "*an accustomed place*" and in the plural may refer to the "*haunts* or *abodes* of animals"; it also may refer to "the abodes of men." The second basic meaning is "*custom, usage*: in pl., *manners, customs, . . .*" Other meanings of various forms include "*disposition, character*" . . . "*moral character*" . . . "*traits, characteristics*" . . . "of outward *bearing*" or "*delineation of character.*" (310)

Scholars generally agree that these two etymologies (of ethos and ēthos) are consubstantial with each other, creating a rationale for combining discussions of character, habit, and abode, thus highlighting the social, constructed, ethical, and agentive aspects of premodern ethos.[9] Miller uses the relationship between character and habit, or ēthos and ethos, to argue that the development of character is a negotiated, communal act rather than an essentialized reputation, "voice," or inborn trait.[10] For instance, he contends, "The *polis* is, then, the social/political environment in which persons are trained in virtuous, habitual conduct—the environment in which a person's character (eethos) is formed" (511).[11] Character is a matter of community values.[12] Portraying "good" character means showing one has made "good" choices intentionally, where "good" is located in the community and the site of the deliberation. As Karlyn Kohrs Campbell explains, ethos "does not refer to your peculiarities as an individual but to the ways in which you reflect the characteristics and qualities that are valued by your culture or group" (qtd. in LeFevre 45). Herein lies the difficulty for women (and other marginalized groups) whose ethos, as "valued by your culture or group," is not recognized as worthy of public participation. Rachel Alicia Griffin powerfully describes the lack of positive ethos for biracial women: "I see images of my body held hostage as Other; entrapped in the controlling imagery of the mammy, jezebel, sapphire, matriarch, and the more contemporary welfare queen, hoodrat, freak, crazy Black bitch, superwoman, or some combination thereof" (147). These kinds of restrictions undercut women's ethē by denying them agency and value. As members of border tribes aware of the ecology of speaking situations, women must understand that there are multiple publics and counterpublics and work to shift values determined by dominant publics.

More recent scholarship on ethos takes up the idea of ethos as "abode" or "dwelling place" that an ecological approach extends further. In the introduction to *The Ethos of Rhetoric*, Michael Hyde

> define[s] ethos as "dwelling places" (ethos; pl. ethea) where people can deliberate about and "know together" (con-scientia) some matter of interest. Such dwelling places define the grounds, the abodes or habitats, where a person's ethics and moral character take form and develop. (xiii)

Individuals, audiences, values, written texts, and physical locations all constitute "dwelling places." Craig R. Smith emphasizes that ethos dwells not just at specific locations but also in the speaker and the audience relationship: "Determining the audience's beliefs is the key to successful adaptation in terms of building credibility. In this way ethos dwells not only in the speaker, as Plato and Isocrates would have us believe, but also in the audience" (6). Likewise, Nedra Reynolds draws on LeFevre's discussion of "betweens" to underscore the spatiality and relationality of ethos.[13] Reynolds envisions ethos as a rhetor's acknowledgment of her social and historical locations. As Judy Holiday points out, "reinvigoration of classical understandings of the social nature of *ethos* troubles modernist notions of intrinsic and consistent character" (389). Not only do these expansive notions of ethos provide more complexity than "voice," "persona," "character," and even "identity" offer, but they also privilege some of the moves and ideals ecological thinking values: a focus on relations, locations, and the relationship of ethics and ethos. As such, the terms "ēthos" and "ethos" and their connection to social relations have weathered historical shifts and retain their usefulness as frames for understanding how rhetoric works.

Defining Feminist Ecological Ethē

In addition to tracing an emergent ecological thread in scholarship on the etymology of ethos, we identify nascent ecological leanings in feminist rhetorical studies that we join with ecological feminism and ecological thinking to develop an alternative ethos construction that can be used by a variety of rhetors, even as we focus on women's rhetorical experiences. The study of ecological systems is not new, but has many historical roots and contemporary disciplinary trajectories.[14] The concept of ecological systems of relations (whether equal or hierarchical) circulates regularly in discourse (even as discussions of systems or networks more broadly), and the study of ecology as a habit of mind now ranges across disciplines from the sciences to the humanities. What we trace here is an iteration of feminist ecological thought in philosophy to develop an argument for the relevance of ecological thinking to women's rhetorics. A feminist ecological notion of women's ethē harnesses the momentum of the "tectonic shift" metaphor Jacqueline Jones Royster and Gesa Kirsch use to argue that "feminist rhetorical studies have broken through habitual expectations for rhetorical studies to be overwhelmingly about men and male-dominated arenas, with the consequence of creating volatility in research and practice, tectonic shifts on the rhetorical landscape" (17). In other words, this collection shifts the understanding of ethos by moving it into a feminist and ecological arena.

This feminist ecological imaginary is emergent in the work of locational feminists. Susan Stanford Friedman characterizes the difference between second- and third-wave feminist concerns as a movement from a "prevailing temporal rhetoric of awakening, revelation, and rebirth to a spatial rhetoric of location, multipositionality, and migration" (18). Such spatial rhetorics situate (most often) marginalized rhetors in place and with ethical stances. Reynolds's 1993 landmark article, "Ethos as Location," draws on the etymology of ethos as "haunts" or "dwelling places" and feminist location theories, including Adrienne Rich's "politics of location" and Donna Haraway's "situated knowledges," to argue "writers construct and establish *ethos* when they say explicitly 'where they are coming from'" (332).[15] With a writer's acknowledgment of her location comes not only an authority to speak, but also a concomitant responsibility to speak from that position with the knowledge conferred by that location, where location refers to "the space of the body, her geographical location, her shifting intellectual positions, her distance or closeness to others, to texts, to events" (Reynolds 335–36). Feminist rhetoricians have used this scholarship on "ethos as location" to theorize race and gender, genre, and personal characteristics as sites of ethos construction (Applegarth; Christoph; Pittman).

Aimee Carillo Rowe offers a different approach to locational feminisms; she advocates for a shift from an emphasis on location to relation. Rowe argues that "in spite of her efforts to position herself as a coalitional subject, Rich fails to locate location within community. In this way she does not hold herself accountable to the allies who enabled her to see from that vantage. So ultimately, 'Notes on a Politics of Location' constructs Rich's identity as 'Enlightened White Feminist' as an *individualized location*" ("Be Longing" 19). Rather than focus on the subject who only acknowledges her own location, Rowe theorizes a politics of relation between complex locations as a means to envision transracial feminist alliances in academia. A feminist ecological imaginary also emphasizes relationality between locations to avoid rendering subjectivity as isolated "individualized locations." Moreover, it entails an ethical orientation toward well-being and integrity that is a regular concern of feminist rhetoricians and characteristic of ecological feminism.

Ecological feminism, a term first used in 1974 by Francoise d'Eaubonne (Warren 21), is generally considered an "umbrella term" for "women-other human Others-nature interconnections" (Warren xiv)—in other words, for the various relations among women and others. In general, ecological feminists analyze the oppression of women and human others as it is intertwined with the domination of "earth Others" (Warren xiv). This work includes a look at the ethical responsibilities of humans to Others (human and earth) and is oriented toward social justice for these others (Warren xiv). The phrase "ecological feminism" rather than "ecofeminism" better characterizes our rhetorical argument following feminist philosophers who reject biological determinism (Cuomo and Code), which "incorrectly locates women as biologically 'closer to nature than men' . . . or assumes a biological essence to women . . ." (Warren 53). Similar to our argument about a feminist ecological imaginary, ecological feminism recognizes the diversity of women's experiences within the shared experience of patriarchal oppression and acknowledges that "values, notions of reality, and social practices are related" (Cuomo 1). Feminist ecologists recognize that "different forms and systems of oppression are interwoven and they therefore strengthen and fuel each other" (7); this observation calls up a corresponding need to develop ways of seeing and critiquing those interconnections as an ethical commitment.[16] Ecological feminism offers a similar framework to our study of ethos construction and should be considered yet another valuable line of inquiry in understanding the ways women develop ecological habits of mind.

We rely strongly on Code's feminist philosophy in *Ecological Thinking* because it articulates the thinking we have traced in rhetorical studies and the contributions to this collection, partly because she focuses on human relations rather than the human-nonhuman relations that dominate ecological feminism. Code places a postmodern yet situated definition of knowledge and intersubjectivity in the wider locations and interrelations of ecologies, where the act of participating in a feminist ecological imaginary calls the current "rhetoric of mastery and possession" into question (35). In an earlier work, she describes subjectivity as a set of shifting, even competing, locations, knowledges, and desires:

> (i) historical location; (ii) location within specific social and linguistic contexts, which include racial, ethnic, political, class, age, religious, and other identifications; (iii) creativity in the construction of knowledge, with the freedoms and responsibilities it entails; and (iv) affectivity, commitments, enthusiasms, desires, and interests, in which affectivity contrasts with intellect, or reason in the standard sense. (*What* 46)

Code's subject accepts the responsibility of situated knowledge making and its related affective and ethical dimensions. In *What Can She Know?*, Code posits this subject as an alternative to the universality and neutrality of the Cartesian subject. By trading a view from nowhere for a partial and located one, she points to her central argument in that text, that subjectivity matters to knowledge making. This scholarship offers a rhetorical sensibility and a commitment to fighting the oppression of women at the level of knowledge making, turning questions that mark positivist philosophy, "knowing that," toward "*who* knows that."

Code's recent scholarship expands this argument to a more ecologically minded one centering on "knowing how well" (*Ecological* 5). "How" takes an explicit rhetorical turn in pointing toward public action. "Knowing how well" exemplifies thinking and acting intentionally and thoughtfully because the ecological knower is "self-critically cognizant of being part of and specifically located within a social-physical world that constrains and enables human practices, where knowing and acting always generate consequences" (5). Shifting subjectivity from "the center of the philosophical-conceptual universe" to an ecological perspective that "emerges from and addresses so many interwoven and contradictory issues—feminist, classist, environmental, postcolonial, racist, sexist—that its implication requires multifaceted chartings" situates ethos in our relations in the world rather than in the individual (3–4). Following the work of Donald Davidson and other American pragmatists, Stephen Yarbrough also acknowledges the value of considering worldly relations.

> When we believe that we must share the same world with our interlocutors, when we believe, in other words, that the same causes that affect their actions, including their speech, writing, and gestures, also may or do affect us, perhaps without our awareness, then we are motivated to enter into the sometimes tedious and difficult inferential labor required to determine what those causes are. (xiv)

This "tedious . . . labor" is part of the process of ethos creation by partial subjects committed to communication: "Ethos is best thought of interactionally—as the set of social relations we project upon a situation that determines how we interact with things" (170). Ethos is a dynamic of multiple ethē among rhetors, audiences, and locations. Undergirded by Code's work on ecologies, subjectivity, and a pragmatic worldview, feminist ecological ethē encourage the flourishing of all people because of a commitment to seeing and communicating relationally and locationally.

Feminist ecological ethē operate as fluid, evolving, and negotiated rhetorical acts with worldly implications. Rhetors with feminist ecological mindsets understand that they are "work[ing] within a social-physical world that constrains and enables human practices, where knowing and acting always generate consequences. For this subject, internal interdependence within communities and their external dependence on one another are a given" (Code, *Ecological* 5). Ecological thinking focuses on partial knowing and taking responsibility for one's "epistemic-moral-political activity" (5). Considering these ethical imperatives, that is, paying attention to consequences and taking responsibility for rhetorical acts, is crucial to ecological thinking and, therefore, the rhetorics of many women in this collection. Ecological thinking is about a way of living in the world oriented toward cohabitation; it acknowledges the dynamic construction of relationships within and across locations and between people as constituting knowledge and values. Ethos is neither solitary nor fixed. Rather, ethos is negotiated and renegotiated, embodied and communal, co-constructed and thoroughly implicated in shifting power dynamics. Many women rhetors and feminist scholars of rhetoric operate in terms of this ecological perspective as they construct ethē and study the rhetoric of others.

Enacting Feminist Ecological Ethē: Interrupt, Advocate, Relate

Collectively, the chapters in *Rethinking Ethos* argue for the multiplicity of women's ethē (conceptually and strategically); they not only draw from and adapt Western masculinist rhetorics and traditions, particularly Aristotelian rhetoric, to reimagine ethos but also create new ways to conceive of ethos outside of that tradition, turning to Chicana rhetorics, Eastern philosophy, transnational feminisms, visual rhetorics, and queer theory. Each is evidence of the "five major strands in the work of feminist rhetorical scholars" that Lindal Buchanan and Kathleen J. Ryan identify: "reclaiming forgotten or disparaged women rhetors," "examining the interrelationships among context, location, and rhetoric," "searching for gender bias and, when it is found, retheorizing (or regendering) rhetorical traditions," "interrogating foundational disciplinary concepts," and "challenging traditional knowledge-making paradigms and research practices" (xviii). While chapters take up different methodologies and offer unique stances on ethos, the shared characteristics of feminist ecological ethē cut across the collection.

Rethinking Ethos highlights different ways women rhetors participate in the feminist ecological imaginary we describe. We organize the chapters into three sections based on the three concepts and strategies that exemplify feminist ecological ethē: interruption-interrupting, advocacy-advocating, and relation-relating. Each section opens with a historical and theoretical look at the three broad rhetorical maneuvers that put feminist ecological ethē into practice. As concepts and acts, these categories name a rhetor's ethos and describe rhetorical maneuvers characteristic of feminist ecological ethē. Kendall Phillips's discussion of rhetorical maneuvers in "Rhetorical Maneuvers: Subjectivity, Power, and Resistance" aptly describes these actions. Phillips defines "rhetorical maneuver" as a rhetorical act operative in the "space between the subject position and the subject form" (325); each of us negotiates the distance between the ways we are positioned by external forces and our own desires for self-positioning. A rhetor performs rhetorical maneuvers when "trading in one's established—or positioned—ethos for one that is not already accepted within a particular space" (327). Rhetorical maneuvers evoke the betweenness of ethos construction and function as a more flexible alternative to Michel de Certeau's concepts of "tactics" and "strategies."[17] Instead of "making do" or merely being tactical, women rhetors in this collection practice deliberative decision-making and push toward transformation. As such, Phillips's notion of rhetorical maneuver offers a broader definition of the actual practices related to ethē construction that this collection explores than de Certeau's work might.

Grouping the chapters according to these three patterns of rhetorical maneuvers follows ecological feminists in looking at "links and patterns" (Cuomo 7) of women's interconnected experiences under patriarchy. Doing so illuminates the hermeneutic and heuristic prospects of seeing connections across rhetorical maneuvers as well as within the particulars of a woman's experiences or a specific group of women's experiences. While each chapter delves into its own particular ecological engagement, these concepts and strategies cut across the chapters to offer concepts with a portability and explanatory power aimed toward seeing and using women's ethē differently.

These three rhetorical maneuvers—interruption, advocacy, and relation—invigorate the prospects of ethos construction for women. Imagine Williams in the desert, dancing at night, with other women "interrupting" a government space with their bodies, "advocating" for each other and other peoples and lives affected by the testing, and then writing and talking about the "relations" required to create this act: "I crossed that line with Jesuit priests, with Shoshone elders, with native people who had also lost lives because of the radiation fallout in the Shivwits' lands" ("Grounding Truth"). Rather than situating women within a narrow interpretation of Aristotelian ethos as "credibility" or "character," these moves highlight the complexity of women knowing and acting in a world characterized by a feminist ecological imaginary. Code ends *Ecological Thinking* with this definition of the act portrayed in her title:

> Ecological thinking, in its commitment to complexity, urges attention to detail, to minutiae, to what precisely—however apparently small—distinguishes this patient, this welfare recipient from that, this practice, this locality from that, as Rachel Carson would distinguish this plant, this species from that, Lucy Candib this heart patient from that, all the while acknowledging and respecting their commonalities, where pertinent. (280)

Feminist ecological thinking is a habit of mind that not only describes what many women rhetors have always believed and done but also offers a new, ethically minded, epistemic and rhetoric for (deliberate) ethos formation. The feminist rhetorical scholars in this collection theorize and historicize ethos to re-imagine rhetorical theory and re-see everyday practices. Adopting ecological thinking as a way of rethinking ethos means we cannot just interrupt, advocate, or relate in isolation. We must consider how we interact within our own environment and with our cohabitants and take responsibility for the ways others are affected by our acts. If women act ecologically and recognize that we all live "in one world," this work can become organic to everyday practices.

Williams makes the case for this approach repeatedly in her prose. In *An Unspoken Hunger*, she writes about testimony she gave "before the subcommittee on fisheries and wildlife conservation and the environment concerning the Pacific Yew act of 1991" (125). In her defense of the pacific yew, a tree whose bark is used exclusively to make an experimental cancer drug, Williams weaves discourse on families, women, and cancer to make an argument for thinking ecologically—for "seeing ourselves as part of the fabric."

> It is not a story about us versus them. That is too easy. It is not a story to pit conservatives against cancer patients. That is too easy also. Nor is it a story about corporate greed against free-market economy. It is a story about healing and how we might live with hope. (130)

Adopting a feminist ecological habit of mind means that decision-making is not easy. The daily practices of interrupting, advocating, and relating require commitment, rigor, and an ethical orientation toward living well with others. Deciding on the "right" course of action is a complex affair, as is constructing attendant ethē to undertake such action.

In shifting scholarly conversations on ethos to account for a feminist ecological imaginary, the definition of ethos shifts to better acknowledge the multiple ways women construct their ethos, while continuing to acknowledge the commonalities these constructions share: a recognition that women as postmodern and rhetorical subjects construct knowledge and selfhood in relationship with others, that such knowledge is located and partial, and that an ethics of responsibility toward and in relationship to others motivates their actions in the world. Such a worldview not only shapes the ways women rhetors analyzed in *Rethinking Ethos* construct their ethos, but also informs the ways that feminist rhetorical scholars contributing to this collection undertake their scholarship.

Notes

1. We use ethē as the plural of ethos (ἔθος) rather than ethea because we are using the Attic Greek of Aeschylus and Aristotle rather the Ionic Greek of Homer.

2. Ryan defines theory as "a method of conceptualizing and systematizing experience through observational, interpretive, imaginative, organizational, and reflective practices" ("Making Pathways," 96). This definition is compatible with

our interest in theorizing feminist ecological ethē because, while normalizing thinking is not a goal, we find systematizing practices to be a productive means of developing habits of mind as repeatable practices.

3. Identifying an imaginary rather than a paradigm reflects our feminist critique of the ways women have tried to negotiate unforgiving patriarchal models of ethos. Instituting imaginaries are more flexible, open systems; instituting rather than instituted imaginaries are creative "vehicle[s] of radical social critique" (Code, *Ecological* 33) that shift us away from "normative meanings, customs, expectations, assumptions, values, prohibitions, and permissions" (245).

4. We join the noun and verb forms of these terms to underscore them as concepts and actions.

5. Warner argues that there are many "publics" rather than "the" public as described by Habermas in his initial conception of the ideal public sphere. Women rhetors also participate in many publics that do not necessarily "counter" dominant publics. Additionally, Fraser notes in "Rethinking the Public Sphere" that counterpublics are sometimes necessary spaces to develop new definitions and vocabularies before taking a particular discourse into the larger public conversation.

6. Copious scholarship and pedagogy, well beyond the scope of this introduction, is based on readings of classical ethos, including Aristotle's discussion of ethos in the *Rhetoric* and the *Nicomachean Ethics*, Cicero's *De Oratore*, and Quintilian's *Institutio Oratoria*. Book I of Aristotle's *Rhetoric* states "[There is persuasion] through character whenever the speech is spoken in such a way to make the speaker worthy of credence" (Kennedy 38). Book II balances the importance of the argument made with the speaker's presentation of self for the audience: "it is necessary not only to look to the argument, that it may be demonstrative and persuasive, but also [for the speaker] to construct a view of himself as a certain kind of person" (112). According to Enos in *Roman Rhetoric*, scholarship tends to focus on Aristotle's theory of ethos versus Cicero's practice and use of *conciliare* as a counterpart to the Greek concept of ethos. Enos argues for a Ciceronian theory of ethos based in specific character traits (123–37). See also May on Ciceronian ethos. The collection *Ethos: New Essays in Rhetorical and Critical Theory* explores what happens to ethos with the poststructuralist death of the author, asking: "Where are we left? Does ethos remain, in any way, a definable (or defensible) rhetorical concept? Is it at all useful?" (J. Baumlin xxvii).

7. These include the well-known though overstated injunction by St. Paul against women preaching publicly, Aquinas's seventeenth-century belief "that women's subordination is due to the necessity for wise government of her weak intellect" (N. Miller 274), and the nineteenth century "'Cult of True Womanhood' [which] enjoined upon women piety, purity, submission to male authority, and

motherly domesticity" (Bizzell 378). Because the ideal Renaissance woman was chaste, silent, and deferential, "any woman who used her tongue forcefully, aggressively, or rhetorically became not an orator or a scholar but lost all virtue—including chastity—and opened herself to a variety of public punishments devised for garrulous women" (T. Baumlin 241). The challenges women of color face increase exponentially, as their morality, if not their humanity, has been "questioned by audiences 'outside their immediate home communities'" (Pittman 44).

8. Such texts that recover and regender women's rhetorics, include, quite recently, Royster and Kirsch's *Feminist Rhetorical Practices* and, earlier, Glenn's *Rhetoric Retold: Regendering the Tradition from Antiquity Through the Renaissance*, and Atwater's *African American Women's Rhetoric*, but also anthologies and collections like *Available Means, Centering Ourselves, Listening to Their Voices, Reclaiming Rhetorica, Rhetorica in Motion, Rhetorical Women, Walking and Talking Feminist Rhetorics*, and *With Pen and Voice*.

9. While Corts critiques scholars who equate ethos and ēthos on the grounds that they are "confusingly equating two separate Greek words" (201), even he acknowledges the "basic consubstantiality" or kinship between these terms whereby the definitions of ethos as "habit" and "custom" are subsumed in the more capacious definition of ēthos (A. Miller 309, 310).

10. A. Miller argues that character (ēthos) finds "its origin in habit and disposition [ethos]" (311). Habits, repeated voluntary behaviors, become character over time: "Such courses of action repeated become habits, and habits repeated until well ingrained become states or dispositions. It is thus that habitual behavior or *ethos* is indicative of a man's character or *eethos*" (313). These actions that become (ideally) virtuous habits are matters of deliberation, of choice, and thus of agency.

11. While we recognize that those Aristotelian scholars who view the *Rhetoric* as a form of practical knowledge consider ethos as a habit of mind, this understanding is contested because of the term's ambiguity within the *Rhetoric*. Kennedy explains this difference between chosen habit and inborn action: Ethos

> is "moral character" as reflected in deliberate choice of actions and as developed into a habit of mind. At times, however, the word seems to refer to qualities, such as an innate sense of justice or quickness of temper, with which individuals may be naturally endowed and which dispose them to certain kinds of action. (148)

12. Reynolds contends, "When ethos is, as in the *Nichomachean Ethics*, a result of experience and instruction, it becomes a shared enterprise among members of the community, and the community decides, in turn, what constitutes justice, temperance, bravery, or ethics" (328).

13. Reynolds suggests,

> Ethos, in fact, occurs in the "between" (LeFevre) as writers struggle to identify their own positions at the intersections of various communities and attempt to establish authority for themselves and their claims. By emphasizing where and how texts and their writers are *located*—their intersections with others and the places they diverge, how they occupy positions and move in the betweens—we can retain the spatial metaphors of ethos without limiting it to arenas of spoken discourse and without assuming that those gathering places are harmonious or conflict-free. (333)

14. Historian Worster explains in his oft-referenced text, *Nature's Economy: A History of Ecological Ideas*, that the two major notions of ecology took root in the eighteenth century: the "Arcadian," which emphasized "coexistence" between "organisms," and the "Imperial," which established "man's dominion over nature" (2). His study follows understandings of ecology as they traversed between these two poles, through Charles Darwin to our current "Age of Ecology," first publicly articulated in Rachel Carson's *Silent Spring* (339). In *Ecology in Ancient Greece*, Hughes traces stirrings of the concept in history, theater, philosophy, and science with a focus on Aristotle's student Theophrastus. Rather than merely cataloguing the world and marking nature's utility to man, Theophrastus "does not consider a plant in isolation, but asks what its relationship is as a living organism to sunshine and exposure" as well as "other plants and animals" (122). See also *Environmental Rhetoric and Ecologies of Place*, edited by Goggin.

15. Similar interest in locations as standpoints, "stopping points," or bordered systems also crop up in additional scholarship on feminism and ethos. In "The Splitting Image: Contemporary Feminisms and the Ethics of *êthos*," Jarratt and Reynolds draw on Reynolds's article to offer feminist standpoint theory's construction of the subject, specifically Haraway's "split" subject, as a way to argue for ethos as an ethical and agentive "admission of a standpoint" (53). In "Constructing Essences: Ethos and the Postmodern Subject of Feminism," Schmertz invokes Diana Fuss's scholarship on the social constructedness of essence to define ethos as "the stopping points at which the subject (re)negotiates her own essence to call upon whatever agency that essence enables" (86). Schmertz uses Rich's politics of location as an example of "a new ethos, a new speaking location" that she calls a "pragmatics of naming" (88, 89). While Fleckenstein does not draw on feminist location theories, she is one of the first scholars in the field to consider ethos as a system and notes that the material world is fused with technology and "non-linear time." She argues for a "cyberethos" that "calls us to act on and judge our inescapable dispersal across osmotic rhetorical and material borders because good character and virtuous behavior are mutually linked" (325).

16. Cuomo elaborates:

> Ecological feminism rests on the claims that women and other Others are full moral agents, that oppression and its correlates ought to be eliminated, and that minimal moral consideration ought to be given to all living things and systems. Acceptance of these premises requires the revision of values, practices, ontologies, and institutions that deny women's full agency and the moral considerability of nonhuman life, and that promote domination and oppression. (63)

17. Our choice to understand the relationship of practice to theory for this collection requires that we see women's ethos as both concepts and strategies that are dialogic, situational, and adaptable. In *The Practice of Everyday Life*, de Certeau is particularly interested in the "tactics" used by regular people to subvert discourses of power. In his formulation, strategies are "an effort to delimit one's own place in a world bewitched by the invisible politics of the other" (36), and the efforts of colonized peoples to remake languages and rituals imposed on them are an example of tactical acts. De Certeau sets strategies and tactics against each other. While we employ the term *strategies*, many of the chapters go beyond de Certeau's notion of "making do" and use language practices in new ways and new spaces to shift the strategies themselves.

Works Cited

Alcoff, Linda Martín. "The Problem of Speaking for Others." *Who Can Speak? Authority and Critical Identity*. Ed. Judith Roof and Robyn Wiegman. Urbana: U of Illinois P, 1995. 97–119. Print.

Applegarth, Risa. "Genre, Location, and Mary Austin's *Ethos*." *RSQ* 41.1 (2011): 41–63. Print.

Aristotle. *Nicomachean Ethics*. Trans. Martin Oswald. New York: Macmillan, 1962. Print.

Atwater, Deborah. *African American Women's Rhetoric: The Search for Dignity, Personhood, and Honor*. Lanham, MD: Lexington, 2009. Print.

Baumlin, James S. "Introduction: Positioning Ethos in Historical and Contemporary Theory." Baumlin and Baumlin, ix–xxxi. Print.

Baumlin, James S., and Tita French Baumlin, eds. *Ethos: New Essays in Rhetorical and Critical Theory*. Dallas: Southern Methodist UP, 1994. Print.

Baumlin, Tita French. "'A good (wo)man skilled in speaking': *Ethos*, Self-Fashioning, and Gender in Renaissance England." Baumlin and Baumlin, 229–63. Print.

Bizzell, Patricia. "Frances Willard, Phoebe Palmer, and the Ethos of the Methodist Woman Preacher." *RSQ* 36.4 (2006): 377–98. Print.

Benson, Thomas W. Series editor's preface. *The* Ethos *of Rhetoric*. Ed. Michael J. Hyde. Columbia: U of South Carolina P. 2004. ix–x. Print.

Buchanan, Lindal, and Kathleen J. Ryan. "Introduction: Walking and Talking through the Field of Feminist Rhetorics." *Walking and Talking Feminist Rhetorics: Landmark Essays and Controversies.* Ed. Lindal Buchanan and Kathleen J. Ryan. West Lafayette, IN: Parlor, 2010. xiii–xx. Print.

Certeau, Michel de. *The Practice of Everyday Life.* Trans. Steven Rendall. Berkeley: U of California P, 1984. Print.

Christoph, Julie Nelson. "Reconceiving Ethos in Relation to the Personal: Strategies of Placement in Pioneer Women's Writing." *College English* 64.6 (July 2002): 660–79. Print.

Cicero, Marcus Tullius. *Cicero on the Ideal Orator (de Oratore).* Trans. J. M. May and J. Wisse. Oxford: Oxford UP, 2001. Print.

Code, Lorraine. *Ecological Thinking: The Politics of Epistemic Location.* Oxford: Oxford UP, 2006. Print.

———. *What Can She Know? Feminist Theory and the Construction of Knowledge.* Ithaca, NY: Cornell UP, 1991. Print.

Corts, Thomas. "The Derivation of Ethos." *Speech Monographs* 35.2 (1968): 201–2. Print.

Cuomo, Chris J. *Feminism and Ecological Communities: An Ethic of Flourishing.* London: Routledge. 1998. Print.

Enos, Richard Leo. *Roman Rhetoric: Revolution and the Greek Influence.* Rev ed. West Lafayette, IN: Parlor, 2008. Print.

Fleckenstein, Kristie S. "Cybernetics, *Ethos*, and Ethics: The Plight of the Bread-and-Butter-Fly." *JAC* 25.2 (2005): 323–46. Print.

Flynn, Elizabeth A., Patricia Sotirin, and Ann Brady. "Feminist Rhetorical Resilience–Possibilities and Impossibilities." *Feminist Rhetorical Resilience.* Ed. Elizabeth A. Flynn, Patricia Sotirin, and Ann Brady. Logan: Utah State UP, 2012. 1–29. Print.

Fraser, Nancy. "Rethinking the Public Sphere: A Contribution to the Critique of the Actually Existing Democracy." *Social Text* 25.26 (1990): 56–80. Print.

Friedman, Susan Stanford. "Locational Feminism: Gender, Cultural Geographies, and Geopolitical Literacy." *Feminist Locations: Global and Local, Theory and Practice.* Ed. Marianne Dekoven. New Brunswick, NJ: Rutgers UP, 2001. 13–36. Print.

Glenn, Cheryl. *Rhetoric Retold: Regendering the Tradition from Antiquity through the Renaissance.* Carbondale: Southern Illinois UP, 1997. Print.

Gold, David. "Remapping Revisionist Historiography." *CCC* 64.1 (2012): 15–34. Print.

Goggin, Peter N., ed. *Environmental Rhetoric and Ecologies of Place*. New York: Routledge, 2013. Print.

Griffin, Rachel Alicia. "I AM an Angry Black Woman: Black Feminist Autoethnography, Voice, and Resistance." *Women's Studies in Communication*. 35:2 (2012): 138–57. Print.

Halloran, S. Michael. "Aristotle's Concept of Ethos, or If Not His Somebody Else's." *Rhetoric Review* 1.1 (Sept. 1982): 58–63.

Holiday, Judy. "In[ter]vention: Locating Rhetoric's *Ethos*." *Rhetoric Review* 28.4 (2009): 388–405. Print.

Houston, Marcia, and Olga Idriss Davis. *Centering Ourselves: African American Feminist and Womanist Studies of Discourse*. New York: Hampton, 2001. Print.

Hughes, J. Donald. "Ecology in Ancient Greece." *Inquiry: An Interdisciplinary Journal of Philosophy* 18.2 (1975): 115–25. Print.

Hyde, Michael J. "Rhetorically, We Dwell." *The* Ethos *of Rhetoric*. Ed. Michael J. Hyde. Columbia: U of South Carolina P, 2004. xiii–xxviii. Print.

Jarratt, Susan, and Nedra Reynolds. "The Splitting Image: Contemporary Feminisms and the Ethics of *êthos*." *Ethos: New Essays in Rhetorical and Critical Theory*. Baumlin and Baumlin, 37–63. Print.

Johnson, Nan. "Ethos and the Aims of Rhetoric." *Essays on Classical Rhetoric and Modern Discourse*. Ed. Robert J. Connors, Lisa S. Ede, and Andrea A. Lunsford. Carbondale: Southern Illinois UP, 1984. 98–114. Print.

Kennedy, George A., trans. Aristotle. *On Rhetoric: A Theory of Civic Discourse*. 2nd ed. New York: Oxford UP, 2007. Print.

LeFevre, Karen Burke. *Invention as a Social Act*. Carbondale: Southern Illinois UP, 1987. Print.

Logan, Shirley Wilson, ed. *With Pen and Voice: A Critical Anthology of Nineteenth-Century African-American Women*. Carbondale: Southern Illinois UP, 1995. Print.

Lunsford, Andrea A., ed. *Reclaiming Rhetorica: Women in the Rhetorical Tradition*. Pittsburgh: U of Pittsburgh P, 1995. Print.

May, James. *Trials of Character: The Eloquence of Ciceronian Ethos*. Chapel Hill: U of North Carolina P, 1988. Print.

Miller, Arthur B. "Aristotle on Habit (ἔθος) and Character (ἤθος): Implications for the Rhetoric." *Speech Monographs* 41 (Nov. 1974): 309–16. Print.

Miller, Hilda, and Lillian Bridwell-Bowles, eds. *Rhetorical Women: Roles and Representations*. Tuscaloosa: U of Alabama P, 2005. Print.

Miller, Nancy Weitz. "Ethos, Authority, and Virtue for Seventeenth-Century Women Writers: The Case of Bathsua Makin's *An Essay to Revive the Ancient Education of Gentlewomen* (1673)." *Listening to Their Voices: The Rhetorical Activities of Historical Women*. Ed. Molly Meijer Wertheimer. Columbia: U of South Carolina P, 1997. 272–87. Print.

Moraga, Cherríe. Foreword. *This Bridge Called My Back*. Ed. Cherríe Moraga and Gloria Anzaldúa. 2nd ed. New York: Kitchen Table: Women of Color Press, 1983. Print.

Phillips, Kendall. "Rhetorical Maneuvers: Subjectivity, Power, and Resistance." *Philosophy and Rhetoric* 39.4 (2006): 310–32. Print.

Pittman, Coretta. "Black Women Writers and the Trouble with *Ethos*: Harriet Jacobs, Billie Holiday, and Sister Souljah." *Rhetoric Society Quarterly* 37.1 (2007): 43–70. Print.

Powell, Malea D. "Down by the River, or How Susan La Flesche Picotte Can Teach Us about Alliance as a Practice of Survivance." *College English* 67.1 (Sept. 2004): 38–60. Print.

Quintilian. *Institutio Oratoria*. Trans. H. E. Butler. Cambridge, MA: Harvard UP, 1920. Print.

Ratcliffe, Krista. *Anglo-American Feminist Challenges to the Rhetorical Traditions*. Carbondale: Southern Illinois UP, 1996. Print.

———. *Rhetorical Listening: Identification, Gender, Whiteness*. Carbondale: Southern Illinois UP, 2005. Print.

Renegar, Valerie R., and Stacey K. Sowards. "Contradiction as Agency: Self-Determination, Transcendence, and Counter-Imagination in Third Wave Feminism." *Hypatia* 24.2 (Spring 2009): 1–20. Print.

Reynolds, Nedra. "Ethos as Location: New Sites for Understanding Discursive Authority." *Rhetoric Review* 11.2 (Spring 1993): 325–38.

———. "Interrupting Our Way to Agency: Feminist Cultural Studies and Communication." 1998. *The Norton Book of Composition Studies*. Ed. Susan Miller. New York: Norton, 2009. 897–910. Print.

Rich, Adrienne. "Notes towards a Politics of Location." *Blood, Bread, and Poetry: Selected Prose*. New York: Norton, 1986. Print.

Ritchie, Joy, and Kate Ronald, eds. *Available Means: An Anthology of Women's Rhetorics*. Pittsburgh: U of Pittsburgh P, 2001. Print.

Rowe, Aimee Carillo. *Power Lines: On the Subject of Feminist Alliances*. Durham, NC: Duke UP, 2008. Print.

———. "Be Longing: Toward a Feminist Politics of Relation." *Feminist Formations* 17.2 (Summer 2009): 15–46. Print.

Royster, Jacqueline Jones, and Gesa E. Kirsch. *Feminist Rhetorical Practices: New Horizons for Rhetoric, Composition, and Literacy Studies*. Carbondale: Southern Illinois UP, 2012. Print.

Ryan, Kathleen J. "Making Pathways: Inventing Textual Research Methods in Feminist Rhetorical Studies." *Rhetorica in Motion: Feminist Rhetorical Methods and Methodologies*. Ed. Eileen E. Schell and K. J. Rawson. Pittsburgh: U of Pittsburgh P, 2010. 89–103. Print.

Schell, Eileen E., and K. J. Rawson, eds. *Rhetorica in Motion: Feminist Rhetorical Methods and Methodologies.* Pittsburgh: U of Pittsburgh P, 2010.

Schmertz, Johanna. "Constructing Essences: Ethos and the Postmodern Subject of Feminism." *Rhetoric Review* 18.1 (Autumn 1999): 82–91. Print.

Smith, Craig R. "Ethos Dwells Pervasively: A Hermeneutic Reading of Aristotle on Credibility." *The* Ethos *of Rhetoric.* Ed. Michael J. Hyde. Columbia: U of South Carolina P, 2004. 1–19. Print.

Warner, Michael. "Publics and Counterpublics." *Public Culture* 14.1: 49–90. Print.

Warren, Karen J. *Ecofeminist Philosophy: A Western Perspective of What It Is and Why It Matters.* Lanham, MD: Rowman and Littlefield, 2000. Print.

Wertheimer, Molly Meijer, ed. *Listening to Their Voices: The Rhetorical Activities of Historical Women.* Columbia: U of South Carolina P, 1997. Print.

Williams, Terry Tempest. *An Unspoken Hunger: Stories from the Field.* New York: Vintage Books, 1994. Print.

———. "The Clan of One-Breasted Women." *Available Means: An Anthology of Women's Rhetoric(s).* Ed. Joy Ritchie and Kate Ronald. Pittsburgh: U of Pittsburgh P, 2001. 402–7. Print.

———. "Ground Truthing." Interview by Devon Fredericksen. *Guernica.* 3 Aug 2013. Web. 3 May 2015. < https://www.guernicamag.com/interviews/ground-truthing/>.

Worster, Donald. *Nature's Economy: A History of Ecological Ideas.* Cambridge: Cambridge University Press, 1985. Print.

Yarbrough, Stephen. *Inventive Intercourse: From Rhetorical Conflict to the Ethical Creation of Novel Truth.* Carbondale: Southern Illinois UP, 2006. Print.

Part One

Ethē as Interruption–Interrupting

Rhetoric scholars have been interested in interruption as a means to grasp agency and shift normative discourses for some time. Reynolds's 1998 chapter "Interrupting Our Way to Agency: Feminist Cultural Studies and Composition" argues that interruption and talking back are ways "women rhetors can draw attention to their identities as marginalized speakers and writers" and "force more attention to the ideological workings of discursive exclusion" (898). To "disrupt" is not an end in itself but a means to break in to conversations, to "[dare] to disagree" (898). Interruption refers to breaks, divides, hitches, disruptions, disturbances, ruptures, or breeches—counters to traditional ways of behaving or conversing—to change the status quo of dominant values and practices. Women who are members of counterpublics interrupt as a means of "tactically speaking in strategic loci" (hooks qtd. in Reynolds, "Interrupting" 907). There are, as Beth Innocenti points out, risks to this rhetorical maneuver; introducing disagreement invites public criticism.[1] Historically, women who "interrupted" gained reputations as nonconformists, rabble-rousers, and traitors to the "feminine" ethos. For example, Kathleen Kendall and Jeanne Fisher point to the tensions surrounding Frances Wright's "incendiary" speech, dress, and actions (65). While Wright's eloquent speech was able to appeal to "particular audiences . . . , historical evidence suggests that her failure to meet societal expectations lowered her ethos and thereby mitigated her effectiveness" (58).

Recent discussions of interruption and ethos offer more promise for this rhetorical maneuver without neglecting the risks entailed in being labeled a "disruption" or "disrupter." Valerie R. Renegar and Stacey K. Sowards, Matthew M. Heard, and Judy Holiday put forward more positive understandings of ethos construction as interruption, where interruptions are a means to uncover and disrupt habits that hinder communication across differences. Renegar and Sowards outline contradiction as a specific kind of interruption. They suggest women use contradiction, a "transcendent term that includes a myriad of other strategies such as ambiguity, paradox, multiplicity, complexity, anti-orthodoxy, opposition, and inconsistency" (6), "to navigate through a world that does not necessarily accommodate their values or rhetorical practices" (3). While Renegar and Sowards admit that contradiction "has long been considered a rhetorical strategy or theoretical position to avoid" (5), they argue that for many third-wave feminists this strategy "enables them to understand their identities, diversity, and feminism on their own terms and to explore new possibilities and options for everyday experiences and activism" (2). Many of the contradictions they identify embrace current, sometimes negative, images of women and reimagine them in ways that force different conversations by juxtaposing new and old concepts. In one example, Renegar and Sowards point to the ways writer Cristina Tzintzún's acknowledgment of her heritage as *both* "colonizer and the colonized" disrupts assumptions about her social and historical locations and, in doing so, creates new conversations about diversity (8). Likewise, Valerie Palmer-Mehta's chapter on Andrea Dworkin's use of a confrontational ethos underscores the difficulty of using disruption rhetorically even as it "provides a new vision of ethos formation for women that is not bound to, or bowed in the face of, patriarchal heterohegemony" (66).

Rather than focusing on interrupting others, Heard uses the sonic metaphor of attunement to describe a means for interrupting a tendency to "seiz[e] alterity—from translating difference, alienness, alterity, and otherness into sounds and sights that represent our own values" (46). Instead of trying to render the "strange" familiar to co-opt another's experience, he encourages us to dwell in the discomfort of "tension, conflict, and failure" (59). Adopting attunement asks us to interrupt our *own* habits, to adopt a "posture of constant engagement with contact that may threaten our most deeply held values and practices" (53). Of course, changing habits, especially our own, as Heard recognizes and pragmatist Charles S. Peirce also argues, is an extremely difficult task.[2] Heard's argument offers an ecological feminist perspective on ethos building in that rhetors must construct ethically responsible rhetorics by disrupting their own habits through listening to others.

Cherríe Moraga enacts attunement in her foreword to the second edition of *This Bridge Called My Back: Writings by Radical Women of Color* when she observes that "to change the world, we have to change ourselves—even sometimes our most cherished block-hard convictions" (iii). Holiday also emphasizes the need to understand interruption as an ethical responsibility. For her, interrupting not only draws attention to what constitutes normal but also reveals the constructed nature of what we consider normal: "the universal begins to become articulated precisely through challenges to its existing formulation, and these challenges emerge from those who are not covered by the existing formulation, who have no entitlement to it" (398). Doing so helps rhetors interrogate normalizing tendencies. Interruptions from members of counterpublics become agentive ways to transform values. Stacey Waite's meditation on queer ethos challenges us to "imagine what doesn't seem imaginable" (88) in turning the concept ethos from being a "dangerous term" to one full of pedagogical possibility.

Notes

1. Innocenti argues that strategies like "crying foul" against a particular argument in a deliberation can run the risk of inviting reciprocal criticism. However, the positive outcomes for a rhetor include remaking the norms of the discourse at hand, making manifest the "badness" of an opponent's rhetorical choices, and demonstrating one's own "forbearance" of this behavior and a willingness to continue participating in an argument as long as things change.

2. Peirce argues explicitly that beliefs develop out of habitual experience. He explains, "we cling tenaciously, not merely to believing, but to believing just what we do believe" (99).

Works Cited

Heard, Matthew. "Tonality and *Ethos.*" *Philosophy and Rhetoric* 46.1 (2013): 44–64. Print.

Holiday, Judy. "In[ter]vention: Locating Rhetoric's *Ethos.*" *Rhetoric Review* 28.4 (2009): 388–405. Print.

Innocenti, Beth. "Countering Questionable Tactics by Crying Foul." *Argumentation and Advocacy.* 47 (2011): 178–88. Print.

Kendall, Kathleen Edgerton, and Jeanne Y. Fisher. "Frances Wright on Women's Rights: Eloquence versus Ethos." *Quarterly Journal of Speech.* 60.1 (1974): 58–68. Print.

Moraga, Cherríe. Foreword. *This Bridge Called My Back.* 2nd ed. Ed. Cherríe Moraga and Gloria Anzaldúa. New York: Kitchen Table, Women of Color P, 1983. Print.

Peirce, Charles S. *Selected Writings: Values in a Universe of Chance.* Ed. Philip P. Wiener. New York: Dover, 1958. Print.

Renegar, Valerie R., and Stacey K. Sowards. "Contradiction as Agency: Self-Determination, Transcendence, and Counter-Imagination in Third Wave Feminism." *Hypatia* 24.2 (Spring 2009): 1–20. Print.

Reynolds, Nedra. "Interrupting Our Way to Agency: Feminist Cultural Studies and Communication." 1998. *The Norton Book of Composition Studies.* Ed. Susan Miller New York: Norton. 2009. 897–910. Print.

1. A Reformer Rides

Radical Photographic Ethos in Frances E. Willard's
A Wheel within a Wheel

Kristie S. Fleckenstein

With a book in her lap, held open with a right hand curled against the page, a pensive Frances E. Willard, long-time president of the Woman's Christian Temperance Union (WCTU), rests her face on her left hand, contemplating some reality beyond the frame and the viewer's gaze. Arrayed in a light-colored, long-sleeved day gown gathered at the bodice with a sprig of flowers, Willard leans against the arm of a richly draped chaise lounge, a figure in reflection, perhaps even a figure of reflection. Against the dark, blurred studio background of the nineteenth-century black and white photograph, Willard glows with an ethereal effulgence, tethered to the reality of mass and movement only tangentially. The almost otherworldly photographic depiction evokes the ethos of the woman eulogized as "Saint Francis" (Bordin 67), "our modern Joan of Arc," "the woman of Christendom" ("In Memory"), for whom love constituted the "ruling principle" of life ("Miss Willard" 4). This serene figure comfortably ensconced within the accoutrements, and protection, of a pseudo-Victorian parlor visually summons forth the credible character of a Willard who, inspired by her "mother-heart," espouses "home protection" through "organized mother love" ("Dawn" 127). Captioned solely with Willard's familiar signature, the studio portrait epitomizes purity, piety, submissiveness, and domesticity, the four virtues of the fading cult of True

Womanhood (Welter), an ideology central to the identity and success of the WCTU (Bordin; Mattingly, *Well-Tempered*). As the frontispiece of the 1895 publication *A Wheel within a Wheel. How I Learned to Ride the Bicycle with Some Reflections by the Way*, the contemplative woman in white, surrounded by the tasteful decorations of a faux domestic scene, creates a visual ethos firmly lodged within the conservative beliefs of late Victorian womanhood.

The visual character of Willard the True Woman, however, contrasts sharply with the remaining five images featured in Willard's charming memoir chronicling her efforts to master the safety bicycle as a means to "to help women to a wider world" (*Wheel* 73). Portraying Willard out of the parlor conquering both bicycle and public roads, these five halftones construct a visual ethos considerably at odds with the serene True Woman of the frontispiece. In a role more evocative of the New Woman than the True Woman, the visual ethos of Willard the cyclist aligns with that of Willard the activist who avers that women "need translating out of passive to the active voice; out of aimless reverie and into resolute aim" (Willard, *What* 147). Tethered to the professional woman, the educated woman, the club woman, and the political woman, the figure of the New Woman represented virtues at odds with the cult of domesticity: secularism vs. piety, sexual freedom vs. purity, independence vs. submissiveness, and emancipation vs. domesticity (Patterson 2). Furthermore, within the cultural imaginary, the fin-de-siècle New Woman and the wheelwoman, became, if not synonymous, then, at the very least, synecdochal, as the wide circulation of images caricaturing the New Woman "perched on bicycles and smoking cigarettes" indicates (Marks 2; see also 174). As a result, both phenomena were subject to the same opprobrium, with the New Woman rebuked as one who "makes a show of herself bicycling up and down the principal thoroughfares of a city in bloomers" ("The New Woman" 183). Given the socially suspect nature of cycling and its visual associations with the derogated New Woman, why would the quintessential True Woman of Willard's frontispiece lend herself in 1893 to such an endeavor, risking social and political fallout?

I address that question in this chapter, arguing that Willard's frontispiece evokes a visual True Woman ethos only if it is isolated from the remaining five photographic halftones strategically positioned throughout the modest seventy-five-page memoir. When perceived as the opening—rather than the sole—image of a visual narrative, the self-portrait of Willard in her studio-parlor contributes to the gradual, but systematic, construction of a radical photographic ethos that literally leaves behind the "aimless reverie" of the parlor and the True Woman ideology. Instead, the memoir's collective photographic ethos advocates the "resolute aim" of the New Woman learning to navigate political and public thoroughfares. By using the photographs both to illustrate and to design a credible character that is also a radical character, Willard effectively generates a visual ethos at stark odds with that of the submissive lady at home in her parlor. In contrast to Willard's reliance on a discursive ethos "wholly feminine, utterly ladylike" with all its attendant limitations (Campbell 129), a choice that results in rhetoric "suited only to reinforce existing beliefs" (129), Willard's photographic ethos constructs a persuasive character resonating with the progressive social reforms the WCTU president began promoting in 1894 and 1895. Before the reader's eyes, the visual of Willard balanced on her steed of steel, her "whimsical and favorite symbol" (*Wheel* 38), crafts an ethos that enacts authority and emancipation as admirable virtues. Thus, as the first plot point in a larger visual narrative, the frontispiece contributes to, rather than resists, the formation of a photographic credible character that rejects socially conservative gender ideologies to promote the reformist notions of a New Woman and her new world order.

The concept of a photographic ethos at the heart of this chapter focuses attention on the intersection of women's ethos and the visual in the nineteenth century when a middle-class white woman's virtue depended to a large extent on her specularity—how, where, when, and with whom she is seen as well as what she is seen doing—a specularity that increased in intensity as the century reached its conclusion in an "explosion of the visual" (Kaestle and Radway 12). Furthermore, complementing work on the rhetorical impact of women's clothing (Mattingly, *Appropriate[ing]*) and delivery (Buchanan), this chapter emphasizes a specific visual technology—photography—as an ethotic resource for late nineteenth-century women, a resource that from its inception in 1839 served as an immensely popular audit of character (Trachtenberg).[1] To demonstrate the daring nature of Willard's use of photography as a rhetorical tool, I begin with the socially hazardous nature of bicycling, highlighting the rhetorical risks intrinsic to visual advocacy of the wheel. Then, in two steps, I examine Willard's collective construction of a persuasive, albeit radical, photographic ethos. First, underscoring the congruence of photographic ethos with Isocratean ethos as "a most honorable name" (Isocrates 278) existing outside of the confines of speech, I focus on the subject matter of the photographs: the various physical moves required to master the bicycle. Depictions of Willard attempting to ride and then actually riding conjure up the reality of an action occurring beyond the covers of the discursive memoir, a reality that recasts authority in public arenas as a feminine virtue. Second, underscoring the congruence of photographic ethos with Aristotelian ethos, which arises from a rhetor's speech separate from his or her reputation in the *polis*, I examine the arrangement of halftones throughout the memoir. Focusing particularly on their sequential design, I argue that the photos interactively form a visual narrative that chronicles and celebrates women's spatial emancipation.

The Radical (Wheel)Woman as Visual Threat

Via the content and arrangement of the six halftones included in this popular memoir, Willard crafts a radical photographic ethos that warrants, without apology, the mobility offered not only by the bicycle but also by gender equality. The process of laying claim to that gender equality began for Willard in late 1893 when, mourning her mother's death and suffering from what she calls "nerve-wear," she takes a bold step. She decides to balance her life by balancing herself on the seat of Gladys, a safety bicycle purchased for her by Lady Henry Somerset, Willard's host in England. Gladys initially serves as a tool for ameliorating Willard's emotional and physical ill health. But her "silent steed so swift and blithesome" (*Wheel* 13) becomes more than a means to realign a life "out of balance" (11) through a regimen of exercise and exposure to the outdoors. It becomes a metaphor for life, especially a life of activism, and an "impetus . . . to that blessed 'woman question'" (38). As Willard struggled to tame Gladys, she documented her experiences in her journal, dictated her reflections to her personal secretaries, and recorded her labors via photography. Eventually, she organized these materials into a best-selling memoir that attracted a significant following and inspired rapid growth in the sale of women's bicycles (Northcliffe 193). However, the memoir, especially its visual advocacy of cycling, constituted a daring rhetorical move for two complementary reasons: cycling's associations with the New Woman as a scandalous "manly woman" and cycling's aggressive public visibility.

Promoting the bicycle, especially promoting the bicycle visually, presented an ethotic dilemma to Willard, who had founded her public persona on the cornerstone of womanly virtue (Bordin; Campbell; Mattingly). With the formation of the national WCTU in 1874, Willard and her WCTU cohort derived their authority to speak publicly from the True Woman ethos. By acting as representatives of "nurturant domesticity" (Bordin 8), temperance activists "scrupulously maintain[ed] the cultural expectations that defined their sphere" (Mattingly, *Well-Tempered* 17). They acted in public, but did so under the aegis of their reputations as True Women, maintaining the salience of the dominant patriarchal ideology as the cost of speaking to and for the good of the community. Troping the True Woman yielded effective results. Under Willard's leadership, the WCTU grew from twenty-seven thousand to over two hundred thousand members, the largest mass mobilization of women in the nineteenth century, wielding considerable clout on local and national levels (Bordin 3). However, the problem with the True Woman ethos—enacted discursively or visually—is that, by reinforcing hegemony, it eroded the efforts to transform that hegemony. In other words, reliance on the True Woman paradoxically undercut Willard's progressive message at the same time it enabled it, vitiating the sweeping social reform that characterized the WCTU under Willard's leadership. Willard's photographic advocacy of the wheelwoman qua New Woman in her memoir constitutes a sharp break with the True Woman tradition, and that break begins with the status of the bicycle in fin-de-siècle America.

The overt problem posed by the bicycle for Willard involved the identification of the wheelwoman with the masculine, with the character of a woman who challenges traditional roles by taking over a technology-coded male. Willard implicitly acknowledges the bicycle's gendered territoriality in her memoir, quoting a naval officer who regrets that women "have no idea of the new realm of happiness which the bicycle has opened to us men" (*Wheel* 11). With precursors dating back to the 1817 *draisine*, or "hobby horse," the bicycle in its various incarnations "seemed to be the design that only men should indulge themselves" (Seymour 706). Dominated by male riders almost exclusively, the early forms of the bicycle were created by and for men. Women taking up early versions of the bicycle were ridiculed and excoriated as semimonstrous (Willard, *Wheel* 13; Wosk 91) not only because they claimed a masculine mobile technology, but also because they embraced unprecedented social and spatial freedom in doing so (Dodge 130; Wosk 94). That dynamic began to shift with the introduction of the safety bicycle in 1886, especially when accommodations were made for women's skirts via the development of the drop frame and the elimination of the cross bar. While popularity soared among men and women, resistance to women riding the new safety bicycle remained entrenched, with critics crying for a return to a more "'patriarchal method of travel'" in which women relied on men for their spatial mobility (Wosk 94). Social conservatives claimed riding weakened a woman's moral fiber, jeopardized her reproductive abilities, and exposed her to social undesirables, all charges Willard courted by her advocacy of cycling (Dodge 130–33; Marks 174). Believing that "actions speak so much louder than the words I set before you," Willard challenges this gender dominance by including visual proof wherein she practices what she preaches (20): she takes over the bicycle despite its masculine coding.

In addition, Willard as masculinized wheelwoman jeopardizes her True Woman ethos because of the bicycle's synecdochal relationship to the New Woman, referred to in the popular press as those "'varmity women,' 'wild women,' 'social insurgents,' and 'manly women'" (Marks 2). Public condemnation of female cycling swelled as the wheelwoman and the New Woman became intertwined in the cultural imaginary, with each disparaged as strong-minded and independent, each censured as a shocking insult to custom and nature. Although the term "New Woman" did not enter the lexicon until 1894, its spirit was in the air a decade before that date as a subject of debate in America, England, and the continent (Marks 2; Patterson 2). In popular periodicals and fiction, the bicycle metaphorically signified women who embraced without apology an active life in public places traditionally denied them, a process that masculinized women as it feminized men. For example, the male protagonist in Frank Dumont's one-act satire *The New Woman's Husband* bemoans his fate as floor scrubber and house cleaner, duties he is forced to take up "because my wife wants to go out riding on her bike. Oh! This is what I get for marrying a new woman" (qtd. in Marks 174). Willard herself implicitly associates the New Woman with cycling. First, in her memoir, she claims that women riding the bicycle presage advancement for "humanity's mother-half" through the changes the riding machine inspires, starting with economics, proceeding to dress reform, and ending with male-female equality (*Wheel* 38–42). Second, in an 1894 interview, Willard frames her complimentary pronouncements on the New Woman with equal advocacy of cycling, implying the two constituted sides of the same coin ("Miss Willard on the 'New Woman'" 138–39).

Finally, the highly public, thus highly visual, performances of the wheelwoman qua New Woman further threatened Willard's social and political stature. While the mere idea of women cycling scandalized socially conservative elements, the visible reality of women actually wheeling in community parks, city thoroughfares, and country lanes constituted the true threat to the culture's gendered social and moral status quo. Maria Ward in her popular 1896 *Common Sense of Bicycling*, a manual for the wheelwoman, concedes as much, claiming in her introduction that women and girls "bring censure upon themselves not for riding but for how they ride" (ix), signaling the importance of the visual—the decorous appearance—that constituted the key challenge for wheelwomen. The obstacles of making an ethotic visual argument for the reform woman replicate those of the wheelwoman because the sight of a woman on the bicycle—just as the sight of a woman on the speaker's platform—was considered an insult to the eye. Visuality presented a key obstacle for the ethos of nineteenth-century women because it was their visibility—how, where, when they were seen, wearing what apparel and engaged in which activities with what companions—that directly affected their ability to construct a credible character in public venues. As Carol Mattingly notes, the visibility of a woman's body and appearance is "crucial to understanding women's participation in public forums" (135) because "women's moving to the platform unveiled the spectatorial and voyeuristic reality of women's place" (*Appropriate[ing]* 138). The perception of female reformers as perverted visual spectacles—as public agitators destabilizing culturally sanctioned identities—directly threatened their persuasive ethos, requiring them to devise visual strategies by which they could divert attention from their identity as rule breakers to their goals as cultural reformers, a conundrum symbolized and exemplified by cycling. Fanny Erskine in her 1897 *Lady Cycling* emphasizes the high priority of visuality for the wheelwoman's respectability, recommending that women avoid reprimand by eschewing two extremes: the scandalous bloomers or knickerbockers at one end of the spectrum and "ridiculous blouses or flower-garden hats" at the other (qtd. in Wosk 109). Each choice rendered the wheelwoman a visual exhibition, exacerbating an already socially risky undertaking. Manuals like Erskine's and Ward's thus advised demure apparel and behavior for women because they recognized, first, that women's reputations for virtue rested on the appearance they presented for visual scrutiny, and, second, that cycling, by its visual nature, imperiled those reputations.

Such is the situation Willard confronts in 1893 when resistance to women as spectacle—either on the wheel or on the dais—remained strong. However, rather than relying on the safe "wholly feminine and utterly ladylike" ethos characteristic of her speeches and her writings, Willard chances the deployment of a starkly different photographic ethos in her memoir, one that visually prefigures the more radical positions she began espousing in 1894 and 1895. Instead of replicating the True Woman ethos, Willard uses the affordances of photography to project a New Woman ethos, thereby asserting social reform through gender reform.

Photographic Ethos as a Reflection of the Real

The photo array in *A Wheel within a Wheel* constitutes an overtly political act. Via a photographic ethos, Willard expresses visually an ideal of radical female excellence that she is justifiably wary of expressing verbally. These half-tones direct the reader's eyes to Willard's mastery of the bicycle at a historical moment when cycling remained a suspect pastime for white, middle-class women. The six halftones begin with the frontispiece, a studio portrait of Willard in a pseudo parlor, perhaps musing on her cycling experience and thus gesturing to the tertiary title of her memoir: "some reflections by the way." The remaining five pictures provide the fodder for Miss Willard's ruminations, capturing Willard in action, either on Gladys or standing by Gladys receiving instruction, always arrayed in the skirts she preferred rather than bloomers. The second halftone finds Willard precariously balanced on a bicycle held in place by three men, followed by a shot of Willard standing beside Gladys. The fourth halftone features Willard mounted and balanced on Gladys. The next image has Willard in motion with only a single preceptor offering minimal aid. Finally, the last photograph presents a shot of Willard pedaling into the camera's lens, riding in solitary splendor while an unidentified male figure stands stationary in the background. Considered collectively, these halftones direct attention to Willard the cultural rule breaker by configuring Willard the cyclist who defies her loved ones' prognostications of disaster to exit her parlor and master the wheel at the age of 53. Unlike Elizabeth Cady Stanton, who published two articles promoting the bicycle but never rode herself, and, unlike Susan B. Anthony, who, in an 1896 interview with *The New York World*, lauded the bicycle as a boon to suffrage but never mounted a wheel herself, Willard follows her own advice: she rides the bicycle and displays proof positive of that venture. By so doing, she crafts and deploys a radical photographic ethos that resonates with Isocratean notions of good character.

Particularly important to the credibility of Willard's radical photographic ethos is the alignment between photography as a record of the real and Isocratean ethos as a reflection of a rhetor's reputation outside of the speech, a concept of ethos that blends the real with the visual. In *Antidosis*, Isocrates explains that a man of "good repute," one who possesses virtue in reality, will be more persuasive than one who lives "under a cloud" (277–78). An "argument which is made by a man's life has more weight than that which is furnished by words," Isocrates notes, suggesting that a rhetor brings to the occasion of speaking a reputation that already serves a persuasive (or counterpersuasive) function (277–78). In this view, the concrete existence and demonstration of excellence in one's life choices—all outside of the speech—are vital elements in establishing a credible character in the speech. Furthermore, this process embraces visibility. In a eulogy for a Cypriot ruler, Isocrates points to the power of painting and statuary to reflect and shape character, for such depictions provide visual paradigms for manly excellence. Although he privileges the power of speech in this regard—because, unlike a stone statue anchored by weight to a particular locale, a rhetor's words can circulate beyond the immediate site—he acknowledges the ethotic arguments presented by visual art (Steiner 278). In addition, that concern with visibility threads throughout his theory of rhetoric. In selecting "from the actions of men" only the "most illustrious and edifying," a rhetor will "feel their influences . . . in all the actions of his life" (277). In other words, by vividly depicting virtue in the text of a speech, a rhetor gestures to his habitual display of virtue through his embodied actions outside of the speech. Verbal rhetoric is reinforced, even made possible, by the rhetor's visual enactment of excellence within the community. Isocratean ethos thus emphasizes the dual importance of a "showing forth": verbally through the speech and visually through one's actions outside of the speech (277–78). Developed more than two thousand years after Isocrates wrote *Antidosis*, photography provides Isocratean ethos with a medium that blends the ethotic power of visual art with the portability of language to embody one's virtuous actions.

One of the most frequently photographed women of the postbellum nineteenth century, Willard carefully monitored and shrewdly deployed her visual image, sensitive to the relationship between photography and character. Like Isocratean ethos, nineteenth-century photography blended reality and character into an ethotic showing forth of the real. The nineteenth-century belief in the "unflattering honesty of the lens" aligned with belief in "theories of congruence between surfaces and depths, appearances and realities" to configure photography as a window into an individual's character (Trachtenberg 59). From its origins, photography was celebrated as an unmediated copy of nature, "the sworn witness of everything presented to her view" (Eastlake, qtd. in Newhall 85). Roland Barthes notes this very characteristic, proposing that a photograph involves "an awareness of its [the phenomenon pictured] *having-been-there*" (44, emphasis original), what Susan Sontag calls a reality "known by its traces" (167). A photographic image testifies to the existence of the object—or individual—pictured. It is, to apply Isocrates, an edifying and illustrious display, and, more specifically, a display of character. For nineteenth-century Americans, photographic portraiture converged with character, a convergence made particularly clear in the kinds of advice offered to portrait photographers. In his popular *The Pencil and the Camera*, Marcus Aurelius Root warns that, whatever deception the sitter might intend, "the inward unworthiness, despite all efforts *will* glare through the fleshly mask" (44, emphasis original) and will replicate itself on the photographic plate. When one submitted oneself to the judgment of the photographic lens, he or she submitted to the equivalent of "fixing character" (Trachtenberg 27). Hearkening to Isocratean ethos, photographic ethos builds its credibility and persuasiveness out of a privileging of the real. Given the prevailing nineteenth-century conviction that the visual offers an index of character, photography as Isocratean ethos presents Willard with a powerful tool by which to assert a credible New Woman character, one that, to contradict Campbell, is neither wholly feminine nor wholly ladylike. The photographic images displayed in her memoir provide evidence of the gradual and systematic process by which Willard claims the male-marked authority to act in public venues. That process begins with mastering Gladys.

The specific content featured in five of the six photographs highlights Willard's radical ethos by depicting her embodied actions within the community and thereby privileging the reality of her mastery of the bicycle. Men only appear two times in the photo array and are never mounted on Gladys in a position of power. Instead, photographic content focuses on women, particularly Willard, conquering Gladys to become the New Woman qua wheelwoman, the manly woman seizing the right to act and speak in public venues. Nor does this mastery come without a struggle. A key aspect of Willard's photographic ethos is the reality of the good character she displays in achieving control over Gladys. As the photographs—all traces of the Isocratean reality—reveal, Willard becomes the wheelwoman only with sustained and arduous effort. Each image takes up the obstacles posed by mastering Gladys and, thus, by extension, obstacles posed by mastering public authority. The content of the memoir's second photograph, "A Lack of Balance," establishes the difficulty of initiating such an endeavor (fig. 1.1).

Fraught with fear and disquiet, "A Lack of Balance" suggests the scope of the contest confronting Willard. Mounted precariously on Gladys, Willard presents neither a graceful figure nor one at ease with her role as wheelwoman. There is no expertise or authority here. Rather, the photo visually exposes Willard's discomfort with a machine so long associated with male pleasure. Her posture is hunched, almost as if protecting herself from a disastrous

Figure 1.1. "A Lack of Balance." Frances E. Willard struggles
for balance. From Willard, Frances E., *A Wheel within a Wheel:
How I Learned to Ride the Bicycle, with Some Reflections by the
Way.* New York: Fleming H. Revell Co., 1895, facing p. 21.

fall from grace, and her facial expression is rigid with apprehension. Her
awkwardness and anxiety are reinforced by the three men who, bent in uncomfortable postures, hold the handlebars and seat. These "three young En-
glishmen, all strong-armed and accomplished bicyclers" (*Wheel* 21) surround
her and control her. Despite their efforts, or perhaps because of those efforts,
Willard tilts one way while Gladys tilts another, her body braced against the
threat of "break[ing] my bones" and "spoil[ing] my future" (20). The various
elements of the content combine to represent not the grace of the True Woman
protected by three True Men, but, instead, the hazardous venture of learning
to be independent of men, true or otherwise. Within the context of this image,

the viewer is confronted with the knowledge that a New Woman is not born; she is made through her struggles to create for herself an authoritative life, an insight reinforced by the third photograph.

If the content of "A Lack of Balance" sets forth in stark physiological and psychological terms the anxiety evoked by the struggle to acquire authority, then the memoir's third photograph, "So Easy—When You Know How," celebrates the rewards—and the virtues—of persevering in the struggle (fig. 1.2). In this image, Willard, sans all evidence of men, yields her place on Gladys to another woman: a female cycling instructor who relaxes on Gladys as if she were an extension of the bicycle. Willard, with her personal secretary and boon companion Anna Gordon, looks on as their friend demonstrates the ease with which a woman can control the wheel. Willard the student stands

Figure 1.2. "So Easy—When You Know How." Willard (*center*) watches the expert. From Willard, *A Wheel within a Wheel*, facing p. 36.

secure on the ground, huddled in a sheltering half-cape that covers clothing inappropriate for riding, watching in doubtful hope the casual almost insouciant expertise the female teacher brings to the art of the wheel. With one foot on a pedal and one foot on the ground, the teacher is the quintessential master of Gladys, the one who, in the seat of power, exercises her command over the wheel with almost negligent dominance. In a scene limited exclusively to women, the mentor's relaxed posture and demeanor visually emblemize the reality of a successful outcome of the struggle to win over a male-marked domain, the struggle to obtain and wield authority in highly visual, highly public ways. As witness to this mastery, Willard offers herself as an acolyte, a potential claimant to a similar dominance that promises "unprecedented liberty of movement and association" (Dodge 130).

If the subject matter of "So Easy—When You Know How" gestures to the rewards of perseverance, the subject matter of the fourth and fifth photos enacts that perseverance, showing forth the reality of Willard's communal excellence. The fourth photo in the memoir, "It's Dogged As Does It," and the fifth, "Let Go—But Stand By," depict the resolute aim required for a True Woman to lay claim to a New Woman's tenacity to implement authority in public ways. In "It's Dogged As Does It," the female instructor from the previous photo has yielded her position of power to Willard (fig. 1.3).

Willard is back on Gladys, learning to operate her nickel-plated steed confidently and decisively. With Gordon lightly holding the seat of the bicycle and the instructor balancing the crossbar, Willard sits upright on Gladys, tilting neither to the left nor right. Instead of the awkward figures—both male and female—portrayed in "A Lack of Balance," the content of this image features all three women in erect postures, suggesting the confidence that Willard is beginning to feel with Gladys, so christened for "the bright spirit of the donor [Lady Henry Somerset], the exhilarating motion of the machine, and the gladdening effects of its acquaintance and use on my health and disposition" (*Wheel* 53). The fifth photo, "Let Go—But Stand By," further tallies up the obstacles and rewards of mastering the wheel in real life (fig. 1.4).

Here, Willard sits mounted on Gladys with both feet on the pedals, precisely balanced and ready to fly. A single female preceptor provides nothing more than a protective presence as Willard begins what seems to be her solo flight on Gladys, the machine by which, Willard notes in her journal, "we well nigh take our leave of Earth" (Gifford 398). With the combination of positions and players, the photographs show forth the Isocratean reality of mastery and the performance of that mastery in public venues. The radical

Figure 1.3. "It's Dogged as Does It." Willard finds her balance.
From Willard, *A Wheel within a Wheel*, facing p. 44.

ethos of a New Woman might come at great cost and only with great effort, but come it does, and with significant rewards. The final image, "At Last," represents the possibilities of a radical ethos for women (fig. 1.5).

In this moment, without any support, Willard confidently pedals into the reader's world, demonstrating the reality of her competence, her grace, and her authority, all displayed in a highly visible public space. She leaves behind not only the parlor but also the governance of the male, indicated by the single stationary male figure who stands far in the background of the speeding Willard. As a credible wheelwoman qua New Woman, Willard in the final image makes a virtue of authority by enacting the reality of that authority in public.

Figure 1.4. "Let Go—But Stand By." Willard takes control.
From Willard, *A Wheel within a Wheel*, facing p. 57.

Photographic Ethos as Artistic Invention

The subject matter featured in five of Willard's six photographs hearkens
to the power of photography to configure and sanction the excellence of a
"manly woman" through an enactment of Isocratean ethos. By including photographic content in which only women, never men, ride the wheel, Willard
violates common photographic practices wherein "the aim was to have each
sitter look like a conventional image of his or her social role" (Trachtenberg
28). Via this violation, she recodes authority and the performance of that
authority in public spaces as female. She makes real the virtues she advocates.
However, Willard's radical photographic ethos also relies for its power on
Aristotelian artistry as much as it does on Isocratean embodiment. Willard

Figure 1.5. "At Last." Willard bicycles on her own. From
Willard, *A Wheel within a Wheel*, facing p. 72.

uses the design options intrinsic to nineteenth-century photography to invent,
not merely enact, a progressive ethos. Through the sequential arrangement of
the six halftones, Willard fabricates a credible character who parlays public
displays of authority into spatial emancipation, promoting a woman's right to
determine what spaces she enters, when, how, and with whom. The progression of photographs mimics the progression of all middle-class white women
from their sequestration in the parlor to their freedom in public spaces.

Nineteenth-century photography and Aristotelian ethos intersect in powerful ways for Willard. In contradistinction to Isocrates, Aristotle claims that
the rhetor uses the resources of a speech to show that he or she possesses the
kind of excellence, good sense, and good will valued by the audience. Ethos,

Aristotle insists, "should result from the speech, not from a previous opinion that the speaker is a certain kind of person" (1.2.4). The rhetor derives persuasive power from the reputation he or she artistically constructs via language's resources. Furthermore, like Isocrates, visuality lurks within the Aristotelian art of character. Aristotle tightly integrates the visual and the rhetorical, perceiving both as the means by which citizens could regulate their "conduct, ēthos and broader 'hexis,' too" (Steiner 280). David Castriota suggests that

> in nearly every instance where [Aristotle] correlates the working of poetry and painting or sculpture, his comparison pertains to the portrayal of ethos, human character, and ultimately his interest has to do with the influence that such ethical representations may exert upon the public. (10)

As an audit of character, portrait photography was configured in nineteenth-century cultural discourses in almost neo-Aristotelian terms: as an artful collaboration between sitter and photographer with the aim of constructing a credible character. A portrait photograph existed as something more than a "solar phenomenon," an image drawn by the sun; it also existed as a cooperative effort among the artist, the sun, and the sitter. Famed photographer Albert Southworth articulates this sentiment, claiming that "nature is not all to be represented, as it is, but as it ought to be, and might possibly have been." Similarly, even as Root protests in his 1864 instruction manual that the flesh of the face always provides a passport to inner character, he simultaneously counsels photographers to shape character artistically by manipulating the expression on the face, position of the body, angle of the head, and direction of the sitter's gaze. Such photographic artistry accords with Aristotle's view of ethos as emerging from the content and style of a discourse. Willard's rhetorical choices, especially in terms of her arrangement of the photographs, reflect her use of design to tell a story of spatial empowerment.

The opening narrative move begins with the frontispiece, "Frances E. Willard," which identifies Willard as the white, middle-class "Everywoman," an Everywoman circumscribed by the walls of the parlor and True Woman ideology (fig. 1.6). As the only formally posed photograph in the memoir, as well as the only one taken indoors, the frontispiece of the semirecumbent Willard seems at first glance to reject the New Woman and the wheelwoman. It dismisses not only the woman who mounts the seat of Gladys but also the woman who crisscrossed the country speaking in more than a thousand venues within a ten-year span, organizing and advocating political reforms that ranged from suffrage and prohibition to kindergartens and child labor

Figure 1.6. Willard sits in a formal pose. From
Willard, *A Wheel within a Wheel*, frontispiece.

(Bordin 73). But this image, in conjunction with the remaining five, functions
to situate Willard as a representative for all women. If she, shackled by ill
health, a sedentary life, and an inflexible body, can leave the parlor to master
Gladys, so, too, can all women. Regardless of age, cultural position, or physical
condition, women can expand the spatial parameters of the authority they
wield by stepping outside the parlor and embracing their inner wild woman.
Thus, Willard recumbent is not a benchmark or the gold standard of what
women should be. Within the context of the remaining five photographs,
Willard recumbent becomes a point of departure for what women could
be. The changes of scene in the remaining five images highlight the gradual
expansion of a woman's sphere of influence.

If the frontispiece emphasizes a woman's ease in the parlor, the second photograph, "A Lack of Balance," emphasizes a woman's initial dis-ease in a public space (see fig. 1.1). The scene takes place outside the cottage where Willard stayed while a guest of Lady Henry Somerset in England. Here, with the cottage in the immediate background and the established pathways plainly delineated, the setting offers a point of spatial transition between the comfort of the domestic parlor and the perils of unknown public venues. It sits on the cusp between the private and the public. Tidy and domesticated, the vista represents a respectable site for a lady, even a lady who seeks to ride a bicycle. Thus, the reader's first glimpse of Willard's wooing of Gladys has the imprimatur of domestic normativity looming in the background and foreground. Furthermore, the spatial potential of the bicycle is constrained by the three men who surround Willard. Hemmed in by the three young males, Willard's first foray into spatial independence is implicitly sanctioned and simultaneously restricted by these men. Willard cannot move with Gladys in any way the three men fail to allow. Finally, the straight lines of the vertical and horizontal path gesture to the strict guidelines that curtail where Willard might go on Gladys when the men release her. Her movement, like that of all women, is curbed and impeded by socially dictated spatial prohibitions. However, by positioning the wheel so that it faces away from the cottage, the site of domesticity, Willard also gestures to the potential of overturning, riding away from, spatial inhibitions. She reduces the sway of those spatial impediments in incremental moves throughout the ensuing photographs.

A seemingly modest change in scene marks "So Easy—When You Know How," the third photo in the memoir sequence (see fig. 1.2). Here, Willard remains situated on the same pathways in front of the same cottage. In addition, her emancipatory potential appears diluted because she is only an observer, firmly planted near the cottage walls as if taking comfort from their protective shelter. However, Willard's gaze focuses her (and the viewer's) attention on the female teacher who comfortably sits on Gladys. Furthermore, the front wheel of the bicycle angles away from the cottage, poised to leave walls and thus protection behind. Even if Willard is not yet ready for such spatial forays beyond the domestic, the young female mentor points the way and illustrates the reality of spatial emancipation. The next photo, "It's Dogged As Does It," reinforces the liberatory promise of "So Easy—When You Know How" (see fig. 1.3). Here Willard is mounted on Gladys but in an entirely different scene, one without the immediate protection of the domestic sphere or the rigid guidelines of the straight and narrow pathways. Instead, the photograph's setting features a more bucolic scene, one that conjures up the "Priory drive" that Willard traversed more than twelve times, marking the experience in her journal as a benchmark moment (*Writing* 388). A step away from the tamed domesticity of the cottage, but without the suggestion of complete freedom, the backdrop of the scene consists of a fence and shrubbery blocking movement on one side. However, while her path to freedom may be curtailed by fences to her left, she possesses open areas in three other directions that invite her to exercise her newly minted ability to choose where to go and how fast. Also, the clearly demarcated paths characteristic of the cottage scenes disappear in this setting. Rather, the landscape invites a range of choices. Within this less cultivated venue, Willard sits upright on Gladys positioned to travel away from the cottage's spatial limitations. That choice is emphasized in the next scene, "Let Go—But Stand By," which returns Willard to the cottage, but a Willard who is now ready to strike off on her own (see fig. 1.4). Only one woman stands near Willard, one who "respects the individuality of another and yet adds one's own, so far as may be, to another's momentum in the struggle of life" (57). This helpmeet encourages the student to explore the possibilities of spatial emancipation while standing by as a bulwark against potential disaster. Subsequently, rather than a point of transition, the cottage now becomes a point of departure, a departure the last photograph illuminates. In "At Last," the rather exhilarating conclusion to the dramatic visual narrative, the cottage and other visual indicators of containment disappear (see fig. 1.5). Willard pedals toward the viewer's world unfettered by parlors or by True Woman ideology. Under her own momentum and guided by her own navigation, she moves toward a destination of her choice. Far behind, left in her wake, a single solitary figure of a man stands with arms lax, watching the figure in front of him recede from view. He is immobilized; she is not. At this moment, through the affordances of photography, Willard designs a radical ethos that aligns with rather than deflects from her reformist agenda. Here, in this visual denouement, Willard's Everywoman, neither wholly feminine nor utterly ladylike, moves and acts in public venues in ways that are both authorized and emancipated.

The Radical on Wheels

Through the reality of the specific content of the halftones and through their arrangement, Willard confronts the challenges posed by the visual for the ethotic arguments of nineteenth-century women. Her multimodal memoir deploys the visual to construct a radical photographic ethos, one that makes a virtue of authority and spatial emancipation, reinforcing her vision of gender equality. "There's more to be taught by the bike than meets the eye & ear," she writes in her journal (*Writing* 390), a sentiment she echoes in her memoir. What Gladys teaches is the accessibility of public authority and spatial emancipation. If, at the end of the day, the wheelwoman qua New Woman returns to the parlor, it is a newly radicalized parlor, one in which the value of what happens in this domestic region is determined by what goes on outside. But, even as this chapter offers intriguing insights into one mode of crafting visual ethotic arguments, it also raises intriguing questions about women and photographic ethos.

First, to what degree might nineteenth-century photography limit Willard's efforts to radicalize the True Woman ethos without losing her credibility or persuasive power? Photography serves as both a tool of conservation as well as a tool of revolution. While photography can act as an agent for change, it is also deeply intertwined with middle-class values and the status quo, a point that Alan Trachtenberg contends is especially true of photography in the nineteenth century. Photography was praised as a window into character because it was celebrated as a mirror of what the culture deemed admirable. During an era of seismic social changes, photography reinforced hegemonic values. By extension, to what degree do the cultural discourses swirling around photography predispose the nineteenth-century viewer to domesticate Willard's radical photographic ethos? Sontag notes that "what an image shows depends on how and where and when and by whom it is seen," indicating the importance of context (20). To a nineteenth-century audience, then, might Willard's wheelwoman qua New Woman ethos be perceived merely as a frivolous, inconsequential diversion from her True Woman character? The parlor is not radicalized by photographs of the wheelwoman qua New Woman; rather, the New Woman is reclaimed by the hegemonic parlor. In brief, then, how and in what ways might a woman's photographic ethos escape control and subvert intent, becoming a tool of the status quo?

Second, what role does discourse play in photographic ethos? While I have positioned both photography and ethos within the cultural discourses of their respective historical eras, I have chosen to separate Willard's photographic content and arrangement from her discursive narrative. However, as Trachtenberg points out, this is at best an artificial separation (xv). Considering the interactivity of images requires more than just considering the images in a visual vacuum. It requires an account of the accompanying and contiguous texts, whether those texts appear as captions or as discursive narrative. Thus, focusing exclusively on photographic ethos leaves unanswered important questions intrinsic to women and ethos. For example, how might the memoir as a whole—as a multimodal interaction of words and images in an ethotic argument—mitigate or reinforce the radical ethos of Willard's photographic performance? How might it underscore the delicate negotiation required of women making ethotic arguments in a culture being gradually dominated by the visual? By considering photographic ethos and its attendant questions, we expand our understanding of the challenges posed by ethos and the remarkable visual strategies women devised to overcome those challenges.

Note

1. Following the lead of Alan Brinton and other scholars in rhetoric and philosophy, I use the term *ethotic* as an adjectival form of ethos. Brinton acknowledges that, while *ethotic* (or ēthotic, in Brinton's case) may be etymologically suspect, it serves as an effective way to evoke the "source characteristics" that comprise ethos as credible character and "influence the receptiveness of hearers" (246).

Works Cited

Aristotle. *On Rhetoric: A Theory of Civic Discourse.* Trans. George A. Kennedy. New York: Oxford UP, 1991. Print.

Barthes, Roland. "Rhetoric of the Image." Trans. Stephen Heath. *Image Music Text.* New York: Hill and Wang, 1977. 32–51. Print.

Bordin, Ruth. *Women and Temperance: The Quest for Power and Liberty, 1873–1900.* New Brunswick, NJ: Rutgers UP, 1990. Print.

Brinton, Alan. "Ethotic Argument." *History of Philosophy Quarterly* 3.3 (1986): 245–58. JSTOR. Web. 10 Oct. 2014.

Buchanan, Lindal. *Regendering Delivery: The Fifth Canon and Antebellum Women Rhetors.* Carbondale: Southern Illinois UP, 2005. Print.

Campbell, Karlyn Kohrs. *Man Cannot Speak for Her: A Critical Study of Early Feminist Rhetoric.* Vol. 1. Westport, CT: Praeger, 1989. Print.

Castriota, David. *Myth, Ethos, and Actuality: Official Art in Fifth-Century B.C. Athens.* Madison: U of Wisconsin P, 1992. Print.

Dodge, Pryor. *The Bicycle.* Paris: Flammarion, 1996. Print.

Gifford, Carolyn De Swarte, ed. *Writing Out My Heart: Selections from the Journal of Frances E. Willard, 1855–96.* Urbana: U of Illinois P, 1995. Print.

"In Memory of Miss Willard." *Kansas City Journal*, Feb. 25, 1898. Library of Congress. Web. 12 Sept. 2012.

Isocrates. *Antidosis.* Trans. George Norlin. Loeb Classical Library, vol. 2. Cambridge, MA: Harvard UP, 1929. Print.

Kaestle, Carl F., and Janice A. Radway. "A Framework for the History of Publishing and Reading in the United States, 1880–1940." *A History of the Book in America*. Vol. 4. Ed. Carl F. Kaestle and Janice A. Radway. Chapel Hill: U of North Carolina P, 2009. 7–21. Print.

Marks, Patricia. *Bicycles, Bands, and Bloomers: The New Woman in the Popular Press*. Lexington: U of Kentucky P, 1990. Print.

Mattingly, Carol. *Appropriate[ing] Dress: Women's Rhetorical Styles in Nineteenth-Century America*. Carbondale: Southern Illinois UP, 2002. Print.

———. *Well-Tempered Women: Nineteenth-Century Temperance Rhetoric*. Carbondale: Southern Illinois UP, 1998. Print.

"Miss Willard." *The Times*, Feb. 19, 1898, 4. Library of Congress. Web. 12 Sept. 2012.

Newhall, Beaumont. *The History of Photography*. 5th ed. New York: Museum of Modern Art, 1982. Print.

"The New Woman." Patterson 183–84.

Northcliffe, Glen. *The Ride to Modernity: The Bicycle in Canada, 1869–1900*. Toronto: U of Toronto P, 2001. Print.

Patterson, Martha H., ed. *The American New Woman Revisited: A Reader, 1884–1930*. New Brunswick, NJ: Rutgers UP, 2008. Print.

Root, M. A. *The Camera and the Pencil: Or the Heliographic Art*. Philadelphia: J. B. Lippincott, 1864. Print.

Seymour, Robert Lew. "The Bicycle—Its Pleasures and Perils." *Chautauquan* 20.6 (March 1895): 703. American Periodicals. Web. 15 Sept. 2012.

Sontag, Susan. *On Photography*. New York: Picador, 1977. Print.

Southworth, Albert S. "An Address to the National Photographic Association," *Philadelphia Photography*, 1871. *Smithsonian American Art Museum*, Helios. Web. 15 May 2010.

Steiner, Deborah Tarn. *Images in Mind: Statues in Archaic and Classical Greek Literature and Thought*. Princeton UP, 2001. Print.

Trachtenberg, Alan. *Reading American Photographs: Images as History, Mathew Brady to Walker Evans*. New York: Hill and Wang, 1989. Print.

Ward, Maria E. *The Common Sense of Bicycling: Bicycling for Ladies*. New York: Brentano's, 1896. Print.

Willard, Frances E. "Dawn of Woman's Day." *Let Something Good Be Said: Speeches and Writings of Frances E. Willard*. Ed. Carolyn De Swarte Gifford and Amy R. Slagell. Urbana: U of Illinois P, 2007. 125–37. Print.

———. "Miss Willard on the 'New Woman.'" Patterson 137–39.

———. *What Frances E. Willard Said*. Ed. Anna A. Gordon. New York: Fleming H. Revell Co., 1905. *Google Book Search*. Web. 17 July 2012.

———. *A Wheel within a Wheel. How I Learned to Ride the Bicycle, with Some Reflections by the Way*. New York: Fleming H. Revell Co., 1895.

———. *Writing Out My Heart: Selections from the Journal of Frances E. Willard, 1855–96.* Ed. Carolyn De Swarte Gifford. Urbana: U of Illinois P, 1995. Print.

Welter, Barbara. *Dimity Convictions: The American Woman in the Nineteenth Century.* Athens: Ohio UP, 1976. Print.

Wosk, Julie. *Women and the Machine: Representations from the Spinning Wheel to the Electronic Age.* Baltimore: Johns Hopkins UP, 2001. Print.

2. Andrea Dworkin's Radical Ethos

Valerie Palmer-Mehta

I'd like to take what I know and just hand it over. But there is always a problem for a woman: being believed. How can I think I know something? How can I think that what I know might matter? Why would I think that anything I think might make a difference, to anyone, anywhere? My only chance to be believed is to find a way of writing bolder and stronger than woman hating itself—smarter, deeper, colder. This might mean that I would have to write a prose more terrifying than rape, more abject than torture, more insistent and destabilizing than battery, more desolate than prostitution, more invasive than incest, more filled with threat and aggression than pornography . . . [My words] would have to stand up for women—stand against the rapist and the pimp—by changing women's silence to speech . . . I'd have to be militant; sober and austere. I would have to commit treason: against the men who rule. (Dworkin, "My Life" 16)

Andrea Dworkin (1946–2005) was the twentieth century's most audacious and controversial feminist. A self-described radical feminist, lesbian, and Jewish American, Dworkin championed women's rights and condemned violence against women as she penned over a dozen books and delivered rousing speeches that prompted Laura Miller to refer to her as the "Jonathan Edwards of radical feminism" (par. 4). When she died in 2005, Catharine MacKinnon stated that Dworkin courageously "exposed the ugliest realities of women's lives and said what they mean" while she served as the "intellectual shock troops, the artistic heavy artillery of the women's movement in our time ... [taking] its heaviest hits" (par. 7).[1] Gail Dines referred to her as an "eloquent writer, passionate orator, and courageous activist. She inspired, challenged, and sparked a movement" (par. 1). Even those who disagreed with her ideas or approach recognized the loss that Dworkin's death presented.

> In a world where teenage girls believe that breast implants will make them happy ... in a public culture which has been relentlessly pornographised, in an academic environment which has allowed postmodernism to remove all politics from feminism, we will miss Andrea Dworkin. (Viner par. 15)

Despite the fact that she has been called "a great political thinker" (Bindel par. 1) and earned a space among the paltry 10 percent of women included in Richard Posner's list of public intellectuals of the twentieth century (168, 196), the broader public, including feminists of varying stripes, have not given due consideration to her life's work and its significance in what some call a postfeminist world.

Although Dworkin's early years with her parents were largely positive, it is clear that she faced a difficult path in life. Dworkin's relationship with the world was shaped by the abuse she received at the hands of numerous perpetrators, which influenced her approach to feminist activism and thought. At the tender age of nine, Dworkin was sexually assaulted (Dworkin, "My Life" 22–23). When she was arrested at age eighteen for demonstrating against the Vietnam War, two prison doctors at the New York City Women's House of Detention sexually assaulted her, giving her a brutal and invasive internal exam that left her bleeding for days. Ariel Levy states that, "Dworkin's response to the incident was her first act of purposeful bravery" (par. 10). She wrote letters to newspapers regarding her sexual brutalization and the deplorable conditions of the prison; a grand jury was instituted to investigate, and Dworkin was subpoenaed to testify (Dworkin, "My Life" 26–27). Even though the grand jury report claimed that nothing was wrong at the prison, years later it was closed and credit was given to Dworkin for cultivating the political winds to facilitate its demise (Dworkin, *Heartbreak* 77–81). After graduating from Bennington College in 1968, she moved to Amsterdam to write, where she married Cornelius Dirk De Bruin, a Dutch anarchist. She subsequently became the victim of domestic abuse: "I remember him banging my head against the floor until I passed out . . . I remember being hit over and over, the blows hitting different parts of my body as I tried to get away from him" (Dworkin, "Battered" 103). When she fled his abuse, she was penniless, homeless, and compelled into prostitution to find a way home to the United States. In her long journey home, she encountered Ricki Abrams, a feminist who not only helped Dworkin find shelter and survive, but also introduced her to radical feminist writings. After returning to the US and immersing herself in feminist activism, Dworkin decided to publicly identify as a lesbian. She moved in with John Stoltenberg, who also was out and gay, and they lived together until her death, marrying in 1999. When an interviewer said, "There are a lot of rumors about your lesbianism. No one quite seems to know what you do with whom," Dworkin replied, "Good" (Levy par. 25). Dworkin embodied the "deliberatively disruptive" approach of queer theory long before Teresa de Lauretis's 1990 use of the term set in motion a whole new mode of inquiry (Halperin 339–340).

Dworkin found feminism's analytical insights enabled her to make sense of the painful experiences that marked her life (Moorcock and Dworkin par. 14). Feminism elucidated a basis for understanding her struggles in systemic, political terms, as a symptom of women's marginality in patriarchal culture, rather than a personal, idiosyncratic experience (Dworkin, "Loving" 63). Dworkin sought to expand upon and share the insights of feminism in her rhetoric by struggling against incest, rape, prostitution, pornography, and violence against women, while also personally challenging injustice wherever she found it. For example, at the memorial service of Petra Kelly, a pacifist, feminist, and German politician who was murdered by her lover, she angered mourners with her unsolicited speech regarding how pacifists had failed to take an appropriate stance in opposition to violence against women; thus, she intimated, they had failed to protect Petra and were, in part, responsible for her death (Dworkin, *Heartbreak* 105–107). As Dworkin examined difficult issues in public forums, she was not averse to making audiences—even ostensibly favorable audiences—angry or uncomfortable. She saw productive confrontation as an integral facet of dismantling the structures that bind women and men in pathological forms of interaction, and she fully recognized that her ideas and approach placed her in the crosshairs of cultural debates: "My work is radical. A lot of people, especially the already comfortable, don't like it" (Moorcock and Dworkin, par. 12). Dworkin's approach even put her at odds with academic feminists, whom she believed held feminism back with their slow approach to social change and their seeming commitment to observing and documenting oppression rather than fighting against it. Consequently, Dworkin was a figure who provoked, as Tanya Serisier notes, "polarized responses" not only from the broader US culture, but also from within feminist debates in the academy, earning her the title of the Malcolm X of feminism (27).

Despite her reach, the field of rhetorical studies has been largely silent on Dworkin, with notable exceptions by Rosa Eberly and Catherine Palczewski. Eberly provides a rich analysis of literary critics' responses to Dworkin's novel *Mercy* (132–159), while Palczewski examines how Catharine Mackinnon and Dworkin cultivated a new definition of pornography ("Contesting" 1–17) and utilized the rhetorical functions of testimony to privilege women's voices ("Public" 461–67). Adding to these important contributions, I argue that Dworkin cultivates a productive, oppositional ethos by deploying radical feminists' rhetoric of confrontation. More specifically, I posit that Dworkin rejects a "pleasing" ethos as a normative and compulsory enterprise by strategically employing radical feminists' specific confrontational modes of symbolic rites, symbolic reversals, and reality structure violations. Drawing on Dworkin's speeches and essays from the 1970s to the 1990s, I first identify how she rebuffs a politics of manners, or the interpellation into an agreeably feminine ethos, through symbolic rites and violating the reality structure by radically defying norms for heterofemininity in her relationships, embodiment, and speech. Second, I demonstrate how she deploys a politics of confrontation through symbolic reversals, in which she strategically uses her ostensibly maligned ethos as a tool to problematize and assail her audiences' ethē, while reversing the responsibility for cultivating a desirable ethos onto them. As Dworkin's bodily practices coalesce with and amplify her rhetoric, she dramatically subverts traditional, masculinized accounts of ethos and invents a productive, confrontational ethos for women—a radical feminist ethos. To begin, I situate Dworkin's contribution within the rhetoric of radical feminism before turning to an analysis of her rhetorical strategies.

The Rhetoric of the Radical Faction of the Women's Movement

Ever since Karlyn Kohrs Campbell identified women's liberation rhetoric as constituting its own unique genre, with distinctive substantive-stylistic features, scholars have worked to delineate the defining rhetorical features of the varying feminist groups that comprise what we now refer to as the second wave of the women's movement (Campbell 74–86; Hancock 264–271; Hope 17–25; Kurs and Cathcart 12–23; McPherson 33–38; Pearce 307–315). Radical feminists, the group with which Dworkin primarily identified, used a range of rhetorical strategies as they endeavored to create an authoritative voice for women at a time when their roles were decidedly traditional, dominated by the domestic sphere, and defined by the duties of being a wife, mother, or sexual partner. Because women were socialized into dependence in their roles as the heterosexual helpmate of men, Campbell states that "the sex role requirements for women contradict the dominant values of the American culture—self-reliance, achievement and independence"—values that were, in practice, reserved for men (75). This practice extended to and complicated women's public voice and their ability to construct viable ethē: "Insofar as the role of rhetor entails qualities of self-reliance, self-confidence and independence, its very assumption is a violation of the female role" (Campbell 75). It was within this context that radical feminists, disillusioned by the slow gains of legal reform, broke off from the reform-minded National Organization for Women, and began to voice their struggle for revolutionary change. In an effort to demonstrate that reforms to the flawed sociopolitical structure were a waste of time, and to illuminate women's oppression, the Women's Liberation Front (WLF) drew upon the rhetorical strategies of metaphors, such as "woman as property," to describe US women's plight; they also employed the strategies of vilifying the patriarchal social order and naming the enemy to construct a positive, prowoman identity as the antithesis of men (Hancock 264–71; Hope 18–20). To promote self-persuasion and agency, as well as to delineate a recurring pattern of oppression, radical feminists used rhetorical strategies such as consciousness raising and self-disclosure (Campbell 78–81; Hope 21–2; McPherson 33–4). Externally, the WLF used shock tactics, which included violating the reality structure by theatrically parodying stereotypical gender roles, and halting communications, which disrupted misrepresentations of women through scorning and refusing to talk to traditional media while creating their own media outlets (McPherson 35–6). A range of radical feminists also appropriated the traditionally masculine manifesto genre as another mode of resistance to patriarchy (Pearce 307–315).

Radical feminists used a prolific range of rhetorical strategies to disrupt the patriarchal social order, but confrontation was the strategy to which Dworkin regularly gravitated. Confrontation emerged with particular force as a distinct rhetorical form from within the radical social movements of the 1960s in general (Cathcart 95–103; Scott and Smith 1–8) and from women's liberation efforts in particular (Campbell 74–86; Kurs and Cathcart 12–23). Reflecting feelings of deep alienation and division, confrontation occurs when rhetors have exhausted normative means of communication with those in power (Cathcart 96–101; Scott and Smith 2). According to Robert Cathcart, "Confrontation is symbolic display acted out when one is in the throes of agon," and it demands "a response that goes beyond the actions of the confrontation itself" (96, 101). As a special mode of suasion, confrontation is not employed liberally in ordinary contexts, but rather it is utilized during "special and limited circumstances, such as periods of societal breakdown or when moral underpinnings are called into question" (Cathcart 97). It requires the coming together of the confronter, who seeks to negate the existing order and identify its evils, and the established order, which responds with polarization and further division as the establishment attempts to paint the confronter as a moral leper in reaction to vociferous challenges to its legitimacy (Cathcart 96–102). Radical social movements gain their identity from acts of confrontation, or "acts of acting together" (Cathcart 102). Indeed, Cathcart argues that confrontational actions "are public statements of conversion which, when coupled with the establishment response, formally commit the individual to the movement, making such individuals dependent on the movement for whatever legitimacy they are to have" (102).

Radical feminists' use of this strategy of confrontation was characterized by "active, outward rhetorical confrontation of the system" carried out using "both verbal and non-discursive forms" (Kurs and Cathcart 19). Campbell, as well as Katherine Kurs and Robert Cathcart, identify varying but overlapping strategies employed, including violating the reality structure, using attack metaphors, and practicing symbolic rites and symbolic reversals. Women's liberation rhetoric worked to violate the reality structure by openly exploring, in stark and provocative ways, taboo subjects typically forbidden from discussion and attacking the culture's psychosocial reality; in so doing, feminists "violate the norms of decorum, morality and 'femininity' of the women addressed" (Campbell 81–82).[2] The use of attack metaphors revealed the ideological construction of sexism in language and thought through shocking juxtapositions—or what Kenneth Burke termed perspective by incongruity—such as positioning a woman as August Rodin's "The Thinker" (Campbell 82). In providing global opposition to patriarchal structures, Kurs and Cathcart argue that lesbian feminists engaged in symbolic rites to exorcise the patriarchal order.[3] This symbolic exorcism occurred through a confrontation with, and the symbolic death of, the old, oppressed self in order to give birth to a new, liberated self. Symbolic rites include personal renaming, head shaving, "adopting dress that is seen as the antithesis of male defined fashion and beauty," and "altering spelling of words such as woman (wommin, wommyn) and history (herstory), as well as repeated execration of the enemy" (Kurs and Cathcart 19). By making the dominant ideology visible via symbolic rites, or as Kurs and Cathcart call it, drawing on Burke—revealing the mystery—feminists work toward dismantling the patriarchal power structure (20). Finally, radical feminists used the strategy of symbolic reversals in order to "transform devil terms society has applied to women into god terms and . . . exploit the power and fear lurking in these terms as potential sources of strength" (Campbell 82). Kurs and Cathcart note that in changing words such as "lesbian and dyke" into god terms feminists deflect cultural negativity, usurp the terms' rhetorical force, and "possess all the confrontational power imbued in these terms as the rhetorical embodiment of the threat" (20).[4] As a radical feminist, Dworkin drew upon the confrontational rhetorical strategies employed within movement rhetoric to create an oppositional ethos.

Dworkin's Rhetoric of Confrontation

Dworkin needed a method of communicating that would allow her to dismantle the cultural habit of invalidating women's voices and experiences; as she said, she needed a "way of writing bolder and stronger than woman hating itself—smarter, deeper, colder" ("My Life" 16). Her method included rejecting a politics of manners through symbolic rites and violating the reality structure and deploying a politics of confrontation through invoking and extending the rhetorical strategy of symbolic reversals. These maneuvers enable Dworkin to construct a radical feminist ethos—an ethos sorely missing in our so-called postfeminist, third-wave world.

Rejecting a Politics of Manners

In contrast to rhetors who strive to project a desirable ethos in relation to the dominant culture, a particularly tenuous rhetorical activity for those situated at the margins of their culture, Dworkin purposefully worked against a normative ethos and instead worked to exorcise, through symbolic rites, the patriarchal social order and its cultural prescriptions for gender and sexuality, effectively constructing a radical ethos. Users of symbolic rites seek to resist the oppressor by symbolically rejecting the practices and thought patterns of the patriarchal order and by making dominant ideologies visible. While symbolic rites typically are conceived as an action to mark a moment, such as a ceremonial initiation that sparks a renaissance and a new feminist life, Dworkin extended these symbolic rites into her everyday practice.

One practice and ideology that Dworkin resists and reveals is heteronormativity and its penultimate goals, marriage and child bearing. She was, as Judith Grant indicates, among the first to argue against the heteronormativity of US culture (976), and she also promoted sexual fluidity rather than gender and sexual polarization, anticipating transgenderism (970). Although she identified as a lesbian, her sexuality was, in fact, ambiguous; Ariel Levy suggests there is little indication that Dworkin had romantic relationships with women (pars. 23–28). It is more likely that she strategically deployed the term lesbian to trouble traditional conceptualizations of gender and sexuality as she worked to achieve positive identification for and with women across their diversity. In so doing, Dworkin deployed symbolic rites in rejecting the dominant ideology of heteronormativity through her public identification as a lesbian, troubling heterosexual marriage through exchanging vows with an out gay man, and resisting the sexual slavery she believed necessarily followed from reproduction. By consciously adopting choices in which she opposed traditional roles, she resisted patriarchal definitions of the self and gender/ sexual relationships. Unlike many second-wave feminists who symbolically committed themselves to change at one moment in time, but went back to normative practices subsequent to the demise of the movement, Dworkin maintained that symbolic resistance throughout her life.

In addition to disrupting a normative ethos relationally, she employed symbolic rites in her resistance to patriarchal norms for fashion and beauty both in her rhetoric and, perhaps more importantly, in her embodiment. She lived what she preached. In *Woman Hating*, Dworkin discusses the stakes involved in policing women's appearance.

> Pain is an essential part of the grooming process, and that is not accidental. Plucking the eyebrows, shaving under the arms, wearing a girdle, learning to walk in high-heeled shoes, having one's nose fixed, straightening or curling one's hair—these things hurt. The pain, of course, teaches an important lesson: no price is too great, no process too repulsive, no operation too painful for the woman who would be beautiful. (115)

Dworkin made sure readers understood the stakes; she explained that beauty norms dictate the relationship that women have with their own bodies (113), and the sheer quantity of time and effort required to adhere to them "forces women to be a sex of lesser accomplishment" (116). Dworkin had a solution: women must make the radical move to reclaim their bodies; they "must stop mutilating their bodies and start living in them" (116). Recognizing the dehumanizing effects of not being able to define the terms and contours of one's own embodiment and having one's body continually regulated and judged, Dworkin purposefully maintained an appearance that was dismissive of feminine norms wearing her hair shaggy and regularly donning oversized jean overalls, regardless of the context. Viner reports that Dworkin would "'go to posh restaurants in Manhattan wearing those bloody dungarees'" (par. 15). She refused to wear makeup and did not pluck, shave, paint, coif, or engage in the numerous rituals women often follow. Melissa August, Elizabeth Bland, and Harriet Barovick refer to her as "unapologetically unfashionable" (par. 3). Her appearance was a subject of admiration, as some "paid tribute to Dworkin's refusal to conform to ideas of attractiveness" (Sayers par. 3), and it was also a source of derision, as MacKinnon notes: "Where the physical appearance of male writers is regarded as irrelevant or cherished as a charming eccentricity, Andrea's was reviled and mocked" (5). Detractors and supporters alike felt qualified to speak about her weight, seeing it as a form of "self-harm" (Moore par. 8) or as an extension of her persona (Gornal par. 2). Derided and admired, Dworkin's embodiment was a strategic rhetorical response to women's oppression, and she used it to reveal, question, and subvert standards of beauty for women.

In her speeches, Dworkin vocalizes her embodiment and relational practices—defiant opposition to society's conventions and sacred traditions. She called on women to reject conforming to what I call, drawing on Dworkin, a politics of manners, or being interpellated into an agreeably feminine ethos, which she describes as "cheerful conformity," "sweet passivity," "submission," and "gratitude" for the "slim options" that face women. By resisting norms for femininity in her relationships, embodiment, and speech, she activates symbolic rites as she subverts normative conceptions of ethos for women who require them to fit into dominant modes. In her rhetoric, she repeatedly discusses the idea that women are offered either the option of being silent ("I Want" 163; "My Life" 16; "Remember" 169–175; "Silence" 235) or of acting "nicely" ("Feminism Now" 325–26; "Night" 17; "Pornography" 201; "Terror" 39). Dworkin urges women to be aware of this positioning and to reject it. In an excerpt published in the *Sunday Times* in 1987 ("Look" par. 19–20), and reprinted in full in her book, *Letters from a War Zone*, Dworkin identifies the women's movement as a location where the politics of manners was manifest, demonstrating no group was beyond Dworkin's reproach.

Will the Women's Movement be an authentic liberation movement for women, a force for the egalitarian redistribution of power, resources, and opportunity; or will feminism be a polite nudge toward superficial reform, mostly of manners, sometimes of social or legal codes or practices? . . . Will feminism continue the difficult and costly politics of confrontation—rebellion against the power of men in public and in private, resistance to a status quo that takes the civil inferiority of women to be natural, sexy, and a piece of political trivia; or will an elite of women, anointed to influence (not power) by the media, keep demonstrating (so that the rest of us will learn) how to talk nice and pretty to men, how to ask them politely and in a feminine tone to stop exploiting us? ("Feminism Now" 325–26)

Dworkin's critique indicates how the radical ideas and approach of the movement were being forced into dominant ideological modes, which Dworkin believed were robbing the movement of its voice and power. She notes that as women were compelled into a politics of manners, they were actively giving up the means of expressing their opposition. Her critique of the movement itself indicates how deeply ingrained the politics of manners is in society, and how it is deployed to limit women's forms of opposition and render them politically ineffectual. Notably, Dworkin makes visible the manufactured process by which those in power strategically select complaisant women to represent women's concerns in the media, with the effect of largely reinforcing the status quo and only superficially questioning practices that work to reify patriarchal hegemony.

Similarly, in a speech delivered at a Take Back the Night event in New Haven, Connecticut, in 1979, Dworkin argues that women are interpellated into "cheerful conformity" as they are compelled to be grateful for their slim options. In this context, she discusses the importance of freedom of movement, by which she means the freedom to be out day or night without worrying about being the victim of sexual violence. She argues that because of the pervasiveness of rape, US women are not "allowed" out after dark. Of course, in some parts of the world, women's freedom of movement is even more restricted. American women, however, are ostensibly lucky because they have the freedom to move about freely during the day. For this, she says facetiously, women are compelled to be grateful.

Especially we must be grateful because jobs and safety depend on the expression of gratitude through cheerful conformity, sweet passivity, and submission artfully designed to meet the particular tastes of the males we must please. We must be grateful—unless we are prepared to resist confinement–to resist being locked in and tied up—to resist being bound and gagged and used and kept and kept in and pinned down and conquered and taken and possessed and decked out like toy dolls that have to be wound up to move at all. ("Night" 17)

Dworkin illuminates the limits placed on women's everyday lives by the un-challenged sexism and complacency toward sexual violence against women in US society. She calls women to recognize the political impotence inherent in politely asking, and being "grateful," for basic rights. Dworkin frequently beseeches women to join her in the struggle for rights and to do so assertively, unapologetically, and without concern for society's judgment. In her key-note speech delivered at the May 1991 Canadian Mental Health Association's Women and Health Conference held in Banff, Alberta, Dworkin said: "I am asking you to stop passing: stop passing and having feminism be part of your secret life. I am asking you to not apologize to anyone for doing it" ("Terror" 42). Because publicly identifying as a feminist undermines a woman's ethos in a patriarchal culture, Dworkin not only subverts traditional notions of ethos formation for herself, but she also encourages women to join her, regardless of what censure the dominant culture may bring.

Discussing taboo topics that people deem unseemly and articulating those topics in stark, provocative, and, in Dworkin's case, dark ways—what Camp-bell has referred to as violating the reality structure—are other methods that Dworkin utilized in resisting a traditionally feminine ethos. Regarding this tendency in her work, Levy states:

> Much of society is set up specifically to assist people in their process of ignoring the horrors of the world. Dworkin's agenda was the opposite. She had little sympathy for anyone with too weak a stomach to dwell with her in the darkness. (par. 9)

In a speech given on April 8, 1983, at Hamilton College, Dworkin indicates that this approach was intentional.

> I represent the morbid side of the women's movement. I deal with the shit, the real shit. Robin Morgan calls it "atrocity work." . . . I deal with what happens to women in the normal course of women's lives all over this planet: the *normal* stuff that is abusive, criminal, violating—the point being that it is considered normal by the society at large. ("Feminism" 133)

In lucid detail, Dworkin talks about pornography, incest, battery, and rape in all its forms. By illuminating the commonplace nature of such abuses and speaking of them in stark terms, Dworkin punctures the normality of abuse by violating the reality structure, which is set up to ignore such topics in public, creating a silence that enables the festering of abuse. In her famous testimony before the Attorney General's Commission on Pornography on January 22, 1986, in New York City, Dworkin demonstrates this approach.

> My name is Andrea Dworkin. I am a citizen of the United States, and in this country where I live, every year millions and millions of pictures are being made of women with our legs spread. We are called beaver, we are called pussy, our genitals are tied up . . . makeup is put on them to make them pop out of a page at a male viewer. Millions and millions of pictures are made of us in postures of submission and sexual access so that our vaginas are exposed for penetration, our anuses are exposed for penetration, our throats are used as if they are genitals for penetration. . . . In this country where I live, there is a trafficking in pornography that exploits mentally and physically disabled women, women who are maimed. . . . Asian women in this country where I live are tied from trees and hung from ceilings and hung from doorways as a form of public entertainment. There is concentration camp pornography in this country where I live, where the concentration camp and the atrocities that occurred there are presented as existing for the sexual pleasure of the victim. ("Pornography Is" 277)

Dworkin's provocative testimony compelled the nation to reexamine the effects of pornography on women. By bringing the realities of porn into polite public discourse, Dworkin violates the reality structure by identifying how women, across their differences, are commodified and presented as degraded, humiliated sexual objects that enjoy their abuse. Her strategic use of plain and direct language to describe the conditions of women in pornography heightens the stakes of the situation and destabilizes the normative, routinized, and mundane nature of women's abuse. Indeed, listening to the description of pornography as if one were describing a list of items on a lunch menu emphasizes that porn is disturbing in its ordinariness and pervasiveness. Juxtaposing the violations with parallelism, Dworkin ties porn directly to the nation state and emphasizes that women's civil rights as citizens of the United States were being grossly violated by pornography.

Dworkin had a deep commitment to rendering visible and interrogating patriarchal ideologies in her rhetoric, while incorporating defiance and resistance to the social order in her relationships and embodiment. She also directly targeted taboo topics that typically were not addressed in everyday conversation because of their ostensible impropriety and difficulty. Using the confrontational rhetorical strategies of symbolic rites and violating the reality structure, Dworkin radically subverts a politics of manners, or being interpellated into an agreeably feminine ethos, and promotes a radical ethos for women. In contrapuntal harmony, she adopts a politics of confrontation.

Deploying Confrontational Symbolic Reversals

Dworkin commanded the floor with force and scarcely devoted time to ingratiating herself with audiences or proving that she was a speaker worthy of having her ideas heard. Instead, she regularly engaged in a symbolic reversal whereby she deflected the need to manage her own ethos by forcing her audience into a position where they needed to edify theirs. She was not concerned with adhering to norms regarding ethos or cultural norms in general; she aimed to dismantle them. This approach was strategic.

> I am not afraid of confrontation or risk, also not of arrogance or error—I am happy not . . . to follow the rules of polite discourse, because I learned to hate them so early—I love what is raw and eloquent in writing but not feminine. ("Loving" 64)

Dworkin refused to adopt what she called a feminine writing ethic, which she associated with stereotypical expectations for women to be polite, nice, and subtle. This was noted by at least one reviewer who called Dworkin the "Leon Trotsky of the sex war. . . . She writes—dare I say it—with an aggressive manner, like a man" ("Andrea Dworkin" par. 11). Dworkin grew up reading male writers, and they had a profound influence on her stylistic choices. Indeed, Dworkin credits the "audacity" she saw modeled by male writers with giving her the means to challenge male power in her own writing ("Loving" 64). However, it was feminists who gave her the model for everyday resistance against patriarchy. "I learned to confront it in life from living feminists . . . who lived political lives not bounded by either female frailty or male ruthlessness; instead animated by the luminous self-respect and militant compassion I still hope to achieve" ("Loving" 64).

Dworkin uses such inspiration in her speeches, where she repeatedly abandons the idea of delivering a pleasing ethos. Instead, adopting and extending the strategy of symbolic reversal, she uses her maligned ethos to problematize her audiences' ethē. She confronts audiences with myriad criticisms that place them in a position where they have to defend their ethē, the contours of which she has defined ("I Want" 163; "Prostitution" 139; "Redefining" 66–67; "Women" 235–36). As she does so, Dworkin raises important issues for consideration. For example, in her 1983 speech in St. Paul, Minnesota, to five hundred men at the Midwest Regional Conference of the National Organization for Changing Men, an antisexist men's organization, Dworkin states:

> I can't come here as a friend even though I might very much want to. What I would like to do is scream: and in that scream I would have the screams of the raped, and the sobs of the battered; and even worse, in the center of that scream I would have the deafening sound of women's silence, that silence into which we are born because we are women and in which most of us die. And if there would be a plea or a question or a human address in that scream, it would be this: Why are you so slow? Why are you so slow to understand the simplest things; not the complicated ideological things. You understand those. *The simple things.* The clichés. Simply that women are human to precisely the degree and quality that you are. ("I Want" 163)

Historically female rhetors have coyly maneuvered around a host of frustrations and obstacles, making conciliatory gestures and accentuating those elements that connect rhetor and audience; Dworkin foregoes the opportunity to create identification around shared values and instead goes directly for the points of contention that exist between them. As the above excerpt indicates, Dworkin was frustrated by various groups' slow approach to social change, especially those groups tasked with achieving justice.

This frustration is evident also in a 1980 speech delivered at a conference of female law students and lawyers at Yale University.

> I must tell you that it is strange for me to be speaking at Yale Law School to lawyers. I once wanted to be a lawyer, but, fortunately or unfortunately, became a criminal first—when I was eighteen, in a demonstration against the Viet Nam War. My visions of myself as Clarence Darrow or Perry Mason were supplanted by the reality of being brutalized in jail and in court both. For a long time after that experience, it did not seem possible to me that one could be a lawyer (for either side) and a decent human being also. The invention of the feminist lawyer in the last several years

has changed my mind—a little. . . . But the real progress of women has been minuscule; and the legal system in which feminists struggle for change is still rotten to the core. ("Women" 235–36)

Dworkin directly takes on the problems she sees with the legal system—problems she believes could be perpetuated or remedied by her audience. Dworkin identifies the flaws of a sexist and unfair system, which barely enables feminists to make a dent in the subjection women face, and she testifies to the problems she personally encountered with the criminal justice system. This might be sufficient to communicate her displeasure with the current state of affairs in the profession, but she further suggests that the whole system is incontrovertibly polluted and that the people who practice in the profession—a good part, if not all, of her audience—are questionable humans. The fact that she once respected the profession, and wished to be part of it, magnifies Dworkin's condemnation, as does her personal experience of brutalization at the hands of the criminal justice system. While it is normative to draw on personal experiences to edify one's ethos, Dworkin uses her maligned ethos—as an ostensible criminal—and her experiences in the system to place her audience's profession, and ethē, in question. In both of the above excerpts, Dworkin engages in a symbolic reversal whereby she deflects the need to manage her own ethos by forcing her audience into a position where they need to edify theirs.

Dworkin makes a similar move in her 1992 speech on prostitution at the Michigan Journal of Gender and Law Symposium at the University of Michigan. Dworkin had a conflicted relationship with academic feminists, who frustrated her with their slow approach to social change. Productive confrontations occur in Dworkin's speech as she critiques perceived flaws in the academic approach to dealing with social problems. Dworkin begins by voicing her reservations about academe, the likely or aspirational vocation of her audience.

I . . . feel an awful lot of conflict about being here, because it is very hard to think about talking about prostitution in an academic setting. The assumptions of academia can barely begin to imagine the reality of life for women in prostitution. Academic life is premised on the notion that there is a tomorrow and a next and a next day; or that someone can come inside from the cold for time to study; or that there is some kind of discourse of ideas and a year of freedom in which you can have disagreements that will not cost you your life. These are premises that those who are students here or who teach here act on every day. They are antithetical to the lives of women who are in prostitution or who have been in prostitution. ("Prostitution" 139)

Dworkin identifies the privileges that academics and students enjoy, noting that they are buffered from the material realities and temporal difficulties faced by the women they wish to study, which complicates their ability to relate to, explicate, and remedy prostitution.

As a former prostitute, Dworkin's embodied experience provides a potent subtext to her speech as she emphasizes the precariousness and unpredictability of prostitutes' lives. Similar to her speech to the Yale Law School, Dworkin's maligned, lived experience, which could undermine her ethos, provides her with tools to problematize her audience's ethē. Dworkin encourages the audience to think of prostitution as a lived, embodied act, rather than an abstraction of ideas.

> I cannot accept—because I cannot believe—the premises of the feminism that comes out of the academy: the feminism that says we will hear all these sides year after year, and then, someday, in the future, by some process that we have not yet found, we will decide what is right and what is true. That does not make sense to me. I understand that to many of you it does make sense. I am talking across the biggest cultural divide in my own life. I have been trying to talk across it for twenty years with what I would consider marginal success. I want to bring us back to basics. Prostitution: what is it?
>
> . . . The minute you move away from what it really is, you move away from prostitution to the world of ideas. You will feel better; you will have a better time; it is more fun; there is plenty to discuss, but you will be discussing ideas, not prostitution. ("Prostitution" 139)

Dworkin probes her audience's presumed values and commitments when she condemns the abstractness of academic feminism and impels her audience to stay grounded with the material experiences of those they wish to study. A crucial tenet of feminism is that ideas should not function in a vacuum but be turned into action in order to make a difference in women's lives. Dworkin was concerned that the buffer of the ivory tower enabled the act of prostitution to become an abstraction and, as it became more remote, the perilousness of the women's lives and the sense of urgency needed to effectuate change are diminished, if not deferred indefinitely. Rather than avoiding points of conflict, Dworkin heads directly to where she and her audience diverge in perspective, particularly areas where they should not if they hope to improve women's status and living conditions in US culture. In this situation, and in the speeches mentioned above, Dworkin repeatedly ensures her own integrity and ethos by striking against her audiences'.

Dworkin's Radical Ethos

Despite efforts to form a strong and supportive collective, Dworkin was not afraid to stand alone, speaking hard and troubling truths in a defiant fashion. Her productive confrontational strategies provided her with a powerful voice that still echoes today. Few could rival her strength or power, and the fortitude that she evinced still serves as an exemplar, particularly in a culture where strong and challenging feminist voices are increasingly hard to find. Although she is no longer with us, Dworkin's radical ethos remains fundamental to the feminist political project because it unfailingly assumes and privileges the value, power, and authority of women's ideas and voices; it questions, and abandons, the compulsion to garner the approval of patriarchal power brokers in society; and it provides a new vision of ethos deployment for women that is not bound to, or bowed in the face of, patriarchal heterohegemony. As she struggled against a politics of manners and cultivated a productive politics of confrontation, Dworkin constructed her vision using radical feminists' rhetoric of confrontation and the distinct rhetorical modes of symbolic rites, violating the reality structure, and deploying symbolic reversals.

Historically, the obligation of the speaker to adapt to her audience has been taken for granted. Dworkin radically reconceptualizes this idea by using the rhetoric of confrontation to cultivate a productive, confrontational ethos by rejecting social convention in her rhetoric, embodiment, and relationships. When she encountered audiences, Dworkin commanded the floor with force, scarcely pausing to justify her presence. Rather than adapting to the audience, or making conciliatory gestures, she called on them to adapt to her way of thinking. Invoking radical feminists' symbolic rites and violating the reality structure, Dworkin purposefully resisted the "politics of manners," or the interpellation into an agreeably feminine ethos, in her defiance of norms for heterofemininity. Adapting symbolic rites into her everyday practices, from her nonnormative relationships to her unruly embodiment, and violating the reality structure by broaching taboo topics in a sharply descriptive manner, Dworkin consistently deconstructed patriarchal normativity while repudiating stereotypical norms for gender and sexuality.

Dworkin also adopted a politics of confrontation through symbolic reversals. Rather than making concessions for her position as a radical feminist, lesbian, criminal, or prostitute, she strategically used her ostensibly maligned ethos as a tool to problematize and assail her audiences' ethē. By engaging in a strategic reversal, she moved the burden of cultivating an appropriate ethos onto her audience, even as she simultaneously determined the contours of that ethos. In so doing, she effectively expands our understanding of symbolic reversals as a strategic mode of managing women's ethē that functions by assailing, rather than assuaging, audiences, and reversing the responsibility of managing ethos—the ethos she, rather than society, has defined—onto them. Dworkin demonstrates that confrontation can be a productive tool in affirming one's identity and challenging entrenched power structures.

As originally conceived, the rhetoric of confrontation was a special rhetorical mode used in limited circumstances. I demonstrate that Dworkin complicates this notion by extending its use, well after the women's movement reached its ultimate demise, as a habituated mode of communication throughout her life to advance the feminist cause. In a sense, Dworkin exceeded the rhetoric of confrontation, as she exceeded the feminist movement. She engaged, informed, and radically challenged audiences long after the rest of the country had fallen back into a normative rhythm. Forging a radical, disruptive ethos for women was one of Dworkin's methods of interrupting that normative rhythm, and it will remain one of her most salient contributions to the feminist political project.

Notes

1. For an analysis of the sexism present in the discourses surrounding Dworkin's death, please see Palmer-Mehta's "A 'Suitably Dead' Woman: Grieving Andrea Dworkin," presented at the 2015 Feminisms and Rhetorics Conference in Tempe, Arizona, and forthcoming in *Communication and Critical Cultural Studies*.

2. McPherson lists, but doesn't classify, this strategy.

3. Kurs and Cathcart make a distinction between radical feminists and their even more radical contemporaries, lesbian feminists.

4. Feminists were not the only movement activists to engage in reversals. Maegan Brooks argues that civil rights activist Fannie Lou Hamer engaged in a strategic reversal by using her powerlessness to gain a voice of authority to speak out regarding the oppression of poor African American Mississippians. In so doing, she constructed an effective oppositional ethos that enabled her to turn "her absence of institutional power into the primary source of her rhetorical authority" (Brooks 530–31).

Works Cited

"Andrea Dworkin." *Times of London*. 13 Apr. 2005: 58. Web.

August, Melissa, Harriet Barovick, and Elizabeth Bland. "Milestones, Apr. 25, 2005." *Time Magazine*. 17 April 2005. Web.

Bindel, Julie. "Andrea Dworkin." *Guardian*, 12 April 2005. Web.

Brooks, Maegan. "Oppositional Ethos: Fannie Lou Hamer and the Vernacular Persona." *Rhetoric & Public Affairs* 14.3 (2011): 511–48. Print.

Campbell, Karlyn Kohrs. "The Rhetoric of Women's Liberation: An Oxymoron." *Quarterly Journal of Speech* 59.1 (1973): 74–87. Print.

Cathcart, Robert S. "Movements: Confrontation as Rhetorical Form." *Readings on the Rhetoric of Social Protest*. Ed. Charles E. Morris and Stephen H. Browne. State College, PA: Strata, 2013. 95–103. Print.

Dines, Gail. "The Porn Buster." *Boston Globe*, 14 April 2005. Web.

Dworkin, Andrea. "A Battered Wife Survives." *Letters from a War Zone*. 100–106. Print.

———."Feminism: An Agenda." *Letters from a War Zone*. 133–52. Print.

———. "Feminism Now." *Letters from a War Zone*. 325–26. Print.

———. *Heartbreak*. London: Continuum, 2002. Print.

———. "I Want a Twenty-Four-Hour Truce during Which There Is No Rape." *Letters from a War Zone*. 162–71. Print.

———. *Letters from a War Zone*. Chicago: Lawrence Hill, 1993. Print

———. "Loving Books: Male/Female/Feminist." *Letters from a War Zone*. 62–64. Print.

———. *Life and Death: Unapologetic Writings on the Continuing War against Women*. New York: Free Press, 1997. Print.

———. "My Life as a Writer." *Life and Death*. 3–40. Print.

———. "The Night and Danger." *Letters from a War Zone*. 13–18. Print.

———. "Pornography: The New Terrorism." *Letters from a War Zone*. 197–205. Print.

———. "Pornography Is a Civil Rights Issue." *Letters from a War Zone*. 276–307. Print.

———. "Prostitution and Male Supremacy." *Life and Death*. 139–51. Print.

———. "Redefining Nonviolence." *Our Blood: Prophecies and Discourses on Sexual Politics*. New York: Harper and Row, 1976. 66–72. Print.

———. "Remember, Resist, Do Not Comply." *Life and Death*. 169–75. Print.

———. "Silence Means Dissent." *Letters from a War Zone*. 247–52. Print.

———. "Terror, Torture, and Resistance." *Canadian Woman Studies* 12.1(1991): 37–42. Print.

———. *Woman Hating*. New York: Dutton, 1974. Print.

———. "Women Lawyers and Pornography." *Letters from a War Zone.* 235–46. Print.

Eberly, Rosa A. *Citizen Critics: Literary Public Spheres.* Urbana: University of Illinois P, 2000. 132–59. Print.

Gornal, Jonathan. "For Ms. Dworkin, Fact Wasn't a Feminist Issue." *Times of London* 18 Apr. 2005: 11. Print.

Grant, Judith. "Andrea Dworkin and the Social Construction of Gender: A Retrospective." *Signs* 31.4 (2006): 967–93. Print.

Halperin, David. "The Normalization of Queer Theory." *Journal of Homosexuality* 45:2–4 (2002): 339–43. Print.

Hancock, Brenda Robinson. "Affirmation by Negation: The Women's Liberation Movement." *Quarterly Journal of Speech* 58 (1972): 264–71. Print.

Hope, Diane Schaich. "Redefinition of Self: A Comparison of the Rhetoric of the Women's Liberation and Black Liberation Movements." *Communication Quarterly* 23 (1975): 17–25. Print.

Kurs, Katherine, and Robert S. Cathcart. "The Feminist Movement: Lesbian-Feminism as Confrontation." *Women's Studies in Communication* 6 (1983): 12–23. Print.

Levy, Ariel. "The Prisoner of Sex." *New York Magazine* 29 May 2005. Web.

MacKinnon, Catharine. "Who Was Afraid of Andrea Dworkin?" *New York Times* 16 Apr. 2005. Print.

McPherson, Louise. "Communication Techniques of the Women's Liberation Front." *Communication Quarterly* 21 (1973): 33–38. Print.

Miller, Laura. "The Passion of Andrea Dworkin." *Salon.* 12 Apr. 2005. Web.

Miller, Stephen. "Andrea Dworkin, 58, Feminist Thinker Wrote against Pornography, Violence." *New York Sun* 12 Apr. 2005. Web.

Moorcock, Michael, and Andrea Dworkin. "Fighting Talk." *New Statesman & Society* 21 Apr. 1995. Web.

Moore, Suzanne. "Diary." *New Statesman* 25 Apr. 2007: 27. Print.

Palczewski, Catherine. "Contesting Pornography: Terministic Catharsis and Definitional Argument." *Argumentation & Advocacy* 38.1 (Summer 2001): 1–17. Print.

———. "Public Policy Argument and Survivor Testimony: Pro-Ordinance Conservatives, Confession, Mediation, and Recuperation." *Argument and the Postmodern Challenge.* Ed. Raymie McKerrow. Annandale, VA: SCA, 1993. 461–67. Print.

Pearce, Kimber Charles. "The Radical Feminist Manifesto as Generic Appropriation: Gender, Genre, and Second Wave Resistance." *Southern Communication Journal* 64.4 (1999): 307–15. Print.

Posner, Richard. *Public Intellectuals: A Study of Decline.* Cambridge, MA: Harvard UP, 2001. Print.

Sayers, Beatrice. "The Editor: The Sunday Columnists." *Guardian* 18 April 2005: 20. Print.

Scott, Robert L., and Donald K. Smith. "The Rhetoric of Confrontation." *Quarterly Journal of Speech* 55.1 (1969): 1–8. Print.

Serisier, Tanya. "Who Was Andrea? Writing Oneself as a Feminist Icon." *Women: A Cultural Review* 24.1 (2013): 26–44. Print.

Sunday Times. "Look: There's still a long way to go." *Sunday Times* [London] 28 June 1987. *Academic OneFile.* Web. 19 Mar. 2013.

Viner, Katherine. "G2: 'She Never Hated Men.'" *Guardian* 12 Apr. 2005. Web.

3. The Unavailable Means of Persuasion

A Queer Ethos for Feminist Writers and Teachers

Stacey Waite

In some ways, the title of this chapter is a contradiction. The moment I say what it might mean to enact a "queer ethos," the terms and definitions shift. "Queer" works like a sheet of ice—whatever we put there slips and slides, impossible to pin down. I hope for this meditation to be one of those moments, where the ice remains ice, but where we might slow down the slippage enough to look closely at what makes a queer ethos possible for the teaching of writing. One thing that can get left out, or tagged onto the end of discussions of queer approaches to teaching, is a connection to our primary project as teachers of composition: teaching students to write and being writers ourselves. I am interested in the questions: what might the notion of a "queer ethos" bring to enactments of pedagogy and writing? Or, put another way, what might queer pedagogies make visible or possible in the teaching of writing as an art form, skill, process, and way of thinking?

In addition to the inherent shifting and movement in the definition of "queer," there are other significant challenges to developing or defining a queer ethos. Because "ethos" as a term has some historical and linguistic ties to ethics and morality, a queer writer like myself can feel repelled by them; after all, "morality" and "ethics" and "good character" are, in many ways, dangerous terms for queers, terms constantly used against us in public debate and in material circumstances. Often times, when I hear ethos, I hear echoes of discourses that construct "right" and "wrong" behavior, discourses that describe my own ethos or location as belonging to the realm of perversion. Additionally, ethos can call up some enduring and conventional ideas— Quintilian's "good man speaking well," for example. This idea is based on the presumption that ethos has something to do with "good" character, with an essential self that can be inherently good and then expressed. But queer theory does not believe in an inherent or essential self; rather, it embraces the self as a shifting and contradictory formation, one that cannot be reduced to "good" or "bad," one that is not one at all, but many. Where Quintilian invokes the "good man speaking well," a queer ethos might invoke an androgynous mind thinking paradoxically. As Virginia Woolf asserts, "the androgynous mind is resonant and porous; . . . it transmits emotion without impediment; . . . it is naturally creative, incandescent and undivided" (81). This "porous" mind, "undivided" by binaries like gender, is precisely where a queer ethos begins, though I would argue that this mind is not tied to character or morality, but finds itself more in line with understandings of ethos that take up questions of location, positionality, and dwelling as their core terms. In "The Splitting Image: Contemporary Feminisms and the Ethics of *êthos*," Susan C. Jarratt and Nedra Reynolds write:

> The ideas of place, position, and standpoint in feminist theory offer us a way of reconceiving ethos as an ethical political tool—as a way of claiming and taking responsibility for our positions in the world, for the ways we see, for the places from which we speak. (52)

In this chapter, I want to extend this work, focusing on ethos as "the ways we see," which seems at first to depend on where we are standing—our position and experience. But what if we could see more possibilities; what if our ethos was not dependent on looking from a fixed location?

A queer ethos, then, calls us to, as Emily Dickinson might put it, "dwell in possibility," to see not only from our own limited positionalities, but to see from elsewhere, to cultivate the ability to imagine elsewhere or otherwise. A queer ethos can interrupt normative ways of looking. And this approach to ethos is intimately bound to writing and rhetorical practice, and therefore also deeply connected to pedagogy. I want to consider what teaching and writing informed by a shifting queer ethos might mean. I want to consider what it might look like to teach others to imagine possibilities that go beyond the limits of their location. In order to establish the ideals or beliefs that might form this queer ethos, recent conversations in queer theory offer a place to begin.

Beginning in the Future

Recent turns in queer theory have shifted many theorists' attention to questions of time and space. In 2004, Lee Edelman makes what some have found to be a startling set of declarations in his book *No Future: Queer Theory and the Death Drive*. In a discussion about how queer relations are characterized by politicians, lawmakers, and the Pope, Edelman writes:

> Queers must respond to the violent force of such constant provocations not only by insisting on our equal rights to the social order's prerogatives, not only by avowing our capacity to promote that order's coherence and integrity, but also by saying explicitly what Law and the Pope and the whole of the Symbolic order for which they stand hear anyway in each and every manifestation of queer sexuality: Fuck the social order and the Child in whose name we're collectively terrorized; fuck Annie; . . . fuck Laws both with capital ls and with small; fuck the whole network of Symbolic relations and the future that serves as its prop. (29)

Influenced by the work of Leo Bersani, Edelman asks queers to fuck the future, to imagine investments that might have little or nothing to do with the future of our lives, the future of our world. Through the figure of the Child, Edelman astutely outlines the ways reproductive futurism positions queerness as the enemy, as the antithesis of the future, as precisely the opposite of the ethical. Edelman invites us to embrace ourselves as this antithesis, as opposition, as antithetical to the future itself. And I must admit, for a teacher (even one working primarily with college students), this is a difficult moment. Can we teach without the future, without a notion of development, a process of becoming that points to a future, a future self, and a future world? Education rests on the notion of future, at least as it's imagined in our current social consciousness.

Judith Halberstam, in a book entitled *In A Queer Time and Place: Transgender Bodies, Subcultural Lives*, creates some interesting layering around Edelman's resistance to the future. Halberstam calls for a "queer adjustment" in how we conceive of time and space. "'Queer time,'" she writes, "is a term for those specific models of temporality that emerge within postmodernism once one leaves the temporal frames of bourgeois reproduction and family, longevity, risk/safety, and inheritance" (6). Halberstam considers what the transgender turn in queer theory has known all along, that "the transgender body has emerged as futurity itself, a kind of heroic fulfillment of postmodern promises of gender flexibility" (18). Queer theorists have been wrestling with these questions: what is queer time and space, and what is their relation to a future? It is in this notion of queer time that I believe a queer ethos offers an intervention in the ways we think about revision (presumably an act invested in a future), organization, and educational notions of improvement.

We might think of improvement as a gradual progression toward something better, a move toward utopia. In his recent book, *Cruising Utopia: The Then and There of Queer Futurity*, José Esteban Muñoz asks us to reconsider the future again, and in contradiction to Edelman, makes the argument that for many queers, and especially for queers of color, the future (and the hope out on the horizon of that future) is a matter of survival. Muñoz writes at the start of his book:

> Queerness is not yet here. Queerness is an ideality. Put another way, we are not yet queer. We may never touch queerness, but we can feel it as the warm illumination of a horizon imbued with potentiality. We have never been queer, yet queerness exists for us as an ideality that can be distilled from the past and used to imagine a future. The future is queerness's domain. Queerness is a structuring and educated mode of desiring that allows us to see and feel beyond the quagmire of the present. (1)

My teaching tells me something about this "horizon imbued with potentiality." While I agree with Edelman's assessment of the cultural problem of futurity as it rests in the hands of procreation, and I agree that queers are often positioned as the enemy to the future, a danger to it, I also think it is the very fact that queerness points toward a future that makes it threatening *to* the future. A queer ethos uncovers and unleashes possibilities—the potentials for ideas that say: *you can do your life differently* or *you don't have to live that way*. And I think it's important to say to students: *you don't have to think that way* and *there are ways of writing you have yet to imagine for yourself*.

There seems to be a pretty lively argument in queer theory about how to think about the future, or whether to think about it. And this question seems deeply connected to the idea of a queer ethos, a queer location from which to look or a queer way of looking. And in terms of the admittedly partial development of a queer ethos here, I think Judith Butler offers one kind of answer to the question of where queerness might be located. Butler's notion of fantasy invites us to think about the future in particularly interesting and contradictory ways. In *Undoing Gender*, Butler writes: "fantasy is part of the articulation of the possible; it moves us beyond what is merely actual and present into a realm of possibility, the not yet actualized or the not actualizable" (28), which is the future, the always fleeting but potential fantasy of this horizon that Muñoz describes. I am drawn to Butler's notion of fantasy here because it requires a "now" (a moment in which the imagining/fantasizing takes place) and a future (that realm of possibility). When, and if, that fantasy becomes "actualized," becomes a "now," a queer ethos would invite us to continue to enact the fantasy, to imagine that queerness that is "not yet here." This way of thinking of time is particularly useful to me as a writer and, I think, particularly useful to students, as well. Aristotle tells us that a writer must establish ethos from the start, but which ethos? A partial answer I want to explore here is this: a writer (established scholar or first-year composition student) must have a complex and even paradoxical relationship to time and location, must hold in their minds the past, the present, and the future. Writing from only one of these temporal locations means writing *without* queer ethos.

Imagine what it means to write without fantasy, without imagination, without the "articulation of the possible." We can imagine it because we read it all the time—that is, we read writing that is not aware of itself, not aware of its time. We read writing that pretends to close down a question or answer it once and for all. A queer ethos means that constant state of revision; it means that the moment the imagined possibility becomes our present, we (as writers and thinkers) are called to imagine another fantasy, another way of thinking about what we think we've just answered. This "educated mode of desiring that allows us to see and feel beyond the quagmire of the present" is precisely what queer pedagogies are for. Fucking the future might mean the kind of antisocial jouissance that Edelman describes, but it also means a loss of another kind of pleasure—the kind that unfolds out of a doing again, or the possibility of doing again, eternally.

The (Un)Available Means of Persuasion

In Edward P. J. Corbett's "Rhetoric, The Enabling Discipline" (and, of course in a variety of other conventional arguments about ethos and rhetoric), we find a very seductive picture of ethos in which we are invited to explore the "vital role that ethos plays in discourse" (32). Corbett describes the question of ethos in terms of Aristotelian notions of "the available means of persuasion," and he connects ethos to an ability to appear as having "good sense, good will, and good moral character" (32). We can further explore Butler's notion of fantasy and the "articulation of the possible" alongside Aristotle's often revisited claim that rhetoric is the "faculty of discovering in the particular case what are the available means of persuasion" (116). It's important, for this particular exploration, to pay attention to the word "available." For Aristotle, ethos, pathos, and logos are the pathways to the formulation of convincing ideas. But in each of these categories, the rhetorician finds herself (if we take up Aristotle's definition of rhetoric) looking for and employing the *available means*. This means, by implication, that there are means *un*available to us—perhaps because of our audience (or our assumptions about them), perhaps because of emotional possibilities we could (or would) not imagine, or perhaps because *not* proving a truth (logos) was not a possibility. But what about the possibility of not proving a truth or the possibility that we cannot, in the end, *know* our audience or our reader? What about those unavailable means, the ways of looking we cannot see from where we are standing?

Butler values "the articulation of the possible" (saying it, naming it) in perhaps a similar sense as Aristotle's "observing the available means"; however, for Butler, the "available means" must answer to fantasy's demand that we also "observe the means" that *seem* unavailable, unimaginable. Butler's attention to drag is particularly useful in thinking about pedagogies that value articulating the possible whereby the imagination can extend and stretch "the available means" by exposing the constructedness (of language, of gender) and opening up the imagination to possibility. But before we (and our students) learn to "articulate the possible," we must first be able to recognize those possibilities that seem impossible. In order for anyone to observe the available means that seem unavailable (like gender bending for example), one must learn to see the means that are barely visible.

What I am characterizing as a Butlerian notion of the "available means of persuasion," or put more aptly, the *un*available means, is closely connected to Heidegger's translation and reading of Aristotle. In *Basic Concepts of Aristotelian Philosophy* (2009), translated by Robert D. Metcalf and Mark B. Tanzer, Heidegger translates and interprets Aristotle's definition of rhetoric as

> the possibility of seeing what is given at the moment, what speaks for the matter that is the topic of discourse, the possibility of seeing at each moment what can speak for the matter . . . it sets forth a "possibility" and cultivates a possibility, a possibility that cultivates in itself the ability-to-see that which speaks for the matter. (78–79)

I am struck by Heidegger's interpretation of Aristotle as being connected to "possibility" rather than "availability." But I am also struck by the temporal marker "given at the moment." Butler's notion of fantasy might enable us to put pressure on the given moment, might demand that we see what is possible *beyond* the given moment. What's available at the moment is not all of what is possible. What's available might be finite, might be regulated or hidden. What is possible is endless. What is possible is fantasy. Possibilities for gender are endless, possibilities for argument, for writing, are also endless.

Unavailable Names

When I think about imagining a future, when I think about the fantasy of that queerness on the horizon, when I think about cultivating a queer ethos, I can't help but think about naming. It is always fascinating to me how much intellectual and creative energy is generated inventing a new name. I spend a great deal of time in class asking my students to invent more names for what a writer might do in an essay. Queer theorist and performance artist Kate Bornstein writes in *Hello, Cruel World*:

> I have this idea that every time we discover that the names we're being called are somehow keeping us less than free, we need to come up with new names for ourselves, and that the names we give ourselves must no longer reflect a fear of being labeled outsiders, must no longer bind us to a system that would rather see us dead. (36–37)

For queer subjectivity, new names are a matter of survival.

When I first began teaching composition courses fifteen years ago, I was (and it seemed at times my students were as well) frustrated with the language already in place to talk about writing and to talk about being in the world. And while, in terms of writing, the name "thesis statement" is not inherently problematic, I think that this particular naming has come to limit rather than expand our ideas about what essays might *do*. In the spirit of "queering the brew," as Harriet Malinowitz put it in her book *Textual Orientations*, I ask students to imagine new names, new kinds of structures, new ways of calling into being what their essays, and the essays they read, can *do*. In my classes, we continue to practice naming together, inventing a common language, a fantasy language, among us. On one particular occasion, I began by handing out the following excerpts—two taken from the final paragraphs of student essays, and one paragraph Bornstein uses to conclude a chapter of her book *Gender Outlaw*, which is a text I, at one time, could only teach in a fantasy! Part of my classroom practice is to blur the boundaries between the student writers and the published writers offered as readings, and this was my goal in constructing this handout. The handout appeared as follows, and all student work and student names are printed here with permission from each student.

The Movement of Concluding: Three Excerpts

If I could go back and have a conversation with little Kelsey, while she was waiting to be rescued by the boys [while playing imaginary Star Wars games], I would give her a couple of pointers on growing up a woman. I would tell her to get up, walk out of the tree house, and go play with her friends. . . . I would understand little Kelsey's reasoning behind allowing herself to be a victim. I would see what influences have brought her to sitting in that house playing the helpless princess. And finally, I would tell her that she should do what she wants. If she would like to be Luke Skywalker, she should go be Luke Skywalker and if she wanted to be Princess Leia waiting to be rescued, then she should be Princess Leia. But I would be sure to ask her one thing: who were those boys to tell her who she could or could not be? She could be Princess Leia, a woman, and still fight the bad guys. No one ever said a Princess couldn't rescue herself.

—Kelsey Fagan "My Journey to Womanhood"

This idea that I am searching for truth, which is ultimately what I believe Bornstein is searching for as well, is never-ending. If I were to think against what I am generally trapped to think, then my truth would indeed be beyond my gender, my skin, or my sexual relations. How would I describe something that is intangible and quite frankly non-existent to our language? After all, our language limits us as well. The basis of gender is even imprinted in how we speak. In search for truth, I am pushing through all the lies that I have been amid. If I drop every lie that I have ever lived, what is left in my hand? That to me is what I fear: the bare-nakedness of what I am made of. I fear this because for once, I would be seeing the truth. If I imagine that truth, I would be an alien—something so queer from our viewpoint of truth that it would be frightening.

—Johnnie Hart "My Queerish Truth"

Our culture is obsessed with desire: it drives our economy. We come right out and say we're going to stimulate desire for goods and services, and so we're bombarded daily with ads and commercial announcements geared to make us desire things. No wonder the emphasis on desire spills over into the rest of our lives. No wonder I get panicked reactions from audiences when I suggest we eliminate gender as a system; gender defines our desire, and we don't know what to do if we don't have desire. Perhaps the more importance a culture places on desire, the more conflated become the concepts of sex and gender.

—Kate Bornstein *Gender Outlaw*

I brought in these three sets of concluding paragraphs with the idea that we might name the moves we saw, describe them rhetorically, aesthetically, even grammatically in order to open up some new possibilities for how we can think about ending an essay or coming to conclusions. I chose these excerpts based on their different moves, and not necessarily because I thought any particular one was a model for concluding. I wanted us to practice, explicitly, the naming of writerly moves. I wanted us to think about the writer's relationship to the past, to the moment, to the future. We started with the first example. I asked students to read the first sentence. *What is Kelsey doing in that first sentence?* Shannon says, "She's talking to herself as a kid." And she's right, though she's not quite getting at the kind of answer I imagined, my pedagogical fantasy answer. Fantasy is sometimes about getting something we didn't imagine. I try again. *Yeah, she is. What would you call that?* Iggy raises his hands and says in a questioning tone, "A hypothetical? Something, like, she can't actually do." I nod my head in agreement, yet still feel confused about how to bring them to new language, so I just keep pushing. *What would you call doing that?* I ask. There are a few silent moments, and finally Kyle raises his hand and says, "I'd call it setting up a conditional, you know like an if/then kinda thing, like in logic proofs." I'm excited by Kyle's answer. Even though the language he is using is familiar, he's using it outside of its usual context, and so its relation to writing is not taken for granted. I am not, at this point in the conversation, quite sure what kind of relation it is, which usually means we're onto something. I paraphrase him on the board writing: *setting up logic proofs—if/then.* I move us on to the following sentence. I read it aloud. *What's she doing now?* I ask. Someone says, "She's repeating the 'then' part of the proof, like the 'if' is still there but she's going on with the 'thens.'"

We describe what they start calling "extending the second part of the conditional," a phrase that also made its way to the board. We talk about how this might be rhetorically powerful. Students notice the repetition of "I would." We focus on its music, on what the repetition did to our reading. And while I do not believe in the separation of form and content, I was excited by the possibilities of what was happening, how we had moved away (in some sense) from what the writing *said* and were moving toward what the writing *did*. Students noticed Kelsey's reintroduction of the "if" part of the proof when she talks about Luke Skywalker, but how she moves not to what she would tell her younger self, but what she would *ask*. We talked about how that might be a "variation" or a branching away from the pattern. "I like it though," Danielle says, "I like how it repeats but then veers away from the pattern slightly. You almost don't notice."

We spent a few class meetings looking at these paragraphs and naming their moves. Students noticed the different ways Johnnie Hart was using the "logical proof." Some of the most interesting moves students noticed in Johnnie's paragraph were "showing his underwear" (which was the name Iggy gave to the idea of admitting one's fears or shortcomings, what I might call self-implication) and "the hard bold truth" (which was the name Danielle gave to Johnnie's short bold claims in the center of his paragraph). We began to talk about how they might imitate some of these moves, how they might use these new names as strategies for writing "conclusions." Then, the conversation turned to Bornstein's piece. The students saw some of the same moves from both Kelsey and Johnnie's essays, noting the repetition of "no wonder" and noticing Bornstein's use of two "hard bold truths" in the first sentence. Toward the end of the discussion, I asked students to note some moves Bornstein makes that they do not see in the other paragraphs. Marie says, "The 'we' thing. Johnnie and Kelsey don't use 'we,' but Bornstein does." Shannon interrupts, "Can you do that? Speak for everyone like that?" I'm intrigued by this discussion, and ask, *Can you? What would you call that?* Kyle says, warmly and laughing a bit, "Well, I mean, I guess you can 'cause there it is." The students all laugh. Jennifer, who rarely speaks up in class, says, sarcastically, I'd call it "gathering the followers." I write this one on the board. I prompt her again. *Great name*, I say, *what do you mean by that?* Jennifer sits up, "I mean, some readers, just if you say 'we' immediately believe they think what you think. It's tricky," she says, smirking a bit. Danielle agrees and says, "Maybe when what you're saying is kinda radical, you use that 'we' because you're really hoping for a world where people see your point of view, you know?"

We spent some time talking this through, this language of coercive inclusion and its possible effects. A discussion of language becomes a discussion of politics. I think of Muñoz. I think for the first time that using that rhetorical "we" isn't just about persuasion, but it's about hope. It's about the fantasy of a time when that "we" might be actualized as a "we." It's about writers imagining a queerer future. A queer pedagogy requires a queer ethos. It doesn't matter if a course is focused around gender or sexuality at all; it matters that students are given the opportunity to see and name new possibilities, to "articulate the possible" beyond their current location as students, or as any of the other identity positions they might see themselves as occupying.

Finally, I ask if there are any other moves in Bornstein worth noting. Johnnie says, "She goes soft at the end." The class bursts out laughing, of course, with all of Bornstein's discussion of sex, gender roles, and her own gender reassignment surgery. I'm laughing too, but try to bring us back to discussion. *Yeah, hilarious Johnnie, but let's attend to the writing part. Because you are serious, right?* Johnnie replies, "Yeah, I am serious. The 'perhaps,' it's super gentle, like maybe or possibly." Danielle chimes in: "It might seem like you shouldn't do that either, like end on saying 'maybe.' Shouldn't you end with something a bit stronger?" The "available means" of the moment seem tied to something stronger, something more certain. *Maybe is a fantasy, an admission of uncertainty, of an uncertain future. I push, Why? Strong how?* Danielle replies, "It's like the 'hard bold truths' feel more like facts. In high school, my one English teacher said to state everything like it's a fact. It's more believable." I feel self-conscious. I try hard not to make high school English lessons seem irrelevant or wrong. I do understand the contexts and value systems informing such lessons. *Let's look back at Bornstein for a second*, I say. *Why might she have "gone soft"?* A few small giggles from the back. "It's tough stuff," Kyle says, "you can't just 'hard bold truth' it the whole time. People will just drop the book and call you a freak."

Imagining an audience is very much like imagining a future. Some writers might say that they "can't think about audience" or don't. Some might say they cannot stop thinking about audience. And like most statements writers make about writing that seem opposite of one another: they're both true. Like imagining a future, imagining an audience is an act of fantasy. *Who is your audience? What is your future?* A queer ethos highlights both the impossibility of answering questions like these and also the imperative of asking them. Queerness is both here and on the horizon (which isn't actually a place). The horizon itself is a fantasy, an imagining of the possibilities of elsewhere.

Queer Grammar Lessons

Amy Winans writes: "Ultimately, queer pedagogy entails decentering dominant cultural assumptions, exploring the facets of the geography of normalization, and interrogating the self and the implications of affiliation" (106). Grammar itself is built on dominant norms and cultural assumptions as it operates under the regulation of what is possible through its syntax, punctuation, and usage rules. Grammar is probably one of the most undercelebrated of the "available means," but it is responsible not only for the rules of how we say things, but sometimes also responsible for literally what it is possible to say or to imagine. And I'd like to say the "grammar lesson" I am about to describe was planned, but it wasn't. In fact, on this particular day, we were supposed to discuss a particular section of Michael Warner's *The Trouble with Normal*, but something else happened instead. As the students arrive at the start of class, Marie raises her hand and says, "Stacey, you know that queer theorist we read sentences by on the board?" I smile, "which one?" Marie looks down at her notebook. "Butler," she says, "Judith Butler." I nod my head. "Well," Marie says sort of smiling,

> she won an award for being, like, a really bad writer. I saw it online. There's a prize for it and everything. And I just thought it was funny that we were looking at sentences by a person who won a bad writing award.

The class giggles. I am laughing too. I know about Butler's sentence from "Further Reflections on the Conversations of Our Time," a sentence that garnered the honor of the worst and most incomprehensible sentence of that particular year. But what do I do here? I'm caught. I'm out of the closet. I am showing them sentences written by people who have been said to be decidedly incomprehensible writers, inaccessible, unavailable, impossible to read.

While I acknowledge the density of Butler's prose, I value a writer trying to say something that feels impossible to say. I value even a writer trying to find out what they are saying while they are saying it. In my teaching, I have noticed students make many grammatical "mistakes" or write jumbled and incomprehensible sentences primarily when they are trying to say something they've never said before, something they've never thought before, something that belongs to the future. I decide, without preparation, to continue with this dialogue. *The bad writing award was for a particular sentence*, I say. *Who has Internet access? Let's find it.* Sure enough, a student is able to call up the sentence on her cell phone. She reads it aloud, and I transcribe it to the board, slowly:

The move from a structuralist account in which capital is understood to structure social relations in relatively homologous ways to a view of hegemony in which power relations are subject to repetition, convergence, and rearticulation brought the question of temporality into the thinking of structure, and marked a shift from a form of Althusserian theory that takes structural totalities as theoretical objects to one in which the insights into the contingent possibility of structure inaugurate a renewed conception of hegemony as bound up with the contingent sites and strategies of the rearticulation of power.

I suspect, as I see the terms appear on the board, that this could be a tremendous pedagogical failure. Can I even define all the words in this passage? Do I have the knowledge to explain something tangible about Althusser's role in this quote? Do I know what Butler is even talking about here? Can I, as someone who is, in some sense, a "professional reader," even read this sentence? We're all staring at it. Some students have given up and seem to be waiting for me. Others, I can see, are reading the passage again and again. I feel proud that they're doing that, but I am deeply fearful they are about to be let down. "What's Althusserian theory?" Johnnie asks. "It's probably made up," Kyle says, laughing a bit. My laugh turns to a nervous laugh. I am filled with the kind of self-doubt that puts the whole exploration in question. How can this sentence, this "bad writing award sentence," teach them something about writing? And, of course, Kyle is right. Everything any of us says is made up, imagined.

I decide it's a mistake to worry about what the passage means. *It's a grammar lesson*, I tell myself, but don't say to them. *I'm a poet*, I tell myself, *I can do this*. I take one of those big breaths. *Let's take it in parts*, I say, *grammatical parts. Let's start with the moves*. I add some slashes to the sentences, like I would in poetry. *What kind of sentence is this?* I ask. There's complete silence. I wait. I wait, as I have been taught by many teaching mentors to wait. Nothing happens. No jokes, no tries. Nothing. I try a different question. *What makes this sentence so hard to read?* I ask. Tearsa says, "You think it's hard to read too, right?" I nod. *Yes, very hard*, I say. I wait again. Danielle speaks up finally, "It's like it has parentheses missing." I ask Danielle to put them in and she does.

The move from a structuralist account (in which capital is understood to structure social relations in relatively homologous ways) to a view of hegemony (in which power relations are subject to repetition, convergence, and rearticulation) brought the question of temporality into the thinking of structure, and marked a shift from a form of Althusserian theory (that takes structural totalities as theoretical objects) to one in which the insights into the contingent possibility of structure inaugurate a renewed conception of hegemony (as bound up with the contingent sites and strategies of the rearticulation of power).

The parentheses appear in some of the same places as my slashes, but they seem to work better, to trigger some discussion. "Whoa," Johnnie says, "that is better actually. I mean, I still don't quite get it, but I feel like I can read it somewhat." I ask Johnnie, *Start with the first two lines. What does Danielle's punctuation do to help?* He sits a moment. He turns to the rest of the class. "I don't know, it's better, isn't it?" he asks them. "It is," Danielle says, "like with my parenthesis, I at least know that what's inside the parenthesis in the first two lines is a definition of 'structuralist account' even though I don't know what the definition means or anything." Kelsey adds, "It means that money controls everything in the same way, I think. Capital is money, right?" They are sorting it through some, and I am just watching. I am doing nothing, mostly because I am still not quite sure what we are doing, or if it will be worth anything in the end. The students talk a few more moments about meaning.

I ask, *Danielle, how'd you know where to put the parentheses?* She walks to the board to show me. "It's just where the pauses are, where she is qualifying stuff. It's like a more convoluted version of Michael Warner," she says. They all laugh. She's right, in a way. It really is. Queer theorists write like this often. "Is it 'cause what she's saying is way complicated?" Kyle asks. "Seems like it," Johnnie says. "I mean, if you could say it an easier way, why wouldn't you?" What gets sparked is an interesting discussion of difficulty, of the ways it might be necessary in order to say what isn't available to you to say, of the ways difficulty obscures *and* illuminates meaning at once. I try something toward the end of class, after we've struggled with this grammar and meaning for over an hour. *You try,* I say to them, *you try a sentence that is grammatically identical to this bad one. Try one and turn it in to me on your way out.* Here are two examples of the sentences I received from students anonymously at the end of class that day:

The move from Australia (in which news is understood to be a way of finding out what funny or strange things happened) to the US (in which news is a way of scaring everyone about tornados, murders and school shootings) brought the question of purpose into our thinking about media, and marked a shift from a form of entertainment and information (that takes important events that encourage a society as the most important subject) to one in which the well-known and accepted human fears are preyed upon as a means of control (as it is bound up in news sources and different cultures).

Coming from my parents' house (in which a late night out is 11 PM) to college (in which a late night out is morning) brought the question of my decision-making to light, and signaled a change from my being motivated by immediate satisfaction (that tells me to do whatever I want) to my being more even-headed (as even headed-ness was previously bound up with my parents' lameness).

Almost every student used parentheses to break up their sentences. And, every single one imitated not only Butler's grammar, but also some of her content—everyone had, for example, understood that the sentence was about a shift in understanding, that the sentence was about movement between a *before* and *after*. Perhaps a queer grammar is always a kind of movement, composing sentences that understand themselves as movement. Perhaps the presence or lack of parentheses has something to do with the ways grammar regulates. It is, after all, a regulatory practice. And it is something queer indeed to *play* with grammar—to put up and take away its markers, to imitate a style that obscures meaning or reflects a meaning already and always obscured. In the same way we might teach ourselves to look at identity differently, to look at structuring an essay differently, we might also look at sentences differently— as having more available possibilities than we initially imagined. I can't help but think (while I acknowledge the denseness and difficulty of Butler's prose) that her queerness and her concern with queer understandings of culture sometimes themselves signal her prose as impossible, incomprehensible, and unavailable itself. Students reported that these sentences were "unlike any sentences" they had ever written—the articulation of the possible, even at the level of grammar. In this sense, Butler's prose is itself queer, imbued with a queer ethos, with the possibility of the horizon. This suggests that the constant qualification characteristic of Butler's prose is a direct result of her trying to say what grammar (dominant culture) might dictate is impossible to say. At one time, for example, articulating the notion that gender is performative might have seemed impossible. That is, until queer theory has a chance to nuance and qualify and until the language quite literally changes what one is able to say about gender, about the body, and about identity.

Imagining a Future

I know none of the classroom moments or student writings I have offered here are earth shattering. There are no conversion moments for students where their perspective drastically shifts from homophobia to acceptance. There are no epiphanies of the most spiritual and political kind. But that's part of my point. Shifts in perspective don't usually (at least, in my experience) happen that way. Most of those written epiphanies aren't real. Enacting fantasy, imagining possibilities that seem unavailable at the present moment, hoping for a revised future moment—these practices can begin as small as inventing alternative ways to end an essay, or strange and unusual ways of forming sentences. After all, if we are able to shift what is possible in form—something shifts in the content as well. That connection is inevitable. In her book *Sexuality and the Politics of Ethos in the Writing Classroom*, Zan Meyer Gonçalves writes, "I suggest we create opportunities in our classrooms for students to examine the beliefs they hold, the beliefs that through language maintain, reproduce, resist, or transform social inequities based on identities" (3). In my experience, this examination doesn't usually happen when we set out to discuss sexuality or gender explicitly; it happens in those small moments when students see how language works, what it makes possible or what it forecloses.

If, as Patricia A. Sullivan suggests in "Feminism and Methodology in Composition Studies," the "contemporary feminist movement and the field of composition studies have, in a sense, grown up together" (124), then perhaps we must imagine together what futures are possible. Part of that imagining is, I want to contend, embracing a queerer ethos. In "The Queer Turn in Composition Studies," Jonathan Alexander and David Wallace remind us that "the particular critical power of queerness remains an underexplored and underutilized modality in composition studies" (301). While Alexander's most recent book focuses on what he calls "sexual literacy" (another significant contribution to queer pedagogies), I want to turn our attention to queer methodologies—those queer ways of looking. These values, I believe, are crucial and significant whether we are writing about gender or sexuality or writing about our "parents' lameness." Partially and provisionally (as is always the case in queer theory), a queer ethos means both a rejection of the future as it is conventionally understood and a yearning for an unimaginable, queerer future—one embedded with (re)visionary possibility. So to enact a queer ethos means to imagine what doesn't seem imaginable, to conclude an essay without an answer, to make a sentence you've never made, to think a thought you are not supposed to think, to think the unthinkable.

As Karen Kopelson reminds us, "*Queer* is a term that offers to us and our students an epistemological position—a way of knowing rather than something to be known" (25). This way of knowing expands the limits of what "senses" can be made. And what senses can be made are intimately bound up with our ability to imagine otherwise. Our ability to imagine otherwise is political, yes, but it is also a matter of imagination itself; in other words, it is a creative matter.

Maxine Greene, in *Releasing the Imagination: Essays on Education, the Arts and Social Change*, discusses the ways in which imagination sparks potential for social transformation. She writes:

> I begin to seek out ways in which the arts, in particular, can release imagination to open new perspectives, to identify alternatives. The vistas that might open, the connections that might be made, are experiential phenomena; our encounters with the world become newly informed. When they do, they offer new lenses through which to look and interpret. (18)

It seems clear to me that the critical promise of Butler's notion of fantasy is only realizable through the cultivation of imagination. In order to "have" a fantasy, one needs to recognize what isn't available in the current moment and, through imagination, project what seems unavailable into a revised future—the untouchable moment of the horizon, queer in its seeming impossibility, yet still, in the end, a name we give to a place we have not yet seen.

Works Cited

Anzaldúa, Gloria. *Borderlands/La Frontera*. San Francisco: Aunt Lute Books, 1999. Print.

Bornstein, Kate. *Hello Cruel World: 101 Alternatives to Suicide for Teens, Freaks, and Other Outlaws*. New York: Seven Stories, 2006. Print.

———. *Gender Outlaw: On Men, Women, and the Rest of Us*. New York: Routledge, 1994. Print.

Butler, Judith. "Further Reflections on Conversations of Our Time." *Diacritics*. 27.1 (1997): 13–15. Print.

———. *Undoing Gender*. New York: Routledge, 2004. Print.

Corbett, Edward P. J. "Rhetoric, the Enabling Discipline." *The Writing Teacher's Sourcebook*. New York: Oxford UP, 2000. Print.

Edelman, Lee. *No Future: Queer Theory and the Death Drive*. Durham, NC: Duke UP, 2004. Print.

Gonçalves, Zan Meyer. *Sexuality and the Politics of Ethos in the Writing Classroom.* Carbondale: Southern Illinois UP, 2005. Print.

Greene, Maxine. *Releasing the Imagination: Essays on Education, the Arts, and Social Change.* San Francisco: Jossey Bass, 1995. Print.

Halberstam, Judith. *In A Queer Time and Place: Transgender Bodies, Subcultural Lives.* New York: New York UP, 2005. Print.

Kennedy, George A., trans. Aristotle. *On Rhetoric: A Theory of Civic Discourse.* 2nd ed. New York: Oxford UP, 2007. Print.

Kopelson, Karen. "Dis/Integrating the Gay/Queer Binary: 'Reconstructed Identity Politics' for a Performative Pedagogy." *College English* 65.1 (2002): 17–35. Print.

Malinowitz, Harriet. *Textual Orientations: Lesbian and Gay Students and the Making of Discourse Communities.* Portsmouth, NH: Boynton/Cook Publishers, 1995. Print.

Metcalf, Robert D., and Mark Tanzer., trans. *Basic Concepts of Aristotelian Philosophy.* Bloomington: Indiana UP, 2009. Print.

Muñoz, José Esteban. *Cruising Utopia: The Then and There of Queer Futurity.* New York: New York UP, 2009. Print.

Reynolds, Nedra, and Susan C. Jarratt. "The Splitting Image: Contemporary Feminisms and the Ethics of *êthos.*" *Ethos: New Essays in Rhetorical and Critical Theory.* Ed. James S. Baumlin and Tita French Baumlin. Dallas: Southern Methodist UP, 1994. 37–63. Print.

Sullivan, Patricia A. "Feminism and Methodology in Composition Studies." *Feminism and Composition: A Critical Sourcebook.* Ed. Gesa Kirsch. Boston: Bedford/St. Martin's, 2003. 124–39. Print.

Wallace, David, and Jonathan Alexander. "The Queer Turn in Composition Studies." *CCC* 61.1 (2009): 300–20. Print.

Winans, Amy E. "Queering Pedagogy in the English Classroom: Engaging with the Places Where Thinking Stops." *Pedagogy* 6.1 (2006): 103–22. Print.

Woolf, Virginia. *A Room of One's Own.* New York: Harcourt Brace, 1981. Print.

4. Changing Audience, Changing Ethos

Beth Daniell and Letizia Guglielmo

We realize the importance of our voice when we are silenced.
—Malala Yousafzai, UN Speech, July 12, 2013

During the 2012 presidential campaign, the congressional testimony of Georgetown law student Sandra Fluke and the debate that followed reveal that misogyny is still an accepted means for discrediting and attempting to silence women's speech. While history illustrates that women rhetors have long suffered similar attacks—many on their characters, some physically violent—Fluke and other women speaking publicly today demonstrate an ethos that differs from the ethos of women speaking publicly in the nineteenth and twentieth centuries. This evolution of women's ethos, we argue, is the result of both the work of feminist activists—those who responded to similar misogyny and silencing in the past—and the impact of social and digital media. Women's ethos in American public life has been marked by shifts in the space of public address and by an opportunity for women's voices to be amplified by the voices of other women in a collaborative exchange.

In this essay we explore the concept of ethos and its troubled relations with women speakers and briefly trace the complications and contradictions of ethos for those women. After exposing how recent misogynistic statements by male politicians mimic antifeminist discourse of the past, we demonstrate how the responses by twenty-first-century feminists to these contemporary statements differ from the rhetoric of nineteenth-century and twentieth-century women rhetors, even while retaining some of the characteristics of women's rhetoric from those centuries. Highlighting this difference, we argue for a new, though perhaps temporary, concept of women's ethos, one that is multivocal, grounded in lived—and shared—experience, facilitated by digital media, and directed at a different audience.

Ethos as a Concept

While in the *Rhetoric* Aristotle may leave us wondering whether ethos resides in the character of the speaker or in the rhetor's words, his explanation is unambiguous that ethos is comprised of good will (in Greek, *eunoia*), good sense (*phronesis*), and good character (*arête*) (182, 213). Classicist and political scientist Danielle Allen takes up these components of ethos in her book *Talking to Strangers*, where she examines the necessity of trust to a functioning democracy. Trust, she argues, derives in large part from good will, good sense, and good character, which are in fact methods by which a rhetor establishes trust between herself and the audience, the community she leads or hopes to lead. As this collection's editors reiterate in their introduction, ethos "is a matter of community values" (introduction, this volume). Etymologically the term *ethos* derives from "custom," "habit," "an accustomed place," according to Nedra Reynolds and others, and the word probably comes from the notion of people gathered in a customary place to discuss the issues before them ("*Ethos*" 327–328). Associating ethos with place and position, Reynolds connects rhetorical ethos and standpoint theory, which validates—and values—the perspective of the marginalized and argues that voices from the margins, voices traditionally excluded from rhetorical theory and practice, offer a different and important perspective (326).

Arguing for the Right to Speak

Changes to the rhetorical tradition came with the Reformation, the rise of science, and revolutionary democratic principles. The Reformation opened up a range of topics for debate. With the rise of science, ethos began to include expertise, and democracy began to allow public speech by those who were not part of the gentry. But "the authority to speak" in eighteenth-century Britain was still open only to those "gendered male and classed with privilege," as Vicki Tolar Burton explains in her study of literacy and rhetoric in John Wesley's Methodism (*Spiritual* 299). Ethos in the eighteenth century lies "outside the canons of invention, arrangement, style, memory, and delivery" (299), according to Burton, residing rather in the social and gendered position of the speaker. However, guided by his passionate belief that God's grace is free to all, Wesley developed an inclusive theology that challenged the classical view of rhetoric by inviting his marginalized followers—women and working class men—to read, write, and speak.

In sharing their own spiritual experiences and the ideas they acquired from reading the books Wesley recommended, eighteenth-century British Methodists created spiritual communities in which the authority to speak—that is, rhetorical agency—derived from invention, Burton argues. She explains that "generating ideas . . . requires that the rhetor feel empowered to speak" (299–300). The ethos established by Wesley's followers grew out of community and place just as had the ethos of the classical rhetors, but the qualifiers of birth or gender did not apply: "The marginalized men and women of Methodism spoke and wrote because they believed God had called them from their lives into speech and because their fellow Methodists affirmed their call by listening, reading, and believing" (300). Women, though not ordained, were allowed, even encouraged by Wesley to lead small groups and even, with what Wesley called an "extraordinary call," to preach (165). Interestingly, almost the minute Wesley died in 1791 the Methodists in Britain set about prohibiting women from speaking (171).

The Methodist belief that God's grace was free to all was embodied in the United States in the nineteenth century by Phoebe Palmer, whose father, Henry Worrall, converted to Methodism before he immigrated to New York City (Bizzell and Herzberg 1085). In 1836, Phoebe and her sister Sarah Lankford began to hold prayer meetings in the home they shared; these meetings attracted many followers over the next several years (1089). Palmer believed that some women received an "extraordinary call" from God to preach and that she was one of them (1087). As Palmer expanded her speaking role to revivals, she and other preaching women faced male criticism, typically in the form of tracts distributed among particular sets of believers (1088). The prohibition against women preaching or speaking publicly on other issues relied on Saint Paul's injunction in Timothy 2:12 that women should not teach men. Citing scripture in turn, Palmer published both a book, *Promise of the*

Father, and a pamphlet, *Tongues of Fire on the Daughters of the Lord*, in 1859 justifying preaching by women (1088–89). In *Tongues of Fire* Palmer points out that the group gathered as witnesses to Christ's ascension into heaven included women (1100). She quotes Joel 2:28–29, where God says,

> I will pour out my Spirit on all flesh; and your sons and your *daughters* shall prophesy, and your old men shall dream dreams, your young men shall see visions. And also upon the servants and upon the *handmaids* in those days will I pour out my Spirit. (qtd. in *Tongues of Fire* 1100, emphasis added)

In these texts, Palmer's knowledge of scripture is her most powerful argument, but she also quotes Latin commentary and references contemporary theologians. These qualities enhance—or at least should have enhanced—Palmer's ethos by demonstrating her good sense. Her good character derives from her powerful words, her broad knowledge, and her reputation. As a nineteenth-century woman, Palmer possessed respectability because her family was well-off, because she was married to a respectable man, because she was known as a highly effective spiritual leader, and because she lived a life of virtue (one of the translations of *arête*), working in what we would now call social justice causes. In the mid-nineteenth century Palmer was speaking to groups who knew her well—first the prayer meeting in New York City, then later in Methodist revivals.

As her reputation grew, Palmer sought to establish her good will toward her male critics by *not* challenging the mores of the culture: her good will is evident in her assertions that preaching the Gospel cannot "despoil a woman of her refined sensibilities" and that religion "brings out to the charmed beholder every thing that is pure, lovely, and of good report" in a woman (*Promise* 1098). In other words, even though she does not expand her argument beyond religious spaces, Palmer claims that preaching in no way damages a woman's femininity. She closes the first chapter of *Promise of the Father* with an overt attempt to show her good will toward the men in her audience and to establish in them reciprocal good will: "It is not our intention to chide those who have thus kept the Christian female in bondage, as we believe in ignorance they have done it" (1099). It must be noted, however, that, even as she absolves men of fault, Palmer does not soft-pedal the status of women in Christianity—"bondage," she calls it. Although she asserts that her right to speak comes from God, she also works to establish good character, good sense, and good will within her nineteenth-century social milieu.

Additionally, Palmer almost always uses the first-person plural pronoun: she is not speaking for herself alone, an unseemly act for a woman in the nineteenth century, but rather for other women preachers and other Christian women as well. Note, for example: "It is not *our* intention to chide those who have thus kept the Christian female in bondage, as *we* believe in ignorance, they have done it" or "*We* believe that hundreds of conscientious, sensitive women have actually suffered" or "*We* sincerely believe, before God, that it is this repulsive doctrine that has so much to do towards keeping Christianity meager" (1099, 1107, 1112, emphasis added). All rhetors try to identify with their audiences—to establish trust and common goals—and thus often use the first-person plural pronoun as part of that effort. For example, in his first inaugural address Abraham Lincoln states, "We are not enemies, but friends. We must not be enemies. We must be friends." In academic writing, scholars assert, "In examining this poem through the lens of reader-response criticism, we see . . ." In syllabi, professors affirm, "Finally, we will explore the question of . . ." The first-person plural in English is ambiguous, one of the indexicals, words whose meaning shifts with context and whose meaning can slip in a single discourse: In the beginning of a political speech, "we" refers to government officials, but by the end it refers to all Americans. The first-person plural pronoun can be either inclusive or exclusive, and sometimes both, as we (the two writers of this chapter) point out in later sections. Women rhetors, especially those writing or speaking to other women about issues of particular concern to women, often use the first-person plural not just to identify with their audiences of women but to speak for that audience as well. As a part of discourse about women's rights or social justice in particular, the first-person plural pronoun seems to be a mark of women's rhetoric—to claim sisterhood, to express grievances that not only are private but shared, to set themselves apart from men as Palmer does.

In the introduction to *Man Cannot Speak for Her*, a study of women's rhetoric in the nineteenth century, Karlyn Kohrs Campbell explains the situation of the woman rhetor who, like Palmer, was speaking from the margins: "In a single speech to men opposed to the very idea of a woman speaking, she cannot succeed in practical terms, even though her speech is powerful and noteworthy" (896). That is, no matter how creative the content or style of the speech, a nineteenth-century woman speaker begins with a damaged ethos at best, a disgraceful one at worst. By virtue of her female body, a woman could never speak for and to the values of the American men who controlled public life and who subscribed to the "cult of domesticity." The binary proclaimed by those subscribing to this "cult" made the female the opposite of the male in every way—he is rational, she is emotional; he operates in the public sphere, she works in the home; men call attention to themselves, women are modest and retiring; he is competitive, she is "the angel in the house"; and so forth (899). Deeply engrained in Western culture, these gender descriptions meant that a woman speaking publicly was defying the natural and divine order of things. When a woman is discounted before she even says a word, she knows that ethos is more complicated than Aristotle's theoretical statement that ethos should come from the *words* of the speaker.

As women in the nineteenth century attempted to speak for abolition and temperance, they realized that they had to argue first for the right to speak publicly (Kohrs Campbell 902). Then using natural rights and expediency arguments, they pressed, finally, for the vote. Male critics expressed horror. A catalogue of such statements is included in the chapter "The Anti-Suffragists: Selected Papers, 1852–1887" in Paula Rothenberg's *Racism and Sexism* (196–201). The charge of sexual impropriety was a typical accusation against nineteenth-century women who spoke in public: Rothenberg includes an 1852 editorial from the *New York Herald* claiming that women who want the vote are "mannish," "having so much the virago in their dispositions" or have been "badly mated" (196). These sexual slurs were printed four years after the Seneca Falls Convention and the Declaration of Sentiments and Resolutions, suggesting backlash and the public's inability to move toward change. This same writer, stating that these women are "mad," ridicules the very idea of women as judges, ministers, or physicians by describing women in such professions suddenly and unexpectedly going into labor and delivering in the courtroom, at church, or in a patient's home (197). In 1869 and 1873, during and after suffragists' arguments that women be included in the Fourteenth and Fifteenth Amendments, Orestes Brownson discusses in journal articles titled "The Woman Question," "the conclusive objection to the political enfranchisement of women [which] would weaken and finally break up and destroy the Christian family" and declares that "women need a head, and the restraint of father, husband or the priest of God" (Rothenberg 197–198).

The increasing obstacles faced by nineteenth-century women speakers, especially those who argued for female suffrage, meant that women did not get the vote until 1920. In America in the nineteenth century, women spoke nonetheless, often out of deep conviction that their causes were just—Elizabeth Cady Stanton, Lucretia Mott, Sarah Grimké, Susan B. Anthony, Maria Stewart, Frances Willard, and Phoebe Palmer, to name only a few. Today, when reading Palmer or Grimké or Cady Stanton, we see the artistry of their rhetoric, the force of their intellect, but the culture they questioned just by standing at a podium was all too often unable to hear them.

Interrupting Discourses of Power in the Twentieth Century

The latter part of the twentieth century saw a resurgence of feminist rhetoric—the result perhaps of those women who went out to work during World War II or who were fortunate enough to attend college and then felt cut off during their child-raising days in the 1950s—the "secret emptiness" as Adrienne Rich describes it (22). In addition, Rosie the Riveter's daughters, who had gone to college in large numbers, were less likely than women in previous generations to keep silent. In consciousness-raising groups during the second wave of the feminist movement and through what bell hooks describes as "talking back," women in the latter half of the twentieth century continued to cast off the masks society seemed to demand, thus creating spaces for discursive exchange. In these spaces women spoke from personal experience to expose dominant systems of oppression acting on women's lives, and as a consequence these silent private realities became significant matters of public political concern. Arguing against discrimination based on sex and race, challenging essentialist notions of women's experiences, and working for reproductive justice, for example, women in the second half of the twentieth century aimed to "reveal the personal," creating with their words not only solidarity among themselves but also impetus for social change (hooks 1). It is no surprise that they were accused of being "angry," "shrill," "man hating," "lesbian," or "needing a good lay."

Within the physical spaces of consciousness-raising groups, sit-ins, and speak-outs, audiences/participants shifted from a center traditionally associated with a white male, granted the authority to speak by virtue of his race, gender, and class, toward women who began to effectively "achieve rhetorical authority from a marginalized position" (Reynolds, "Ethos" 330). Unlike women rhetors before them, these women did not invoke a divine right to speak but focused instead on a civil right to speak publicly. For women during the second half of the twentieth century, a shift in ethos was connected to two significant shifts in place: First, women both reframed and inserted themselves within "publics," creating their own collaborative spaces for collective discussion and exchange, "occupying" spaces in large numbers to amplify their voices (the Miss America protest of 1968, for example), and daring to publish the realities of women's lives in texts such as

Susan Brownmiller's *Against Our Will: Men, Women, and Rape* and *Ms.* magazine. Second, in describing "where they [were] coming from," women "challenged the dominant discourse" (Reynolds, "Ethos" 332) as well as the gendered authority presumed to embody ethos; in turn, they connected with audiences of women in order to move toward social action.

In claiming agency through lived and shared experience, these women and their audiences together built an ethos that empowered women to "intervene" and to "interrupt" dominant discourses (Reynolds "Interrupting" 59), particularly within public spaces. Both hooks and Reynolds discuss the potential danger in these acts of interruption, "interpreted as rude behavior, especially for women and children" (Reynolds "Interrupting" 59), yet these powerful acts of "talking back"—inserting themselves into discourses that were meant to exclude them—served as "an act of resistance, a political gesture that challenge[d] politics of domination that would render [them] nameless and voiceless" (hooks 8).

In her 1971 essay "When We Dead Awaken: Writing as Re-Vision," for example, Rich boldly interrupts the traditional, detached, objective discourse of the academy with personal experience and observation. Crediting the feminist movement and the work of lesbian and black feminists with creating significant change in writing and literary scholarship, she describes a moment of "awakening consciousness" (18). Like women rhetors before her, Rich speaks to, about, and for many women, of a "collective reality" made possible by the women's movement, one that "has drawn inescapable and illuminating connections between our sexual lives and our political institutions" (18). As part of a panel titled "The Woman Writer in the Twentieth-Century," Rich first delivered this paper at the 1971 MLA convention in the wake of calls for radical change within the organization, particularly on the status of women in the profession. Described as "one of the strongest and most dramatic talks of the convention" (Barber 26), Rich's words serve as an interruption on various levels. First, in describing her own experience as a wife, mother, and writer in the 1950s, she effectively breaks the silence about women's lives, validating women's "secret emptiness, their frustrations" (22); doing so in a space traditionally coded as male goes one step further in making this reality public. Second, she names men's privilege to "tolerate" or to "reject" women's "words and actions" (20), even with men presumably as part of her audience. In her guest editor's introduction for the October 1972 issue of *College English* in which Rich's essay was published along with those of her fellow panelists, Elaine Hedges remarks,

> What strikes me as especially important is the anger—healthy, construc-
> tive anger—that the writers of these four articles express. Rich angry at
> the male influences—fathers, teachers, and prescribed male poets—who
> for years unconsciously prevented her from finding her own voice. (2)

By Hedges's estimation and likely that of other audience members, this anger
does not appear to undermine Rich's good sense nor her good character and
may, in fact, lend authenticity to her words.

Finally, in an act of solidarity, Rich confronts the academic women with
their privilege while admitting her own, and, in so doing, she uses the first-person plural to unify herself with this audience.

> Every one of *us* here in this room has had great luck—*we* are teachers,
> writers, academicians; *our* own gifts could not have been enough, for *we*
> all know women whose gifts are buried or aborted. *Our* struggles can have
> meaning and our privileges—however precarious under patriarchy—can
> be justified only if they can help to change the lives of women whose
> gifts—and whose very being—continue to be thwarted and silenced. (21,
> emphasis added)

Rich does not mince words. She identifies the place from which she speaks,
draws upon a collective experience by naming her own and connects these
problems to larger systems of oppression. Unlike Palmer, Rich is not attempting to justify her right to speak nor to appear benign to her audience nor to
hide her individual experience. Yet like Palmer, Rich's message is more potent
with the use of first-person plural pronouns.

Feminist scholars have long debated the potential danger—the co-opting of voice and experience, the colonization—possible in speaking for the
"other," and while we heed these cautions, we also acknowledge that the
women whose words we quote share their personal experience in order to
create identification, and thus solidarity, with other women. In revealing
the realities of their lives, particularly when other women are not in positions to speak publicly, and in sharing these experiences, they begin to
create rhetorical spaces within which other women may add their voices of
support or dissent. Rhetors, unlike researchers or theorists, are always—by
definition—speaking for others.

And we see this again in the 1977 Combahee River Collective (CRC)
Statement, which offers a keen articulation "that major systems of oppression
are interlocking" (292), particularly for black women. The authors describe

a feminist movement of false universalism that has alienated black women, calling audiences of privileged women to confront their own "racism and elitism" (293). Here, too, the authors use first-person plural pronouns to indicate collective struggle, yet in this context their use of "we" and "us" is at the same time deliberately exclusionary given their larger claims within the text.

> *We* realize that the only people who care enough about *us* to work consistently for *our* liberation are *us*. *Our* politics evolve from a healthy love for *ourselves, our* sisters and *our* community which allows *us* to continue to struggle and work. (294, emphasis added)

In naming their own "otherness" within a predominantly white middle- and upper-class women's movement, the members of the collective effectively break this silence by identifying the challenge in "separat[ing] race from class from sex oppression because in our lives they are most often experienced simultaneously" (295). Using the language of the feminist movement—including "the personal is political" and "consciousness-raising sessions"—the collective asserts that they have "gone beyond white women's revelations" (295–96) to "inclusiveness" and "concer[n] with any situation that impinges upon the lives of women" (299). In attempting to speak to and for audiences of women of color, the collective believed ethos was determined by shared experience within a group, their group now being a community of women of color whose experiences had been excluded by privileged white women. More powerful still, argues Brian Norman, "The group's Statement articulate[d] a 'we' that is simultaneously particular and inclusive, both historically specific and future oriented," allowing the first-person plural to include audiences not yet envisioned by the CRC, who would read, claim, and identify with their words in numerous anthologies and future printings (103). With Rich and the CRC, women had, by the end of the twentieth century, prompted significant change in redefining ethos by expanding notions of who speaks when, to whom, and within what context.

Collective Ethos and Digital Media in the Twenty-First Century

In the early part of this millennium, feminists enact different interruptions because they no longer doubt their right to speak, and like the members of the Combahee River Collective, they often speak as a group. Sometimes these women are invited to speak by women who themselves created earlier interruptions and who have attained positions that now allow them to do the inviting. In these public spaces, women often speak with, about, and for the experiences of other women as women rhetors did before them. This unapologetic rhetoric, no longer focused solely on claiming public space, allows women to challenge male discourse openly and to collectively talk back, amplifying their voices by means of digital and social media and interrupting without embarrassment.

In the last two decades much of the scholarship on writing with/in digital media has highlighted the participatory possibilities of communicating in digital environments, particularly the opportunities for sustained collaboration and community-building. Cynthia Selfe, for example, points to the potential of digital media to "offer marginalized groups a forum in which to discover their own voice, to reinterpret and reconstruct their experience, and to make meaning that reflects their own cultural and intellectual contributions" (127). Equally important, however, have been the cautions against these ideals, specifically about an assumed "egalitarian space" within online environments. In their 1994 study of academic women online through the group woman@waytoofast, Gail E. Hawisher and Patricia Sullivan argue, "Because of the attractiveness of the egalitarian narrative and the persuasiveness of the research that supports it, feminists have needed powerful stories of gender deception, violence, and harassment to counter prevailing notions about the utopian possibilities of e-space" (175). Subsequent analyses by cyberfeminists have prompted critical reflection on the dualities of digital spaces—their potential both to foster equitable exchange and to reinforce hierarchies and hegemonic distributions of power. Although computers were long considered "masculine" tools of hierarchical military and business structures, scholarship in cyberfeminism indicates that online digital spaces also have the potential to foster feminist rhetorical practices, particularly in terms of decentered spaces and multivocal texts and exchanges. In other words, these spaces become significant locations for feminist action because they offer a place for feminist resistance and interventions, long the hallmark of women's political and discursive interruptions. Most significantly, however, digital and social media prompt us to reexamine our notions of speaker, audience, and authorship, changes that likewise facilitate important shifts in our understanding of ethos.

Because audiences are not merely consumers of information in the cyberspaces of Web 2.0 but also producers, commenting on and contributing to digital texts within various media, these audiences—now speakers—foster community and collaboration while disrupting traditional centers of power. As anyone who has read an online article posted to the Web can attest, comment sections and tools for sharing these texts allow readers to add their voices to a discussion, often borrowing the original author's ethos and speaking from personal experience, sometimes disagreeing with or refining the original author's position. Audiences may be physically absent yet ever present, and in the tradition of consciousness raising, this coordination and collaboration certainly can promote social action informed by multiple voices and perspectives.

Digital and social media have facilitated two important developments in terms of women's ethos: the redefinition of rhetorical spaces and a new "version" of the woman rhetor as a woman drawn from the margins who may not be invited to speak but who may choose to speak nonetheless, sometimes anonymously. According to Vicki Tolar Collins (Burton),

> When women's lives are formed and women's voices are managed and silenced by the ways a production authority uses their discourse and the forms and forums in which it is published, who is speaking and who controls the materiality of the message matters very much—culturally, rhetorically, and ethically. ("Speaker" 146)

Within digital and social media, women now have greater opportunities not only to control the context of their messages, but also to distribute and access them. With increased opportunities to reach audiences of women, women's appeals to ethos have shifted. In digital spaces, they do not ask permission to include themselves in the conversation or justify their right to speak.

In their introduction to *Webbing Cyberfeminist Practice: Communities, Pedagogies, and Social Action*, Kristine Blair, Radhika Gajjala, and Christine Tulley reinforce the importance of sharing stories—of making the personal public—in moving toward social change. Their contributors describe the cyber-opportunities women have used to work *against* social norms "while foregrounding women's lives as mothers, consumers, and workers" (8). In her work on infertility blogs, for example, Angela Haas analyzes the capacity of these blogs to "humanize the women writing them" (76) and to work against the dominant voice of the medical community often present in online infertility resources, predominantly white male "experts." Rather than being asked to speak, these bloggers simply create new spaces within which to recount their experiences and allow other women to contribute to multivocal texts by adding their stories. Ethos is granted not by medical expertise but by lived experience.

Cyberfeminist scholarship suggests that one way to ensure women's interests are served online is to promote digital authorship among women and girls, calling on women to reinvent digital spaces (Hocks; Takayoshi, Huot, and Huot). Within these spaces, women engage in acts of resistance, and "across the globe [they] use internet technology to create and claim identities, agency, and political activism outside of the circulation of one-third-world, U.S.-centric rhetorics of power" (Queen 264; see also Somolu). Cyberfeminist scholar Anita Harris examines how women, particularly young women, engage politically through "online DIY culture and social/personal uses of new technologies" (482). Significantly, many examples of digital and social media, to borrow Lisa Gerrard's words, "offer images of powerful competent women—speaking in confident voices and promoting political action, scholarly discourse, vehement challenges to misogyny, and boisterous irreverence" (298).

Examples of Women Warriors

The 2012 election offers a number of examples that identify the ongoing evolution of women's ethos and the role of social and digital media in facilitating women's public voices. Probably because of significant political gains by women in office—especially liberal women—the 2012 election sparked a backlash, deemed by liberals a war on women waged by those on the far end of the conservative spectrum. An explanation for the misogynistic statements from conservatives occurs in Krista Ratcliffe's examination of what happens when women attempt to demonstrate the realities of their lives.

> Grounded in women's private/public experiences and skeptical of major/ minor distinctions, feminists' arguments frequently emerge as emotional pleas that are too often received . . . as *improbable* impossibilities—that is, improbable within the consensus of public opinion and impossible within the logic of dominant discourse. That these improbable impossibilities (read "private emotional pleas") might possess logics of their own is an unpopular notion that public opinion is not often willing to acknowledge, let alone explore. (93)

And while these improbabilities may have been more common during the nineteenth century and before the breaking of silences common during the late twentieth century, one such "plea" occurred in early 2012. Sandra Fluke, a Georgetown law student, was not permitted to speak before the overwhelmingly male House Oversight and Government Reform Committee on the topic of birth control during ongoing debates involving the Affordable Care Act and its requirement that birth control be covered in the health care plans of companies and institutions. Later, she was invited by former House Speaker Nancy Pelosi to testify at the House Steering and Policy Committee because Pelosi believed that a woman's voice should be heard amid the male discourse on the topic.

In her statement, Fluke shares the lived experiences of other women, creating a multivocal testimony intended to challenge assumptions about birth control and the regulation of women's bodies by conservative male politicians. Like Rich and the Combahee River Collective before her, Fluke reminds her audience that the personal is political. Confident of her own ability and her position, Fluke does not doubt her right to speak nor does she make the case for occupying the space. Simply, she states the place from which she speaks: "My name is Sandra Fluke, and I'm a third-year student at Georgetown Law, a Jesuit school. I'm also a past president of Georgetown Law Students for Reproductive Justice, or LSRJ." Acknowledging her own privileged position as a law student, Fluke turns her attention to allowing other women to "speak" through the experiences they have shared with her, and she relies on borrowed and collective ethos.

> When I look around my campus, I see the faces of the women affected, and I have heard more and more of their stories . . . On a daily basis, I hear from yet another woman from Georgetown or other schools or who works for a religiously affiliated employer who has suffered financial, emotional, and medical burdens because of this lack of contraceptive coverage.

Here and throughout her remaining testimony, Fluke uses personal stories to humanize the ongoing debate regarding contraception and the Affordable Care Act, a debate whose House version had allowed only male testimony up to that point. The stories she recounts illustrate how "denials of contraceptive coverage impact real people." She states, "And so, I am here to share their voices, and I thank you for allowing them to be heard."

Following her statement, Fluke was verbally assaulted by the political right, most vocally by Rush Limbaugh, in a manner resembling the attacks on women rhetors during the nineteenth century but with cruder language. Limbaugh, calling Fluke a "slut" and a "prostitute" who wanted "taxpayers to pay her to have sex," attempted to characterize the women's lives described by Fluke in her testimony as private, personal pleas, or as Ratcliffe puts it, "improbable impossibilities" (Wilson). To privatize such pleas is to deny the political, social, and economic forces that constrain women's lives. Yet unlike responses to nineteenth-century women rhetors, Limbaugh's misogyny, although somewhat predictable given his flavor of public commentary, resulted not in silencing women's voices but in a powerful public effort not only to condemn him and his words but also to amplify Fluke's message. Beyond the news and print media coverage, Fluke's message and "53 of Rush Limbaugh's Most Vile Smears Against Georgetown Law Student Sandra Fluke" (Wilson) circulated throughout social media sites, prompting sponsors to withdraw support for Limbaugh's radio show and women to add their voices to Fluke's.

In one particularly notable example, in May 2012, a man named George Tierney of South Carolina took to Twitter with obscene comments about Fluke. Once the comments reached Fluke, she tweeted a response, which many of her thirty-six thousand Twitter followers retweeted and responded to. Before long, Tierney was demanding his comments be removed from Google. The response from cyberspace? "Here's the thing, George: Thanks to the strange powers of the World Wide Web, we are *all* Sandra Fluke. So whatever you say to her, you say to us" (qtd. in Murdoch). Other women borrow Fluke's ethos, speak from where they are, and not being invited or asked to respond, they add their own voices to this exchange. A few months later in her remarks at the Democratic Convention, Fluke acknowledged this public response as well as the invitation to speak during prime time: "And then, instead of trying to silence her, you invite me here—and give me a microphone—to amplify *our* voice" ("DNC 2012," emphasis added). Again, she makes rhetorical use of the first-person plural pronoun to call on collective experience, and her ethos is thus sanctioned by the group.

In a similar replication of the nineteenth century, during the 2012 Missouri senate race, Republican candidate Todd Akin, best known for his misogynist comments on "legitimate rape," accused incumbent Claire McCaskill of not being "ladylike" in her campaign, equating her with "a wildcat [let] out of the cage" (qtd. in Camia).[1] The response was swift and public with Akin's comments repeated via social and digital media. Unlike women rhetors during the nineteenth century, McCaskill did not argue for the authority to speak nor did she soften her speech in an act of good will toward men. She did display good sense and good character, however. Asked about Akin's comments on MSNBC's *Morning Joe*, McCaskill stated firmly,

I don't know exactly what his accusation that I am not "ladylike" means. I am a former courtroom prosecutor and I try to be strong and informed.

The debate was tough for Todd because I went through the list of his very, very extreme positions and . . . maybe he wasn't prepared to answer. (qtd. in Camia)

Rather than defending her actions—or her right to speak—McCaskill effectively cast doubt on her opponent's abilities while reinforcing her own ethos. If McCaskill's ethos failed in Akin's assessment, his criticism was inconsequential with her intended audience, the voters of Missouri.

Beyond adding their voices to support other women, women are using digital and social media to identify, and sometimes ridicule, male politicians whom they see as offensive or condescending, as they did in responding to Mitt Romney's now famous "binders full of women" remark, a statement made during the second presidential debate of the 2012 election. By the end of the debate, the newly created Romney's Binder Twitter account and "Binders Full of Women" Facebook page each had generated over 30,000 followers and likes, respectively, and would increase to 274,000 likes by the next morning ("Romney 'Binders'"; "Binders Full of Women"). One of the most memorable sites was a Tumblr blog titled *bindersfullofwomen* created by Veronica De Souza. According to a *Mashable* article, "De Souza ensured submissions were enabled so people could help generate content," and within thirty minutes the blog had three thousand followers and by the next morning more than twenty-seven hundred submissions of binders full of women memes (Haberman). In addition to generating content, women also were adding their voices to this very public conversation on the topic by reblogging, retweeting, reposting, liking, and commenting on various posts circulating through cyberspace, reinforcing and sharing one another's ethos in this exchange.

In 2013, Texas state senator Wendy Davis was the impetus for similar cyberfeminist action. Davis's thirteen-hour filibuster successfully stalled a bill designed to significantly limit abortion rights in the state, and although Davis, like women rhetors before her, shared her personal experience—in this case with an ectopic pregnancy—what became even more powerful in her hours-long testimony were the voices of other women whom she had invited to share personal stories on her website. Over thirteen thousand people throughout Texas responded to her call. During her speech in the Texas Senate, their words amplified Davis's message and she, in turn, made visible the lived experiences of many women (Sherman). Her ethos was borrowed and shared in collective action. Like Fluke, Davis acknowledged this shared victory.

Less than a week ago you were at the crux of a turning point in Texas history. You joined the ranks of brave men and women who love this state and fought for their liberties and preserving Texas values. It was your voices—lent to me—that made it possible for me to stand those 13 hours. (qtd. in RHRC)

Beyond the invitation to add their voices to Davis's, another surprising act of public testimony appeared on Amazon.com in the days following the filibuster. The hot pink sneakers worn by Davis during her testimony became an instant sensation, and "[b]uried in the hundreds of reviews . . . are also some stories about abortion and reproductive rights" (Sherman). The space for public address has shifted, with room for various voices from the margins, and although these women may never stand before a government body to tell their stories, they have found a way to add their voices to this public discussion.

Like Phoebe Palmer, we believe—or would like to believe—that the resistance to and outrage about women's public speech derives from ignorance. But we are forced to wonder whether perhaps like their nineteenth-century predecessors, some twenty-first century men seem threatened by seeing continuing cracks in the patriarchy. We speculate that the misogyny we recount here and experience in our lives has its sources in what Michael Kimmel calls "aggrieved entitlement"—that is, "that sense that those benefits to which you believed yourself entitled have been snatched away from you by unseen forces larger and more powerful" (18). Because of women's speech, our culture now has experts who know the conditions of women's lives. Those experts offer immediate challenges to such inane remarks as the one about how during a rape a woman's body "shuts that whole thing down" so that no pregnancy results. We like living in a world where women can speak out against injustice, cruelty, and mindlessness, yet we also recognize our own privilege to do so and the privilege of many of the women whose words we cite throughout this chapter.

One has only to look to the example of Malala Yousafzai, the young Pakistani advocate for girls' education and now Nobel Peace Prize winner, who, encouraged by her teacher-activist father, shared the details of her life under Taliban rule through a blog for the BBC. Because she told the truth of her own life and of other girls' lives to a large audience, she was shot by the Taliban, an incident demonstrating that grave danger still exists for many women who dare to make public the realities of women's lives. Yet also remarkable in Malala's story was the response through social and digital media and the global impact of her story and her words, particularly on women and girls. Even more remarkable perhaps is Malala's invited speech at the United Nations on July 12, 2013, in which she makes clear her commitments.

> I speak—not for myself, but for all girls and boys. I raise up my voice—not so that I can shout, but so that those without a voice can be heard. Those who have fought for their rights: Their right to live in peace. Their right to be treated with dignity. Their right to equality of opportunity. Their right to be educated.

As the editors of this collection contend, "Ethos is neither solitary nor fixed. Rather, ethos is negotiated and renegotiated, embodied and communal, co-constructed, and thoroughly implicated in shifting power dynamics" (introduction, this volume). If the ethos required for women to speak against injustice means, at least for right now, speech directed primarily to audiences of other women, then so be it. If the ethos created by this community of women is not—for a while—perceived as "ladylike," but is, rather, unapologetic and forceful, then so be it. What we see in this short retrospective is that the ethos of women rhetors has changed, and, as more and more women speak to and for one another, we can be confident that it will continue to change.

Note

1. Although originally broadcast as part of MSNBC's *Morning Joe*, McCaskill's comments were later quoted and rebroadcast in a variety of print and online media, including *USA Today*, *CBS News*, the *Washington Times*, the *Huffington Post*, and *Politico*, among other sources.

Works Cited

Allen, Danielle. "Rhetoric, a Good Thing." *Talking to Strangers: Anxieties of Citizenship since Brown v. Board of Education*. Chicago: U of Chicago P, 2004. 140–59. Print.

"The Anti-Suffragists: Selected Papers, 1852–1887." Rothenburg. 196–201. Print.

Aristotle. From *Rhetoric*. Trans. W. Rhys Roberts. Bizzell and Herzberg. 179–240. Print.

Barber, Virginia. "The Women's Revolt in the MLA." *Change* 4.3 (1972): 24–27. Print.

"Binders Full of Women." *Wikipedia: The Free Encyclopedia*. Web.

Bizzell, Patricia, and Bruce Herzberg. Headnote "Phoebe Palmer." Bizzell and Herzberg. 1085–95. Print.

Bizzell, Patricia, and Bruce Herzberg, eds. *The Rhetorical Tradition: Readings from Classical Times to the Present.* 2nd ed. Boston: Bedford/St. Martin's. 2001. Print.

Blair, Kristine, Radhika Gajjala, and Christine Tulley. Introduction. Blair, Gajjala, and Tulley. 1–19. Print.

———, eds. *Webbing Cyberfeminist Practice: Communities, Pedagogies, and Social Action.* Cresskill, NJ: Hampton, 2009. Print.

Brownmiller, Susan. *Against Our Will: Men, Women, and Rape.* New York: Ballantine, 1993.

Buchanan, Lindal, and Kathleen J. Ryan, eds. *Walking and Talking Feminist Rhetorics: Landmark Essays and Controversies.* West Lafayette, IN: Parlor, 2010. Print.

Burton, Vicki Tolar. *Spiritual Literacy in John Wesley's Methodism: Reading, Writing, and Speaking to Believe.* Waco, TX: Baylor UP. 2008. Print.

Camia, Catalina. "McCaskill Rips Akin for 'Ladylike' Comment." *USA Today* 28 Sept. 2012. Web.

Collins [Burton], Vicki Tolar. "The Speaker Respoken: Material Rhetoric as Feminist Methodology." Buchanan and Ryan. 146–69. Print.

Combahee River Collective. "Combahee River Collective Statement." Ritchie and Ronald. 291–300. Print.

"Declaration of Sentiments and Resolutions, Seneca Falls Convention, 1848." Rothenberg. 192–96. Print.

"DNC 2012: Sandra Fluke's Speech at the Democratic National Convention (Full text)." *Washington Post* 5 Sept. 2012. Web.

Fluke, Sandra. "Written Testimony of Sandra Fluke, Past President of Georgetown LSRJ." *Law Students for Reproductive Justice* 16 Feb. 2012. Web.

Gerrard, Lisa. "Beyond 'Scribbling Women': Women Writing (on) the Web." *Computers and Composition* 19 (2002): 297–314. Print.

Haas, Angela. "Wired Wombs: A Rhetorical Analysis of Online Infertility Support Communities." Blair, Gajjala, and Tulley. 61–84. Print.

Haberman, Stephanie. "Talking Internet Gold with Creator of 'Binders Full of Women' Tumblr." *Mashable* 17 Oct. 2012. Web.

Harris, Anita. "Young Women, Late Modern Politics, and the Participatory Possibilities of Online Cultures." *Journal of Youth Studies* 11.5 (2008): 481–95. Print.

Hawisher, Gail E., and Patricia Sullivan. "Women on the Networks: Searching for E-Spaces of Their Own." Jarratt and Worsham. 172–97. Print.

Hedges, Elaine. "Women in the Colleges: One Year Later." *College English* 34.1 (1972): 1–5. Print.

Hocks, Mary. "Cyberfeminism Intersects Writing Research: Studies in Digital Rhetoric." Blair, Gajjala, and Tulley. 235–53. Print.

hooks, bell. *Talking Back: Thinking Feminist, Thinking Black.* Boston: South Bend Press, 1989. Print.

Jarratt, Susan C., and Lynn Worsham, eds. *Feminism and Composition Studies: In Other Words.* New York: MLA, 1998.

Kimmel, Michael. *Angry White Men: American Masculinity at the End of an Era.* New York: Nation Books, 2015.

Kohrs Campbell, Karlyn. Introduction to *Man Cannot Speak for Her: Reading Rhetorical Theory.* Ed. Barry Brummett. Fort Worth: Harcourt College, 2000. 895–903. Print.

Lincoln, Abraham. "First Inaugural Address of Abraham Lincoln." 4 Mar. 1861. *The Avalon Project: Documents in Law, History, and Diplomacy.* Lillian Goldman Law Library. Yale Law School. Web.

Murdoch, Cassie. "Unintelligent Male Attacks Sandra Fluke on Twitter, Wants His Name Magically Scrubbed from Google." *Jezebel* 22 May 2012. Web.

Norman, Brian. "'We' in Redux: The Combahee River Collective's Black Feminist Statement." *Differences: A Journal of Feminist Cultural Studies* 18.2 (2007): 103–32.

Palmer, Phoebe. "The Promise of the Father" and "Tongues of Fire on the Daughters of the Lord." Bizzell and Herzberg. 1095–113. Print.

Queen, Mary. "Consuming the Stranger: Technologies of Rhetorical Action in Transnational Feminist Encounters." Blair, Gajjala, and Tulley. 263–86. Print.

Ratcliffe, Krista. "Bathsheba's Dilemma: Defining, Discovering, and Defending Anglo-American Feminist Theories of Rhetoric(s)." Buchanan and Ryan. 80–107. Print.

Reynolds, Nedra. "*Ethos* as Location: New Sites for Understanding Discursive Authority." *Rhetoric Review* 11.2 (1993): 325–38. Print.

——. "Interrupting Our Way to Agency: Feminist Cultural Studies and Composition." Jarratt and Worsham. 58–73. Print.

RHRC Staff. "What Wendy Said: Sen. Wendy Davis' Remarks at 'Stand with Texas Women' Rally." *RH Reality Check* 1 July 2013. Web.

Rich, Adrienne. "When We Dead Awaken: Writing as Re-Vision." *College English* 34.1 (1972): 18–30. Print.

Ritchie, Joy, and Kate Ronald. *Available Means: An Anthology of Women's Rhetoric(s).* Pittsburgh: U of Pittsburgh P, 2001. Print.

"Romney 'Binders Full Of Women' Debate Remark Inspires Tumblr, Facebook Page, and Twitter Account." *Huffington Post* 17 Oct. 2012. Web.

Rothenburg, Paula S. *Racism and Sexism: An Integrated Study.* New York: St. Martin's, 1988. Print.

Selfe, Cynthia L. "Technology in the English Classroom: Computers through the Lens of Feminist Theory." *Computers and Community: Teaching Composition in the Twenty-First Century.* Ed. Carolyn Handa. Portsmouth, NH: Boynton/Cook. 118–39. Print.

Sherman, Renee Bracey. "How Wendy Davis—and an Amazon Reviews Page—Helped Women Share Their Abortion Stories." *RH Reality Check* 1 July 2013. Web.

Somolu, Oreoluwa. "'Telling Our Own Stories': African Women Blogging for Social Change." *Gender and Development* 15.3 (2007): 477–89. Print.

Takayoshi, Pam, Emily Huot, and Meghan Huot. "No Boys Allowed: The World Wide Web as a Clubhouse for Girls." *Computers and Composition* 16 (1999): 89–106. Print.

Wilson, John K. "Rush's 53 Smears against Sandra Fluke." *Daily Kos* 4 Mar. 2012. Web.

Yousafzai, Malala. "Speech to the United Nations." *Guardian* 12 July 2013. Web.

Part Two

Ethē as Advocacy–Advocating

The dilemmas of advocacy entail rhetors advocating for their own right to speak authoritatively and negotiating the complexities of speaking for others.[1] Activists who are members of minority groups have to negotiate a perceived lack of authority and identification with the normative expectations of dominant publics. Coretta Pittman's study of African American women rhetors shows the difficulties Harriet Jacobs, Billie Holiday, and Sister Souljah had "try[ing] to assert a good and respectable ethos in an American society that continually questions their moral character" (44). These women "resisted, adopted, and then adapted elite white women's virtues and claimed them as their own" to advocate for themselves and for other black women who otherwise would not have opportunities to do so (48, 49). Paige Conley describes the complex subjectivities at play in the way Zitkala-Ša is "able to move fluidly between subject positions now located both within and beyond dominant culture" (188) as well as "advancing indigenous interests in the early decades of the twentieth century" (189). More recently, Rachel Alicia Griffin acknowledges the ethical responsibility she feels to speak for herself and other biracial women. She advocates for her right to be "blistering mad," "frustrated," and "enraged" in a reputable academic journal, a public space more often reserved for "civil" and "rational" discourses, and acknowledges the importance she places in speaking for women like herself. Griffin asserts, "I feel obligated to use my access to class and academic privilege to advocate for women who look like me to have access to voice" (142). Being an advocate seems less problematic when one member of a group speaks on behalf of other members of the same group who might not encounter publics otherwise. Advocating can be riskier when rhetors differ in power, access, and agency, such as Harriet Jacobs speaking to white women as mothers or when first world feminists advocate for third world women.

Since advocacy requires continuous ethical consideration and adjustments to power, relationships, experiences, and imagined versus real needs, rhetors speaking from privileged positions must take special care when they speak for others to avoid misrepresenting or co-opting others for their own ends. Wendy Hesford and Wendy Kozol articulate this problem for feminists doing transnational work: "The challenge that feminist critics face . . . is how to avoid reproducing the spectacle of victimization while also not erasing the materiality of violence and trauma, and recognizing the interdependence of material and discursive realms" (13). The dilemma is particularly salient when, as Gayatri Chakravorty Spivak famously stated, the "subaltern cannot speak" and "the practice of privileged persons speaking for or on behalf of less privileged persons has actually resulted (in many cases) in increasing or reinforcing the oppression of the group spoken for" (Alcoff 99). Linda Martín Alcoff offers four "interrogatory practices" for speaking ethically on behalf of others: (1) the rhetor's "*impetus* to speak must be carefully analyzed and, in many cases (certainly for academics), fought against" (111); (2) the rhetor examines how her subjectivity and context explicitly inform the content of her discourse; (3) the rhetor is accountable to and responsible for speaking (112); and (4) the rhetor "analyze[s] the *probable or actual effects of the words on the discursive and material context*" (113). These practices push rhetors toward feminist ecological ethē to construct ethical, located ethē as they examine the consequences of speaking and not speaking. Hesford's examination of ethos and campaigns against acid violence shows the complexity of ethos and transnational advocacy in the ways privilege, rights, and ethics circulate for different stakeholders. We also see the benefit in privileged women using Matthew Heard's notion of attunement to advocate cautiously for others, bringing together the strategies of interruption and advocacy.[2]

Notes

1. As an alternative to speaking for others, Jarratt offers speaking alongside or beside others, where speakers "plac[e] themselves not at the head of some silent group of followers but rather beside themselves" (60).

2. See also Myers's "Western Women's *Ethos.*"

Works Cited

Alcoff, Linda Martín. "The Problem of Speaking for Others." *Who Can Speak? Authority and Critical Identity.* Ed. Judith Roof and Robyn Wiegman. Urbana: U of Illinois P, 1995. 97–119. Print.

Griffin, Rachel Alicia. "I am an Angry Black Woman: Black Feminist Autoethnography, Voice, and Resistance." *Women's Studies in Communication* 35:2 (2012): 138–57. Print.

Heard, Matthew. "Tonality and Ethos." *Philosophy and Rhetoric* 46.1 (2013): 44–64. Print.

Hesford, Wendy, and Wendy Kozol. *Just Advocacy? Women's Human Rights, Transnational Feminisms, and the Politics of Representation.* Piscataway, NJ: Rutgers UP, 2005. Print.

Jarratt, Susan C. "Beside Ourselves: Rhetoric and Representation in Postcolonial Feminist Writing." *JAC* 18.1 (1998): 57–75.

Myers, Nancy. "Western Women's *Ethos* and a Response to Privilege: Advocacy in Hillary Rodham Clinton's 'Women's Rights Are Human Rights.'" *Political Women: Language and Leadership.* Ed. Michele Lockhart and Kathleen Mollick. Lanham, MD: Lexington, 2013. Print.

Pittman, Coretta. "Black Women Writers and the Trouble with *Ethos*: Harriet Jacobs, Billie Holiday, and Sister Souljah." *Rhetoric Society Quarterly* 37.1 (2007): 43–70. Print.

5. Ethos as a Social Act

The "Unauthorized" Susanna Wesley

Lynée Lewis Gaillet

Susanna Wesley (1669–1742), mother of Methodist founders John and Charles Wesley, gained notoriety as an exemplar mother within religious circles. However, by studying her letters and journals, we find a woman admirable in her own right. She not only lays foundations of what will become Methodism through her character and actions, but also advocates for women's education and subverts prevailing notions that Christian women should keep silent and obey. Susanna Wesley (referred to hereafter as "SW" to avoid confusion with other family members) recognized and studied largely in conjunction with the famous men in her life, such as her well-known Dissenting minister-father, her less prominent Anglican minister-husband, and her two sons who went on to found Methodism, a fact explicitly noted on her tombstone at the Bunhill Fields Dissenter's cemetery in London. However, SW's actions and writings merit a second look and scholarly attention outside the religious circles that typically characterize her as, according to Charles Wallace (editor of her papers), "the Methodist Madonna" (4).[1]

Throughout her lifetime, SW reacts against her husband, local ministers, and the Church of England. She finds herself in a precarious situation for a woman of her day, as she must deftly balance claims of reason and intelligence as justification for her right to speak (a male act) in harmony with the community-oriented and inventive ethos that draws local parishioners into her home (a feminine act), all while cleverly maintaining the church in the absence of a familial patriarch and local effective minister. Intentionally or not, SW claims the right for women to become leaders in the emerging Methodist denomination. Her son John Wesley, who would go on to found Methodism, initially merely observes his mother's actions, but later recognizes the methods of her rhetorical praxis. Learning from her example, he subsequently affords women the right to church leadership positions and establishes small-group study that still defines tenets of Methodist education.

Countering reductive contemporary definitions of ethos as ethics or the authority of a speaker, Nedra Reynolds encourages scholars to pay "attention to the etymology of *ethos*—its connections to space, place or location" in order "to reestablish *ethos* as a social act and as a product of a community's character" (327). Likewise, Susan Friedman claims that "feminism has moved to a concern with location—the geopolitics of identity within differing communal spaces of being and becoming" (3). These contemporary claims for reinscribing feminist study are illustrated in the character and actions of SW, who wrote, taught, and preached from her home in the rectory at Epworth, England. Although John Wesley is recognized as the founder of Methodism, he remained a lifelong Anglican, always insisting that his Methodist "movement" fell within the boundaries of the established church. The same cannot be said for his Dissenter-mother. Like her son, she embraced tenets of Methodism, leading by local example, but SW made a point of joining the new faith. Specifically, SW's determination to speak despite censure from her husband and local clergy, her role as a woman who was willing to fill in recognized gaps in local religious instruction, and the role she adopted in her own community garnered local admiration while also providing a sustained model of women as agents within emerging notions of Methodism. In SW's correspondence, she actively counters criticism from local clergy (including her husband), critiques of her clergyman-son, and notions that a wife must support her husband's political views.

By modeling ways women can redefine and construct notions of their stance and authority, Susanna Wesley creates new venues for women speakers and religious leaders. Wallace suggests that she is becoming something of a foremother for latter-day Christian feminists and an example of early "writing women" who employed intellect and spirituality to subvert (however gently) some of the very religious-based conventions that ordinarily worked to keep women modest, chaste, and silent. (3)

I agree. Through an examination of SW's rhetorical actions, thoughts on women's education, teaching methods, and ideas about women's roles in society found in her journals and correspondence, I propose to cast SW as a forerunner of the mid- to late-eighteenth-century intellectual bluestockings, clearly illustrating Wallace's claim. As I detail below, her interest in intellectual pursuits for both herself and the edification of her family and local citizens reflects later characteristics of bluestockings. For this study, the relationship between bluestocking women and Anglican clergymen is of particular interest, given SW's role as daughter, wife, and mother of clergymen, her defense of early Methodist actions and beliefs, and her influence upon what will become tenets of Methodism—specifically, reliance upon small group educational meetings and support of women teachers and preachers.

Susanna Wesley: A Brief Biography

Susanna Wesley (January 20, 1669–August 1, 1742) was the youngest of twenty-five children.[2] Reared in London by Puritans—her father, Samuel Annesley, was a Church of England Dissenter—she chose at age thirteen to return to the Church of England. Notably, her father supported her decision (although it contradicted his own departure from the Anglican Church), and she remained a favored child, the recipient of his books and papers upon his death. Accordingly, her early upbringing and the Dissenter spirit of freethinking and piety characterized her adult actions. Typical of the times, Susanna Annesley received little formal education, but, instead, her father supervised her rigorous studies at home. He introduced her to current theology and encouraged literate practices through both the analysis of printed texts and frequent gatherings of prominent clergy who assembled in their home. In 1688, Susanna Annesley married Samuel Wesley, a visiting son of a Dissenting minister. Both Susanna and Samuel had returned to the Anglican Church after Dissenting. They were married forty-six years, and Susannah gave birth to a total of nineteen children, including multiple sets of twins. Only ten children lived to adulthood: Samuel, Emilia, Annesley, Jebediah, Mehetabel, Anne, John (nicknamed Jacky), Martha, Charles, and Kezia.

Of immense importance was the fact that SW educated her children at home in a structured and consistent manner. This methodical approach shaped son John Wesley's creation of Methodist principles, including novel ideas about education and women's roles in countering and enacting public policy. John Wesley's later facets of Methodist educational pedagogy were greatly influenced by his education at the feet of SW and her local and highly visible example of women (re)inventing their ethē to include public places in which to speak and teach, despite dominant cultural expectations and in defiance of outright male opposition. SW's creation of a public ethos, one that permitted teaching of and by women and which allowed space for local citizens to learn and worship outside the bounds of Sunday morning church services, is echoed in her educational plan for children. As an adult, John Wesley once asked his mother to outline her educational plan, which she did with some hesitation (Letter to Jacky/John; 21 February 1732): "The writing anything about my way of education I am much averse from" (150). Vicki Tolar Burton explains that in hesitating to describe her rigorous home school educational plan, SW insinuates that few women would devote their lives to such an intensive pedagogy, suggesting that "there may be no real audience for her system" (40). In addition to pedagogy, SW developed her own well-articulated theology, which she taught to her children along with more traditional school subjects. In a July 1732 essay, written as a letter to her son John, SW provides the details of her comprehensive educational plan. John was impressed and disseminated the essay after his mother's death in his published *Journal* and in *Armenian Magazine*, where he integrated her advice in one of his sermons (Wallace 367).

In detailing her educational plan, SW references both Locke's *Essay concerning Human Understanding* (sections copied in her journals) and *Some Thoughts concerning Education* (journal entries 5 and 103). Wallace suggests that in her teaching philosophy we see a unique blend of "evangelical and Lockean ideas, one that also goes a long way toward explaining the remarkable [Wesley] children . . . and that illustrates the zeal with which Susanna Wesley pursued an educational vocation within the bounds of contemporary social constraints" (368). SW's literary and intellectual interests become evident in her teaching plan and, in turn, her journal writings as well as public and private letters published posthumously. In her letter/essay to John (whom she called "Jacky") outlining her educational theories and pedagogy, SW describes her educational method from cradle to graduation, including: rules for infant napping, instilling fear of the rod, nutritional information, rules for dining, bedtime rituals, advice for conquering a child's will, instilling mannerly speech, methods for learning to memorize important passages, guidelines for teaching children their letters (in just one day, at age five) and how to read (mastered in four months), classroom discipline, peer learning among siblings, punishment for sinful actions, commendations for obedience, rules of ownership and propriety, and the strict enforcement of promises and rewards. The final entry of this 1732 letter-essay concerns the education of girls.

> That no girl be taught to work till she can read very well; and then that she be kept to her work with the same application, and for the same time, that she was held to in reading. This rule also is much to be observed; for the putting children to learn sewing before they can read perfectly is the very reason why so few women can read fit to be heard, and never to be well understood. (373)

This advocacy on the part of all her children is unique and emphatic, illustrating Susan Friedman's claim in *Mappings: Feminism and the Cultural Geographies of Encounter* that feminism depends upon "a turning outward, an embrace of contradiction, dislocation, and change" (4). Certainly, Susanna Wesley practiced what she preached, evidenced by her willingness to reinvent the traditional role of not only mother and wife, but also of teacher. SW was willing to commit to a pedagogy that demanded much of both teacher and pupil in the same ways she committed to defying conventional expectations in fighting for her own right to speak publicly and hold assemblies in her home. In her educational plan, we find a model mother-teacher willing to sacrifice herself to principles she held dear. Her plan was not typical of the day (she thought few would find it interesting or have the wherewithal to commit to it) and was not slavishly devoted to common educational practices of the time (particularly regarding the education of girls), but was instead a blended mixture of discipline and regard for human dignity and rights. SW's strict rules for governing children are motivated and tempered by what she thinks is best for them, but love is also at play in her curriculum (journal entry 72): "This we may be assured of, that love is the strongest passion, the affection that excites and leads the rest to action" (248).

This familial educational philosophy bleeds over into her small group pedagogy as well, and is clearly evident in tenets of later Methodist educational practice. Current Methodist small groups (for example, United Methodist Women, community action committees, social Methodist groups including monthly dinner gatherings and Bible discussion and study groups) regularly meet in congregation members' homes, following to some degree the example set by SW. Characterized by care for fellow group members, these small group meetings follow prescribed meeting formats, denomination-sanctioned study guides (often published by Cokesbury, a Methodist Press), and tenets found in the Methodist *Book of Discipline.*

Susanna Wesley's rigid teaching plan also allows time for one-on-one conferencing. She sets aside one pedagogical hour per week to spend individually with each child (journal entry 79): "Molly on Monday; Hetty on Tuesday; Nancy on Wednesday; Jacky, Thursday; Patty, Friday; Charles, Saturday. Blessed by God! One for every day of the week and two for Sunday" (255). During this hour, she speaks confidentially with the children about the states of their souls, fears, and future plans. For all her children, but perhaps specifically for John, we learn (from his diaries and journals) that this questioning initiated lifelong habits of regular self-examination. In emulating his mother's closely examined lifestyle, he formulated practices and beliefs that become apparent in the Methodist movement: living the closely examined life, early morning time for prayer and reflection, and making time for small group instruction. Interestingly, before instructing her children, SW set aside an hour for herself each morning for scripture reading, prayer, and recording her thoughts. Typical of Puritan practice, she advocated meditation and reflection at least three times a day (journal entry 17): "Make an examination of your conscience at least three times a day and omit no opportunity of retirement from the world" (216–17). In revisiting the life and work of SW, Wallace sees these practices, evident in her "religious writings as discourse that encouraged woman's education and afforded some psychic space, some 'room of one's own,' for her own self-expressions and self-development" (4). Claiming this personal time was particularly important since SW was solely responsible for the daily instruction of her children and later answered the spiritual needs of members of the local community. Her husband Samuel was often away for extended periods of time, leaving her to act as a single parent and manager of household finances despite her own ill health as a result of constant childbirth and child rearing; yet, she still had to fill in as spiritual shepherd for the parishioners he had abandoned.

The family, too, was plagued by financial problems. From the very beginning of their marriage, Samuel was often absent for months at a time: to serve in the government, to explore his own interest in creative writing, to serve time in debtors' prison. Sometimes, it seems, he just wanted to be away from home. SW writes in a lengthy letter to her oldest son, Samuel Jr.: "Truly my health and fortune is much alike, neither very good or extremely bad. I have constantly pain enough to mind me of mortality and trouble enough in my circumstances of fortune to exercise my patients" (11 October 1709). Obviously, Samuel Wesley Sr. was a bad financial manager and inattentive husband and father, as evidenced in SW's lengthy letter to her brother, Samuel Annesley, dated 20 January 1721. In this missive, she explains to her brother, who offered her family continued financial support, her meager and destitute circumstances. SW's personal trials at home and in her community lead her to reconsider her role, ultimately setting the stage for her to bravely engage in novel action in answering the needs of her family and fellow worshipers. In two noted cases, SW defies her husband in matters of government and ecclesiastical authority (see below). By acting hopefully and resolutely, Susanna Wesley enacts feminist change characterized two centuries later by Jacqueline Jones Royster and Gesa E. Kirsch in *Feminist Rhetorical Practices*:

> This feminist view of hope calls instead for sharp analytical skills. With a positive outlook as a driving force, the effort is to assess current situations, contexts, and institutional forces; to recognize the strengths, limits, and challenges of present arrangements; to inhabit a sense of caring about the people and processes involved in the use of language by immersing ourselves in the work, spending time thinking broadly and deeply about what is there, not there, and could be there instead. The effort is to think beyond the concrete in envisioning alternative possibilities in order that we might actually work, often collaboratively, toward enacting a better future. (145)

Spoken about twenty-first-century-feminist researchers, Royster and Kirsch's words aptly capture SW's thoughts and detailed plans for meditatively reenvisioning literacy and communicative practices to improve the lives of those she encounters. She looked outside her isolated community for inspiration. For example, in countering her absent husband's admonishment to adhere to local societal conventions, SW responds by comparing her novel works to that of Danish missionaries (Letter 6 February 1711).

> Soon after you went to London, Emily found in your study the account of the Danish missionaries . . . I was never, I think, more affected with anything than with the relation of their travels, and was exceeding pleased with the noble design they were engaged in . . . For several days I could think or speak of little else. At last it came into my mind, though I am not

a man nor a minister of the gospel, and so cannot be employed in such a worthy employment as they were; yet if my heart were sincerely devoted to God, and if I were inspired with a true zeal for his glory and did really desire the salvation of souls, I might do somewhat more than I do. (80)

Upon studying the Dutch missionaries, she resolves to augment her actions both at home and in the community to include a greater focus on the soul of the individual: immediately, she amends her pedagogical plan for her children to include an individual hour with each and begins leading unsanctioned spiritual gatherings in her home. This resulting reinvention of both her self-conception and the parameters within which she can act represents an important turning point in SW's developing ethos.

As a boy and young man, John Wesley witnessed his mother's methodical plan for daily life, her appreciation of education for both boys and girls, her rational responses to theological beliefs and practices, which she thought to be in conflict with reason, her expression of strong opinions, and her devotion to journal keeping. Wesley's early literacy practices, learned from parents who were both opinionated writers and speakers, influenced him in numerous ways, many of which have been documented by Tolar Burton (62–65). Regardless of his often complicated ways of viewing women as leaders in the church, Anglican clergyman John Wesley would ultimately create venues and liminal spaces for women to speak, serve, and lead (Tolar Burton xv), particularly when these women expressed an authentic call to public action (this is seen clearly in his support of Mary Bosanquet's public preaching). Revisiting John Wesley's writings makes clear the ways in which his early educational experiences at his mother's direction and her public actions played a key role in his support of women preachers and church leaders.

Susanna Wesley and Rhetorical Agency

For the subject of this treatise—ethos—Susanna Wesley's willingness to counter conventional notions of a woman's place and expected behavior in public is decisively significant. In the foreword to Michael Hyde's *The Ethos of Rhetoric*, Calvin O. Schrag explains the "originative meaning of *ethos* as the dwelling or abode from which our communicative practices of entwined discourse and action take their rise and to which they return for their validations of sense and reference" (vii). The present edited collection strives to break down disciplinary understandings of ethos, arguing that the term is historically wide-ranging and asking why academics so often pigeonhole the concept. This stance applies to my goal in writing about SW. While she is well known in Methodist circles as the mother of Methodism, I wish for deeper understanding of her contributions to rhetorical practice. SW embodies an understanding of ethos that moves it beyond definitions of mere credibility; instead, ethos becomes a concept "central to place, community, identity, and moral action" (Benson ix). Hyde's 2002 concept of ethos "to refer to the way discourse is used to transform space and time into 'dwelling places' (*ethos*; pl. *ethea*) where people can deliberate about and 'know together' (*con-scientia*) some matter of interest" (xiii) is remarkably apropos. Hyde's exploration of the architectural functions of *ethos*—"how, for example, its practice grants such *living room* to our lives that we might feel more *at home* with others and our surroundings" (xiii)—isn't just a metaphor when applied to the rhetorical agency of Susanna Wesley, but a physical reality. She literally invited the community into her home, created an ethical space for establishing community, and arranged boundaries and new spaces for speaking and listening.

The earliest extant letters preserved in the collection of SW papers provide understanding of the motivations behind her rhetorical actions. In these letters, thirty-three-year-old SW is called to defend her actions of wifely insubordination, her right to speak publicly, and her choice to gather parishioners in her home. These acts and her subsequent justification of her actions (seen in the excerpts from her letters below) illustrate SW's difficulty in balancing competing ethē, taking on the role of male parishioner leader on the one hand juxtaposed with that act occurring in the most domestic of spaces, her home. As SW becomes a spiritual shepherd, she engages in male acts of public speaking, but these acts take place in community-defined female spaces. Her role as leader clearly makes space for her original thoughts and opinions; however, by enacting the male right to speak freely, SW clearly violates the long-held biblical and community belief that the husband is head of his household. This juxtaposition becomes problematic, as illustrated in her letters justifying her actions and pleading for understanding.

A 1701–1702 example concerns the first of two rectory fires and surrounding events. An independent SW disagrees with her husband's political leanings; she refuses to say "amen" at the end of Samuel's prayer blessing William and Mary. Instead, she advocates that James II has a divine right to the throne. Samuel becomes furious and refuses to sleep with SW until she recants her political views. He flees to London, abandoning her and six young children, saying: "You and I must part; for if we have two kings, we must have two beds" (qtd. in Wallace, 12). SW seeks counsel from political allies—an acquaintance who lived near Epworth, Lady Yarborough, and Reverend George Hickes, whom Lady Yarborough recommends as advisor to SW. Interestingly, these letters addressing female resistance and sexual politics were not discovered until 1950. In a 7 March 1701 letter to Lady Yarborough, SW justifies her actions in regard to Samuel, "since I'm willing to let him quietly enjoy his opinions, he ought not to deprive me of my little liberty of conscience" (35). She earnestly asks Lady Yarborough to speak with "Divines" on her behalf, explaining that her husband has abandoned her bed:

> I'm almost ashamed to own what extreme disturbance this accident has given me, yet I value not the world. I value neither reputation[,] friends or anything in comparison of the single satisfaction, of preserving a conscience void of offence towards God and man; and how I can do that if I mock almighty God, by begging pardon for what I think no sin, is past my discerning. (36)

With support from her two confidantes, SW doesn't give in or recant her actions to Samuel. As a result, he applies for a position as chaplain on a ship, planning to desert SW, but a rectory fire changes his mind. He returns to Susanna and the children. Was the fire a case of divine intervention? Many followers of Methodism believe so; upon Samuel's return, John Wesley is conceived.

Another more devastating fire occurs at the rectory in 1709. Unfortunately, Susanna Wesley's writings are lost in this blaze. Her convictions strengthen as a result of this calamity. We witness a pivotal event, at least for the study of ethos, in 1711–12. Samuel is again absent, this time serving in London as a delegate to an Anglican convention. Not only was Samuel absent and financially unsupportive, but an inadequate substitute minister, the Reverend Mr. Inman, is hired to serve the needs of the parishioners in his stead. In the following account, SW opposes her husband along with much of the rest of the church. In his absence, SW begins holding supplementary Sunday evening spiritual gatherings at her home (where she reads devotionals and publishes sermons) for her children and servants. Local citizens hear about these gatherings and join in. The crowd swells to between two hundred and three hundred, according to SW in a 25 February 1711/1712 letter to her husband (82). Eventually, local churchgoers boycott the ineffectual Sunday morning church services led by the Reverend Mr. Inman, Samuel Wesley's replacement, in order to spend more time at the rectory with SW. Inman becomes angry and writes to Samuel requesting that he ask his wife to desist.

Samuel does so, and we have two letters, dated 6 February 1711/1712 and 25 February of the same period, from SW to Samuel in which she defends her rights to speak and assemble parishioners in her home.

In the first letter, Susanna Wesley answers three of her husband's concerns about the Sunday meetings: "First, that it will look particular; secondly, my sex; and lastly, your being at present in a public station and character" (79). Below are excerpts from her letter in which she responds to these issues respectively:

As to its looking particular, I grant it does; and so does almost everything that is serious, or may in any way advance the glory of God or the salvation of souls, if it be performed out of pulpit, or in the way of common conversation; because in our corrupt age the utmost care and diligence have been used to banish all discourse of God or spiritual concerns out of society, as if religion were never to appear out of the closet, and we were to be ashamed of nothing so much as of professing ourselves to be Christians.

To your second, I reply that as I am a woman, so I am also mistress of a large family. And though the superior charge of the souls contained in it lies upon you as head of the family and as their minister, yet in your absence I cannot but look upon every soul you leave under my care as a talent committed to me under a trust by the great Lord of all the families of heaven and earth. And if I am unfaithful to him or to you in neglecting to improve these talents, how shall I answer unto him, when he shall command unto me to render an account of my stewardship? . . .

Your third objection I leave to be answered by your own judgment. We meet not on any worldly design. We banish all temporal concerns from our society; none is suffered to mingle any discourse about them with our reading or singing; we keep close to the business of the day, and as soon as it is over they all go home. And where is the harm of this? . . . Therefore, why any should reflect upon you, let your station be what it will, because your wife endeavors to draw people to the church and to restrain them by reading and other persuasion from their profanation of God's most holy day, I cannot conceive. . . . For my part, I value no censure on this account . . . As for your proposal of letting some other person read. Alas! You do not consider what a people these are. I do not think one man among them could read a sermon without spelling a good part of it; and how would that edify the rest? (79–81)

In the next letter to her husband, SW further comments upon the complaints against her, asking her husband to reflect upon his criticism of her actions. She lists good consequences of the gatherings in her home: the swelling numbers of attendees, the reformation of parishioners, the presence of families who never before attended church, and the friendships developing among neighbors. This justification of her actions illustrates the tension found between her effectiveness as a public speaker and the male-prescribed limits placed on the roles she is allowed to adopt within the community. To this end, SW adds a powerful and effective admonishment to her husband:

> If you do after all think fit to dissolve this assembly, do not tell me any more that you desire me to do it, for that will not satisfy my conscience; but send me your positive command in such full and express terms as may absolve me from all guilt and punishment for neglecting this opportunity of doing good to souls, when you and I shall appear before the great and awful tribunal of our Lord Jesus Christ . . . I pray God direct and bless you. (82–83)

Susanna Wesley continues holding public meetings in her home, setting an example for other women (and men) in her community and for her highly educated children. While her actions and rationalized defiance of her behavior is important for this study of feminist ethos, her claims for small-group study and the authority of women to teach/preach take on even greater significance as they become an integral practice in the formation of Methodism. The Methodist meetings held by John and Charles throughout their lives would become famous, but the gatherings held in her home and led by SW were actually the first Wesley-organized Methodist meetings.

In this new method of religious practice, John Wesley, like his mother, advocated small-group study and classes, along with spiritual meetings, all in addition to weekly sermons. Wallace explains that these "innovations that he likewise did not intend to rival the official church worship, may have had an unconscious model in his mother's earlier experiment" (79). Furthermore, Susanna Wesley's staunch defense of her religious actions, both to her husband and to the local clergy, as well as the significance of her continued willingness to teach and preach to a large local congregation (albeit in her home) didn't go unrecognized:

> Summing up her life at the time of her death, [John Wesley] was ready to place her in the same category as her many male clerical relatives and grant her the biblical title a "preacher of righteousness." The effectiveness of his mother presiding at a public religious gathering may also have made him more receptive to the work of women in his own societies. (79)

Unfortunately, Anglican clergyman John Wesley was way ahead of his time. The Church of England did not recognize women priests until over two hundred years following the Methodist founder's 1791 death. In fact, it was not until 12 March 1994 that the Anglican Church ordained its first female clergy. While women deacons were allowed in 1987, the debate over ordaining women bishops continued. Female bishop legislation was rejected in July 2012. In stating the "deep degree of sadness and shock that they had felt as a result of that vote and also of the need to affirm all women serving the church—both lay and ordained—in their ministries," the Archbishops' Council of the Church of England insisted "that a process to admit women to the episcopate needed to be restarted at the next meeting of the General Synod in July 2013" ("Women Bishops"). As of 14 July 2014, the Church of England voted to allow women to become bishops for the first time, after a vote passed the General Synod by 81 percent. While the resolution of the fate of women leaders in the Anglican Church is still not quite resolved (the 2014 vote and resulting legislation is still awaiting final approval), the story of Methodist ordination of women illustrates John Wesley's vision and Susanna Wesley's practice.

Of course, various factions of Methodism have been in place since John Wesley's founding of the denomination. Since the inception of the 1956 formation of the current United Methodist organization (in which the earlier factions were brought together), women clergy have been sanctioned to preach and hold leadership positions. The United Methodist website explains:

> Clergywomen have been part of Methodism since John Wesley licensed
> Sarah Crosby to preach in 1761. Although women were ordained in the
> Methodist tradition as early as the late 1800s, it was the May 4, 1956
> General Conference vote for full clergy rights that forever changed the
> face of ordained clergy.

Today, women serve in every capacity of Methodist leadership, from local pastors to bishops. And on 1 May 2012, the United Methodist General Conference voted in a landslide election (889 to 20) to grant the United Methodist Women (UMW) organization an autonomous status within the United Methodist Church. "The historic vote separates the national policymaking body of women organized for mission within the denomination from the church's mission agency for the first time in more than 70 years," according to a United Methodist press release. This legislation strengthens connections between global mission projects, which rely upon the support of local groups and local UMW circles found within most Methodist congregations. Yvette Moore explains how this action "will provide more flexibility to local, district, conference and jurisdictional United Methodist Women as they organized for mission in their respective communities." Fittingly, scores of local UMW circles are named in honor of Susanna Wesley—a fitting tribute to her eighteenth-century community leadership—and now, in the twenty-first century, church legislation opens new avenues for women's local/global initiatives. SW, along with other early Methodist female preachers encouraged by Methodist/ Anglican ministers, would be proud.

Bluestocking Women and Anglican Church Patronage

Susanna Wesley's writings, particularly her journal entries and letters, argue for reexamining her life and work from a feminist and literary perspective. SW is an example of what later will become known as the bluestockings— high-minded, morally astute women credited with literary or intellectual interests. This eighteenth-century group includes leading lights such as Mary Astell, Elizabeth Carter, Elizabeth Elstob, Hannah More, Catherine Talbot, Anna Seward, Mary Bosanquet, and Sarah Trimmer. Although not typically counted in the roster of traditional bluestockings, SW certainly exhibits many of the literary, intellectual, and feminist traits associated with this later group. However, it is her association with Anglican ministers and their patronage that most clearly echoes the prevailing descriptions of bluestocking women. Like later women who published with the assistance of Anglican ministers, SW also benefited (even when she was young) from the willingness of these clerics to educate women and promote their intellectual development. Furthermore, aligning SW with other bluestockings, such as Hannah More, strengthens the argument for viewing her as a feminist thinker, casting her as a woman willing to rival male clergymen (not only as the mother of Methodism), and reexamining her role in paving the way for women to be ordained as clergy.

Bluestocking women—a name derived from the less formal blue woolen stockings (rather than the formal black silk ones) worn by some intellectual women (and earlier by intellectual men) in social gatherings—are often associated with the patronage of clergymen of the Church of England. In many cases, the male patrons were relatives or family friends of the bluestockings. Church of England clergy, including John Wesley, served as sponsors (although not always ardent supporters) of women's literacy practices as well as proponents of small-group education and temperance. We must keep in mind that although John Wesley is the father of Methodism, he was also, throughout his entire adult life, an Anglican clergyman.

I adopt the lens of Susan Staves, author of "Church of England Clergy and Women Writers," for viewing SW as a bluestocking. Staves astutely explores the reasons Anglican clergy supported intellectually ambitious and virtuous women. She explains that the clergymen were charitable. These men believed they had a Christian duty to help and promote the writings of virtuous women. They also saw ways women could assist in pastoral initiatives and goals, including providing social and spiritual responsibility for children; founding schools to educate the poor, such as the Sunday school movement; and encouraging women to minister to other women (see Mary Astell's *Serious Proposal to the Ladies* [1694, 1697], Hester Chapone's *Letters on the Improvement of the Mind* [1705], and Hannah More's *Strictures on the Modern System of Female Education* [1799]). Furthermore, according to Staves, Church of England clergymen wanted to spotlight models of both Anglican female piety and learning that were worthy of imitation and that would enhance the reputation of the church (94). Despite mutual benefits of this patronage (each side publicly supported the writings and works of the other), tensions certainly arose between bluestocking women and clergymen. Sources of this tension include: illicit love affairs (although not frequent); conflicts arising over differences concerning publishing matters; differences in theology and biblical hermeneutics; class patronage when the wealthy women were patrons of the clergy, evangelism, and Dissenters; and gender issues and blurred lines between the duties of ordained men and ordained laywomen leading to a gendered hierarchy of duties and venues for rhetorical action (Staves 96–101). SW's biographical history and rhetorical actions illustrate both this patronage and the accompanying tension.

In casting Susanna Wesley as an early bluestocking, we find that she fits Stave's profile of an intelligent woman "sponsored" by clergy in a number of ways. First, SW is educated by her minister-father, marries a minister, and fathers ministers. Second, she is an author of letters and tracts, including "The Apostles' Creed Explicated in a Letter to her Daughter Susanna" and "A Religious Conference between Mother and Emilia"—both of which were designed to educate her daughters on philosophical and theological matters. Later, upon posthumous publication, these tracts instructed other young women as well, encouraging women to question the role of reason in religion. SW also develops a detailed and methodical home school program for her children, reflecting the bluestocking emphasis on pastoral education and care of young children and women. Third, SW is passionately devoted both to her children and her religious principles. She is pious, methodical, and independent. Indeed, as a young woman, she returns to the Church of England after being reared as a Dissenter (representing the model Anglican woman).

Likewise, the life and career of Susanna Wesley illustrate tensions between sponsoring clergymen and intelligent women in several significant ways. First, SW comes forth as "proxy champion" of doctrinal beliefs in "Some Remarks on a Letter from the Rev. Mr. Whitefield to the Rev. Mr. Wesley, In a Letter from a Gentlewoman to her Friend" (1741). She also attacks White-field's Calvinism in this piece, which is, incidentally, the only work published during her lifetime. Additionally, she challenges the Church of England in her disregard for the visiting Pastor Inman and defies her own husband, as seen in her response to his demand that she cease holding home meetings. In matters of appropriate venues for education and roles of leadership for women, SW is contentious, to say the least. Finally, she disagrees with her husband over political and religious matters, leading to separations throughout their marriage.

In the end, for Susanna Wesley, the tensions between herself and clergymen forced acceptance—or at least tolerance—for gendered speaking. This recognition does not occur for all bluestocking women. Staves claims that in many instances, Anglican patronage "bound women like Astell, Elstob, Carter, Talbot, Trimmer, and More to the Church," thus maintaining the status quo of male gender supremacy. As these women compared their education to that of the divines, they came to realize "their own amateurism," according to Staves (103). SW was no shrinking violet. She persevered, citing her own conscience, God's word, and her allegiance to improvement of the mind and spirit in defense of her actions. She was guided ultimately by God, not by man.

Royster and Kirsch contend that imaginative and hopeful feminist "inquiry strategies allow us to engender an *ethos* of humility, respect, and care—an *ethos* we consider critical to achieving qualities of excellence" (21). Susanna Wesley imagined a community where people acted in the best interest of others, including children, church members, Dissenters, servants, and women. She stayed committed to her personal sense of values throughout her lifetime, despite the clergy's expectations of women's obedience and public silence. In revisiting SW's letters, journal entries, missives, and published work, we find a thoughtful, morally responsible woman advocating intense self-examination and accountability. She is never self-promoting or self-righteous, but instead acts in the best interest of those for whom she feels responsible (journal entry 66): "Make not your own esteem or reputation the end of your thoughts, words or actions" (244). Her influence in the world is manifested in the work of her children, and it is ironically only the significance of her famous sons that make access to her papers possible.

However, closer study of these materials reveals a well-educated woman exerting influence within her local sphere. She is neither afraid to appeal to those in power for assistance and justification of her actions nor to criticize the empowered and privileged who, for misguided reasons, prevent the advancement and learning of others. She is outspoken when justified and necessary and acquiescent and accepting of her fate when her spiritual well-being is at stake. In a now-famous quote taken from an 8 June 1725 letter to Jacky/John, Susanna Wesley advocates leading the examined and spiritual life at whatever physical cost in order to avoid sin, defined by her as

[w]hatever weakens your reason, impairs the tenderness of your conscience, obscures your sense of God, or takes off your relish for spiritual things; in short, whatever increases the strength and authority of your body over your mind; that thing is sin to you, however innocent it may be in itself. (109)

Location determines identity in many ways. Susanna Wesley's formulation of ethos as a community and familial construct and her contributions to education and the developing denomination of Methodism are a byproduct of her own education as well as her sometimes contentious reciprocal sponsorship by and of Anglican clergymen. While SW's public actions occur locally and in response to exigent circumstances (both familial and communal), she has studied broadly and intently throughout her life, all the while engaging in intense communal observation and self-reflection. Her immediate actions are in every instance influenced by this close study of educational, spiritual, and rhetorical thought, along with her own detailed method of examining her private and public actions. Throughout this journey, SW strives for spiritual excellence at whatever physical cost, always encouraging her family members and neighbors to embrace similar standards. In SW, we find an eighteenth-century contextualized model of one who enacts a Christian-feminist pedagogy of both male and female ethē, made visible in her social interactions with family and community members. Studying the example of Susanna Wesley's life and work helps present-day readers imagine what an alternative to the patriarchal, religious pedagogues of the eighteenth century might look like.[3]

Notes

1. I wish to thank the librarians and archivists at the Arthur J. Moore Methodist Museum and Library located at Epworth by the Sea, St. Simon's Island, GA, for their kind assistance in introducing me to Wesley family papers and archives.

2. Charles Wallace, editor of SW's writings, offers an interesting feminist reading of the life of SW: 4–17. See also Vicki Tolar Burton's *Spiritual Literacy in John Wesley's Methodism*, chapter 2.

3. I wish to thank Don Gammill, Stephanie Little Rountree, and Helen Gaillet, along with the editors of this volume, for close readings of this chapter and their excellent advice.

Works Cited

Benson, Thomas W. Preface. *The* Ethos *of Rhetoric*. Ed. Michael J. Hyde. Columbia: U of South Carolina P, 2004. Print.

Burton, Vicki Tolar. *Spiritual Literacy in John Wesley's Methodism*. Waco, TX: Baylor UP, 2008. Print.

Friedman, Susan Stanford. *Mappings: Feminism and the Cultural Geographies of Encounter*. Princeton, NJ: Princeton UP, 1998. Print.

Hyde, Michael J. Introduction: "Rhetorically, We Dwell." *The* Ethos *of Rhetoric*. Ed. Michael J. Hyde. Columbia: U of South Carolina P, 2004. Print.

Moore, Yvette. "General Conference Approves United Methodist Women Autonomy." *United Methodist Women*. UMW. Web. 4 Apr. 2013.

Reynolds, Nedra. "*Ethos* as Location: New Sites for Understanding Discursive Authority." *Rhetoric Review* 11.2 (1993): 325–38. Print.

Royster, Jacqueline Jones, and Gesa E. Kirsch. *Feminist Rhetorical Practices*. Carbondale: Southern Illinois UP, 2012. Print.

Schrag, Calvin O. Foreword. *The* Ethos *of Rhetoric*. Ed. Michael J. Hyde. Columbia: U of South Carolina P, 2004. Print.

Staves, Susan. "Church of England Clergy and Women Writers." *Huntington Library Quarterly*. 65 (2002): 81–103. Print.

Wallace, Charles, Jr., ed. *SW: The Complete Writings*. Oxford: Oxford UP, 1997. Print.

Wesley, Susanna. *SW: The Complete Writings*. Ed. Charles Wallace, Jr. Oxford: Oxford UP, 1997. Print.

"Women Bishops." *Church of England: A Christian Presence in Every Community*. Web. 3 Apr. 2013.

"Why Does the United Methodist Church Ordain Women?" *United Methodist Church*. Web. 3 Apr. 2013. Print.

6. Hospitality as Kenosis

Dorothy Day's Voluntary Poverty

Sean Barnette

In 1935, the radical Catholic social activist Dorothy Day wrote to a friend about a man she described as her "greatest and most miserable worry."

> Mr. Breen is at present downstairs, with his clothes hanging off him, cursing and swearing and raving at us all. . . . He would not stay with us, not caring for "kikes and dingos," as he says, so we've been paying for a room around the corner and he has spent his days with us. Now his landlady has put him out, and he still refuses to stay with us. We don't know what to do. He sits at the lower window like a Cerberus and growls and curses at everyone who comes in for a bite of food or some clothing. He hates us all, he hates this place, and he says he is going to die, yet he won't have the Sacraments, etc. He won't bathe, he won't dress. I have to ask one of the men to button him up. He is going to sit right there. He won't go to a hospital. He won't be comforted. . . . It's the hardest problem we have yet. ("To Catherine de Hueck" 77)

By "we," Day meant the residents of the Charles Street house of hospitality, a two-story tenement on the west end of Greenwich Village, temporary headquarters for the Catholic Worker Movement (CWM). That movement, which Day had helped begin in 1932, was a lay organization that aimed to ameliorate social and economic injustice by publicizing and trying to live out the social teachings of the Roman Catholic Church. The CWM's goal was not modest: Day and her comrades frequently cited their desire to "build a new world in the shell of the old." To that end, the CWM worked on a number of fronts, the most visible of which were publishing a newspaper, the *Catholic Worker*, and running a series of houses of hospitality, where members of the movement lived with and cared for people who came seeking food, shelter, clothing, or other necessities.

As Day's letter makes clear, life in a Catholic Worker house was not always easy or pleasant, yet Day felt compelled to receive guests like Edward Breen with hospitality because she believed that it was her Christian duty (see Maurin). And while Day and other members of the CWM certainly believed that offering hospitality to others earned spiritual benefits for themselves, they also saw hospitality as a rhetorical act addressed to a broad public. Indeed, Day constantly stressed that practicing hospitality was not merely a way to address short-term, individual needs, but an essential means of fostering the CWM's hoped-for social revolution. Day was, therefore, eager to press on with this "hardest problem" of hospitality.

In this chapter, I explore how the hospitality of the CWM in the 1930s worked rhetorically, focusing on how Day's practice of hospitality made use of a rhetorical strategy that I label *kenosis*. My goal is to suggest how rhetoricians might understand kenosis as an ethical strategy—that is, as a means of establishing and using ethos. The word kenosis means "emptying," and I use it to refer to a strategy of divesting oneself of any essential concept of self or preconstructed ethos, enabling oneself to enter more fully and responsively into relationships with others and with the material world. Drawing on Maurice Hamington's notion of feminist hospitality, I argue that this responsiveness marks kenosis as a particularly feminist strategy. While kenosis has been an important concept in Christian moral theology since the first century—and has in recent years been critically examined by feminist theologians—scholars of rhetoric have not yet explored how kenosis might work as a feminist ethical strategy.

To understand the relationship between hospitality and kenosis, I consider Day's practice of hospitality as a material rhetoric, with elements "that signify not through language but through their spatial organization, mobility, mass, utility, orality, and tactility" (Dickson 297).[1] My analysis draws on Carole Blair's heuristic for analyzing material texts, in particular her question, "How does the text act on people?" (30). Like Blair, I understand a text's action "on people" to refer not only to the intellectual or affective state of an audience's mind, but to the physical state of their bodies. While Blair's use of the term "text" might suggest a single physical entity (whether verbal or material), the subject of my analysis is not one object but the ecology of objects and practices involved in offering guests space, shelter, food, and other materials. These objects and practices are what allow hospitality to do rhetorical work.

That rhetorical work is best understood as promoting what Kenneth Burke calls *identification*. Traditionally, the goal of rhetoric has been seen as persuasion. However, persuasion is a problematic goal for material rhetoric because it is propositional: a speaker tries to convince an audience that such-and-such is or is not true (and, perhaps, to act on that conviction). Given that material rhetoric acts not only on audiences' intellects but on their bodies as well, it is insufficient to see persuasion as the end of this sort of rhetoric. Identification, in contrast, involves highlighting or constructing similarities among participants in a discourse in order to move those participants to act in a desired way. This definition of identification leaves room for material rhetoric: similarities that form the basis of identification might easily be physical, spatial, or experiential. For instance, the fact of being in the same room as someone or wearing the same uniform facilitates identification. As Gregory Clark explains, the act of sharing spaces and experiences "gathers [people] together with others in an environment of shared perspectives, values, and commitments to reconstitute them as members of a community" (144). Of course, identification can be merely a means of accomplishing persuasion, but because identification is a reciprocal act of ethos construction, a rhetor "can succeed [at persuasion] only insofar as he [or she] yields to that audience's opinions" (Burke 56). In other words, when we participate in rhetorical discourse, we construct an ethos (or, in the case of kenosis, we divest ourselves of an ethos) in relation with our interlocutors, and that act changes us. Thus the end of rhetorical hospitality is more than the mere persuasion of a guest or an outside audience; it also effects a change in the rhetorical identity of the speaker.

Feminist Hospitality as Rhetoric

It is something of a commonplace to begin discussions of hospitality by observing that twenty-first-century Western culture has largely commercialized or outright abandoned the practice of hospitality (e.g., Haswell, Haswell, and Blalock; Jacobs; Murray; Nouwen; Pohl). But hospitality has long been an important practice in human societies, often serving to establish the identities of host and guest within a hierarchical social structure. A host receives a guest into her (or, more often, his) home or homeland, and hospitality consists in providing the guest with food, protection, information, and other necessities and comforts. Lavish generosity toward one's guests demonstrates—and maintains—one's advanced social standing in two ways. Most obviously, it provides an opportunity for a host to showcase her material wealth. (In modern American discourse, this showcasing often prompts an acknowledgment of appreciation from the guest, something like, "You have a lovely home.") More subtly, receiving a guest also shows that a host is secure enough, both physically and socially, to accept the risk posed by an encounter with a stranger who may very well present a threat.

The word *hospitality* itself preserves the tension inherent in the act of welcoming a potentially threatening stranger. As the linguist Emile Benveniste has argued, the Latin *hospes*, from which the modern word derives, is a compound of roots with apparently contradictory meanings: *hostis*, meaning "guest" or "host," and *pet* or *pot*, meaning "master" (71). One the one hand, the hostis root implies a reciprocal, interdependent relationship, as is evident from the fact that both host and guest are designated by a single term. In Roman custom, a *hostis* was a particular class of outsider who enjoyed the same rights as a citizen, and the relationship between *hostes* was ratified by an exchange of gifts (77). On the other hand, the pet root implies power, especially self-mastery or self-sufficiency—exactly the opposite of the reciprocity inherent in the idea of a hostis. Hospitality, thus, involves both interdependence and independence, the giving of oneself to an Other and the maintenance of clear boundaries between the self and the Other. Furthermore, as Tracy McNulty has pointed out in *The Hostess: Hospitality, Femininity, and the Expropriation of Identity*, traditional hospitality "constitutes identity: the identity of the host, but also that of the group, culture, or nation in whose name he acts" (viii). Hospitality thus weaves host and guest into a social fabric that extends beyond either of them. Consequently, the practice of hospitality inevitably has social effects, whether conservative or subversive.

Most traditional forms of hospitality have been limited in ways that promote hospitality's conservative effect. For instance, hospitality is offered with the understanding that a guest's presence is temporary—a guest is not a permanent resident—and ultimately the separation between host and guest remains clear. However much a host may insist that a guest "make herself at home," she is, by definition, not at home. Furthermore, traditional hospitality is not open to just anyone; only certain members of a society may be received as guests, such as the *hostes* in Roman society or members of the warrior class in Homer (Haswell, Haswell, and Blalock).

Nevertheless, more subversive forms of hospitality are also possible. Haswell, Haswell, and Blalock describe what they call "nomadic hospitality," in which a traveler is welcomed into the temporary home of another traveler. In such a situation, the statuses of guest and host are more contingent, and therefore more truly egalitarian. Others have cited the Benedictine tradition of hospitality, in which guests are welcomed with profound respect as though they were Christ (Jacobs; Rudd; Want). One model of subversive hospitality that I wish to explore in some detail is what women's studies scholar Maurice Hamington has called feminist hospitality, which like nomadic and Benedictine hospitality "mitigates the expression of power differential, while seeking greater connection and understanding for the mutual benefit of both host and guest" (23). For Hamington, feminist hospitality holds the key to a more just society because it enacts feminist, nonviolent principles and "reflects a performative extension of care ethics" (24). Hamington identifies four qualities of feminist hospitality that make it potentially subversive: first, it is inclusive, in that anyone may participate; second, it is nonhierarchical, in that the host/guest relationship is one of equals, and therefore is dynamic; third, it is based on forgiveness rather than on justice and revenge; fourth, it is an embodied, material practice rather than an abstraction.

I argue that two of these qualities of feminist hospitality are particularly important to an understanding of Day's hospitality as a feminist rhetorical practice: its nonhierarchical nature, and its materiality. Given hospitality's natural association with domesticity, its practice can easily be seen as merely feminine, rather than feminist. However, when hospitality is practiced with a sincere spirit of mutuality, hosts and guests enact "a commitment to pluralism and valuing diverse voices" that makes it transformative, rather than conservative (Hamington 29). In Day's case, a key mechanism by which this transformation occurs is hospitality's material nature. Feminist hospitality cannot be practiced at a distance, by proxy. Whereas in traditional hospitality a host might dispatch servants or employees to tend to a guest's needs, feminist hospitality can operate only when a host eschews such detachment and makes herself truly, physically present to her guest. This embodied presence "facilitates a concretizing of the Other" (32) that enables a host to identify more fully with guests than she otherwise might; guests cannot be abstractions, but real people, and therefore true participants in the rhetorical exchange of hospitality. Furthermore, Hamington explains, as an embodied practice, feminist hospitality contributes to the development of moral habits that make up a rhetor's ethos: "if one exercises and practices hospitable acts, there is a reflective and imaginative dimension to human corporeal existence that makes it easier to respond accordingly to new and unexpected guests" (32). Finally, as a result of the equality inherent in feminist hospitality, a host's embodied habits of hospitality can be learned by a guest, who then, in future encounters, can act hospitably toward others. In other words, the materiality of feminist hospitality affects the way that both host and guest construct rhetorical identities for themselves and how they may interact with others in the future.

Kenosis as a Rhetorical Strategy

To clarify the relationship between feminist hospitality and ethos, I turn to the vocabulary of Day's spiritual tradition to borrow the term *kenosis*. As mentioned above, the term itself—from the Greek adjective *kenos*, meaning "empty"—refers simply to the act of emptying or the state of emptiness. When the term appears in ancient Greek manuscripts (e.g., in Plato's *Philebus* and Sophocles's *Oedipus Tyrannus*), its use is unremarkable. The term's significance arises instead from its use in the Christian tradition, first found (as a verb) in St. Paul's letter to the Christians at Philippi.

> Fulfill ye my joy, that you may be of one mind, having the same charity, being of one accord, agreeing in sentiment. Let nothing be done through contention, neither by vain glory: but in humility, let each esteem others better than themselves: Each one not considering the things that are his own, but those that are other men's. For let this mind be in you, which was also in Christ Jesus:
>
> > Who being in the form of God,
> >   thought it not robbery to be equal with God:
> > But emptied [i.e., *ekenosen*] himself,
> >   taking the form of a servant,
> >   being made in the likeness of men,
> >   and in habit found as a man.
> > He humbled himself,
> >   becoming obedient unto death,
> >   even to the death of the cross.
> >   (*Douay-Rheims Bible*, Phil 2:2–8)

As is evident from the line structure, beginning in verse 6 ("Who being . . ."), Paul's writing style changes considerably. Biblical scholars believe this change indicates that Paul is quoting a preexisting liturgical hymn that would have been familiar to his first-century readers. Paul's reference to Christ's kenosis, therefore, is not his own as much as it is a commonplace that he uses to persuade his readers to act in a particular manner. This means that, while Paul is often credited with shaping much of early Christian doctrine, the concept of kenosis clearly predates Paul's writing, and indeed it has remained a central spiritual imperative for believers who have been instructed to "deny themselves" in imitation of Christ's self-emptying.[2] To be clear, kenosis involves more than simple self-denial in the common ascetical sense of denying oneself certain comforts or necessities. That sort of self-denial places the self in the grammatical role of beneficiary or indirect object. Kenosis, in contrast, places the self in the role of direct object of the denial; one's very identity is what is denied. Kenosis is thus more radical than mere asceticism.

Obviously, this understanding of kenosis is fraught with potentially problematic gender associations. In fact, the theologian Daphne Hampson suggests that kenosis's prominence in Christian thought is due precisely to the fact that it responds to a particularly male problem (i.e., agonistic self-assertion). But for women, Hampson argues, "the theme of self-emptying and self-abnegation is far from helpful as a paradigm" (155). Indeed, as a moral imperative, kenosis has the potential for abuse, and a teaching that promotes self-denial can be (and has been) used to oppress and silence women and other traditionally disempowered people. Kenosis, in this line of thinking, may be an appropriate path to holiness for someone who has worldly power to give up, but to encourage women or other groups with relatively less social power to give up what power they have only perpetuates injustice in the name of religion. Furthermore, just as feminist theologians like Hampson have raised concerns about the idea of kenosis in Christian tradition, feminist rhetoricians might rightfully be concerned with the notion of kenosis in rhetoric. If feminists want to resist patriarchal rhetorical traditions that concentrate rhetorical agency among only a few individuals, then what use is a rhetorical strategy by which one gives up one's rhetorical standing? In other words, why should feminist rhetoricians draw the idea of kenosis from Christian tradition into rhetoric?

One answer to that comes from theologian Sarah Coakley, who argues that kenosis is actually "not only compatible with feminism, but vital to a distinctively Christian manifestation of it" (*Powers* 4). Coakley suggests that critiques such as Hampson's both ignore the complicated variety of possible theological understandings of kenosis[3] and, more importantly, represent a "failure to embrace a feminist reconceptualizing of the power of the cross and resurrection" (33). In other words, kenosis can be seen not simply as the condescension of a patriarchal God or as that God's feigning weakness in order to identify with humanity, but as the paradoxically self-constituting action of an inherently peaceful, nurturing God. To explain how such a feminist understanding of kenosis might play out in human behavior, Coakley looks to the practice of contemplation, the "act of silent waiting on the divine in prayer" (34). She continues:

> This rather special form of "vulnerability" is not an invitation to be battered; nor is its silence a silenc*ing*. (If anything, it builds one in the courage to give prophetic voice.) By choosing to "make space" in this way, one "practices" the "presence of God"—the subtle enabling presence of a God who neither shouts nor forces, let alone "obliterates." . . . This special "self-emptying" is not a negation of self, but the place of the self's transformation and expansion into God. (35–36)

It is in this type of prayer that Coakley sees the potential usefulness—for men or women, regardless of the degree of power they wield in relation to their social situation—of the kenotic imperative.

While Coakley's recuperation of kenosis as a spiritual practice may be useful for Christian feminists, I believe kenosis can be similarly reconsidered as a feminist ethical strategy, especially given the context in which Paul initially refers to Christ's self-emptying. Before quoting the hymn, Paul exhorts his readers to "be of one mind" and "of one accord, agreeing in sentiment" (2:2). These are, arguably, the precise ends of rhetorical discourse: to move an audience toward mutual identification and consensus.[4] Christians' imitation of Christ's kenosis thus becomes a strategy for doing exactly what rhetoric aims to do.

But kenosis, as an ethical strategy, is not connected merely with the ends of rhetoric but also with the means used to achieve those ends, so a rhetorical strategy grounded in kenosis would differ in important ways from more traditional forms of rhetoric. For instance, when Quintilian, writing just one generation after Paul, famously echoed Cato's assertion that a rhetor must be a "good man," he argued that goodness of character is actually more important for a rhetor than skill in speaking (12.1.1). Kenosis, in contrast, calls for a rhetor not to build up character but to divest herself of it. It promotes emptiness, rather than goodness. Another important difference between kenosis and more traditional rhetorical strategies has to do with the degree to which these strategies promote particularly feminist rhetorical practices. For example, as Sally Miller Gearhart has pointed out, traditional rhetoric assumes that a rhetor must take an agonistic, patriarchal stance toward an audience: rhetoric is thought to be effective when a rhetor gains and exerts control over an audience. Gearhart proposes a "womanization" of rhetoric in which rhetorical discourse is seen as an act of cocreation rather than of conquest. Similarly, Sonja Foss and Cindy Griffin suggest that traditional rhetoric's narrow focus on persuasion ignores other possible and less patriarchal goals for rhetoric.[5] In light of these calls for alternative ways of conceptualizing and practicing rhetoric, Paul's initial endorsement of kenosis becomes especially significant: Paul urges that consensus should arise without "contention" (Greek *eritheia*). In other words, kenosis as a rhetorical strategy requires a definition of rhetoric that includes noneristic discourse. Consequently, kenosis may be a particularly apt strategy for feminist rhetors who wish to avoid agonistic rhetoric because of its ties to violence and male-dominated discourse.

Day's Use of Kenosis: Voluntary Poverty

Although she was clearly a skilled rhetor, Day was no scholar of rhetoric, and never described the CWM's efforts at propaganda and indoctrination in the technical vocabulary of rhetoricians.[6] Nonetheless, Day was familiar with the various ways that the kenotic imperative had been articulated throughout Christian tradition, such as St. Paul's exhortation for Christians to offer their bodies as "a living sacrifice" to God (Romans 12.1), or the various means of mortification recommended by saints and spiritual writers, such as fasting and almsgiving. Indeed, Day frequently wrote of the necessity of mortification; however, her preferred term for the rhetorical strategy I am naming kenosis was "voluntary poverty."

In her writing, Day was careful to differentiate between poverty and destitution (e.g., *House* Conclusion). The latter she understood to describe an extreme material and spiritual privation, whereas the former connoted only a lack of material security. Poverty was a condition that could be embraced, trusting that God would provide for one's true needs. In Day's understanding, therefore, poverty was ultimately a solution to the problem of destitution, but only if one's poverty was voluntary. What was essential was not the lack of control over one's situation that poverty signaled, but the voluntary giving up of the control that one had—in other words, kenosis. Thus anyone, regardless of material conditions, could chose to embrace voluntary poverty.

The idea of poverty, while it has much in Christian tradition to recommend it, was not always one for which Day could garner support. Ostensibly, part of the reason for the CWM's existence was to combat poverty, and Day was sensitive to how exhortations to poverty would be received by the readers of the *Catholic Worker*. Especially in the early days of the movement, Day was concerned that the importance of voluntary poverty was "a thing delicate and precious and hard to convey" because her readers—"the embittered, fallen away Catholic,—the man on the street,—the poor mother of many children, the father out of work"—were already too familiar with the consequences of involuntary poverty (Day, "To a Jesuit" 60). Day also wanted to avoid giving credence to the communist objection that religion was only a means of pacifying poor people (and keeping them poor) by getting them to accept their condition as somehow worthy of eventual, eternal reward. The difficulty of writing about poverty may explain why Day did not use the phrase "voluntary poverty" in any signed article in the *Catholic Worker* until 1937. When she finally did, however, her wording indicates she expected the idea of voluntary poverty should already be familiar to her readers.[7] Through the late 1930s and especially into the 1940s, Day more and more cited voluntary poverty as a central tenet of the CWM's revolutionary program.

The distinction Day draws between voluntary poverty and involuntary destitution shows that she was sensitive to the potential dangers of encouraging those without social power to "empty themselves" through kenosis.[8] But Day also used voluntary poverty as a rhetorical foil to critics who accused her of being soft and sentimental (i.e., too feminine) in her views.

> But let those who talk of softness, of sentimentality, come to live with us in cold, unheated houses in the slums. . . . Let them live with rats, with vermin, bedbugs, roaches, lice (I could describe the several kinds of body lice).
> Let their flesh be mortified by cold, by dirt, by vermin; let their eyes be mortified by the sight of bodily excretions, diseased limbs, eyes, noses, mouths.
> Let their noses be mortified by the smells of sewage, decay and rotten flesh. Yes, and the smell of the sweat, blood and tears spoken of so blithely by Mr. Churchill, and so widely and bravely quoted by comfortable people.

Let their ears be mortified by harsh and screaming voices, by the constant coming and going of people living herded together with no privacy. (There is no privacy in tenements just as there is none in concentration camps.)

Let their taste be mortified by the constant eating of insufficient food cooked in huge quantities for hundreds of people, the coarser foods, the cheaper foods, so that there will be enough to go around; and the smell of such cooking is often foul.

Then when they have lived with these comrades, with these sights and sounds, let our critics talk of sentimentality. ("Why")

Day's defense dwells on the material elements of poverty; to be voluntarily poor was to be at the mercy of these material conditions, and the mortification Day writes of is exactly the sort of difficult kenosis that allowed her and other workers to use hospitality as a critique of social injustice.

Kenosis and Feminist Hospitality in Action

How, then, did this critique work? As I have argued, Day's ethical strategy of kenosis allowed her to practice feminist hospitality, which served to critique unjust social structures by realigning the identifications of hosts and guests in the CWM, as well as those of outside audiences, such as readers of the *Catholic Worker*. A story that Day relates to biographer Robert Coles offers an especially clear illustration of the materiality of feminist hospitality in action, and how this worked rhetorically within the CWM. As her description of the dirty, unsafe, and unsanitary conditions in some houses of hospitality makes clear, one of Day's perennial complaints about the CWM houses was the distraction of the constant noise. Many times, Day relates, people would come in to the house "agitated and noisy, so noisy, that they quieted everyone else down. In a strange way, they could be a relief." She continues:

A very drunk sailor, who was a notoriously angry man, came to us, and he told all the people in the room to shut up, and he told a few men if they didn't get out of the room, he'd kill them. I was serving soup and bread, and I went to him and told him he was a great friend to us that day, and we were grateful, *very* grateful. He looked at me. I'll never forget those blue eyes of his; they were moving away from me, then closing in on me; they were dancing all over, then they were so still and penetrating I was more afraid of them than any knife or gun he may have had. (qtd. in Coles 123)

Confronted with a dangerous situation, Day attempts to neutralize the threat by means of rhetoric. She names the man as a friend, hoping to identify with him so that he will not attack anyone, but the man's shifting and threatening eyes indicate his resistance to Day's rhetorical advances. So she tries again.

> He would move his right hand through [his] thick, curly hair and then he'd wipe his hand on his trousers, as if he'd touched something dirty. Mind you, his trousers were fairly dirty themselves. He saw me following that hand, looking at his trousers, and he bellowed, "What are you looking at?" . . . I said, "At you." He shouted back, "Why are you looking at me?" I answered, "Because I'm standing here talking with you." He shouted back, "Well, who are you?" I gave him my name and asked him who he was. He told me—his first name, at least, Fred. I offered my hand to him and he offered his, but before he let us shake, he asked me if I was worried that he was dirty. I said no, and besides, I hadn't washed my own hands, and there was all sorts of crud on them, from the kitchen, and would he excuse me, and he said yes, and then we shook. (qtd. in Coles 123)

When her verbal rhetoric fails, Day engages the man's material existence, apparently hoping that drawing attention to their physical proximity will lead the man to interact with her in a less threatening manner. The man perceives her looking at him to be an inappropriately intimate act, and she counters that the fact that she is "standing here" justifies it; their physical proximity constitutes their intimacy, and her looking at him is thus warranted. Day further identifies with the man through their physical similarities—they are both dirty—and based on this identification, the man is persuaded to acknowledge their connection by shaking hands. Two acts of kenosis make this identification possible. First, by leaving the space where she had been working, Day literally distances herself from the site of rhetorical power that would have designated her as a host. Second, Day further denies her identity as host by showing that she is just as dirty as her guest.

Day then thanks Fred for quieting the room down, calling him "a life-saver." But Fred resists her thanks:

> He gave me a strange look. He lowered his eyes, stared at the floor, and talked to me without looking at me. He said he didn't *want* to be called a lifesaver, I must not call him that. He was growling. (qtd. in Coles 124)

Again Day's attempt to bring Fred into her circle of identification through verbal rhetoric fails, so she takes a material approach:

I asked him if I could give him some soup. He asked me what was in it. I told him lots of good vegetables. He asked me if I would have some. I said I was hungry, and I sure would. So we sat down, and he wouldn't start until I did. He watched me swallow a few tablespoons, and then he was about to start his, when all of a sudden he changed his mind and asked me if he could have *my* soup. I said sure, and he gobbled it up!

Meanwhile, I had a flash of intuition, because I saw him staring at his soup! I asked him if I could have that soup. He said yes, that he *wanted* me to have it, as a matter of fact. . . . I took the bowl and slurped it up, hungrily. I *was* hungry. He sat there watching me, as intently as I had ever been watched. (qtd. in Coles 124)

This exchange involves yet another instance of kenosis. By serving soup to her guest, Day performs a traditional act of hospitality that places her in the role of host. But in exchanging the bowls, Day transgresses the expectations of her role, divesting herself to an extent of the ethos associated with her role. The soup that Day and Fred then share cements their identification. Importantly, though, their identification does not affect only Fred. The emphasis in Day's comment, "I *was* hungry," suggests that her kenotic interaction with Fred made her aware of her own need, an emptiness that she was somewhat surprised to discover within herself. Although she had been serving food to guests when Fred came in, it was by sitting down and eating the soup with him that Day allowed herself to recognize and satisfy her own hunger. Both host and guest are transformed by Day's practice of hospitality.

After the soup was finished, Fred became threatening again, and Day asked him if there was anything else he wanted. She continues:

I picked up a piece of bread, broke it in half, took part of one half in my mouth, and offered him the other half—and he took it. He said thank you, and I said . . . "Oh, do come here, anytime; we'd love to have you as our guest." Then I excused myself. . . . As I left, I could hear the room getting noisier and noisier, and I'll tell you, I was never happier to hear all that rattle. . . . The next day that man came early in the morning with bags full of celery and carrots and onions and potatoes. I asked him, please, come and have lunch, taste the soup with his vegetables in it, and he said he would. He became one of our regulars. (qtd. in Coles 125)

The language Day uses to describe the three-part action of sharing bread with her guest (i.e., picking it up, breaking it, and offering it) clearly echoes the language Christians use to describe the institution of the Eucharist (e.g., in Matthew 26.26: "And whilst they were at supper, Jesus took bread, and blessed, and broke: and gave to his disciples"). And, just as in Roman Catholic teaching the Eucharist is closely associated with hospitality and is seen as the consummation of the communicant's inclusion in the Body of Christ (see Pohl 30), Day's act of sharing soup and bread completes Fred's shift of identification from threat to member of the group. Day's hospitality leads to a reciprocal gift from Fred, one that blurs the line between host as provider of food and guest as recipient.

Throughout her encounter with Fred, Day enacts feminist hospitality, voluntarily becoming more and more powerless as she gives up the social and material markers of her role as host. Through that kenosis, she is able to identify with Fred. For example, by asking Fred to excuse her for being so dirty, she puts herself on the same level as her guest, stepping out of her role as host and asking his indulgence, enacting the equality Hamington names as one quality of feminist hospitality. Next, while the act of giving Fred her soup is not really any different from traditional hospitality (a host is expected to provide food to a guest), when Day asks if Fred will give her his soup, she again empties herself of the rhetorical power associated with her role as host and places the roles of host and guest on the same level. In this encounter, then, Day and Fred begin in clearly defined roles: Day is the host and Fred is the guest (and a threatening one). However, throughout their interaction, Day repeatedly moves to divest herself of the power associated with the role of host. This divestment takes different forms in response to the changing situation of their encounter, but in each instance Day's kenosis helps to establish her credibility with her interlocutor, and it is therefore an important aspect of her ethos. Through her verbal and material self-emptying she creates a situation that facilitates her and Fred's mutual identification.

Kenosis and Love

Day was not especially interested in feminism. In later life, she was quite critical of the women's movement in the United States because she saw it as exclusively concerned with the middle class, whereas she felt "the struggle . . . was still a class struggle and the big issue today was world poverty" ("On Pilgrimage—June"). And as her writings make clear, she held to essentialist views on gender differences, arguing that women "by their very nature are more materialistic, thinking of the home, the children, and of all things needful to them, especially love" (*Long* 60). Nonetheless, as I have argued, Day was committed to practicing hospitality in a way that can be described as feminist, and the fact that Day places love at the climax of her observation about material concerns highlights the close ties between love and feminist hospitality.

To practice feminist hospitality, one must be open to the threat that guests such as Mr. Breen or Fred inevitably present, and that very openness is itself also a threat. Openness to others, achieved by kenosis, disrupts a host's social status and, consequently, her very identity. But that disruption, for Day, was exactly the point. If rhetoric involves the shifting of identifications, then a rhetor's kenosis provides a necessary, hospitable space in which guests and hosts are invited to realign their identifications—hopefully in ways that promote the principles of care and love.

Notes

1. There was, of course, an important verbal component to CWM hospitality; Day and other members of the movement regularly referred to the homeless, hungry, and sick people who came to them as "ambassadors of God"—a significant act of renaming. For insightful analyses of the CWM's verbal rhetoric, see Dana Anderson's *Identity's Strategy*, Carol Jablonski's "Dorothy Day's Contested Legacy: 'Humble Irony' as a Constraint on Memory," Kristine Johnson's *Meeting When He Asks to Be Met: Public Religious Discourse in the* Catholic Worker, Sabrina Marsh's "'The Odds and Ends of Things': Dorothy Day's 1930s *Catholic Worker* Columns and the Prudent Translation of Catholic Social Teachings," and June O'Connor's "Dorothy Day as Autobiographer."

2. The fact that Christ's kenosis was evidently a very early concept in Christian theology highlights an ambiguity in the text: it is not clear whether the reference to Christ's kenosis here describes an act prior to or synonymous with his "humbl[ing] himself" in accepting crucifixion. In other words, while Christian orthodoxy came to see this text as describing the incarnation of a preexisting divine Logos, some critics have pointed out that such a reading anachronistically assumes a more fully systematic theology of the incarnation than the first Christians espoused (Coakley "Kenosis" 194).

3. A detailed overview of these different theological perspectives is beyond the scope of this chapter, but Coakley identifies five distinct (and sometimes contradictory) understandings of kenosis that have been prominent throughout Christian history (*Powers* 3–14).

4. Rhetoric can also be disruptive, of course, interrupting or contesting normative discourses. In this text, however, Paul clearly sees kenosis as leading to peaceful ends, rather than disruptive ones.

5. While Burke offers identification as an alternative to persuasion, it is not clear that identification necessarily avoids the problems that Gearhart and Foss and Griffin identify in traditional approaches to rhetoric.

6. When Day used the word "rhetoric" in her writings, it was always with its popular meaning of "manipulative speech," with one illustrative exception. Writing in the *Catholic Worker* in 1973, Day recalled: "Today I had interesting conversations with Jo von Gottfried, a teacher of rhetoric in Berkeley, a great lover of St. Thomas and St. Augustine. I tried to understand what "rhetoric" really means and she explained, but I cannot now remember" ("On Pilgrimage—September").

7. In reporting on an interview with Michigan governor Frank Murphy, she wrote, "Evidently voluntary poverty was part of the Governor's credo, too" ("Interview").

8. Coakley, in arguing for a kenotic form of contemplative prayer, makes the same distinction "between this 'right' vulnerability and mere invitation to abuse; between this contemplative 'self-effacement' and self-destruction or self-repression" (*Powers* 36).

Works Cited

Anderson, Dana. *Identity's Strategy: Rhetorical Selves in Conversion.* Columbia: U of South Carolina P, 2007. Print.

Benveniste, Emile. *Indo-European Language and Society.* Trans. Elizabeth Palmer. London: Faber and Faber, 1969. PDF file.

Blair, Carole. "Contemporary U.S. Memorial Sites as Exemplars of Rhetoric's Materiality." *Rhetorical Bodies.* Ed. Jack Selzer and Sharon Crowley. Madison: U of Wisconsin P, 1999. 16–57. Print.

Burke, Kenneth. *A Rhetoric of Motives.* New York: Prentice Hall, 1952. Print.

Clark, Gregory. *Rhetorical Landscapes in America: Variations on a Theme by Kenneth Burke.* Columbia: U of South Carolina P, 2004. Print.

Coakley, Sarah. "Kenosis: Theological Meanings and Gender Connotations." *The Work of Love: Creation as Kenosis.* Ed. John Polkinghorne. Grand Rapids, MI: Eerdmans, 2001. 192–210. Print.

———. *Powers and Submissions: Spirituality, Philosophy, and Gender.* Malden, MA: Blackwell, 2002. Print.

Coles, Robert. *Dorothy Day: A Radical Devotion.* Cambridge, MA: Da Capo, 1987. Print.

Day, Dorothy. *House of Hospitality.* 1939. *The Catholic Worker Movement,* n.d. Web. 6 Apr. 2010.

———. "Interview with Murphy." *Catholic Worker* Oct. 1937: 1, 3. *The Catholic Worker Movement.* Web. 10 May 2013.

———. *The Long Loneliness: The Autobiography of Dorothy Day.* 1952. New York: Harper Collins, 1980. Print.

———. "On Pilgrimage—June 1971." *Catholic Worker* June 1971: 1–2, 5–6, 8. *The Catholic Worker Movement*. Web. 23 Nov. 2010.

———. "On Pilgrimage—September 1973." *The Catholic Worker* Sept. 1973: 1–2, 6. *The Catholic Worker Movement*. Web. 10 Aug. 2013.

———. "To a Jesuit Priest." 7 May 1934. Ellsberg 60–61. Print.

———. "To Catherine de Hueck." July 1935. Ellsberg 76–78. Print.

———. "Why Do the Members of Christ Tear One Another?" *The Catholic Worker* Feb. 1942: 1, 4, 7. *The Catholic Worker Movement*. Web. 30 Oct. 2010.

Dickson, Barbara. "Reading Maternity Materially: The Case of Demi Moore." *Rhetorical Bodies*. Ed. Jack Selzer and Sharon Crowley. Madison: U of Wisconsin P, 1999. 297–313. Print.

Douay-Rheims Bible. DRBO.org. 2013. Web. 9 May 2013.

Ellsberg, Robert, ed. *All the Way to Heaven: The Selected Letters of Dorothy Day*. Milwaukee: Marquette UP, 2010. Print.

Foss, Sonja K., and Cindy L. Griffin. "Beyond Persuasion: A Proposal for an Invitational Rhetoric." *Communication Monographs* 62 (1995): 2–17. Print.

Gearhart, Sally Miller. "The Womanization of Rhetoric." *Women's Studies International Quarterly* 2 (1979): 195–201. Print.

Hamington, Maurice. "Toward a Theory of Feminist Hospitality." *Feminist Formations* 22.1 (2010): 21–38. *Project Muse*. Web. 25 Aug. 2010.

Hampson, Daphne. *Theology and Feminism*. Oxford: Blackwell, 1990. Print.

Haswell, Janis, Richard Haswell, and Glenn Blalock. "Hospitality in College Composition Courses." *CCC* 60.4 (2009): 707–27. *Literature Online*. Web. 16 Aug. 2010.

Jablonski, Carol J. "Dorothy Day's Contested Legacy: 'Humble Irony' as a Constraint on Memory." *Journal of Communication and Religion* 23.1 (2000): 29–49. Print.

Jacobs, Dale. "The Audacity of Hospitality." *JAC* 28.3/4 (2008): 963–81. Print.

Johnson, Katherine. *Meeting When He Asks to Be Met: Public Religious Discourse in the* Catholic Worker. Diss. Purdue U, 2009. Print.

Marsh, Sabrina. "'The Odds and Ends of Things': Dorothy Day's 1930s *Catholic Worker* Columns and the Prudent Translation of Catholic Social Teachings." *Rhetoric Society Quarterly* 42.4 (2012): 330–52. Print.

Maurin, Peter. "The Duty of Hospitality." *A Collection of Peter Maurin's Easy Essays*. The Catholic Worker Movement, n.d. Web. 30 Sept. 2010.

McNulty, Tracy. *The Hostess: Hospitality, Femininity, and the Exploration of Identity*. Minneapolis: U of Minnesota P, 2007. Print.

Murray, Harry. *Do Not Neglect Hospitality: The Catholic Worker and the Homeless*. Philadelphia: Temple UP, 1990. Print.

Nouwen, Henry J. M. *Reaching Out: The Three Movements of the Spiritual Life*.

Garden City, NY: Doubleday, 1975. Print.

O'Connor, June. "Dorothy Day as Autobiographer." *Religion* 20.3 (1990): 275–95. *ScienceDirect.* Web. 1 June 2010.

Pohl, Christine. *Making Room: Recovering Hospitality as a Christian Tradition.* Grand Rapids, MI: Eerdmans, 1999. Print.

Quintilian. *Institutio Oratoria.* Laccus Curius: Into the Roman World. 30 July 2013. Web. 2 Oct. 2013.

Rudd, Anthony. "Learning in Comfort: Developing an Ethos of Hospitality in Education." *The Educational Conversation: Closing the Gap.* Ed. James W. Garrison and Anthony G. Rudd. Albany: State U of New York P, 1995. 119–28. Print.

Want, Joanna Lin. "Listen to Strangers: A Response to Dale Jacobs' 'The Audacity of Hospitality.'" *JAC* 31.1/2 (2011): 241–48. Print.

7. Powerlessness Repurposed

The Feminist Ethos of Judy Bonds

Mary Beth Pennington

In 2003, just four years after joining the Coal River Mountain Watch (CRMW) activist organization, West Virginian Julia "Judy" Bonds won the international North American Goldman Environmental Prize, which is awarded annually to "grassroots environmental heroes from the world's six inhabited continental regions . . . for sustained and significant efforts to protect and enhance the natural environment, often at great personal risk" ("About the Prize"). This achievement in such a short time is notable because of Bonds's background: At forty-seven years old, she was already a grandmother when she joined the movement against mountaintop removal (MTR). A former Pizza Hut waitress and "coal miner's daughter," she never attended college, but as an Appalachian activist, she managed to make audiences of the United Nations, Congress, and a number of environmental, academic, corporate, and governmental organizations listen so much so that she became "one of the most visible faces" in the anti-MTR movement (Barry 51).[1]

Although she never talked about her activism as rhetoric and never identified as feminist, her distinct rhetorical strategies apparent in the few artifacts that preserve her voice (primarily YouTube videos and interview and speech transcripts) are clearly feminist. Bonds enacts ethos in ways that only a woman activist can, but she also offers a blueprint for leveraging powerlessness that can be useful to any environmental justice activist. In her public discourse, she constructs authority through her first-person experience as she also invites audiences to analyze the contingency of that authority. She uses emblems of powerlessness as a way to convey the urgency of her message. While she draws audiences' attention to immediate environmental threats, Bonds calls on them to think about how they conceive of her as a victim activist, how they make decisions about her rights to authority as a speaker, and how their prejudices of class, age, gender, and culture inevitably affect those decisions. Central to Bonds's ethos, then, is an abiding concern with relationships and power. The exigency of the environmental threat she faces down makes this ethos possible.

The ease with which Bonds confronts the rhetorical complexity of her message as she also pleads for support in the anti-MTR campaign suggests that feminist, ecological ethos finds its resonance in grassroots activism. Environmental injustice, especially, provides an opportunity for someone like Bonds to take the stage as an effective feminist rhetor for several reasons. First, environmental/social justice rhetoric, like some feminist epistemologies, is predicated on personal testimony with the same understanding that the private is very much a part of public matters (Capek 8). Victims of environmental injustice are more times than not poor and marginalized, so their grassroots activists often rely primarily on personal experience as opposed to the privileged discourse of academics and pundits (Capek 7). By using personal experience as evidence, activists such as Bonds express the second-wave feminist strategy of "making the personal political," a 1968 slogan attributed to feminist activist Carol Hanish that helped to propel the women's movement forward (Rosen 196). Further, the entrance of the poor and marginalized to public forums can only work if those representatives self-identify as such in order to reveal the complex social hierarchies and prejudices that make environmental injustice possible. This move corresponds with another tenant of feminism—that individuals must reveal how longstanding prejudices are embedded in our social institutions and how these prejudices direct injustices. Finally, because instances of environmental injustice are more times than not imminent threats to individuals, there is an urgency underlying this rhetoric that makes the transformation of the personal to the political and the entrance of unlikely activist figures into the public spotlight all the more essential. This understood urgency is especially valuable for women activists from marginalized backgrounds who can leverage common stereotypes that their culture of origin may hold regarding their "place" as keepers of the home and family. By publicly rejecting these expectations, women such as Bonds are able to demonstrate the acuteness of the environmental threat—it is so grave that women have been shaken from their preferred way of living and thrust into the spotlight against their will—as they are also able to preserve their cultural values. Subsequently, women activists who make such rhetorical moves join a tradition of female activists, including Mary Harris "Mother" Jones, Fannie Lou Hamer, Lois Gibbs, and countless others.[2] For Bonds this resemblance serves as further legitimization among the audiences of environmental and social justice activists, lawmakers, and other supporters to whom she speaks.

By isolating the touchstones of Bonds's rhetoric that find resonance in feminist theory, I articulate a praxis of feminist, ecological ethos, which may serve as a model for victims of environmental injustice who often find themselves with nothing to rely on but their personal experience. This chapter traces Bonds's focus on relationships and power by examining how she: (1) shares her personal experiences to establish motivation for her activism; (2) prompts audiences to view how they themselves play a part in the MTR problem; and (3) positions MTR as the exigency for a national conversation about the causes of environmental injustice. Section one demonstrates how Bonds rhetorically constructs the story of her entry into grassroots activism as one of necessity. After years of Big Coal's environmental and economic damage to her family and community, she points to her loss of power as matriarch and protector as the motivating factor for her involvement in anti-MTR efforts. Section two focuses on Bonds's rhetoric of identification, how she works to establish commonalities between herself, her audiences, and the environment using familiar and distinctly female, activist traditions. Section three highlights the ways in which Bonds calls attention to rhetorical constraints instead of diffusing them, asking her audiences to take ownership of their prejudices as a way to best address environmental injustice. Bonds's feminist ethos, engendered by her rhetorical strategies, can inform future environmental justice efforts.

Personal Experience as Rhetorical Exigency

Judy Bonds's first response to the effects of MTR was triggered by the horror of seeing her grandson and other children wading in a stream full of dead fish.

There was fish kills in which kids, my cousin's kids, and my own grandson, you know, were standing in the stream and found these dead fish. Then I started to notice as my neighbors moved out, there was coal trucks running constantly and it just devalued our property, our quality of life. . . . I was afraid for my family. I became angry. I became frustrated because I couldn't find any help. (qtd. in Barry 51)

She would often recount this experience in interviews as a way to explain why her participation in the anti-MTR effort was unavoidable. For Bonds, this experience operates not just as her impetus for environmental activism but also as kairic rhetoric, a strategy of exigency. Carl C. Herndl and Adela C. Licona identify "kairos" as "the moment in time when speaking and acting is opportune and when this opportunity has important implications for a concept of agency" (3). They tie kairos to ethos, which "implies the authority to speak and act with consequences . . . a legitimating function for a rhetor or subject" (3). Bonds uses the story of her grandson and the dead fish to validate her right to speak and act. Like many grassroots activists, Bonds began speaking out publicly against MTR because she felt she had no choice. In her hometown of Marfork Hollow, West Virginia, Massey Energy Corporation, the largest producer of coal in Central Appalachia, formerly headed by the infamous CEO, Don Blankenship, had just begun MTR operations near her home when she noticed what she called "white gooey stuff on the bottom of the water" (qtd. in Barry 51).[3] Bonds frames this moment as the lighting of the fuse for her activist efforts, a motivation not unlike that of other environmental justice activists, often women, who burst on the activist scene as political "naives." Women are often the first to speak out against environmental threats because so many environmental disasters literally "strike home" (see Stein). Joyce Barry explains:

[F]eminist political ecologists argue that women have a unique connection to environmental issues, not based solely or exclusively in biology, but primarily in the work they perform in their homes and communities. Because women are often responsible for providing and managing life's basic necessities, such as food, clothing, child care and elder care, they view environmental problems in unique ways. (10)

Implicit in this reasoning is the foundational belief that a mother has a biological right to protect her children, if not an automatic reflex to do so. This belief is heteronormative and conservative, but its persistence among certain audiences makes it useful for rhetorical leveraging.

Bonds uses motherhood as a rhetorical commonplace, embracing the knowledge and values commonly shared by audiences to establish the relational awareness she calls for in her audiences and reflects in her ethos, signaling a kind of kairic "permission" to enter public debate at the grassroots level. Even though the opportune moment enables agency, it is the audience who ultimately determines whether or not that moment is opportune and whether or not the speaker has the authority or permission to seize it. Phillip Siporia traces this understanding of kairos to Doro Levi's 1924 essay, "The Concept of Kairos and the Philosophy of Plato," wherein Levi finds in Plato's "philosophic rhetoric" that kairos involves a linking together of ethics and aesthetics. In this way, "kairos establishes the moral value of human actions" (6). Bonds appeals to the moral sensibilities of her audience by sharing her personal experience as a concerned mother, a form of discourse that is harmonious to their understanding of health and order. This moral appeal trumps whatever reservations audiences may have about her credibility as a speaker. As Siporia reveals through Isocrates, who had not yet considered women as viable public figures, "kairos is a principle that guides men to do, not what they are entitled to do, but, rather, what they should do" (12). Bonds's testimony reveals to the audience why she has no choice but to act.

Audiences grant Bonds "permission" to serve as spokesperson not only because her motherly instinct provides a socially accepted explanation for her interest, but also because her identification as "mother" casts her as part of a tradition of other women activists who legitimate their activism in similar ways. In an interview addressing the fact that women outnumbered men in the anti-MTR movement early on, Bonds argues that:

> It's a protection issue. . . . A woman just feels that she has to protect her children and her grandchildren and her homeplace. And that's why there is so many women involved in this because we have that instinct inside of us and that stubborn streak and the convictions to protect. . . . Through the traditional people I've studied, the women has been the ones that managed things, that protected things, that basically did what they needed to do to protect their children. (qtd. in Barry 35)

In her response, Bonds appeals to the traditional norm of the woman defending the domestic space and the health of the family in order to publicly legitimize her interest in anti-MTR issues. Her use of the word "instinct" indicates that she has little choice in the matter and associates that motivation to all women activists with her use of "we." Her repeated use of "protect" emphasizes that she is taking the position of defender, not aggressor, establishing that her activism as a woman has been provoked and is not such an unusual response. Her reasoning clearly operates relationally by connecting motherly duty and crisis to grassroots activism.

Bonds's nod to a familiar and established rhetorical commonplace grants her permission to enter public debate in at least two ways. For some audiences, it is a justification of her activism. In central Appalachia, a woman's interest in her home and family is not just understood, it is expected. Consequently, the anti-MTR movement has been largely organized and populated by working class women whose activism has been informed by "entrenched gender ideologies shaped and solidified by coal in the region," namely that women are responsible for the household and men are responsible for work outside the home (Barry 53). As a woman and mother, Bonds claims a right that few would question. Although progressive societies no longer suggest that women are solely responsible for domestic matters, the basic premise remains, and while many raise alarm at the association in matters of policy, most audiences are certainly not alarmed when a woman herself embraces this role. Many view the response as "natural" in fact—a commonplace that women rhetors who are mothers may do well to note.

For audiences who are sympathetic to her cause and familiar with the history of activism in America, Bonds's maternal rhetoric evokes memories of notable activist figures. Mari Boor Tonn reports that "early women reformers at times assumed maternal roles to bolster their ethos and deflect criticism of their speaking and independent lifestyles" (2). Bonds joins the ranks of such activists. Tonn specifically discusses labor activist Mother Jones's strategy of "militant motherhood" as grounded in "physical care and protection and in a feminine rhetorical style that is at once affirming and confrontational" (3). When Bonds assumed a similar stance in her speeches before academics, environmental action organizations, legislators, and even local coal workers, surely she evoked images of Mother Jones in the audiences' minds. Such an association prompts not only nostalgia, but a sense that Bonds understands the tradition in which she is participating, even borrowing from the ethos of the activists whose strategies she uses, especially Mother Jones, while building beyond them. In short, when Bonds identifies as a mother she appeals to both traditional and progressive audiences, achieving the agency to speak publicly of the injustices she has witnessed.

Bonds's rhetorical exigency and ethos evolve from her life experiences in a coal-mining community and from her conviction about the injustices of the economic and social systems around her. She refers to Central Appalachia as "an energy 'sacrifice zone,' where the lives and environment of the few are sacrificed for the good of the many" (qtd. in Barry 106). Most of the coal extraction in Appalachia that provides electricity for much of the United States comes from southern West Virginia, eastern Kentucky, and western Virginia, which are areas nationally recognized for their poverty and economic depression. Over the years, Appalachia has existed in the national consciousness as either a culture in dire need of charity—a place of poverty and illiteracy—or as a culture defined by defiance and pride as illustrated by the great Coal Wars at the turn of the century and the ensuing United Mine Workers of America labor battles of the late 1980s. Tapping into this national consciousness, Bonds refers to the economy in southern West Virginia as a "private serfdom" (Shapiro 70). As the "only job in town," coal mining has provided many people with well-paying jobs over the years, but the industry has also held residents hostage economically. With the fall in labor union involvement and subsequent drop in health and safety regulations, as well as the widespread weakening of the economy, Appalachians are clinging to the coal industry more desperately now than ever. The problem, of course, is that the demand for coal has led to new developments of extraction in the coal industry that require fewer workers but are making a far more pronounced impact on the environment. As traditional underground mining techniques struggled to meet increased demand, coal companies developed different surface-mining methods over the years as a way to more cheaply access coal deposits.

Bonds employs specific local examples to emphasize the kairos of rhetorical exigency for her audiences. An often-used example of the recklessness of the coal operators is the coal processing plant built directly behind Marsh Fork Elementary School in Raleigh County, West Virginia, where a "385-foot-earthen dam holds more than a billion gallons of slurry, a black, chemical-laden liquid waste from coal processing," or as Bonds calls it "waste holding back waste" (Shapiro 10). The reality that several Marsh Fork Elementary teachers and students have contracted unusual cancers heightens this exigency for Bonds's audiences (Shapiro 10).[4] Bonds's examples demonstrate the effects of coal companies' increased use of a large-scale form of coal mining called "mountaintop removal"—a surface-mining method that far surpasses strip mining in its destructive effects. MTR involves the literal blowing up of mountaintops for the purpose of accessing coal deposits underneath. Once these mountaintops have been blown away, enormous machinery scoops up the coal and pushes waste into "valley fills," which serve as containment sites (Barry 4). Barry explains that "an average MTR site removes 600–800 feet of mountain, stripping roughly 10 miles, dumping the waste from this process into 12 valley fills that can be as large as 1,000 feet wide and a mile long" (4). Author-activist Tricia Shapiro draws attention to the extent of the natural destruction and contamination: "Runoff silt clogs thousands of miles of mountain streams—and hundreds of miles of streams are now completely buried under debris. Aquifers are cracked by blasting, wells dried up or poisoned. Flash floods run off the stripped mountaintops" (3). The size and scope of these extraction sites alone should explain why MTR has become a serious concern for environmental scientists and local residents, but it is what Bryan McNeil refers to as the "accompanying social denigration of communities" and the "complex array of social, economic, and political pathogens" that have had an even more devastating effect (20). Those who live near these extraction and waste sites find their quality of life affected in a number of ways. Mortality rates are elevated in communities near surface-mining locations, and there is a pronounced increase in chronic pulmonary disorders and lung cancers among residents in these areas (Barry 4–5). Coal dust and chemicals from coal-processing facilities plague residents.[5]

Bonds recognized the direness of the environmental situation, and in her delivery one senses discomfort and anger at being forced into the role of activist. The spotlight was inevitable but certainly not sought. While Appalachian women are traditionally strong and outspoken when it comes to local knowledge, they are understandably less strident when it comes to issues extending beyond their immediate community. Any perceived awkwardness in Bonds's performance, such as reading from a folded piece of paper, stumbling over her words, and using colloquial speech, signals her discomfort with civic discourse, yet she does not apologize for being unpolished or for relying heavily on her personal experience. The unconventionality of her appearance at events, the sound of her dialect, the inelegance of her language, all suggest Bonds is a woman at once out of place and right at home as an activist. In those moments when Bonds seems uncomfortable before her non-Appalachian audiences, she enlightens them to the fact that not all American women find it easy to speak out, especially those from popularly denigrated cultures. Bonds approaches her activism as a woman whose adherence to tradition is surpassed by the rhetorical exigency she claims in the face of the Big Coal crisis. In the process, she invites her audiences to consider the agency Appalachian women have historically been afforded and how much agency they themselves are willing to grant her in the rhetorical situation.

At the Capitol Climate Action event in 2009, Bonds roars, "I don't mind being poor and I don't mind being made fun of, but I draw the line at being blasted and poisoned" ("Capitol Climate Action"). Just as her maternal rhetoric served to at once justify and interrogate the necessity of justification for her entrance into the public forum, so the phrase "I don't mind" prompts her environmentally conscious audience to consider how environmental injustice works, how it strikes those cultures that are most ignored and seemingly most disposable. As a marginalized cultural group, Appalachians have endured social and economic hardship without much sympathy from their fellow Americans, but for every Appalachian, just as for every mother, there is a moment of crisis-induced kairos. This repetition of "I don't mind," aside from its stylistic value, asks audiences to consider the daily injustices that Appalachians, women, blue collar workers, any marginalized group, really, must face and to ask themselves, "how much is too much?"

Bonds's rhetorical exigency combines with her awkward rhetorical style to manifest in an ethos of advocacy and expression. From kairos, agency is born. Herndl and Licona note, using Foucault, that agency, like power,

> does not reside in a set of objective rhetorical abilities of a rhetor . . . rather agency exists at the intersection of a network of semiotic, material, and yes, intentional elements and relational practices . . . agency is a social location. (7–8)

To find agency to speak out, Bonds has to first establish a personal exigency that her audience can acknowledge as warranted. Few would dispute a grandmother's concern for the health and welfare of her grandchildren, thus the rhetorical situation becomes ripe for intervention. The biological certainty of a mother's love has a transcendent power for audiences, which Bonds, like other environmental justice activists, uses as an agentive platform.

Rhetorical Exigency as Public Memory and Responsibility

Bonds uses the analogy of motherhood to self-identify or, as Nedra Reynolds suggests, to "locate" her ethos for her audience and to tap into greater traditions of female activism as a rhetorical strategy (326). Bonds finds power in a seemingly powerless situation by relying on analogies of motherhood and spirituality, historically significant commonplaces used by the environmental and labor movements. She assumes the authority of a mother as a way to establish power that she does not have with her audiences; in addition, she uses spirituality and the authority of God to grant her influence she would not otherwise have. Her version of motherhood is both militant and meditative, and, as such, embodies a broad spectrum of female activist traditions (see Hamilton; Maathai). In demonstrating an understanding of activist precedent, Bonds builds credibility. Lorraine Higgins and Lisa Brush articulate how difficult it can be for "subordinated narrators" to achieve this goal:

> The credible public narrator or protagonist must demonstrate agency, countering assumptions about her own passivity, ignorance, and impugned character. She needs to avoid casting herself or others in extreme hero or victim roles, and she must be willing to engage the substantive and moral terms of the dominant discourse without capitulating to them. (701)

To strike this delicate balance, Bonds attends to the rhetorical canon of memory, prompting audiences to not only associate her call to act with effective activist strategies from the past, but also with memories of the vested authority of all mothers and grandmothers. In these ways, she appeals to both personal and public memory.

Bonds often likens the environmental consequences of MTR and other destructive energy practices to a child's mess. At the 2010 Treehugger's Ball in Orange County, California, she warns:

> Our children are going to know whether or not we acted; your children will know whether or not we acted . . . we partied on our children's future . . . you know what, we told our children to clean up their rooms, but look at the mess we're leaving them to clean up, look at the mess we're leaving them to clean up. How dare us! Shame on us. Hey kids . . . look at your mom and your dad and your grandparents and look at 'em and say "hey now looka here Mom and Dad help me clean up this mess you done made. Help me clean this mess up. Save something for me." ("Treehugger's Ball")

Note that Bonds calls attention to the multiple generations her audiences represent. She begins by referring to her audience as "we," as in her generation, but then shifts into calling out the "kids" in the audience, prompting them to make their parents accountable. One gets the impression that the onus of responsibility is shared in Bonds's paradigm, as she diffuses the assignation of blame. In some ways, she plays the role of disapproving mother, shaming her audience for not cleaning up their "mess," one of the earliest and most basic social responsibilities a child learns. Further, in likening sites of environmental destruction to messy rooms, Bonds summons the frequently used environmentalist metaphor of the earth as a "home" that everyone bears some responsibility for keeping up under a universal and unspoken set of "house rules."

Bonds frames the environmental/energy crisis as a relational problem, not a scientific one. She draws attention to the personal places from which she speaks as she also locates those places in a political context, an ethos in keeping with the feminist model of constructed subjectivity, necessarily dynamic and openly dependent on relationships among speaker, audience, and context (LeFevre 45–46). She sometimes antagonizes her audiences as a way of drawing attention to rarely interrogated perceptions of relationships among victimizers, victimized, and advocates. At the Appalachian Studies Association conference in 2008, Bonds tells an audience of scholars, "If you get your electricity from a coal-fired power plant, then yes, you do have coal mining issues" ("ASA"). By removing the critical distance most of her audiences are afforded and making her issue essentially their issue, she forces them to reconsider where they "stand." Davis Bourland maintains that "rather than positioning MTR mining as a mere regional issue, Bonds describes an integrated national problem regarding manufacture of American energy" (91). Not only is the energy problem literally shared by everyone, Bonds suggests that those social and political problems that have enabled environmental injustices also belong, in some way, to everyone, as well.

Driving home the issue of MTR, Bonds seeks to make the *political* personal for her audiences, just as she makes the *personal* political for herself. At the Treehugger's Ball there would be little need to encourage her listeners to value nature. At the Appalachian Studies Association conference there would be little need to encourage her listeners to value the experience of Appalachians, so Bonds is calling attention to something else. Her rhetoric here emphasizes her audience's responsibility to one another and the importance of acknowledging and honoring human relationships, ideas that are distinctly feminist in tone. By using the analogy of the family, Bonds likens environmental justice to domestic tranquility, neither of which is possible without empathy and love. Her rhetoric hints that she is keenly aware of how even the most sympathetic audiences might appreciate a problem but not really act on its behalf. The devastation of MTR and other outrages of Big Coal in recent years are no longer "their" problems but "our" problems in Bonds's paradigm. Bonds often uses the metaphor of "battered wife" to describe coal communities' dysfunctional relationship with Big Coal (qtd. in McNeil 20), yet another way of shifting the onus to the audience that, by inaction, risks becoming the sympathetic but quiescent bystander to domestic violence.

Bonds's references to spirituality are also driven by relational awareness and call to mind familiar tropes in environmental activism. In the essay, "Fighting for My Appalachian Home," Bonds articulates that, as Appalachians, "We are part of these mountains and they are a part of us: we are one. We are connected to this ancient, reverent land" (183). References to spirituality are not uncommon in environmentalist rhetoric, but in environmental justice rhetoric, activists do not typically rely on these metaphors, as they pragmatically seek to identify those "powerful social actors" who are responsible for injustices (Capek 8). While Bonds does not hesitate to call attention to the evils of Massey Energy and Big Coal generally, she also attends to a higher power and the roles her audience should play as stewards of the land. Just as Bonds borrows ethos by assuming the strategies of former "militant mother" activists, she also establishes credibility with environmental groups by showing awe and tenderness toward nature. Yet, just as she reconciles her ethos with her audiences' expectations, she also provokes them.

Bonds recognizes that many of her environmentalist sympathizers were nonreligious, but that does not stop her from using "hellfire and brimstone" in her delivery. In an interview with Shapiro, she specifically discusses the EarthFirst! Organization, which she claims to be "doing God's work," although "they just don't realize it and won't acknowledge it" (62). Knowing that she was often speaking to nonbelievers did not stop her from relying on overtly religious rhetoric. At the 2010 Treehugger's Ball, Bonds declares portentously, "God gonna judge us for what we did for his creation" ("Treehuggers"). Her words of warning are especially noteworthy considering that her audience is comprised of environmentalists who are manifestly on her side, many of whom may not be religious and may not appreciate her thundering Free Will Baptist tone. Bonds warns against complacency and thinking that sympathizing is enough. She includes herself in this Judgment Day roll call ("God gonna judge us"), implicating and incriminating everyone, even those on her side. In taking this ominous tone, Bonds appears to be provoking her audience, setting herself up as a kind of seer infused with the power of God. This tone conveys the urgency of the situation by calling for confession of sin, compelling audiences to assess what part they may play in anti-MTR practices. She implies that action is available to everyone, that this movement, no matter how idiosyncratic, touches all humans as part of a greater story of social responsibility.

Using relational politics, a feminist rhetor acknowledges the location from which she speaks and the dynamics that dictate the rhetorical situation (see Adrienne Rich). Interestingly, Bonds's more meditative use of spiritual rhetoric offers a direct natural analogy for the interconnectedness of human experience and its implicit hierarchies, which nicely illustrates the importance of relational dynamics in advancing a cause, or in the case of the geese she uses as an example, in swiftly and efficiently heading to warmer climes. At a 2008 Powershift rally, Bonds once again commands her audience.

> I want you to notice nature, how geese are in flight, and they form a V in a leadership role. And when that leader, of that flight, the lead goose, when he gets tired of flapping his wings, he drops to the back, and the next goose comes up front and becomes the leader, without stopping, without fussing, without whining. He becomes that next leader, he or she, and that's what we have to do, we have to move in those positions. ("Powershift")

This analogy echoes traditional environmentalist tropes of personifying nature and calling upon a higher power to emphasize the direness of environmental abuse, but it does more than that when considered as part of a feminist, ecological agenda. The geese analogy demonstrates the ways in which relationships define, direct, and qualify human action. It illuminates the kind of leadership associated with female activism, driven by consensus, cooperation, and humility. Bonds defines leadership here as modeling and cultivating awareness as well as empathy for the other that includes reflexive questions such as: what distance am I maintaining from the others; am I keeping up; am I falling behind; when is it the right time to advance into the lead; when is it the right time to drop back? This analogy also illustrates the kind of dynamic rhetorical situation Bonds creates with her audiences. She makes audiences uncomfortable, which prompts them to meaningfully contemplate her ability to lead and the ways they themselves might find responsibility in the Big Coal crisis.

In mobilizing her audiences by revisiting and refining familiar commonplaces, Bonds enacts an undeniable resemblance in ethos to the labor activist Mother Jones, of whom both Appalachian and non-Appalachian audiences would likely know. Mary Harris "Mother" Jones was not originally from Appalachia, although during the labor movements of the early twentieth century, she spent a good deal of time in the region generating support for the United Mine Workers of America. During the most violent period in US labor history, Mother Jones made the decision to cultivate a distinctly maternal persona, and in her physical characteristics and rhetorical strategies, one finds unmistakable likenesses to Bonds. However, unlike Jones who primarily addressed those workers she wished to organize, Bonds focused her energy not on the victims of environmental injustice but on those with the power and influence to assist in the anti-MTR movement.

Physically, both Jones and Bonds looked the part of mother for their respective time period and audiences. Short and animated, Jones wore her white hair in a traditional bun, wore rounded eyeglasses, and dressed in the modest fashion of an Edwardian gentlewoman; one can imagine that Mother Jones looked the way her coal workers' mothers would have looked. Bonds, however, looked more the part of a working mother, demonstrating the evolution of roles mothers have assumed since the turn of the twentieth century. Bonds's short, gray hair and modest jeans and T-shirt mark her as a typical blue collar mother or grandmother. The grittiness of her dress proves especially important in emphasizing the location of her agency as related to class, region, culture, and gender. The visual juxtaposition for both activists was deliberate. Jones's strategy was to stand out, prompting audiences to consider "why is someone's mother here?" since an angry mother usually indicates children in trouble or in danger. Bonds's strategy was to stand out, prompting audiences to consider, "why should we listen to this kind of mother?" since a woman with her look and sound seemed conspicuously out of place in many of the public forums in which she spoke.

In her public addresses, Bonds's tone is strikingly similar to Mother Jones's—scolding and resolved. Of Mother Jones's rhetoric, Tonn writes:

> Stylistically, Jones's militant maternal persona took form through her use of personal experience and personal provocation, narrative and inductive strategies, intimate and familial terms of address and *ad hominem* attacks, empathy and shaming, and opportunities for audience imitation, including enactment and dialogic dialectics. In concert with her physical mothering, these stylistic properties nurtured a collective "familial" identity for her audience and equipped them with skills and confidence sufficient to resist their oppression. (3)

Bonds's style reads almost identically to Jones's and perhaps not by accident. By co-opting Jones's persona, Bonds taps into a viable and successful theme. However, she offers a variation on that theme by not simply enacting the role of symbolic mother to MTR victims. She offers herself as an emblem of a historically powerless culture and region and, in this way, sabotages a bit of that earned ethos as a means of making powerlessness the point for her audiences.

Bonds's adoption and adaptation of Jones's visual and linguistic rhetoric also resonates in the titles Bonds acquired during her activism. Not surprisingly, to Boone County, West Virginia, resident, Tommy Jarrold, she was "Little Mother Jones" (Shapiro 133). Scholars called her a "folk celebrity"; fellow activists called her "the godmother of the anti-MTR movement," and she has been known as "Hillbilly Moses" by those both sympathetic and unsympathetic to her cause. Bonds preferred to refer to herself as a "little old gray-haired hillbilly woman," a title perhaps telling of the sexism and ageism she faced during her activism in addition to the frequent Appalachian stereotyping. These descriptors suggest that Bonds was successful in putting her finger on what Karen LeFevre calls the "in-between," acknowledging audience knowledge, values, and needs as she also aimed to reinvent them.

Rhetorical Exigency as Personal, Public, and Political

At a 2008 Appalachian Studies Association conference, Bonds cites a West Virginia University study on the effect of coal pollution on communities and follows up with the not so subtly sarcastic line, "Well, we hillbillies have known that for over a hundred years; what took you so long?" ("ASA"). Identifying as a "hillbilly" is generally a risky move, especially if one wishes to be taken seriously in public debate. Even the most riveting first-person account can prove ineffective if the audience believes the speaker to be incompetent. Public deliberation necessarily involves what Robert Asen calls "indirect exclusions," which "function tacitly through discursive norms and practices that prescribe particular ways of interacting in public forums" (345). Asen's argument suggests that civic discourse by its nature discourages participation from speakers who have not been formally trained. Foucault calls this "rarefaction among speaking subjects: none may enter into discourse on a specific subject unless he has satisfied certain conditions" (224–225). This problem is compounded for speakers whose discursive style announces socio-demographic markers that can unearth deeply seated prejudices in the audience, profoundly weakening their trust in a speaker's authority and competency. In the above example, Bonds is addressing a sympathetic audience who likely understands the "hillbilly" as a cultural concept, but she and the CRMW organization did not limit their celebration of the hillbilly to safe crowds.

Just after Bonds's death in 2011, Bob Kincaid, president of the CRMW board, describes her in a *Huffington Post* article as "our Hillbilly Moses," who "knew better than anyone that we will make it to the Promised Land: out of the poisonous bondage of coal companies" (qtd. in Biggers 1). Considering the way that Bonds liked to shift her pronouns from "I" to "we" to "you," Kincaid's "we" here does not just describe CRMW members but all Americans who, as Bonds so often pointed out, are just as much a slave to coal as any Appalachian. Kincaid's association casts Bonds as a "vessel for moral truth" whose life and premature death closely follows the story of Moses (Bourland 102). The spiritual association of the nickname, "Hillbilly Moses," is significant in that it describes Bonds's ethos among fellow activists, an association explored by Bourland, Barry, and others. I draw attention instead to the "hillbilly" qualification since it best describes Bonds's ethos—a charismatic leader who knew that her agency was determined by her audience's willingness to accept her grassroots knowledge and perceived incompetence as an Appalachian.

Some years ago, understanding the futility of escaping the cultural stereotype, CRMW began what they call the "save the endangered hillbilly" campaign, printing the slogan on T-shirts and protest signs. The slogan is both comic and disturbing, a combination that invites audiences to chuckle and, if the aim is successful, think about *why* they chuckle. Bonds also uses the term for its subversive effect as well as to educate audiences about what it actually means to be Appalachian. In a personal interview, Bonds responded to a question about her use of the term.

> I'm proud to be called a hillbilly. . . . It's what you use before the word "hillbilly" that we have a problem with. You know it's the derogatory statements of dumb, lazy, stupid, hillbilly, ignorant, inbred hillbilly. . . . It's all those adjectives that you put on it that makes it the bad word. (qtd. Barry 107)

When considering the importance of "relevant knowledge and competency" in civic discourse (Dahlgren 337), one can see why those individuals who identify as "hillbilly" find it difficult to establish credibility as public figures. It is a fraught term for Appalachians. As the culture has been denigrated over the years, the expression has become a source of embarrassment as well as cultural pride. The term illustrates the standard view of the culture and conjures images of bearded and overall-wearing Hatfield and McCoy types. Recent horror movies and growing media coverage of prescription drug abuse in the region have contributed a gothic element to the stereotype that has shifted the "hillbilly" image from friendly and lazy to depraved and alien (see Satterwhite). Implicit in any interpretation of the term is ignorance and lack of sophistication.

Bonds is often aggressive and angry when she identifies as Appalachian in her speeches, citing the negative cultural connotations as partially if not wholly responsible for the exploitation of the area and people. She asks,

> Why would anyone care about a bunch of hillbillies? . . . We are living with domestic terrorism from these coal barons, and our lapdog politicians are working hand-in-hand with corporations that put them in place to destroy our children's world. (qtd. in Barry 106)

She further claims that the coal industry has "robbed us our humanity, mis-interpreted our culture, maligned our heritage" (qtd. in Barry 116). This tone, directed to a group of scholars who are mostly sympathetic to her cause, indicates her desire for audiences to confront their own prejudices and to consider the ways in which their personal biases may contribute to the problem.

By pointing to those very aspects of her identity that may compromise her authority, Bonds essentially invites the audience to consider why she is powerless and why social identifiers come to be liabilities in the first place. Elizabeth S. D. Englehardt identifies feminist theory as an effective way for Appalachians, particularly, to analyze the complex power dynamics that drive cultural stereotypes (3). She describes feminist scholarship as moving constantly between "individual and institutional structures of power . . . being attentive to how race, class, gender, and other identity categories combine to shape individual lives and institutions" (7). Bonds enacts a feminist ethos that allows for such analysis. At the ASA conference, Bonds points out that,

> The Appalachians is the only ethnic group left that America can still make fun of and get by with it, the only one left. America still rapes the land and people of Appalachia and doesn't think twice about it. Government agencies still hold contempt for us Appalachians, they want us extinct—they want us to go away. ("ASA")

Appalachian marginality is, arguably, so deeply embedded in the national consciousness that resorting to bald observations that make audiences uncomfortable is perhaps the most effective way to make obvious these power dynamics.

Identifying not only from *where one is coming* but also how that *from where* constrains the message places responsibility on the audience to reflect on their personal contribution to the meaning of the rhetorical moment. The negotiation of private and public, the individual and institutions, then, is not reserved for the speaker in her performance as communicator. Kate Ronald finds ethos in the "tension between private and public self" for the speaker (qtd. in Reynolds 37); I contend that drawing attention to this tension as a speaker invites the same negotiation for the *audience*. Joanna Schmertz defines ethos as "the stopping points at which the subject (re)negotiates her own essence to call upon whatever agency that essence enables" (86). As agency is dependent on the audience, ethos must, then, necessarily invite that same negotiation on their part. Schmertz reasons:

> When we attend to our own ethos in a postmodern rhetoric, we are both constructing a subjectivity for ourselves and retroactively reconstructing or recuperating that subjectivity in a process that is never finished because it is always already shaping its own critique, shifting to a new position or location. And as this subject we have made moves, it pulls upon the rest of rhetorical situation, creating new points of convergence among its elements. (89)

This fluid definition of ethos opens up the possibility for speakers to conceive of their audiences as co-constructors and co-investigators, meaning the process of address is not about persuading as much as it is about transparently probing the institutional power dynamics that determine individual persuasive success as enacted by ethos.

In calling herself a "hillbilly," Bonds acknowledges that the audience may perceive her as ignorant, so she uses that disparity to her benefit. Instead of attempting to elide the cultural stereotype that will no doubt appear the moment she speaks, Bonds calls it up first. Calling attention to this rhetorical constraint proves that she is aware of social assumptions about dialect and appearance that her audiences may have. Drawing attention to these assumptions becomes a rhetorical strategy that grants her a certain agency. Her rhetoric generally addresses where she is "from" as an over-fifty, Christian, Appalachian mother without a college education. As her self-labeling attests, a speaker who addresses the relational politics that determines the success of her message as she speaks can in fact strengthen her ethos. Adrienne Rich calls this a "politics of location," which Schmertz describes as a "practice of identifying and acknowledging the position (social, personal, institutional, etc.) from which one speaks" (82). Bonds understood the "politics of location," as she also critically analyzed her perceived credibility as a rhetor, which is perhaps the strategy that most qualifies her as feminist.

Bonds invites audiences to examine hierarchies implicit in the rhetorical situation that translate as those exclusionary standards that prevent marginalized people from securing civic agency. She meets the feminist responsibility of identifying the limits of her power as a speaker, but she does not stop there. She presses for a dialogue about her limits of power by making her audiences, which at times included well-meaning environmentalists, feel partially accountable for destructive cultural and economic power differentials. Bonds's exigency and ethos ask audiences to confront their own prejudices and to acknowledge and analyze her powerlessness as she also persuades them to act.

As Bonds demonstrates, to effectively address the economic and cultural complexity of environmental injustices such as MTR practices, a rhetor must draw attention to not only the physical effects but also to the historically ignored discrimination that has made environmental decimation possible. Activists may look to these moves as inspiration for their own ethical orientation as speakers. Admitting one's powerlessness signals a global awareness of the institutional dynamics at work that can, in fact, strengthen one's ethos. When activists offer personal testimony and identify power dynamics among audiences and speaker, they can invite listeners to meditate on marginalization and discrimination. Most importantly, activists can prompt audiences—even the most sympathetic—to consider the role they may personally play in the environmental exploitation of populations, which almost always results from deeply engrained and unexamined cultural biases.

Despite their powerlessness, Bonds and the anti-MTR activists in Appalachia have elevated the status of the marginalized rhetor by constructing an ethos that invites deliberation of not only the social injustice at hand but also of those values and beliefs that tacitly direct the rhetorical exchange. Through a relational ethos, Bonds makes it clear that everyone has a role to play in cleaning up Appalachia, and that role begins not when he or she calls his or congressman or volunteers to pass out brochures, but at the very moment Bonds's words are heard and she is judged as a post middle age, inarticulate, Appalachian woman. Bonds makes the moment of judgment regarding her ethos the point and, in this way, demonstrates how discrimination and cultural biases become insidious and ultimately responsible for environmental/social injustices.

Bonds's ethos arises from her rhetorical awareness of location and relationality. She offers an environmental justice rhetoric that demands that the speaker: (1) publicly recognize where she stands, both geographically and culturally (in this case, in relation to her audience and within her social milieu); and (2) leverage that relational awareness as a way to effect change, creating a dialogue in the process about the ways in which existing power structures obstruct change. When Bonds tells her audience "from where she is coming," she shifts the audience's focus to where they stand in relation to her, prompting them to find accountability in the message, as well. The added element of accountability—rhetors inviting audiences to consider how "from where they both are coming" affects the success of the message—is especially important. As Henry Giroux claims, environmental justice rhetoric must move toward a more "biopolitical" orientation in which the activist not only describes the practical effects of an environmental threat but also brings into question the apparent large-scale "disposability" of certain populations. Giroux points out that "in the aftermath of Hurricane Katrina, the biopolitical calculus of massive power differentials and iniquitous market relations put the scourge of poverty and racism on full display" (191). Hurricane Katrina was ostensibly a natural disaster, but the homogeneity of its victims (black and poor) was hard to ignore. Unlike Hurricane Katrina, which was a large-scale, highly televised, one-time disaster, many forms of environmental injustice go unnoticed by the national media and occur quietly and destructively over time. In order to get at the "biopolitical orientation" that makes environmental injustice possible, rhetors need to discover a way to bring those sociodemographic inequalities into relief without losing the audience's trust in the speaker's communicative competencies. Taking notes on Bonds's enacted ethos can help environmental justice activists to achieve this goal.

Notes

1. For recent developments in the movement against mountaintop removal, see Sorkin's "A New Tack in the War on Mining Mountains: PNC Joins Banks Not Financing Mountaintop Coal Removal" and the *Washington Post* editorial "The Dirty Effects of Mountaintop Removal Mining."

2. For Fannie Lou Hamer, see Brooks and Houck; for Lois Gibbs, see Goodwin and Jasper.

3. Don Blankenship has since been indicted by federal prosecutors on a number of charges. See Berkes's "Feds Add Coal Dust Coverup Allegation to Mine CEO's Indictment."

4. In January 2013, a new Marsh Fork Elementary School opened in a less dangerous part of Raleigh County. Massey Energy donated $1.5 million to help

pay for the construction. See Lilly's "New Marsh Fork Elementary Part of Legacy" and Holdren's "Marsh Fork Elementary Dedicated."

5. Bonds died of cancer at the surprisingly young age of fifty-eight, a death that some have conjectured to have been a result of her exposure to toxins (Biggers 1).

Works Cited

"About the Prize." *The Goldman Environmental Prize*. Goldman Environmental Foundation, n.d. Web. 20 April 2015.

"ASA 2008 Judy Bonds (w/intro by Shirley Stewart Burns; Part 1)." *Online Posting*. YouTube, 10 Apr. 2008. Web.

"ASA 2008 Judy Bonds (Part 2)." *Online Posting*. YouTube, 14 Apr. 2008. Web.

Asen, Robert. "Imagining in the Public Sphere." *Philosophy and Rhetoric* 35.4 (2002): 345–67. Print.

Barry, Joyce. *Standing Our Ground: Women, Environmental Justice, and the Fight to End Mountaintop Removal*. Athens: Ohio UP, 2012. Print.

Berkes, Howard. "Feds Add Coal Dust Coverup Allegation to Mine CEO's Indictment." National Public Radio. 10 Mar. 2015. Web.

Biggers, Jeffrey. "Thousands Pay Tribute to Judy Bonds: She Has Been to the Mountaintop—and We Must Fight Harder to Save It." *Huffington Post* 4 Jan. 2011. Web.

Bonds, Julia. "Fighting for My Appalachian Home." *The Appalachians: America's First and Last Frontier*. Ed. Mari-Lynn Evans. Charleston: West Virginia UP, 2012. Print.

Bourland, Davis. "Chronotopic Figurations of Coal Mining at Blair Mountain." MA thesis. Wake Forest U, 2011. Print.

Brooks, Maegan Parker, and Davis W. Houck. *The Speeches of Fannie Lou Hamer: To Tell It Like It Is*. Jackson: UP of Mississippi, 2011. Print.

Capek, Stella. "The 'Environmental Justice' Frame: A Conceptual Discussion and an Application." Spec. issue of *Social Problems* 40.1. (Feb. 1993): 5–24. Print.

Dahlgren, Peter. "The Internet and the Democratization of Civic Culture." *Political Communication* 17 (2000): 335–40. Print.

"The Dirty Effects of Mountaintop Removal Mining." Editorial. *Washington Post* 21 Oct. 2014. Print.

Englehardt, Elizabeth S. D. "Creating Appalachian Women's Studies: Dancing Away from Granny and Elly May." *Beyond Hill and Hollow: Original Readings in Appalachian Women's Studies*. Ed. Englehardt. Athens: Ohio UP, 2005. 3–7. Print.

Foucault, Michel. The Archaeology of Knowledge *and* The Discourse on Language. New York: Pantheon, 1972. Print.

Giroux, Henry. "Reading Hurricane Katrina: Race, Class, and the Biopolitics of Disposability." *College Literature*. 33.3 (Summer 2006): 171–96. Print.

Goodwin, Jeff, and James M. Jasper. "Biography—Lois Gibbs, Housewife Warrior." *The Social Movements Reader: Cases and Concepts.* Ed. Goodwin and Jasper. 2009. 234–35. Print.

Hamilton, Heidi E. "Feminine Style and Militant Motherhood in Antiwar Discourse: Cindy Sheehan as Grieving Mother and/or Left-Leaning Radical." *Media Depictions of Brides, Wives, and Mothers.* Ed. Alena Amato Ruggerio. Lanham, MD: Lexington, 2012. 115–27. Print.

Herndl, Carl G., and Adela C. Licona. "Shifting Agency: Agency, *Kairos*, and the Possibilities of Social Action." *Communicative Practices in Workplaces and the Professions.* Ed. Mark Zachry and Charlotte Thralls. Amityville, NY: Baywood, 2007. 133–53. Print.

Higgins, Lorraine D., and Lisa D. Brush. "Personal Experience Narrative and Public Debate: Writing the Wrongs of Welfare." *College Composition and Communication* 57.4 (2006): 694–729. Print.

Holdren, Wendy. "Marsh Fork Elementary Dedicated." *Register Herald* 19 Jan. 2013. Web.

"Judy Bonds at Capitol Climate Action." Online posting. YouTube, 4 May 2009. Web.

"Judy Bonds at Powershift07!" Online posting. YouTube, 31 Jan. 2008. Web.

LeFevre, Karen. *Invention as a Social Act.* Carbondale: Southern Illinois UP, 1987. Print.

Lilly, Jessica L. "New Marsh Fork Elementary Part of Legacy." *West Virginia Public Broadcasting.* 27 Aug. 2012. Web.

Maathai, Wangari. *Unbowed: A Memoir.* New York: Anchor, 2007. Print.

McNeil, Bryan T. *Combating Mountaintop Removal: New Directions in the Fight against Big Coal.* Urbana: U of Illinois P, 2011. Print.

Reynolds, Nedra. "Ethos as Location. New Sites for Understanding Discursive Authority." *Rhetoric Review* 11.2 (1993): 325–38. Print.

Rich, Adrienne. "Notes towards a Politics of Location." *Blood, Bread, and Poetry: Selected Prose, 1979–1985.* London: Virago, 1986. 210–232. Print.

Rosen, Ruth. *The World Split Open: How the Modern Women's Movement Changed America.* New York: Viking, 2000. 196. Print.

Satterwhite, Emily. "Horror in Appalachia, or What Happens When Suburban Whites Take a 'Wrong Turn.'" Paper presented at the annual meeting of the American Studies Association Annual Meeting, Hilton Baltimore, Baltimore, MD. 20 Oct. 2011.

Schmertz, Johanna. "Constructing Essences: Ethos and the Postmodern Subject of Feminism." *Rhetoric Review* 18.1 (1999): 82–91. Print.

Shapiro, Tricia. *Mountain Justice: Homegrown Resistance to Mountaintop Removal for the Future of Us All.* Baltimore: AK Press, 2010. Print.

Siporia, Phillip. "Introduction: The Ancient Concept of Kairos." *Rhetoric and Kairos: Essays in History, Theory, and Praxis.* Ed. Phillip Siporia and James S. Baumlin. Albany: State U of New York P, 2002. 6–12. Print.

Sorkin, Andrew. "A New Tack in the War on Mining Mountains: PNC Joins Banks Not Financing Mountaintop Coal Removal." *New York Times* 9 Mar. 2015. Print.

Stein, Rachel, ed. *New Perspectives on Environmental Justice: Gender, Sexuality, and Activism.* New Brunswick, NJ: Rutgers UP, 2004. Print.

Tonn, Mari Boor. "Militant Motherhood: Labor's Mary Harris 'Mother' Jones." *Quarterly Journal of Speech* 82 (1996): 1–21.

8. Strategically Negotiating Essence

Zitkala-Ša's Ethos as Activist

Paige A. Conley

> *O sisters, work to that end; work in cooperation that the stain upon*
> *our country in the treatment of my people may be wiped out.*
> —Zitkala-Ša, addressing the General Federation of Women's Clubs

Known primarily as an early twentieth-century writer, Zitkala-Ša also served as editor of a national publication, taught school, performed as a concert violinist, coauthored an opera, worked as a community organizer, and perhaps most significantly, engaged in indigenous activism for most of her adult life.[1] Working specifically for more than two decades as a political advocate, Zitkala-Ša penned manifestos, waged prolific letter-writing campaigns, testified before national legislative hearings, served as a government-appointed investigator, and made a large number of public speeches before her death in 1938, striving all the while to improve conditions for many Native American communities. Emerging histories within rhetoric and composition continue to recover generally ignored or previously marginalized voices, but we still lack studies specifically examining public speeches made by individuals, particularly women, who sought to both survive within dominant American society, and simultaneously maintain, if not advance, sovereign forms of identity, community, and culture. A careful review of Zitkala-Ša's early twentieth-century efforts to advance indigenous concerns provides scholars with rich opportunities to examine rhetoric from perspectives beyond the Western Eurocentric canon. Her rhetorical maneuvers as an orator, particularly between 1920 and 1925, frequently invoked Dakota culture and continually reworked Western Eurocentric rhetorical forms—specifically epideixis and ethos—as sites of agency and resistance. Recovering this overlooked history enriches our understanding of *survivance* as articulated by Gerald Vizenor and continues to expand our conceptions of effective multivalent, cross-cultural forms of rhetorical production.

The historical record for Zitkala-Ša indicates that on February 22, 1876, a young woman living near the Yankton Agency in Dakota Territory named Táte I Yóhin Win, who also went by the name of Ellen Simmons, gave birth to a daughter she named Gertrude. This daughter, Gertrude ("Gertie") Simmons, chose to adopt the name Zitkala-Ša in her early twenties.[2] Zitkala-Ša began her life within the Yankton community in 1876, but left her home in 1884 when Christian missionaries recruited children for White's Manual Labor Institute, a Quaker boarding school in Wabash, Indiana. A national policy of forced assimilation and the barbaric conditions of many boarding schools carrying out this far-reaching agenda have been clearly documented. Zitkala-Ša's own writing about this period in *Old Indian Legends* highlights shock, trauma, and abuse related to issues of language, articulation, and voice. Despite these initial and substantial challenges, Zitkala-Ša grew to become a gifted, multilingual writer and speaker.

Recent scholarly work examining Zitkala-Ša's record of indigenous activism frequently references her exceptional abilities as a public speaker, particularly through her work for the Society of American Indians (SAI), but little is known about the specific performances that worked to establish Zitkala-Ša's reputation as an effective orator. There is a dearth of scholarship examining the advocacy efforts Zitkala-Ša undertook for decades from the speaker's podium even though she worked tirelessly on a number of causes, speaking frequently, and often engagingly, to many audiences located comfortably within dominant American society. Researchers working within the field of Native American or American Indian Studies, particularly Robert Warrior, argue that the value of Zitkala-Ša's work as an early twentieth-century Native American intellectual and advocate is difficult to assess, given the assimilationist stance generally associated with members of the SAI. Yet this view fails to account for the complex rhetorical strategies Zitkala-Ša developed and deployed as an indigenous *female* speaker. In many Western Eurocentric cultures—and clearly during late nineteenth- and early twentieth-century America—women seeking to participate in public discourse had to first invent ways to speak within dominant sociocultural contexts of continually being "silenced and rendered invisible as persons" (Ritchie and Ronald xvii).

This chapter specifically builds upon feminist standpoint theory as theorized by Susan Jarratt and Nedra Reynolds to enlarge our understanding of Zitkala-Ša's rhetorical legacy and reconceive prevailing views of ethos. By using a feminist lens to closely examine one of Zitkala-Ša's speech acts before the General Federation of Women's Clubs (hereafter GFWC) in June 1921, this discussion contends that ethos can operate as an expansive rhetorical concept with fluid, dynamic capacities for facilitating authority and legibility within environments hostile to certain forms of rhetorical production.[3] This essay specifically argues that by invoking and subsequently moving between multiple discursive constructions as standpoints or "essences" during a particular rhetorical event, Zitkala-Ša successfully deployed ethos as a rhetorical tool for agency and resistance, carefully linking popular discourses regarding particularly "American" forms of citizenship to common perceptions of the "Indian" or "Indianness" and "Indian Princess." These discursive linkages created interest in a new, more inclusive civic agenda, which Zitkala-Ša termed "Americanize the First American!" Her new rhetorical agenda, as a form of political rhetoric, helped to raise awareness for Native concerns and ultimately facilitated widespread GFWC support for the Indian Citizenship Act of 1924 and the Indian New Deal of 1934. Recovering this rhetorical history allows contemporary scholars to rethink conceptions of ethos as a fixed and stable rhetorical construct. Indeed, a close examination of one particular performance given by Zitkala-Ša to leading members of the GFWC in 1921 reveals how ethos can operate in multivalent ways—credibly and effectively—within the space of a single speech act in order to address a myriad of shifting (and often competing) rhetorical exigencies.

Ethos as Strategically Negotiating Essence

The methods of research and analysis found here draw primarily from feminist rhetorical theory in order to invoke a more expansive view of ethos and more fully assess Zitkala-Ša's ability to access and utilize the limited discursive platforms available to women doubly or multiply marginalized due to prevailing notions of race, ethnicity, and gender. This scholarship focuses on contingency and fluidity in order to examine how forms of rhetorical ethos might be constructed, negotiated, and revised to support rhetorical efficacy. Thus, despite its patriarchal, Western Eurocentric origins, feminist recovery in rhetoric continues to embrace ethos as a useful theoretical construct. Instead of abandoning this concept, feminist scholars maintain that closely reviewing ethos as it shifts or expands to account for communication from marginalized positions within social formations can be a powerful analytical tool (Foss, Foss, and Griffin 130).

Leading feminist rhetorical scholars, Jarratt and Reynolds in particular, envision ethos as a kind of contingent essence that speaks from constantly changing "sites" as the person engaging in an utterance is being positioned by one's audience and simultaneously seeking to reposition oneself and one's listeners. Jarratt and Reynolds look to Linda Martín Alcoff to define "positionality" and "stance" as a place from which values are interpreted and constructed rather than the locus of an already determined set of values (50). They find that

> the ideas of place, position, and standpoint in feminist theory offer a way for reconceiving ethos as an ethical political tool—as a way of claiming and taking responsibility for our positions in the world, for the ways we see, for the places from which we speak. (52)

This view of ethos continues to account for ethics in the sense that a speaker must still take responsibility for assuming an albeit contingent position. With this view, ethos becomes a force that constructs, constitutes, and reconstitutes the rhetorical self through the choices made within each discursive or rhetorical performance, creating and recreating the speaker/writer in an ongoing process of self-fashioning.

Relying on Donna Haraway's feminist reading of the subject as "a split and contradictory self," Jarratt and Reynolds further argue that subjectivity is always multidimensional: the "knowing self is partial in all of its guises, never finished, whole, simply there and original; it is always constructed and stitched together imperfectly and *therefore* able to join with another, to see together without claiming to be another" (Haraway qtd. in Jarratt and Reynolds 55). Thus, within rhetorical ethos, these split selves are guises as constructed essences, but they are not distortions or lies—they are recognitions of the ways one is positioned multiply and differently (55). This rhetorical construction allows speakers and writers to identify themselves authoritatively within complex, shifting networks of race, gender, class, and power. As they articulate differences between and within multiple viewpoints to fashion discourses that build upon specific points of commonality with audiences, they both "split and resuture" their speaking selves (57).

Johanna Schmertz further argues that these "splitting and resuturing" forms of subjectivity create "essences" or ontological forms of being in the world, which are contingent and reveal themselves fundamentally through language. According to Schmertz, an understanding of essence is critical for a feminist rethinking of ethos in order to view this rhetorical construct "as neither manufactured, nor fixed, neither tool nor character, but rather the stopping points at which the subject (re)negotiates her own essence to call upon whatever agency that essence enables" (86). Schmertz's postmodern view of essence avoids fixed locations and essentialism by locating this philosophical term more closely within language through acts of naming as performative utterances: "naming creates identity—essences—from the contexts that envelope it. . . . when we speak . . . we create an essence—a subject—that demands response from our rhetorical environment" (88–89).

Zitkala-Ša's ability to produce and navigate key discursive shifts as she presented multiple forms of essence appears in her speech given at a national GFWC meeting held in 1921. In order to engage and interest her largely white, female audience in the political concerns of early twentieth-century Native communities, Zitkala-Ša needed to both "stand within" and simultaneously resist the homogenizing, popular rhetoric of "Americanization" and prevailing, totalizing cultural views of "Indians" and "Indianness" as well as unstable, gender-based perceptions frequently deployed around fantastical notions of the "Indian Princess." Fluid forms of rhetorical production—specifically ethos as multiple forms of essence—allowed Zitkala-Ša to engage in key forms of resistance and activism, even as she appeared comfortingly to her GFWC audience to generally support hegemonic ideologies and oppressive cultural discourses. This discussion analyzes historical context and Zitkala-Ša's oral performance in order to more fully demonstrate her carefully crafted rhetorical efforts to engage in extended forms of indigenous activism.

Early Twentieth-Century Reform Efforts and the GFWC

An interest in "Indian Reform" focused primarily on complete assimilation began to take hold in the United States during the 1880s, spurred to national heights with the publication of Helen Hunt Jackson's scathing tract, *A Century of Dishonor*, in 1881. Women's groups participating in these early reform efforts tended to focus on education, missionary work, and the transformation of

Indian homes to more closely resemble white, middle-class Victorian ideals. These assimilationist policies proved disastrous for Native communities who found themselves under even greater threat from provisions of the Dawes Act, which continued to allow land speculators to acquire millions of acres of previously "reserved" land.[4] With the closing of the frontier, a growing interest in greater expansion for both public and private interests continued to threaten land allotments held by Native individuals throughout the first two decades of the twentieth century, greatly undermining tribal communities and deeply threatening their already fragile economies.

In reaction, the late 1910s brought national calls for different kinds of federal Indian policy—greater political rights, the restoration of tribal lands, freedom of religion, and some forms of self-determination. One key reform group, led primarily by John Collier, continued to pursue Progressive policies over the next two decades, which ultimately would lead to the Indian New Deal of 1934. John Collier found an early ally in Stella Atwood, a wealthy GFWC clubwoman from Riverside, California, who worked to establish "Indian Welfare" committees in her home state and hoped to secure additional support for her reform efforts through the national GFWC organization.

Distinguishing GFWC clubwomen from other female associations of the period, historian Karin Huebner argues that most members of the GFWC supported a wide range of efforts aimed at social or civic improvement and "Indian" concerns became a small part of these much broader aims. Founded in 1890, by 1921 the GFWC had become perhaps one of the most prestigious women's organizations in the country (Welch 373).[5] The *Official Register and Directory of Women's Clubs* from 1921 states that the GFWC consisted of more than two million members by this time, all hailing from community clubs located throughout the United States (10). Not all clubwomen within the GFWC shared Atwood's level of interest or concern. As Huebner explains, "many clubwomen demonstrated varying degrees of Anglo ethnocentrism. Some were Progressives, others were radicals, and many were split on the issue of assimilation" (342). Certainly, support for Native concerns varied from region to region, and locale to locale. Nonetheless, seeing great potential for widespread, national support from more than two million newly enfranchised voters, Atwood managed to convince the executive board of the GFWC to place her reform interests on the agenda for further consideration at the 1921 national meeting.[6] Clearly Atwood and Zitkala-Ša shared similar aims, and both women certainly understood that a substantial amount of public interest and publicity could be mobilized through women's groups like the GFWC.

The 1921 GFWC National Meeting and Americanization

Organized more generally around the themes of "Americanization" and "American Citizenship," the GFWC held their 1921 biennial council meeting at the Hotel Utah in Salt Lake City from June 13 through June 18. The GFWC's national print publication, the *General Federation News*, later reported that attendance during the week reached over six hundred clubwomen representing more than thirteen thousand local and regional GFWC clubs ("General Summary" 12). The federation meeting opened with a reception in the portico of the Utah State Capitol building on Monday night and concluded in Assembly Hall on Friday with a formal evening session. While Zitkala-Ša spoke at several events throughout the week, she achieved perhaps her greatest prominence as she appeared on stage before GFWC members during the formal closing session on Friday, June 18.

Seeds for a national GFWC theme addressing "Americanization" had been sown at least three years before during a national board of directors meeting held in 1918. At that time, the GFWC board directed all of their clubwomen to adopt Americanization as a "special line of work" to be undertaken by all departments within the federation ("Suggested Program" 2, 4). Between 1918 and 1921 the GFWC had implemented a number of far-reaching initiatives designed to "reconstruct" American society. These efforts included developing prescribed reading lists for children and adults, preparing strictly formatted club programs and discussion questions for local clubs to implement, and producing patriotic plays and pageants. The GFWC hoped these efforts would contribute usefully to an ongoing national dialogue regarding citizenship and acceptable forms of American identity. These concerns continued to grow after World War I, as a perceived threat from immigration prevailed well into the 1920s with displaced eastern and southern European populations seeking refuge and asylum in the United States. This population influx led to an intense national focus on assimilation and cultivation of a particular kind of "good" and "obedient" American citizen produced through efficient forms of mass education.[7]

Prevailing discourses of Americanization intimately connected to proper notions of citizenship reached well beyond concerns for immigrants and tended to influence "scientifically proven" race-based aims for social reform as well. Francis Paul Prucha and others clearly document the ways that these discourses of Americanization supported ethnocentrism and policies of total assimilation with respect to Native populations throughout the country during the late nineteenth and early twentieth century.[8] Arguably, GFWC's campaign for Americanization reinforced these race-based hierarchies but also provided a limited platform for new voices seeking to enter into this conversation.[9] For Zitkala-Ša, the GFWC interest in Americanization provided a means for sparking interest in Native concerns, but this rhetorical opening would need to be negotiated carefully. Initially Zitkala-Ša needed to avoid unnecessarily reinforcing the totalizing aspects of Americanization working to destroy Native culture. Then, she had to navigate other widely circulating discourses that constructed and positioned the "Indian," or "Indianness," and "Indian Women" in limiting ways.

Navigating Race and Discourses of Americanization

During the early twentieth century, discourses and ideologies addressing what it meant to be "American" worked to renounce, erase, or appropriate Native identity and Native culture. Connecting fantasies related to race with prevailing notions of national identity began well before America's founding and certainly continue today. As Philip Deloria notes, the dominant American culture frequently constructs, claims, and enacts a variety of myths or fantasies about "Indians" and "Indianness" as it struggles to define itself as a nation, and as individuals within that nation. These racial fantasies cast "Indians" as part of a romantic past, a past that emphasizes the passing of a vanishing race to make way for others, "more progressive" or "more modern" or "more fit" races. Deloria points out that the emergence of "science," particularly ethnography, allowed for an acknowledgment of the ongoing presence of "Indians," but still defined those individuals as part of a distant, primitive, and romanticized past, rather than the present (91). The dominant American culture consistently employs these false constructions to empower itself and deny power to actual people. While these hegemonic practices produce powerful tensions in American society between the ideal of equality on the one hand and the real inequalities engendered by hierarchical constructs of race on the other, they also cause marginalized individuals to live within a series of unstable symbolic fields. As she appeared before the GFWC members gathered in Salt Lake City, Zitkala-Ša had to engage, refashion, and redeploy these symbolic fields of representation in order to impart a larger message regarding the need for concern, interest, and civic action designed to improve actual conditions for indigenous communities. Working through these fields of representation meant that Zitkala-Ša had to act appropriately

"Indian" enough to gain her audience's trust—she had, in fact, to embody a fantasy—and simultaneously invoke a credible, believable *presence* as an indigenous woman in order to (re)focus her audience's attention on authentic, urgent concerns needing political redress.

Further Navigating "Indian Play" in Order to Play the Indian (Princess)

Speaking from an already unstable discursive position as a socially constructed "Indian" figure appearing on stage before a largely white, female audience, Zitkala-Ša's speech before the GFWC on Friday night also followed a performance by two non-Native individuals who opened the evening ceremonies by "performing" as "Indians"—white individuals who enacted "Indian" roles as theatrical play. News summaries of the Friday program praise the "group of Indian songs sung in costume by Harold Frasee, a noted dramatic tenor, and Mrs. C. C. Dailey, [who] concluded the [week-long] program, leaving lasting memory of the pathos of the real Westerner, the American Indian" ("Remarkable" 8). Thus, discourses and ideologies of Americanization, already circulating at the GFWC meeting, mapped neatly onto prevailing conceptions of the "Indian" and "Indianness," helping to fuel another unstable discursive field for Zitkala-Ša to navigate that evening: dominant society's fondness for "Indian play."

Deloria reminds us that socially constructed views of the "Indian" and "Indianness" function as a foundation for imagining and subsequently performing domination or power in American culture. Notions of "the Indian" and "Indianness" have historically invoked identities that are unquestionably viewed within the dominant culture as quintessentially "American," for this social construction continually references a timeless, unchanging, nonthreatening world. For generations of Americans caught up in relativisms that challenged nation, community, and selfhood, fantasizing about "Indians" as markers of something undeniably real also allows for a kind of psychic space associated with "Indianness" that provides opportunities within the dominant culture for transformation, rebellion, and creation (183–184). "Indian play" becomes a space within dominant culture for working out contradictory longings for freedom and fixed truth. Moreover, engaging in play—through singing, dressing in costume, staging a pageant—makes racial imaginings seem true; this physical play makes race-based fantasies appear to be real (184).

Thus, to be read legibly by her GFWC audience, Zitkala-Ša faced at least two significant performance-related hurdles. First, she had to distinguish herself, or set herself apart from the simulated "real Indians" who were "played" by Harold Frasee and Mrs. C. C. Dailey. Then, Zitkala-Ša had to act appropriately "Indian" enough to gain her audience's trust, as both a Native person, and as a Native woman often perceived by the dominant culture to function primarily as an "Indian Princess." Rayna Green explains how racialized "Indian" constructions in American culture *further* impose a particular kind of gendered construction upon many Native women: "Always called a Princess (or Chieftain's Daughter), she, like Pocahontas, has to violate the wishes and customs of her own 'barbarous' people to make good the rescue. . . . often out of 'Christian sympathy'" (704).[10] Zitkala-Ša was no stranger to this "Princess" construction, for women's organizations continued to advertise Zitkala-Ša's speaking engagements during this era as the appearance of an "Indian Princess."[11] A February 1924 newspaper clipping from the *Indianapolis Star*, for example, notes that "Princess Zitkala-Sa" will be speaking during an upcoming luncheon for the local Women's Department Club (fig. 8.1).

Viewed from these perspectives, we begin to understand how perceptions of Zitkala-Ša at the GFWC national meeting in Salt Lake City shifted continually between Zitkala-Ša and essentializing forms of the "Indian," "Indianness," "Indian play," and the "Indian Princess" as social constructions. Zitkala-Ša appearing in the flesh assumes rhetorical agency with her GFWC audience as a "full-blooded Sioux Indian" crying tears of gratitude for the "saving" impulses that she engenders for her GFWC audience. However, the construction is at least partially false, particularly as Zitkala-Ša is read by her audience to be a fantastical figure from the past, standing before them as "Princess," a helpless, maiden-like figure in need of their rescue. Her presence on stage confirms false, unstable ethē—that is to say, Mrs. C. C. Dailey in costume and Zitkala-Ša are viewed with the same equivalency—dressed up, Mrs. Dailey is a "play Indian," and Zitkala-Ša is the "full-blooded" version. Zitkala-Ša becomes more "real" than the simulated presentation by Frasee and Dailey, which the audience "knew" to be "play," but she still remains a fantasy as she appears to her audience as an "Indian" or as an "Indian Princess"—both unstable, sentimentalized, romanticized constructions associated with weakness and a vanishing, or a vanished, past.

Oddly, this complex sociocultural mapping onto Zitkala-Ša provides a certain kind of legibility and agency, if not authority, for Zitkala-Ša as she speaks from within dominant culture. Paradoxically, these hegemonic projections

Women to Hear Indian Princess.

PRINCESS ZITKALA SA.

The Indian Princess Zitkala Sa will be one of the speakers for the birthday anniversary luncheon of the Woman's Department Club, which will be given Friday in the Riley room at the Claypool hotel. She is officially connected with the General Federation of Women's Clubs as research agent of the Indian welfare committee.

Zitkala Sa is a Sioux Indian woman, directly descended from one of the greatest Indian chiefs of the past, Sitting Bull. She is the author of "Old Indian Legends," which is used in the Brooklyn training school of teachers, both in its theory department and in its model school, and is a member of the League of American Pen Women, a national organization.

Figure 8.1. "Women to Hear Indian Princess—Princess Zitkala-Sa."
Indianapolis Star, February 21, 1924. L. Tom Perry Special Collections, Harold B. Lee Library, Brigham Young University, Provo, Utah.

ultimately could all be fused together in productive ways in order to create a significant rhetorical opening for Zitkala-Ša. Indeed, as Schmertz notes, in scenarios where some sort of essentialism is necessary for political action, we need ways of speaking for ourselves and others that expand the conditions under which we may exist (88).

The specific context in Salt Lake City that week called for Zitkala-Ša to engage in a series of discursive maneuvers, to essentially oscillate between her multiply perceived selves—at a minimum as the false "Indian" or "Indian Princess" and something more "real"—in order to craft a coherent, meaningful message for her audience that worked to do more than just reinforce ideologies of essentialism, dominance, and oppression. This kind of legibility required a multidimensional form of rhetorical subjectivity—an ability to invoke multiple selves, speaking from multiple positions—credibly—within the space of a single speech act.

A Series of Strategic Maneuvers

News accounts summarizing Zitkala-Ša's Friday evening appearance before the GFWC highlight the engaging nature of her performance as she appeared on stage under the billing, "Indians of Today." According to the *General Federation News*, Zitkala-Ša created one of the "most dramatic and touching incidents of the convention" and the opening moments of her speech on Friday evening are described in the *News* as follows:

Zitkala-Sa, a full-blooded Sioux Indian of high culture . . . said in an emotional way:

The Great Spirit knows my heart is full! Words are so deep in my heart I cannot utter them without tears. As an educated woman I have tried as interpreter to make America, which is so generous to all other races of the world, understand the longing of her own people, the first Americans, to become citizens of this great republic. Children of the Great Spirit they are, the same as you, and as worthy as any other race of recognition. ("Indian Welfare" 9)[12]

From this account, we observe that the *News* writer, and certainly perhaps the GFWC audience, needed to frame Zitkala-Ša from the start and label or categorize her as that of a "full-blooded Indian," but an exceptional one—of "high culture." This latter phrase affirms Zitkala-Ša's fluency with Eurocentric ideals and values, her essential ability to "pass" in the dominant culture, but it simultaneously distances and sublimates the Dakota or "Sioux" culture she also embodies.

With this reported opening, Zitkala-Ša's strategic rhetorical maneuvers related to ethos operate as a multifaceted construction right from the start, as she draws simultaneously from the discursive fields shaping "Indians," the "Indian Princess," "Indianness," and "Americanization." Zitkala-Ša's initial reference to the "Great Spirit" and her mention of a heart filled with gratitude gently positions her audience as Christian saviors and Zitkala-Ša as part of a community in need of help and rescue from other, more powerful entities. Her use of the term "Great Spirit" cleverly broadens and refigures "God" by simultaneously infusing or injecting a/the presence of more indigenous forms of spirituality and religiosity, but this shift would not have been too disruptive for her audience, particularly if they continued to perceive her as an "Indian" figure.

Building upon these anticipated "Indian" constructions, Zitkala-Ša re-positions herself slightly, reminding her audience that she is "educated" and serves as a "translator." Both of these references establish her currency and authority, again, as a woman who moves between social spaces—a figure able to understand the dominant culture and also speak effectively for others. But rather than dwell in the (often nonproductive) discursive space of "Indianness," Zitkala-Ša pushes forward, linking her audience's othering immediately to the *topos* of Americanization—a potentially much more generative, less solidified space, ideologically and discursively, for challenging or refiguring dominant perceptions. Working efficiently, within the space of a few sentences, Zitkala-Ša reminds the GFWC women of their commitment to social activism as benevolence, their "generosity to other races," but then swiftly creates a distinction between the foreign-born and existing indigenous communities by noting that the clubwomen's "own people" are in need of assistance. This association becomes enhanced by her subsequent use of the phrase, "the First Americans" which, by implication, neatly aligns (marginalized) indigenous communities more closely (than immigrants) to GFWC clubwomen but also keeps Native individuals comfortably distant from these same women, as indigenous communities are perceived as "First"—but not quite contemporary or modern "Americans"—equating them still as part of a romanticized past. Zitkala-Ša frequently deploys the term, "First Americans," perhaps as a kind of catchphrase for quickly referencing and indexing indigenous concerns as distinct from others, and their "right" as more or less "real" Americans to more attention, if not more concrete forms of help or aid.

Having established sufficient legibility and a unique rhetorical space for her message related to indigenous populations—i.e., we can be served by the GFWC interest in Americanization, but we have different needs—Zitkala-Ša speaks from a new rhetorical position as policy advocate and activist when she begins to address specific governmental policies, but she frames them in more palatable, less threatening phrases designed to motivate her audience to act in particular ways, and not alienate them:

> At present they are but prisoners of the state, without citizenship rights, ruled by superintendents who are given almost unlimited powers over them. They are kept in ignorance instead of being trained to useful labor. Our dear friends here have asked you to establish an Indian Departemnt [sic] in your federation. O sisters, work to that end; work in cooperation that the stain upon our country in the treatment of my people may be wiped out. This is the happiest day of my life and you have just taken the greatest step made in American civilization toward uplifting the aborigine. ("Indian Welfare" 9)

Here, we see Zitkala-Ša begin to address ward status, but casting this complex topic as first a problem of ignorance that can be remedied through education and hard work—two concepts near and dear to members of the GFWC.

To bolster her authority to speak on these policy issues, Zitkala-Ša repositions herself as an ally of Atwood and resutures herself to members of the GFWC as a "sister,"—a cherished (non-Indian) family member speaking from a shared (geopolitical) space known as "our country"—then switching slightly again to enlarge this vision, to reference "my people," who by implication, have now become "our people." Gently implying shameful treatment in the past, Zitkala-Ša also ingratiates—"this is the happiest day of my life," you have taken "the greatest" step, you are "civilizing" and following your aims for Americanization. Then Zitkala-Ša makes yet another turn back to speak from her position as "Indian" figure by referencing the "aborigine." A term that resonates with more respected forms of indigeneity today, during the early twentieth century the word "aborigine" may have primarily invoked notions of primitivism and "Indianness." This last discursive turn arguably becomes a means for Zitkala-Ša to earn more trust and comfort from her audience as she begins to address more of her policy concerns in specific detail. Throughout this entire section of Zitkala-Ša's speech, we observe deliberate forms of naming and renaming or the invocation of ethos in multiple forms as a political tactic, for as Schmertz observes, the "naming of ourselves and others . . . acknowledges the essences that naming creates and attempts to be aware of both the possibilities and limitations entailed in that naming" (88). Invoking both "Indianness" and her identity as a cherished "sister" of the GFWC becomes a discursive means for reassuring her audience and simultaneously presenting aspects of her message most certain to threaten the status quo.

The *News* article goes on to present eight additional paragraphs of speech text, reportedly presenting Zitkala-Ša's utterances word for word. The first sentences at the start of this next, extended section, illustrate how her tone and character shift yet again to engage in a more pointed, policy-focused discussion, with concrete requests for political action: "You have enfranchised the black and are now waging a campaign of Americanization among the foreign born. Why discriminate against the noble aborigines of America— they who have no father-mother-land?" ("Indian Welfare" 9). Playing with her audience's essential sense of fairness, Zitkala-Ša argues that "Indians" are at least as deserving as other enfranchised groups, then positions herself and the people she speaks for as "noble aborigines," childlike, and in need of parenting. Already positioned by her audience as an "Indian of high culture," with these latter references, Zitkala-Ša sutures herself—her essence(s)—more fully to discourses of "Indianness" circulating in Salt Lake City that week, creating the kind of legibility and credibility that her audience continued to expect. While this maneuver upholds prevailing racial hierarchies and dom- inant views of Native individuals as primitive, or less modern, it nonetheless conveys to her audience that she can be believed as she takes up a sustained critique of the status quo. Assuming yet another ethos that further embraces Christianity, Zitkala-Ša repeatedly reminds her audience of their messianic impulses, but links these impulses to a much larger, more radical agenda:

> The gospel of humanitarianism, like charity, must begin at home. Amer- icanize the first Americans! Give them freedom to hold open forums for the expression of their thought, to do their own thinking, to exercise their own judgement [*sic*], to manage their own business, and finally, to become citizens of this republic whose constitution entitles each individual to life, liberty and pursuit of happiness. We, the American Indians, insist upon recognition of the fact that we are really normal and quite worth-while human beings. ("Indian Welfare" 9)

Repeating her established catchphrase for indigenous communities as "First Americans," Zitkala-Ša gets here to the heart of her message. She radically refigures "Indian"—she humanizes and concretizes indigenous existence. Arguing that humanitarianism, even as charity, must embrace certain principles, Zitkala-Ša demands enhanced opportunities for voice, agency, sovereignty, and self-determination, linking these demands to the most overused American motto of all: "life, liberty, and the pursuit of happiness." Finally, she insists on presence—we are here, we are visible, we are worthy of consideration.

Establishing this final, crucial shift, Zitkala-Ša recasts her constructed self—in all of her multiple forms of essence—to those indigenous communities now discursively rendered present through her speech act. A member of this otherwise marginalized community now speaks meaningfully from within the dominant culture. Indeed, ethos—now completely unmoored from any one, fixed identity—effectively multiplies the positions from which Zitkala-Ša may speak. Able to move fluidly between subject positions now located both within and beyond the dominant culture, the final portions of Zitkala-Ša's speech text make specific demands and outline specific means for achieving political reform on behalf of indigenous communities often excluded from or overlooked within this discursive space.

> *We* want American citizenship for every Indian born within the territorial limits of the United States. *We* want a democracy wheel whose hub shall be an organization of progressive educated Indian citizens and whose rim shall be the Constitution of your American Government. . . . *I* would suggest business schools for the Indians, together with a voice in their own affairs. . . . *I* would suggest that Congress enact more stringent laws to restrain [Bureau of Indian Affairs employees] and further, that the Bureau of Indian Affairs, which through 90 years has steadily enlarged itself, regardless of the diminishing Indian population, be relieved of its practically unlimited autocratic supervision of an orderly people now kept prisoners on small remnants of land not shown on our maps in a prolonged warship [*sic*], never intended to be permanent, but assumed by the Government as an emergency measure and not compatable [*sic*] with the idea of American freedom and American ideals, and contrary to the very constitution itself of the "land of the free." ("Indian Welfare" 9, emphasis added)

Moving carefully through a series of related but different rhetorical positions, Zitkala-Ša stands within discourses of the "Indian" and "Americanization," but has completely reworked them. Popular notions of "Americanization" as embraced and envisioned by the GFWC have been substantially enlarged to include creating more sovereign space for indigenous concerns,

concerns that include providing opportunities for voice and self-autonomy in determining social policy, a dismantled ward system, and enfranchisement. Indeed, to do any less would be "un-American." To achieve this rhetorical feat, Zitkala-Ša deploys ethos as a series of "ever-shifting points of convergence" or discursively creates "stopping points" where moment-to-moment, Zitkala-Ša (re) negotiates her own essence(s) in order to call upon whatever agency any given essence might enable (Schmertz 86). By appearing multiply within the space of a single speech act—as Mrs. Gertrude Bonnin, as Zitkala-Ša, as an Indian Princess, as a member of the Yankton Dakota community—Zitkala-Ša speaks simultaneously from both within, and back to, dominant culture.

Zitkala-Ša's complex rhetorical strategy becomes a critical means for advancing indigenous interests in the early decades of the twentieth century. Immediately following this appearance in Salt Lake City, Zitkala-Ša became a popular speaker at many local and regional GFWC meetings. She also spoke at national conventions held by the GFWC in 1922 and 1924. Due in large part to the initial interest sparked by Zitkala-Ša in 1921, the GFWC continued to agitate for federal reform for the next thirteen years. While levels of commitment and support varied from club to club throughout this extended period, the GFWC continues to receive credit for generally advancing advocacy efforts at the federal level, most particularly, for supporting the Indian Citizenship Act of 1924 and the enactment of the Indian New Deal in 1934.[13] Beyond this successful work within the GFWC, Zitkala-Ša's appearance in 1921 helped to launch her reputation as a national policy advocate, and this reputation continued to provide key discursive platforms to her for many years to come. Her work within the GFWC reached millions of women throughout the country and provided greater forms of visibility for her concerns, nationally, regionally, and locally. Zitkala-Ša's speech act in 1921 ultimately led to the successful crafting of limited but sustainable and moderately successful forms of indigenous activism.

This key moment within the early twentieth-century history of advocacy undertaken by Zitkala-Ša to advance indigenous concerns, particularly through her use of oration and oratory performance, enriches our understanding of rhetorical production from feminist viewpoints, extending and enhancing epistemic views of ethos. Recovering and reexamining this portion of Zitkala-Ša's rhetorical legacy allows us to reconsider ethos from expanded, if not more complex, perspectives. Her ability to speak credibly and effectively as she strategically negotiated between multiple discursive standpoints as essences successfully demonstrates that ethos can function in fluid, dynamic, and diverse ways, particularly for rhetors speaking from doubly marginalized locations.

Notes

1. This chapter is an excerpted section from my doctoral dissertation entitled, "Stories, Traces of Discourse, and the Tease of Presence: Gertrude Simmons Bonnin as Orator and Indigenous Activist."

2. After marrying Raymond T. Bonnin in 1902, Gertrude Simmons used the names Zitkala-Ša, Gertrude Simmons Bonnin, and Mrs. R. T. Bonnin throughout her life, continuously and interchangeably. My review of existing archival records located throughout the country led me to conclude that Bonnin often self-identified as "Mrs. Bonnin," "Gertrude Bonnin," or "Gertrude Simmons Bonnin" while engaging specifically in political advocacy work. I try to honor naming choices supported through archival evidence; however, the editors and publishers of this collection have insisted on "Zitkala-Ša." Existing scholarship on Zitkala-Ša as Gertrude Simmons Bonnin is significant and easily accessed in most scholarly databases. See generally, Carpenter; Hafen; Johnson and Wilson; Newmark; Warrior; Wilkinson. As a related consideration, this chapter does not generally reference tribal affiliations for historical figures and, for the sake of consistency, extends that choice to contemporary scholars referenced here as well, even though there is wide agreement that it is most appropriate to use naming practices that reference specific tribal affiliations for Native individuals. Despite certain editorial choices, this scholarship remains committed to affording respect and marking critical distinctions within Native experience.

3. Certainly, as Karma R. Chávez and Cindy L. Griffin openly acknowledge, the first four decades of feminist research generally ignored, resisted, or marginalized concepts of otherness and often produced scholarly work that universalized the experiences of elite, heterosexual, white women (xi). Indeed, in her essay, "There Is No Word for Feminism in My Language," Laura Tohe observes: "When Indian women joined the feminist dialogue in the 1970s, we found that equality for women was generally directed toward white women's issues. The issues that were relevant to our tribal communities were not part of white feminist dialogue" (109). Tohe's essay concludes with the following observation: "There was no need for feminism because of our matrilineal culture. And it continues. For Diné women, there is no word for feminism" (110). This discussion, as a feminist examination of discursive opportunities provided to an indigenous woman within *dominant* culture, aligns with and does not dispute Tohe's understanding of the relationship between feminism and tribal cultural formation(s).

4. See generally, Hertzberg; Philp; Prucha.

5. For GFWC history, see generally, Houde; Wells; White.

6. How Atwood and Zitkala-Ša began to work together remains unclear. Zitkala-Ša may have encountered Atwood in 1917 as she toured California on SAI business and gave a series of lectures in and around Riverside, Atwood's home base. Alternatively, Zitkala-Ša may have met Atwood in Washington D.C. at a women's rights meeting sponsored by the National Woman's Party. See generally, Vertical File for "Gertrude Bonnin," Women's History Resource Center. How Zitkala-Ša came to attend the GFWC meeting in Salt Lake City remains a bit of a mystery as well. Susan Dominguez asserts that Zitkala-Ša appeared as Atwood's guest (xx). Deborah Welch also states that Zitkala-Ša agreed to appear with Atwood in Salt Lake City in order to encourage members of GFWC to support Atwood's reform efforts (179).

7. See generally, Barrett; Olneck; Van Nuys.

8. See e.g., Prucha, *Americanizing*.

9. Kristin K. White argues that the GFWC campaign for Americanization fostered racist notions but also provided rhetorical openings for new voices—particularly the voices of immigrants, newly naturalized citizens, and young adults.

10. See also Castañeda at 75–77, 87–88 who calls for feminist scholars to write from new points of view, attending to these racialized complexities in more specific ways, exploring both the hegemonic and counterhegemonic strategies, roles, and activities that women developed and employed in response to colonialism in order to reclaim women as active subjects, not passive objects or victims. Malea Powell and Carolyn Sorisio argue that viewing Sarah Winnemucca (one of Zitkala-Ša's contemporaries) as an "Indian Princess" limits our ability to understand the complexity of her self-representation and obscures other more resistant, more activist facets of her early twentieth-century articulations or performances within the dominant culture.

11. See also, Carpenter, "Detecting Indianness."

12. This essay works specifically with the speech text as reported within the *General Federation News* as the most reliable evidence of articulations made by Zitkala-Ša and subsequently interpreted by her primary audience, women of the GFWC.

13. For an extended discussion of these efforts, see generally, Downes; Hertzberg; Holm; Huebner; Prucha; Tyler.

Works Cited

Barrett, James R. "Americanization from the Bottom, Up: Immigration and the Remaking of the American Working Class, 1880–1930." *Journal of American History* 79 (Dec. 1992): 996–1020. Print.

Carpenter, Cari M. *Seeing Red: Anger, Sentimentality, and American Indians*. Columbus: Ohio State UP, 2008. Print.

———. "Detecting Indianness: Gertrude Bonnin's Investigation of Native American Identity." *Wicazo Sa Review* 20.1 (2005): 139–159. Print.

Castañeda, Antonia I. "Women of Color and the Rewriting of Western History: The Discourse, Politics, and Decolonialization of History." *Pacific Historical Review* 61.4 (1992): 501–33. Print.

Chávez, Karma R., and Cindy L. Griffin. *Standing in the Intersection: Feminist Voices, Feminist Practices in Communication Studies*. Albany: State U of New York P, 2012. Print.

Deloria, Philip J. *Playing Indian*. New Haven, CT: Yale UP, 1998. Print.

Dominguez, Susan Rose. "The Representative Indian." Introduction to *American Indian Stories*. Lincoln: U of Nebraska P. 2003. Print.

Downes, Randolph C. "A Crusade for Indian Reform, 1922–1934." *Mississippi Valley Historical Review* 32.3 (Dec. 1945): 331–54. Print.

Foss, Karen A., Sonja K. Foss, and Cindy L. Griffin. "Transforming Rhetoric through Feminist Reconstruction: A Response to the Gender Diversity Perspective." *Women's Studies in Communication* 20 (1997): 117–35. Print.

"General Summary of Program Heard at Salt Lake City." *General Federation News* 2.1 (Aug. 1921): 2, 10–12. Print.

Green, Rayna. "The Pocahontas Perplex: The Image of Indian Women in American Culture." *Massachusetts Review* 16 (1975): 698–714. Print.

Hafen, P. Jane. "Help Indians Help Themselves: Gertrude Bonnin, the SAI, and the NCAI." *Studies in American Indian Literatures* 25.2, The Society of American Indians and Its Legacies: A Special Combined Issue of *SAIL* and *AIQ* (Summer 2013): 199–218. Print.

———. "Gertrude Simmons Bonnin: For the Indian Cause." *Sifters: Native American Women's Lives* (2001): 127–140. Print.

Hertzberg, Hazel W. *The Search for an American Indian Identity: Modern Pan-Indian Movements*. Syracuse, NY: Syracuse UP, 1971. Print.

Holm, Tom. *The Great Confusion in Indian Affairs: Native Americans and Whites during the Progressive Era*. Austin: U of Texas P, 2005. Print.

Houde, Mary J. *Reaching Out: A Story of the General Federation of Women's Clubs*. Washington, DC: GFWC, 1989. Print.

Huebner, Karin L. "An Unexpected Alliance: Stella Atwood, the California Club Women, John Collier, and the Indians of the Southwest, 1917–1934." *Pacific Historical Review* 78.3 (2009): 337–66. Print.

"Indian Welfare Work Will Be Undertaken." *General Federation News* 2.1 (August 1921): 1, 9. Print.

Jackson, Helen Hunt. *A Century of Dishonor: A Sketch of the United States Government's Dealing with Some of the Indian Tribes*. 1881. Norman: U of Oklahoma P, 1995. Print.

Jarratt, Susan C., and Nedra Reynolds. "The Splitting Image: Contemporary Feminisms and the Ethics of *êthos*." *Ethos: New Essays in Rhetorical and Critical Theory*. Ed. J. S. Baumlin and T. F. Baumlin. Dallas: Southern Methodist UP, 1994. 37–63. Print.

Johnson, David L., and Raymond Wilson. "Gertrude Simmons Bonnin, 1876–1938: 'Americanize the First American.'" *American Indian Quarterly* 12.1 (Winter 1988): 27–40. Print.

Newmark, Julianne. "Pluralism, Place, and Gertrude Bonnin's Counter-Nativism, from Utah to Washington D.C." *American Indian Quarterly* 36.3 (Summer 2012): 318–47. Print.

Official Register and Directory of Women's Clubs in America. Vol. 23. Boston: N. A. Lindsey, 1922, Print.

Olneck, Michael R. "Americanization and the Education of Immigrants, 1900–1925: An Analysis of Symbolic Action." *American Journal of Education* 97.4 (1989): 398–423. Print.

Philp, Kenneth R. *John Collier's Crusade for Indian Reform, 1920–1954*. Tucson: U of Arizona P, 1977. Print.

Powell, Malea. "Princess Sarah, the Civilized Indian: The Rhetoric of Cultural Literacies in Sarah Winnemucca Hopkins's *Life among the Piutes*." *Rhetorical Women: Roles and Representations*. Ed. Hildy Miller and Lillian Bridwell-Bowles. Tuscaloosa: U of Alabama P, 2005. Print.

Prucha, Francis Paul. *Americanizing the American Indians*. Cambridge: Harvard UP, 1973. Print.

———, *The Great Father: The United States Government and the Indians*. Lincoln: U of Nebraska P, 1984. Print.

"Remarkable Musical Programs at Council Meeting." *General Federation News*. 2.1 (August 1921): 7–8. Print.

Ritchie, Joy, and Kate Ronald, eds. *Available Means: An Anthology of Women's Rhetoric(s)* Pittsburgh: U of Pittsburgh P. 2001. Print.

Schmertz, Johanna. "Constructing Essences: Ethos and the Postmodern Subject of Feminism." *Rhetoric Review* 18.1 (Autumn 1999): 82–91. Print.

Sorisio, Carolyn. "Playing the Indian Princess: Sarah Winnemucca's Newspaper Career and Performance of American Indian Identities." *Studies in American Indian Literatures* 23.1 (Spring 2011): 1–31. Print.

"Suggested Program for Americanization." General Federation of Women's Clubs Americanization Committee, 1918–1920. San Francisco: California Commission of Immigration and Housing, 1920. Print.

Tohe, Laura. "There Is No Word for Feminism in My Language." *Wicazo Sa Review* 15.2 (2000): 103–10. Print.

Tyler, Lyman S. *Indian Affairs—A Study of the Changes in Policy in the United States toward Indians.* Provo: Brigham Young UP, 1964. Print.

Van Nuys, Frank. *Americanizing the West: Race, Immigrants, and Citizenship, 1890–1930.* Lawrence: UP of Kansas, 2002. Print.

Vertical File, "Gertrude Bonnin." General Federation of Women's Clubs. Women's History Resource Center, Washington, DC.

Vizenor, Gerald. *Literary Chance: Essays on Native Survivance.* Lincoln: U of Nebraska P, 2011. Print.

———. ed., *Survivance: Narratives of Native Presence.* Lincoln: U of Nebraska P, 2008. Print.

———. *Fugitive Poses: Native American Indian Scenes of Presence and Absence.* Lincoln: U of Nebraska P, 1998. Print.

———. *Manifest Manners: Narratives on Postindian Survivance.* Lincoln: U of Nebraska P, 1994. Print.

Warrior, Robert. *Tribal Secrets: Recovering American Indian Intellectual Traditions.* Minneapolis: U of Minnesota P, 1994. Print.

Welch, Deborah Sue. "Zitkala Sa: An American Indian Leader, 1876–1939." Diss. U of Wyoming, 1984. Print.

Wells, Mildred White. *Unity in Diversity: The History of the General Federation of Women's Clubs.* Washington, DC: GFWC, 1953. Print.

White, Kristen K. "Training a Nation: The General Federation of Women's Clubs' Rhetorical Education and American Citizenship, 1890–1930." Diss. Ohio State U, 2010. Print.

Wilkinson, Elizabeth. "Gertrude Bonnin's Rhetorical Strategies of Silence." *Studies in American Indian Literatures* 25.3 (Fall 2013): 33–56. Print.

"Women to Hear Indian Princess—Princess Zitkala-Sa." *Indianapolis Star,* 21 Feb. 1924. Print.

Zitkala-Ša (Gertrude Simmons Bonnin). *Old Indian Legends.* Boston: Ginn, 1901. Print.

Part Three

Ethē as Relation–Relating

Relation-relating draws attention to the ways in which women's ethē are socially constructed; rhetors construct their identities and texts in relation to others and their environments. Subjectivity is better characterized as intersubjectivity, and relation-relating invokes a range of relationships: collaboration, connection, and coalitions or alliances. Moreover, ethē of relation highlight the ethical motives of this feminist ecological approach: reflecting on one's own subjectivity makes a rhetor mindful of others, and working together is understood as necessary and desirable though sometimes difficult. Because feminist rhetoricians generally place a high value on collaboration, this practice has played a significant role in feminist rhetorical studies, even through the collaborations of feminists editing collections, books, and articles in the field, as Andrea Lunsford and Lisa Ede and Karen Foss and Sonja Foss have done throughout their careers. More recently, Jacqueline Jones Royster and Gesa E. Kirsch

> proclai[m] that feminist rhetorical scholarship (and other work as well) is being done quite regularly by colleagues working together rather than alone, as indeed we are doing in this volume, thus defying a dominant image in the history of rhetoric, that is, an individual *genius* at work alone and often in solitude. (43)

Their description of collaboration as offering a "much-enlivened space" (43) describes our experience as coeditors composing this text together, along with contributors, to make for a richness of perspectives and depth of work. Risa Applegarth's study of "an imbalanced, inequitable collaboration" points to the "messy relations of power" that may characterize collaboration and calls up additional ways of considering relation-relating (217).

In addition to seeing relation as collaboration, relation describes the "betweens" that characterize the metaphorical distances between rhetors and their readers, audiences, or publics (LeFevre 46). Such relations are often fraught; women, even when talking to other women, compose not necessarily in the context of Burkean identification, where rhetor and reader/listener are consubstantial, but rather in the context of dis-identification or non-identification (Ratcliffe, *Rhetorical*). Burkean identification does not serve subjects who differ, particularly in terms of power, because "the 'I' with the power" is the one "who decides which differences to bridge and which differences must be deemed excess and relegated outside the consubstantial place of identification" (59). That kind of thinking can erase differences, reinforce misogyny and racism, and engender miscommunication. An ethē of relation entails rhetors negotiating the gaps between people in meaningful ways.

An ethē of relation allows for embracing Adrienne Rich's politics of relation and pressing past this orientation largely focused on the rhetor's individual location and moving toward alliances and coalitions that focus on the dialogic potential and practices between people. Her politics of location reflects an understanding that subjectivity is epistemically salient and constantly shifting even in its multiplicity because contexts change: "Rich's politics of location admits its situatedness, its multivocal contradictions, and its interests" (Ratcliffe, *Anglo-American* 126). The recognition of social locations as a category to acknowledge, value, and negotiate spurs the potential for transformation, for re-vision of the self and world (126, 127). For many feminists, especially white feminists, Rich's politics of location has taught us to identify "where we stand" in order to disrupt the belief that a view from nowhere is preferable to one that is located. Kendall Leon and Stacey Pigg draw on Chicana theory to address two challenges to this hopeful concept: "that actively voicing and naming one's commitments means simultaneously being positioned by others" and "understanding ethos as located can be reductive if we understand 'locations' as static spatial containers" (259–60). They read Gloria Anzaldúa's concept of conocimiento to offer a "rhetorical vocabulary to help account for dynamic networks of ethos without overstabilizing locations from which we invent" (260).

Like Leon and Pigg's discussion of conocimiento, Aimee Carillo Rowe's politics of relation offers a more explicit ecological stance that better considers the dynamism of relationality and locatability and the difficulty of such positioning for women of color. Rowe describes the necessary movement from a politics of location to relation as a shift "from a binaristic vision in which white women and women of color are neatly divided (and eternally opposed) to one in which feminists are joined (or divided) over politics and, by extension, through shared (or segregated) experience" (9–10). The hope she places in feminist alliances is visualized through a metaphor of power lines: "We build alliances to link our lives together, to transmit power, and potentially for the purpose of transforming power" (1). Malea Powell also advocates for an alliance model for its transformative potential. She advocates modeling disciplinary alliances on the historical alliances of the Miami Confederacy, whose "strength was, and is, in alliance and in the ability to adapt to rapidly changing worlds" (39).[1] Powell is motivated by the belief that "We need, I would argue, an alliance based on the shared assumption that 'surviving genocide and advocating sovereignty and survival' has been a focus for many of the people now on this continent for several centuries and, as such, should also be at the center of our scholarly and pedagogical practices enacted in these United States" (41). It is no wonder then that feminists, "first world," "third world," and global or transnational, are moving toward definitions of ethos as ecological in the name of ethics and in recognition of the need to "reconcile attention to difference with the equally vital desire for—and urgent necessity of—connection and alliance" (Adams 2).

Note

1. Powell offers a "rhetorical sketch" of Susan La Flesche Picotte to model prospects for contemporary alliances grounded in an ethics of trust, solidarity, and respect (44).

Works Cited

Adams, Katherine. "At the Table with Arendt: Toward a Self-Interested Practice of Coalition Discourse." *Hypatia* 17.1 (Winter 2002): 1–33. Print.

Foss, Karen, and Sonja Foss. *Women Speak: The Eloquence of Women's Lives.* Long Grove, IL: Waveland, 1991. Print.

LeFevre, Karen Burke. *Invention as a Social Act.* Carbondale: Southern Illinois UP, 1987. Print.

Lunsford, Andrea A., ed. *Reclaiming Rhetorica: Women in the Rhetorical Tradition.* Pittsburgh: U of Pittsburgh P, 1995. Print.

Powell, Malea D. "Down by the River, or How Susan La Flesche Picotte Can Teach Us about Alliance as a Practice of Survivance." *College English* 67.1 (Sept. 2004): 38–60. Print.

Ratcliffe, Krista. *Anglo-American Feminist Challenges to the Rhetorical Traditions.* Carbondale: Southern Illinois UP, 1996. Print.

———. *Rhetorical Listening: Identification, Gender, Whiteness.* Carbondale: Southern Illinois UP, 2005. Print.

Rowe, Aimee Carillo. *Power Lines: On the Subject of Feminist Alliances.* Durham, NC: Duke UP, 2008. Print.

Royster, Jacqueline Jones, and Gesa E. Kirsch. *Feminist Rhetorical Practices: New Horizons for Rhetoric, Composition, and Literacy Studies.* Carbondale: Southern Illinois UP, 2012. Print.

9. Ethos Righted

Transnational Feminist Analytics

Wendy S. Hesford

In *Feminist Rhetorical Practices: New Horizons for Rhetoric, Composition, and Literacy Studies*, Jacqueline Jones Royster and Gesa E. Kirsch ask us to consider contemporary feminist configurations of the "ethical self" and the terms of our engagement with both the texts we study and produce. They call to feminist scholars to "engender an ethos of humility, respect, and care," and, in so doing, they prompt us to think of ethos in relational terms (21). Although the qualities of "humility, respect, and care" suggest a nonagonistic feminist stance, the *means* to this *end* are far less demure. Among the reflexive practices that have gained traction in contemporary feminist rhetorical studies and that Royster and Kirsch endorse, are those that involve the "critique [of] our analytical assumptions and frames" (14), demonstrate multidirectional thinking (86), and extend "the boundaries of locally defined assumptions" (112). Royster and Kirsch do not frame ethos as a mode of inquiry per se; but the terms of critical engagement that they espouse provide a set of tactics that feminist scholars might ostensibly adopt in pursuit of the enviable "ethical self" (14).

Transnational feminist studies exhibit qualities of critical engagement similar to those that Royster and Kirsch reference; yet transnational feminists also foreground methodological challenges that the authors do not explicitly address that are vital to a relational understanding of ethos. Assuredly, ethos is a "component of rhetorical argument" (Hyde xvi). But instead of defining ethos in modernist terms as an attribute of the speaker prerequisite to persuasion, I aim to reinvigorate classical notions of "*ethos* as a social act" and argue for an understanding of ethos as an analytical orientation to thought and action (Holiday 389). Specifically, I turn to transnational feminist studies for a more robust theory of ethos as both a mode of inquiry (epistemology) and as a site of struggle (political action). Transnational approaches to feminist scholarship developed as a critical response to the universalizing tendencies of global feminism, namely the sisterhood-is-global model (Morgan) that emerged in the 1980s and 1990s, criticized for privileging gender as a category of analysis and for its near exclusive focus on women's sexual victimization and reliance on a Western liberal legal framework.

Transnational feminist scholarship cannot be reduced to a single methodology; but generally transnational feminist methods aim to illuminate cultural, political, and economic processes of globalization and the inequalities that shape geopolitical alignments. Although transnational feminists question the sanctity of the nation-state as an analytical category, they do not abandon analyses of the global force of the world's most powerful nations.[1] Attuned to the contingencies that generate seemingly incommensurable differences among women across contexts, transnational feminist analytics dislodge ethos from its moorings in liberal notions of the polis (inattentive to cultural stratification and inequalities) in order to attend to the asymmetrical terrain of feminist politics and political economies. This includes attention to how political economies differently shape the domestic oppression of racial and ethnic minorities (see Chowdhury, "Locating"). In offsetting uncritical cosmopolitan feminisms, transnational feminisms return us to the classical sense of ethos as "a habitual gathering place" (Holiday 389), with renewed questions about the ideological frameworks that underwrite the formation of political alliances. Specifically, feminist studies that examine the multiple layers of power operating in transnational movements for gender justice and local feminist responses to these movements call forth a relational ethos that is neither lodged in complicity (determinism) nor in the ideals of ethical purity (idealism). In focusing on women's navigation of contesting material-discursive fields, recent transnational feminist studies of social movements summon postmodern notions of ethos as an "element of the discourse itself, not simply its origin" (Holiday 389). Transnational feminist analytics animate ethos as a struggle with norms, including the regulatory structures of liberal internationalism and its moral paradigm of rescue and repudiation of "third world" women and children and construal of certain populations as objects of recognition onto whom rights must be conferred.

In *Transnationalism Reversed: Women Organizing against Gendered Violence in Bangladesh*, Elora Halim Chowdhury skillfully charts the movement of narratives of multiple actors involved with local and transnational campaigns against acid violence and demonstrates how privilege is consolidated through multiple axes of power and unevenly distributed across these campaigns. I turn to *Transnationalism Reversed* because its methodological and ethical imprint can usefully inform our discussions about ethos in feminist rhetorical studies. In her analysis of Naripokkho (translated "For Women"), a women's advocacy group founded in 1983 in Bangladesh, and the conceptual groundwork that the organization provided for the internationalization of campaigns against acid violence (namely, the construal of acid violence as a gendered human rights violation), Chowdhury brings a much needed rhetorical approach, primarily narrative interpretation, to the transnational study of feminist advocacy. She does not explicitly engage the concept of ethos, but her focus on survivor-activists' struggles for justice, the strategic deployment of women's narratives of violence in international politics and popular media, and the consequences of transnationalism to local women's advocacy campaigns deepens our understanding of how globalization has reset the parameters of feminist praxis and ethical deliberation. I use the phrase "ethos righted" in my title as both a descriptor and an analytic to characterize the genealogy of modern notions of the "ethical self" in liberal humanism, a formulation of ethos that contrasts with the transnational feminist movement of rights arguments toward a more critical humanism. Three variations of feminist ethos emerge in *Transnationalism Reversed*: the ethos of the compassionate cosmopolitan whose privileged mobility enables recognition of the rights of the disempowered; the survivor of acid violence and activist, who must repeatedly assert her rights, lest they be denied; and the transnational feminist ethnographer, who strives to document these recognitions and denials while mindful of her inescapable influence on the representational process.

Transnational Rights Narratives and Visibilities

I had heard about barbaric acts of violence against women in the third world, but I had no idea that hundreds of young women in Bangladesh were being attacked with sulfuric acid simply because they dared to say no to men. . . . I saw a portrait of one victim that was truly extraordinary. It showed a woman's head completely covered by a veil, except for one eye staring out. . . . The woman behind the veil was a 17-year-old named Bina and the more I learned about her, the more I realized that we had to tell this story through her eyes. . . . Ironically, Bina was one of the first acid survivors to take off her veil. Most of the victims are too ashamed to show their faces . . . But Bina was different. . . . For the first time in Bangladesh, a girl burned by acid was demanding justice. (Connie Chung)

Television journalist Connie Chung's report "Faces of Hope," which aired on ABC's *20/20* on November 1, 1999, and is the focus of Chowdhury's media analysis, features the stories of two teenage acid-violence survivors—Bina Akhter and Jharna Akhter (no relation)—and their trip to the United States for medical treatment. Chung and her camera crew follow the girls from Bangladesh to the United States and introduce them to their host family in Cincinnati. Bina was fourteen years old when a gang broke into her home to abduct her older cousin, Makti. The men brought acid with them to use if they encountered resistance. During a struggle, Bina was severely burned. The attack had left her blind in her left eye (Chowdhury 93). Neither "Faces of Hope" nor *Transnationalism Reversed* offers details about the circumstances of Jharna's attack; readers of *Transnationalism Reversed* only access Jharna's story through Bina's recollections. (Given the common surname, I will refer to Bina Akhter as Bina from here on.)

In "Faces of Hope," Chung presents acid violence as a "little-known crime" and assumes that with greater international visibility the problem will diminish (ABC News 1999). Chung reports that she

had heard about barbaric acts of violence against women in the third world, but [she] had no idea that hundreds of young women in Bangladesh were being attacked with sulfuric acid simply because they dared to say no to men. (ABC News 1999)

Underlying Chung's compassionate cosmopolitan ethos as a reporter is an epistemology of saving third world women; a strategy of representing the suffering "other" that transnational feminists have long argued against. In response to Chung's newfound knowledge of the extent of the problem in Bangladesh, Chowdhury asks a key question: "Little known to whom?" (xviii). Chowdhury explains, "Acid violence was certainly not 'little known' in the context of Bangladesh" (xviii). Bangladeshi activists had documented hundreds of cases of acid violence and played a key role in supporting victims and mobilizing medical, legal, state, and media professionals to intervene (xviii). In its absence of coverage of local activists, Chowdhury argues "Faces of Hope" "essentialize[d] rescuers and victims on either side of the North-South divide" (xix). The report made acid attacks against women and girls in Bangladesh intelligible to U.S. audiences through the highly gendered and racialized rescue narrative of liberal internationalism, wherein, as Gayatri Chakravorty Spivak legendarily put it in 1994, "white men . . . sav[e] brown women from brown men" ("Can the Subaltern" 93). Ethical discussions based on essentialist identities and geographies are clear oversights of ethos as a mode of inquiry alert to contextual variables, contingencies, and particularities.

The close-up photograph of Bina's scarred face that accompanies ABC's *20/20* online report sets the parameters for the audience's ethical engagement in terms of a visual rhetoric that attributes to spectators the privilege of incorporating the victimized foreign "other" as a subject within the liberal international imaginary, wherein human rights subjectivity is established on the basis of its violation. The unsettling photograph establishes the scene of rights recognition in dialectical (self-other) terms, while maintaining the fantasy of transnational intimacy for distant audiences. That international recognition of "third world" women's human rights is founded on subjection partly explains the prominence of spectacular images of women's scarred bodies in campaigns against acid violence. But the high profile acid-attack cases reported in US popular media are also driven by international development narratives that depict women of the global South not only as victims of gendered violence but as victims of cultures and political systems perceived as hindering their emancipation. Here international human rights meets its sister discourse—neoliberal development.

The rhetoric of recognition that underlies these discourses, as I discuss elsewhere (*Spectacular Rhetorics*), is one in which our "seeing" Bina's scarred face becomes a mandatory element of her projected progress and promise of liberation. But, as Arabella Lyon persuasively argues in *Deliberative Acts: Democracy, Rhetoric, and Rights,* "Recognition, a self-willed engagement with another, is more than the condition of seeing and being seen" (49). Lyon usefully broadens "the concept of recognition from one of making people politically visible to one of enacting the human" (49). "Performative deliberation," she argues, "would have us understand recognition as a matter of being and becoming rather than one of seeing and representing or witnessing" (49). To reorient the concept of recognition from the "*condition of possibility* (to have rights)" to "its *actual performance* . . . (the right of engagement)" may unsettle human rights' ocular epistemology, but this shift does not retire the rhetorical critic of the task of investigating the link between visibility and structures of subjection (49). Indeed, as "Faces of Hope" illustrates, the ethos of US internationalism is deeply entrenched in hierarchical scenes of recognition and the visual production of violated and righted subjects.

The cultural weight attributed to the face as a conveyer of meaning (Omizo) becomes evident in Chung's emphasis on Bina's removal of her veil. Unveiling is read as a highly charged act in the post 9/11 context, where images of unveiled "liberated" Afghan women circulated as justification for US military interventions in the region (some of these images were reportedly staged by Western journalists). "Faces of Hope" partakes in the Western Orientalist fantasy of imagining what is behind the veil as a project of reimagining Muslim women as subjects with rights and dignity. However, the Orientalist fantasy of seeing behind the veil is complicated in this instance because the face revealed is scarred by gendered violence. The photograph of Bina's scarred face that accompanies the article serves as the "before" image (not the typical afterimage of Western liberation) and points toward the sought "after" image of the reconstructed and "liberated" face. The medical promise of liberation overwrites acid-violence survivors' subversion of cultural norms and risk in public unveiling within the context of their own communities, where removing the veil works against the shame of disfigurement. Women's advocacy groups, such as Naripokkho, encourage acid victims to show their faces in public and to partake in public forums to share their stories (Chowdhury, *Transnationalism* 36). Indeed, the "visibility of the survivors became a key strategy in the efforts to make public the anti-acid violence campaign" (35). In its stress on the afterimage, ABC's *20/20* "Faces of Hope" deflects attention from acid survivors' ethos as political agents engaged in the disruption of cultural norms and shaming tactics.

Sensational depictions of gendered violence prevail in international human rights campaigns and popular media. Amirita Basu rightly notes that the most visible and apparently successful transnational campaigns for women's rights have been those that prioritize sexual victimization, especially when the focus is on "women from the south who experience genital mutilation, stoning, or public humiliation" (82). Predictably, Chung characterizes Bina as a victim of "barbaric acts of violence in the third world," invoking the savage-victim-savior metaphor (Mutua). But in depicting Bina as an "extraordinary" survivor who demands justice, Chung extends the savage-victim-savior trope. The victim turned survivor-activist narrative facilitates Bina's incorporation into the liberal international imaginary as a transformed (righted) subject. Metonymically, victims of acid violence are "righted" (redirected, remedied, rehabilitated) by the global North, who confer rights onto women of the global South and presumably place them on the correct path. Here the "liberal apparatus of the human rights identity machine" sets up dualistic oppositions that permit the narratability of only certain identities and social relations (Chowdhury, *Transnationalism* 141).

In *Trafficking Women's Human Rights*, Julietta Hua investigates the protocols that circumscribe legal personhood and liberal subjectivity and thus advances our understanding of the genealogy of the ethical self—ethos—as a righted subject. She asks: "What are the terms through which subjects can become legible as victims of trafficking? What do these terms tell us about the ways gender, sexuality, and race are working to help shape notions of national and global belonging" (xxi–xxii). Although "becoming legible is necessary to garnering aid like legal status, food, and shelter," as Hua rightly notes, and as we see in popular media depictions of acid-violence survivors, the normative frameworks of legibility often reiterate troubling configurations of the "third world." Within the context of international and domestic US trafficking legislation, women who are trafficked are (inadvertently) required to produce themselves as victims without agency in order for their experience to be categorized as a human rights violation. Hua therefore asks: "How useful is human rights as a site through which to address global gender violence, given the fact that human rights talk threatens to resurrect these colonial configurations of power?" (xxiii).

At various points in the history of human rights, certain groups have been cut off from the category of the "human," namely women, children, slaves, the "insane," and the disabled. One common response to the dialectical (self-other) philosophical framework of human rights law and its history of exclusion has been the call for a more inclusive history. Yet, as Hua remarks, countering the colonial hierarchies of human rights past and future is not simply a matter of the inclusion of heretofore excluded voices and perspectives. Hence transnational feminist scholars and activists consider the conditions of legibility that render certain populations visible and audible and others invisible and inaudible. In tackling these multifaceted conceptual issues, *Trafficking Women's Rights* reveals the limits of the commonplace liberal feminist paradigm of inclusion as a political solution to the problem of human trafficking. For Hua, and for transnational feminist scholars more broadly, the challenge of difference for rights advocacy is not just one of "accurate representation" (Lyon 3) or inclusion, but about how difference shapes recognition—that is, as Lyon puts it, "the moment of the conferring of subjectivity and humanity" (2).

Transnationalism Reversed illustrates how women's advocacy groups skillfully navigate the international moral economy of human rights and how individual acid-violence survivor-activists, such as Bina Akhter, unsettle moral dichotomies (victim/agent) as they take on shifting identities and positions in narrating their struggle for power within their multifaceted particularities. In contrast to the savage-victim-savior narrative told by elite popular media, Bina's story, as conveyed to Chowdhury, is much more fragmented and contested. Bina discloses that while she was grateful for the generosity of her host family, for example, there were serious cultural and religious tensions in the home. The host family required Bina and Jharka—both are Bengali Muslims—to attend church and pressured them to convert to Christianity. Chowdhury also reveals Bina's shifting relationship with and eventual estrangement from Naripokkho, the advocacy group for which she once played a leadership role. Chowdhury's explication of contesting cultural and institutional expectations enables her to make visible Bina's struggle for representation without reproducing the static spectacle of the suffering "other" (16). Through comparative ethnographic, oral history, and media analysis, Chowdhury elucidates how the internationalization of the campaign against acid violence confounded the rescue and rehabilitation narrative customary to global feminist and neoliberal development discourses and how Bina and other Naripokkho activists negotiated competing antiviolence discourses and agendas.

In contradistinction to the sisterhood-is-global model of community ethos, Bina's ethos as survivor-activist and her shifting relationship to Naripokkho unsettle universalized notions of women's experience and feminist resistance. Chowdhury puts it well, "the feminism of Bina and alternative ways she crafted her own narrative of victimization, empowerment, and choice could not be given voice within the larger script of global feminism" (*Transnationalism* 183). Bina first met Naripokkho activists at the burn unit in Dhaka Medical College Hospital. After attending an acid workshop organized by Naripokkho in 1997, Bina was named coordinator for the nationwide acid survivors' network (85). Bina's relationship to Naripokkho, however, changed after she left Bangladesh to obtain medical treatment in the United States, a trip made possible by Naripokkho, and US-based organization Healing the Children, UNICEF, Shriner's Hospital in Cincinnati, and a host family.

Prior to coming to the United States, Bina played a prominent role in Naripokkho's acid campaign. But when she began to pursue options for staying in the United States, Naripokkho activists felt betrayed. If Bina were to stay in the United States beyond two years, she would defy the contractual understanding that she had with her sponsoring organizations and further compromise Naripokkho's legal case against the men who had attacked her. However, by the end of the two-year period, Bina's medical treatment was not yet complete. Moreover, Bina thought that she and her family were at risk in Bangladesh from her attacker and his associates (97). In 2000, she applied for political asylum in the United States (98). As Bina started the political asylum process and after Healing the Children relinquished sponsorship of both girls, she moved in with a Bangladeshi expatriate family in Cincinnati. Shriner's hospital continued to care for both Bina and Jharna. Two years later, Bina moved into her own apartment and began to tour the country to share her experiences. At a speech she delivered at Boston University's Take Back the Night rally in 2002, Bina again drew the attention of the international community. Chowdhury observes, "She had the ability to draw crowds, to stir emotions, and to question people about their own assumptions and beliefs" (100)—transnational feminist ethos extraordinaire.

Initially, Bina found herself the star of Naripokkho's acid campaign, but once she transgressed the conduct of a "good victim," she was blamed for the campaign's loss of local and international support (114). Bristi Chowdhury, who worked closely with Bina at Naripokkho, criticizes the organization's decision to place Bina in such a prominent role.

> I believe it was a mistake to choose Bina as the Naripokkho intern. We should have groomed someone else. We knew from the onset that she was a star. But, she was also a child. We should have known better. (B. Chowdhury qtd. in Chowdhury *Transnationalism* 117)

In other words, Bina was shunned for acting "as the ungrateful and wayward child of the campaign: the very campaign that had brought her into the limelight" (118). The infantilization of Bina points to the class-based tensions within Naripokkho. Moreover, Bina's ethos and agency are tied to class-based expectations. While the middle-class women of the organization construe Bina as unprofessional, Bina's decision to stay in the United States is based partly on her desire for economic security.

During the course of her extended ethnographic study, Chowdhury learns that Naripokkho's organizational hierarchy was also driven by the dictates of

international funding agencies. Additionally, the more the campaign interna-
tionalized, the more tensions between "funders" and "recipients" and among
individuals within the organization grew (*Transnationalism* 118). Naripokkho
began to systematically campaign to bring public attention to the problem
of acid attacks in the mid-1990s. As a result of its success in conceptualizing
acid violence as a gendered human rights violation, the campaign attracted
a diverse set of international actors, which by 2003 had set in motion the creation of the Acid Survivors Network in Bangladesh. The network eventually
took over the service role of the campaign by assisting acid-violence survivors.
In short, Chowdhury's attention to the rise and fall of Naripokkho's involvement in the international campaign against acid reveals the unintended and
lesser-known consequences of transnational movements at the local level, a
process that Elizabeth Friedman refers to as "transnationalism reversed,"
from which the title of Chowdhury's study is derived (109).

Chowdhury's invocation of the concept "transnationalism reversed"
points to her important complication of feminist critiques of neoliberalism
that either construe development as a deterministic megadiscourse or un-
critically espouse neoliberal development visions in women's empowerment
projects. Chowdhury suggests that the Acid Survivor's Foundation (ASF) falls
into the latter category in that it "strives to 'empower' individual survivors
by channeling them into service activities without an attendant deeper focus
on social transformation" (*Transnationalism* 57). Although Chowdhury acknowledges the important services that ASF provides, she points out that it
is limited "by its structural location as a local NGO funded by international
development organizations that subscribe to a mission that replicates a neo-
colonial vision of women's empowerment" (57). *Transnationalism Reversed*
defines development as the practice of negotiating normative structures and
expectations. Of course, Chowdhury also has a stake in these negotiations; her
research depends on her access to development organizations. She does not
explicitly engage questions of narrative distance or reliability; rather she fore-
grounds Bina's self-narration as a mechanism through which readers might
see its potential offering of "decolonizing" and "oppositional knowledges"
(88). Yet Chowdhury is well aware that "experiences are mediated by active
narrative construction[s]" (88), her study's analytical frameworks among
them. To point out that experiences are discursively mediated is far from a
new revelation. *Transnationalism Reversed*, however, is distinct in the preci-
sion with which Chowdhury explicates the mediation of experience and the
insights that her multisited narrative ethnography yields for understanding

the intricacies of acid violence and the survivor-activist ethos as a struggle for representation, subjectivity, and agency.

In a 2004 interview with Chowdhury in Boston, Bina recollected events that she thought were particularly important to document (88). Chowdhury frames Bina's willingness to retell her story as a strategy to reach out to Naripokkho activists from whom she had become estranged (89). Eight years after the attack, Bina narrates her experience.

> I saw the men with a bucket and jar advancing towards Mutkti. I shook her awake. At that moment the contents of the jar splashed on my out-stretched hands, and the bucket on my feet. I screamed. . . . Then, Dano poured the entire contents of the bucket on my face. I felt my ears burning and touched it. The skin was peeling off in to my hands, and the acid was dripping in to my mouth—I could taste it. It was like the room was alight with fire. I cannot describe, and you cannot imagine what it was like. I tried to grab the man, and in the struggle, Dano's mask fell off . . . I think he also got burnt by the acid on my hands. At that point, he took out a pistol and aimed it at me. "If anyone tried to stop me, I will shoot you. Just look outside," he threatened. There were at least 10 more men outside the house in addition to the four inside the room. I let go of him. I thought, if I lived I would be able to get him later. But, if he shot me and I died, my family died, nobody would be able to do anything about the crime that had just taken place. (qtd. in Chowdhury 90)

Bina's ethos as narrator lies in her construal of herself as an agent, as a subject with rights who fought her attacker and made prudent decisions in the midst of the attack.

> I let go of him. I thought, if I lived I would be able to get him later. But, if he shot me and I died, my family died, nobody would be able to do anything about the crime that had just taken place.

Bina's ethos is also located in the *act* of self-narration and in the *narratability* of her story. Bina's narrative is encumbered by the difficulty in describing her pain and suffering to another, but her narrative agency is not. She explicitly cordons off the listener from either knowing or identifying with her pain and suffering: "You cannot imagine what it was like," as if to say, "You are not me. I am I." Authorial distance is minimized, however, in her acquiescence to a community-based ethos of justice—crime and punishment—with which her audience presumably identifies. Bina's assertion of difference within identification raises a larger question about what's at stake in upholding identification as a precondition for ethical deliberation. That Bina cordons off the listener from sharing her pain might also be read metaethically as procuring a collective response to human suffering directed at systemic solutions.

Linking ethos to method brings ethics to the foreground—a connection that is not new to feminist ethnographers, especially those working in the field of rhetoric, composition, and literacy studies (Royster and Kirsch), who call for increased self-reflexivity on location and power imbalances between researchers and their subjects. Chowdhury attends to similar concerns. But transnational feminists also point to the limits of self-reflexivity and its risks. In *Transnational Feminism in the United States*, Leela Fernandes observes that "self-reflexivity too often becomes reduced to static conceptions of social locations or unduly elaborate representations of the researcher/writer's own self in relation to the subjects of study" (128). As an alternative to mechanistic acts of self-reflexivity, Fernandes turns to Donna Haraway's notion of the "feminist writer as a 'modest witness' who observes, participates in, and shapes the world she writes about" (128). According to Haraway, "Critical reflexivity, or strong objectivity, does not dodge the world-making practices of forging knowledges with different chances of life and death built into them" (qtd. in Fernandes 129).

In the "Faces of the Hope" report, Chung's ethos as a compassionate cosmopolitan emerges as a response to her construal of Bina as a victim turned humanitarian subject. In other words, Chung's ethos emerges as a byproduct of the incorporation of Bina's struggle into the normative structures of liberal-humanist internationalism. In contrast to Naripokkho's construal of Bina as the ungrateful and disloyal global sister, Bina's ethos as a survivor-activist within the context of Chowdhury's study resides in her pragmatic response to and contextual negotiation of shifting material realities and personal desires. Indeed, Bina's diverse encounters with development structures serve as a counterpoint to scholarly critiques of development as an all-encompassing megarhetoric. Bina's ethos emerges as an analytic, as praxis, as she strategically negotiates social norms and institutional expectations. Finally, Chowdhury claims an ethos similar to that of the "modest witness" that Haraway describes. Chowdhury attempts to establish narrative reliability through reflexive commentary, yet she is also clearly invested in women's struggle for justice and sees her research as a form of transnational feminist advocacy. In the next section, I expand on the concept of transnational feminist ethos as a mode of inquiry committed to the formation of transnational publics primed for both ethical deliberation and political action.

Transnational Feminist Ethos

> Just before we headed for Bangladesh, we learned that Bina was coming to America. An organization called Healing the Children had arranged for Shriner's Hospital in Cincinnati to donate surgery for two acid survivors. We timed our trip to arrive in Dhaka a few days before she flew to Cincinnati—and then we flew back with her to America. As we got on the plane to come to America, she was grinning ear-to-ear. She knew this was a once-in-a-lifetime chance—her only hope for a normal life. She would be treated by the best surgeons in America. Could they give her back what she had lost? (Connie Chung)

Chung's reflection on her "discovery" of the extent of the problem of acid violence in Bangladesh might seem a qualifying instance of an "ethical self." But Chung is not engaged in a critique of normative frameworks; rather Chung repeats the dominant rescue narrative in her description of normalcy as a gift bestowed by American medicine. There is a reflexive moment later in the report, however, which is triggered by one of the few plastic surgeons in Bangladesh. In response to Chung's enthusiasm for increased philanthropy to support the movement of burned victims from Bangladesh to Europe and America for medical treatment, the surgeon Dr. Samanta Lal Sen replies:

> We cannot send all the girls to Spain, America, Australia or Italy. We must do the treatment here in Bangladesh. . . . And we have got the skill. If we get the facilities, we will be able to do this surgery here. We must stand on our own feet.

That Chung includes this "correction" in her report is perhaps an indication of critical reflexivity, a process that Royster and Kirsch argue can mitigate the risks of "overidentification and romanticization" (78). Yet "Faces of Hope" illustrates that practicing certain modes of inquiry will not guarantee the comprehensive mitigation of *what is not known*. Nancy Tuana argues, and I concur, "far from being a simple lack of knowledge that good science aims to banish, [ignorance] is better understood as a practice with supporting social causes as complex as those involved in knowledge practices" (195). Chung precisely does not question the supporting social causes that enable "not-yet-knowing" (Holiday 403), nor does she interrogate the oppressive practices that work "through and [are] shadowed by ignorance" (Tuana 195).

To posit ethos in epistemological terms as a mode of inquiry is not to forestall ethical deliberation about "what is" and "what should be." Transnational feminist methods are not limited to the analysis of representational practices but can involve direct action and collaboration between researchers and activists (i.e., Sangtin Writers and Richa Nagar, *Playing with Fire*). In *Transnationalism Reversed*, however, Chowdhury presents transnational feminist praxis largely in methodological terms. She engages the ethical in terms of the "politics of fieldwork" (Fernandes 127). She is explicit about the need for transnational feminist ethnographers to be accountable to the communities with which they are engaged. Chowdhury's ethos as an ethnographer emerges as dynamic and relational. Chowdhury discloses her multifaceted relationship to Bina Akhter, for example, as well as how certain stakeholders capitalized on her long-term relationship to Bina to advance their own narratives. She explains,

> I was at once an insider to Bina's circle of friends from Bangladesh, and therefore a witness to the trajectory of her arrival in the United States, and at the same time an outsider to her newer circle of American patrons, to whom I was a "native informant" from which to seek affirmation for their progress narrative. (11)

In her attention to how she and her subjects navigate the "script[s] of global feminism and local contingencies" (17), Chowdhury illustrates how women activists and researchers together "shape the dynamic terrain of transnationalism" (4).

Like Margaret E. Keck and Kathryn Sikkink's award-winning study *Activist beyond Borders*, Chowdhury's attention to the communication infrastructure of transnational advocacy unsettles commonplace assumptions about collective rhetorical action by explicating advocacy's multidirectionality. Chowdhury elucidates the "paradoxical moments" that define transnational feminist praxis (14) and "contradictory consequence[s] of global women's organizing efforts, whereby new kinds of hierarchies emerge" (176). The NGO boom in Bangladesh, for instance, has largely benefited middle-class women, because NGOs create jobs for development professionals (130); consequently, poor women are further marginalized (174). *Transnationalism Reversed* demonstrates how NGOs reproduce local power structures and how transnational nongovernmental advocacy groups' reliance on donor-driven mechanisms engenders codepdent relations and competition among groups (142). In Bangladesh, these "contradictory consequences" are symptomatic of increasing socioeconomic disenfranchisement and part of a larger phenomenon known as the "silent revolution," namely the disruption of existing social structures and male-dominated public spheres as more women become integrated into the economy and labor force (25).

Transnationalism Reversed illustrates the "unexpected even unlikely alliances and trajectories that transnational feminist projects may engender" (21) and the contradictory and shifting ways in which collaborations take shape, and, in this way, inadvertently responds to Royster and Kirsch's call to "renegotiat[e] . . . the paradigms by which we account for rhetoric as a dynamic phenomenon" (132). Similarly, transnational feminist media scholars have argued for the potential of moments of "transnational incommensurability" as a "potent critical nexus" from which feminism may reconstitute itself (Imre, Marciniak, and O'Healy 386–7). These incommensurabilities push beyond the Hegelian (self-other) dialectic of recognition that haunts human rights politics and representations of gendered violence. *Transnationalism Reversed* teaches us that transnational feminist methods and practices "cannot be assumed a priori but [are] always contingent" and "shaped by . . . specific historical and institutional realities" (9). The same might be said about ethos as a mode of inquiry. It too is contingent. Chowdhury animates these contingencies in her resistance of "analytical closure" (10) and through her deliberate "multiaxial analysis of diverse women's positionalities and realities" (178).

Transnational feminist perspectives challenge narrow configurations of ethos as an individual attribute (moral character) or audience-conferred recognition (credibility). Such attributes and recognitions certainly have an effect on diverse rhetorical situations, but the ethos of transnational feminist praxis and research, as *Transnationalism Reversed* illustrates, is not rooted in an individual's moral development or in the promise of consensus. The ethos of transnational feminist methods, which includes recognition of the historical and cultural production of ethical principles, sets the stage for more informed ethical deliberations. Fernandes puts it well: "Ethical action is not a self-evident or innocent realm" (130). Instead of deference to individualist liberal notions of ethos as an acquisition or universalized model of community ethos ("global sisterhood"), transnational feminist analytics (relational, comparative, and historical) engender ethos, like rights, as a site of struggle.

Note

1. For an excellent overview of transnational feminist methods see Fernandes. Among the most prominent scholars working in the area of transnational feminist studies (including those who navigate intersections among postcolonial and transnational feminisms) are: Alexander; Alvarez; Basu; Chowdhury; Dutt; Grewal; Grewal and Kaplan; Hesford and Kozol; Hua; Keck and Sikkink; Marciniak, Imre, and O'Healey; Merry; Mohanty; Naples; Ong; Shohat; Spivak; Swarr and Nagar. Scholars in rhetorical studies engaged in transnational feminist projects include Dingo; Hesford; Lyon; Queen; Schell; Wingard; among others.

Works Cited

Alexander, M. Jacqui. *Pedagogies of Crossing: Meditations on Feminism, Sexual Politics, Memory, and the Sacred.* Durham, NC: Duke UP, 2005. Print.

Alvarez, Sonia E. "Translating the Global: Effects of Transnational Organizing on Local Feminist Discourses and Practices in Latin America." *Meridians* 1.1 (2000): 29–67. Print.

Basu. Amrita. "Globalization of the Local/Localization of the Global: Mapping Transnational Women's Movements." *Meridians* 1.1 (2000): 68–84. Print.

Chowdhury, Elora Halim. *Transnationalism Reversed: Women Organizing against Gendered Violence in Bangladesh.* Albany: State U of New York P, 2011. Print.

———. "Locating Global Feminisms Elsewhere, Braiding US Women of Color and Transnational Feminisms." *Cultural Dynamics* 21.1 (2009): 51–78.

Chung, Connie. "Faces of Hope." *ABC News Internet Venues.* 1 Nov. 1999. Web. 30 April 2013. <http://www.pandys.org/escapinghades/acidvictims.html>.

Dingo, Rebecca. *Networking Arguments: Rhetoric, Transnational Feminism, and Public Policy.* Pittsburgh: U of Pittsburgh P, 2012. Print.

Dutt, Mallika. "Reclaiming a Human Rights Culture: Feminisms of Difference and Alliance." *Talking Visions: Multicultural Feminism in a Transnational Age.* Ed. Ella Shohat. 225–46. New York: New Museum of Contemporary Art, 1998. Print.

Fernandes, Leela. *Transnational Feminism in the United States: Knowledge, Ethics, Power.* New York: New York UP, 2013. Print.

Friedman, Elizabeth. "The Effects of 'Transnationalism Reversed' in Venezuela: Assessing the Impact of UN Global Conferences on the Women's Movement." *International Feminist Journal of Politics* 1 (1999): 357–81.

Grewal, Inderpal. *Transnational America: Feminisms, Diasporas, Neoliberalisms.* Durham, NC: Duke UP, 2005. Print.

Grewal, Inderpal, and Caren Kaplan. *Scattered Hegemonies: Postmodernity and Transnational Feminist Practices.* Minneapolis: U of Minnesota P, 1994. Print.

Hesford, Wendy. *Spectacular Rhetorics: Human Rights Visions, Recognitions, Feminisms*. Durham, NC: Duke UP, 2011. Print.

Hesford, Wendy S., and Wendy Kozol. *Just Advocacy? Women's Human Rights, Transnational Feminisms, and the Politics of Representation*. New Brunswick, NJ: Rutgers UP, 2005. Print.

Holiday, Judy. "In[ter]vention: Locating Rhetoric's *Ethos*." *Rhetoric Review* 28.4 (2009): 388–405. Print.

Hua, Julietta. *Trafficking Women's Human Rights*. Minneapolis: U of Minnesota P, 2011. Print.

Hyde, Michael J. "Rhetorically, We Dwell." *The Ethos of Rhetoric*. Ed. Michael J. Hyde. Columbia: U of South Carolina P, 2004. xiii–xxviii. Print.

Imre, Anikó, Katarzyna Marciniak, and Áine O'Healy. "Transcultural Mediations and Transnational Politics of Difference." Special issue of *Feminist Media Studies* 9.4 (2009): 385–90.

Keck, Margaret E., and Kathryn Sikkink. *Activists beyond Borders: Advocacy Networks in International Politics*. Ithaca, NY: Cornell UP, 1998. Print.

Lyon, Arabella. *Deliberative Acts: Democracy, Rhetoric, and Rights*. University Park: Pennsylvania State UP, 2013. Print.

Marciniak, Katarzyna, Anikó Imre, and Áine O'Healy, eds. *Transnational Feminisms in Film and Media*. New York: Palgrave, 2007. Print.

Merry, Sally Engle. *Human Rights and Gender Violence: Translating International Law into Local Justice*. Chicago: U of Chicago P, 2006. Print.

Mohanty, Chandra. *Feminism without Borders: Decolonizing Theory, Practicing Solidarity*. Durham, NC: Duke UP. 2003, Print.

Morgan, Robin. *Sisterhood Is Global*. Garden City, NY: Anchor/Doubleday, 1984. Print.

Mutua, Makau. "Savage, Victims, and Saviors: The Metaphor of Human Rights." *Harvard International Law Journal* 42 (2001): 201–45. Print.

Naples, Nancy. "Changing the Terms." *Women's Activism and Globalization: Linking Local Struggles and Transnational Politics*. Ed. N. A. Naples and M. Desai. New York: Routledge, 2002. 3–14. Print.

Omizo, Ryan. "Facing Vernacular Video." Diss. Ohio State U, 2012.

Ong, Aihwa. *Flexible Citizenship: The Cultural Logics of Transnationality*. Durham, NC: Duke UP, 1999. Print.

Queen, Mary. "Transnational Feminist Rhetorics in a Digital World." *College English* 70.5 (2008): 471–89.

Royster, Jacqueline Jones, and Gesa Kirsch. *Feminist Rhetorical Practices: New Horizons for Rhetoric, Composition, and Literacy Studies*. Carbondale: Southern Illinois UP, 2012. Print.

Sangtin Writers Collective and Richa Nagar. *Playing with Fire: Feminist Thought and Activism through Seven Lives in India*. Minneapolis: U of Minnesota P, 2006. Print.

Schell, Eileen "Gender, Rhetorics, and Globalization: Rethinking the Spaces and Locations of Women's Rhetorics in Our Field." *Teaching Rhetorica: Theory, Pedagogy, Practice*. Ed. Kate Ronald and Joy Ritchie. Portsmouth, NH: Boynton Cook, 2006. 160–74. Print.

Shohat, Ella. *Taboo Memories, Diasporic Voices*. Durham, NC: Duke UP, 2006. Print.

Spivak, Gayatri Chakravorty. "Can the Subaltern Speak." *Colonial Discourse and Post-Colonial Theory. A Reader*. Ed. Patrick Williams and Laura Chrisman. Hertfordshire: Harvester Wheatsheaf, 1994. Print.

——. "Righting Wrongs." *Human Rights, Human Wrongs: The Oxford Amnesty Lectures, 2001*. Ed. Nicholas Owen. Oxford: Oxford UP, 2003. 164–227. Print.

Swarr, Amanda Lock, and Richa Nagar, eds. *Critical Transnational Feminist Praxis*. Albany: State U of New York P, 2010. Print.

Tuana, Nancy. "Coming to Understand: Orgasm and the Epistemology of Ignorance." *Hypatia* 19.1 (2004): 194–232. Print.

Wingard, Jennifer. *Branded Bodies, Rhetoric, and the Neoliberal Nation-State*. Lanham, MD: Lexington, 2012. Print.

10. Working With and Working For

Ethos and Power in Women's Writing

Risa Applegarth

I told her that I had never agreed to work FOR *her, that I was willing to collaborate when her material supplemented mine, but that my sand-paintings were mine and not hers. I also said that I was all through doing anything* FOR *or* WITH *her on any Indian work whatever—that she could publish hers and I would publish mine as I saw fit. (Frances Newcomb to Gladys Reichard, 7 November 1938)*

Anyone who has written collaboratively can relate to the distinction that amateur researcher Frances (Franc) Newcomb draws between working *for* someone and working *with* someone. Writers who understand their shared work as an intellectual partnership understandably bristle at the suggestion they are subordinate gatherers of data rather than contributors of expertise, and in this 1938 letter to her friend, professional anthropologist Gladys Reichard, Newcomb relates her sense of injury at having been treated as an employee by a person she viewed as a collaborator. Newcomb's possessive pronouns—*her* material, *my* sand paintings were *mine* and not *hers*—further emphasize the stakes of such delicate negotiations: Who ultimately will see her name on the spine of a book? Whose publications will garner payment and citation? Whose claims to intellectual property will be granted? The intricate negotiations that attend collaborative writing, this chapter argues, underscore and make visible the situated and power-saturated nature of ethos.

I investigate an imbalanced, inequitable collaboration: not the one that Newcomb complained about in her 1938 letter to Reichard, but instead a collaboration *between* Newcomb and Reichard that was structured by both parties' social and spatial positions and shaped by their complex rhetorical negotiations. Examining correspondence between Newcomb and Reichard during and after their collaborative publication of an expensive, richly illustrated volume of Navajo sand paintings in 1937, I employ contemporary theories of ethos to analyze the messy relations of power that shape how this collaboration unfolds, as each woman seeks to garner and stabilize a persuasive public ethos and to translate collaborative activity into material and symbolic rewards.

Newcomb, an amateur researcher who developed her expertise and reputation through informal practice rather than formal training, was particularly attentive to collaborative negotiations, as she worked to establish her identity as a researcher and to translate her experiences into material and intellectual opportunities. Reichard, a professional anthropologist who held a teaching position at Barnard College, who had trained with Franz Boas and maintained connections to a powerful network through her affiliation with Columbia University, entered into a collaborative partnership with Newcomb because of the expertise Newcomb had developed as a collector of Navajo sand paintings. The relatively straightforward social positions reflected in these characterizations—amateur vs. professional, informal vs. formal training, unpaid vs. paid research activity—are complicated by both writers' *spatial* positions. In particular, Newcomb's geographical location in the Southwest was both an asset and a liability in this partnership. They each conducted research among the Navajo[1] in relatively adjacent territory in New Mexico and Arizona; Newcomb lived and worked at the town of Newcomb, New Mexico, where her husband ran a trading post, some sixty miles north of Gallup, while Reichard conducted her research in an area south of Ganado, Arizona, about sixty miles west of Gallup. Reichard, however, had a teaching position that kept her for most of the year in New York, while Newcomb largely lacked access to the centers of intellectual power and the informal publication networks that Reichard experienced through her professional affiliations with Boas and Elsie Clews Parsons.

Despite these initial differences, their shared object of study, Navajo religious ritual and its reflection in sand paintings, made a collaboration seem mutually advantageous. Sand paintings are ephemeral works of ceremonial art, part of an intricate system of religious ritual among the Navajo. Within the context of a "chant" or "sing," a healer or chanter creates sand paintings as a component of a community-wide ceremonial event that might last from one to nine days. This event is performed on behalf of the health and blessing of a particular individual, the "one-sung-over," but is experienced by a broader audience of community members who participate in the sing, as well as by the chanter and his assistant, who prepares many of the materials used during the ceremonies (Newcomb and Reichard 2). Over the course of a sing, a healer uses colored sand to compose an image on the floor of a hogan; the ceremonial creation of the image is itself performative and deeply inflected with meaning, and the image, once created, is erased through subsequent activity; indeed, a longstanding prohibition against allowing sand paintings to be reproduced in more permanent form was being debated among healers and other community members during these decades in the early twentieth century. Specific sequences of images are affiliated with each chant, and healers select from this sequence as they compose sand paintings during the sing. Certain chants are rarely performed, others are performed more routinely, and the duration and timing of any chant varies considerably, as these events emerge in relation to the needs of specific individuals for healing and blessing rather than in accordance with a yearly ritual calendar.[2]

Their artistic as well as religious dimensions made sand paintings powerfully appealing to artists, anthropologists, and collectors in the early twentieth century, even as this highly ephemeral, variable, and context-specific event posed challenges for anthropologists, like Reichard, who wanted to gain access to these forms of art and ritual for anthropological study. In particular, the ephemeral and contextual quality of sand paintings made Newcomb's year-round presence in the Southwest valuable, as did the techniques Newcomb developed for recording these works of art. As a white woman who was known within her neighboring Navajo community as a collector, Newcomb was often invited to rituals, where she would observe the colors, patterns, and practices used to construct each sand painting. Immediately after the ceremony, she would sketch the painting from memory and would then consult with the healer who created the painting to correct errors or gaps in the sketch. She subsequently produced precise, full-color illustrations as reproductions of the ceremonial paintings. The expense of traveling to sings and procuring paints and paper for her full-color reproductions made Newcomb's technique costly as well as time-consuming, but her participation and process helped her establish a reputation for accuracy among the healers and other members of the Navajo community in her area. Newcomb's combination of technical expertise, longstanding habitation in a particular location, and well-regarded reputation granting her access to privileged cultural information proved significant assets in her collaboration with Reichard as Newcomb worked to convert these resources into a persuasive and durable ethos.

Feminist scholars have understood ethos as a crucial mechanism by which women who have historically lacked access to more privileged forms of argumentation nevertheless influence public life. As the editors of this collection outline in the introduction, ethos is a fundamentally *located*, *situated*, and *social* act. Understood in this way, ethos "requires attention to the mediation and negotiation that goes on in the spaces between writers and their location" (Reynolds 333). That is, viewing ethos as ecological—created in negotiations among writers, audiences, and material and symbolic environments—demands precise attention to the intricate relations of power that characterize human communication, as the case below demonstrates. Attending to rhetors' negotiations with (sometimes hostile) audiences, (often limiting) social norms and scripts, and (frequently devalued forms of gendered, raced, and classed) embodiment reminds us forcefully that a rhetor is never fully in control of her ethos construction.

This chapter builds from these insights to examine how relations of power are negotiated during collaboration, constructed within a coauthored text, and compounded beyond the initial collaboration. The textual negotiations between Newcomb and Reichard illustrate how differentially located researchers deploy their rhetorical ingenuity to establish their claims to authority, status, and expertise, yet this case also reveals that the relations of power that inflect these negotiations persist and accumulate, influencing writers' future opportunities for garnering symbolic and material rewards as a result of their rhetorical performances. This study ultimately underscores the high stakes that attend ethos negotiations and the power-saturated nature of ethos as a textual accomplishment.

Collaboration in the Context of Professional Anthropology

Historical and sociological studies of science have firmly established the significant role played by knowledge networks, resource sharing, and other collaborative activities in the knowledge-making practices of scientific and social scientific disciplines.[3] Anthropology, in particular, through its emphasis on participant observation in ethnographic fieldwork, has long been understood as a fundamentally collaborative endeavor, requiring myriad participants to accomplish its feats of knowledge making.[4] Among women participants in early professional anthropology, collaboration took a number of forms, ranging from mutually supportive to deeply exploitative relationships. Collaborative relationships among peers—such as Ruth Benedict and Margaret Mead's well-known intellectual and personal partnership—were sometimes long-lasting and mutually sustaining. More broadly, many women in professional anthropology in the early twentieth century provided financial and intellectual support to one another and engaged in practices of community formation that created a network of recruitment and support.[5]

In contrast to these horizontal relationships, professional women also—like their male counterparts—established hierarchical relations with the many Native and non-Native informants, interpreters, traders, and collectors with whom they worked. These relationships created what Bernard Fontana called the "quadripartite" structure of anthropological collaboration in the early twentieth century, typically "comprised of an Indian (the informant), a wealthy dilettante (usually an Easterner), an academic advisor (normally someone from the East with doctoral or professorial status), and a data-gathering go-between (trader, Indian Service employee, or missionary)" (567). Anthropologists' relationships with Native communities have been critically examined in scholarship that underscores not only anthropologists' intellectual and material exploitation but also the active and creative work of Native researchers.[6] Ethos scholars might notice the clear imbalances of power that characterize relations among all four of these positions, the differential status of terms such as "dilettante," "informant," "professor," and "trader" and the unbalanced relationship scripted by pairing "professor" with "informant," for instance. To reshape these familiar relationships requires one to shift identifications—to move, for instance, from the status of "informant" to that of "anthropologist," or from "data-gatherer" to "researcher." These familiar and imbalanced relations thus shape the ethos maneuvers of participants, who are engaged in a rhetorical wrangle to garner position relative to other participants.

Negotiating Ethos: Expertise, Authority, and Intellectual Status

Amateur researcher Franc Newcomb's correspondence with professional anthropologist Gladys Reichard—over the course of a collaboration that both writers initially viewed as mutually beneficial—underscores the negotiated nature of Newcomb's ethos and the high stakes that attend that negotiation. I contend that Newcomb's letters show her shifting between assertions of independence and markers of subordination as she seeks to negotiate a persuasive ethos in relation to a collaborator whose academic and geographic location—as a professor of anthropology at Barnard College in New York— marks their statuses as unequal.

At many moments in their correspondence, Newcomb casts herself in the role of subordinate, assuming the division of labor that typically inhered between "academic advisors" and "data-gathering go-betweens" that Fontana describes. For instance, Newcomb often seeks Reichard's approval for work she has submitted or apologizes for her slowness in sending Reichard drawings or responses to research questions. Newcomb reports, for example, that the "first two sketches . . . have been forwarded to you from the store. I guess that you thought that I was never going to get them finished," and repeats that she "hop[es] that the sketches arrive in good condition and are satisfactory" (5 April 1932). In another letter, Newcomb apologizes for having

> been very slow at getting this done, but first we were trying to get
> the water chant for Mary [Wheelwright] . . . and then I was all in a
> mess moving to Albuquerque, then I had the flu for ten days and so it
> seemed to be one thing right after another. (n.d.)

Newcomb seeks Reichard's guidance to ensure that Reichard will find her work satisfactory, as when she offers to "continue with wind [the Wind Chant] until that is cleaned up, unless you want me to change" (n.d.), or asks, "Do you want me to draw them in order—or do you want one snake picture—and then skip to the next 'teaching' and get a Thunder-bird sketch" (22 January 1932). These moments reveal Newcomb ceding to Reichard the authority to determine the timing and direction of her work.

Newcomb's positioning as Reichard's subordinate is especially clear when Newcomb explicitly compares herself with Reichard or acknowledges the status differential between them. For instance, early in their relationship, Newcomb expresses astonishment at Reichard's productivity, writing, "And so you are writing on South Sea Island Art—too!! How do you do it?? You make me feel quite like a flat tire with the little that I do!!" (22 January 1932). Newcomb pursued research into Navajo sand painting despite lacking the resources available to a professor affiliated with a powerful institution like Columbia. Even though she was responsible for the care of her children and worked significant hours at the trading post she ran with her husband, her research productivity despite these material disadvantages indicates her determination. Later, Newcomb writes again, "I can't tell you how glad I am to have the privilege of knowing you—and with what pride I say—'my friend Gladys R'" (28 September 1932). Such comments cast their relationship within a script that represents an amateur researcher as the grateful recipient of attention from a legitimate, institutionally sanctioned scholar—reinforcing rather than questioning the differential value accorded to these statuses.

Newcomb's attention to material dimensions of her partnership with Reichard both solidifies and complicates Newcomb's positioning as a subordinate.[7] On one hand, Newcomb's (sometimes implicit) requests for payment from Reichard suggest a subordinate status, in line with the relationships Fontana outlines, in which a *real* researcher employs a *paid* data gatherer. Paying someone for data involves a transfer of ownership and a clear demarcation of responsibilities that renders such relationships quite different from intellectual partnership. In one letter that reports on a recent research excursion, for instance, Newcomb recounts,

> *I was certainly glad to get these sketches, even if it did cost me the price of a woman who stayed with the children while I was at the Post. Also my time for six days, groceries for the Sing, a dollar each day for the medicine man, besides about a dollar and a half each day spent for cigarettes for the painters. Then the afternoon that he was at the house I gave him $3.00 and the interpreter $2.00. If I count in the expense of running the car it brings the total up to more than I can afford. So I hope there are not any more until I get back to living on the Reservation. (5 April 1932)*

Although the letter contains no explicit request for compensation, Newcomb's "hope" at the end of this account—that Reichard will request sketches of no other ceremonies until Newcomb is in a better (geographic *and* financial) position to collect them—reinforces her implicit request for repayment. Indeed, Reichard responds to this implicit request, for Newcomb's next letter thanks Reichard for her "promptness in sending the check," noting that Newcomb's daughter Lynette "has so many extra graduation expenses" (15 April 1932). Including details of her *need* for money further identifies Newcomb as a paid data gatherer rather than an independent researcher, for it offers financial exigency as a motive for Newcomb's work, as when she asks Reichard to check whether Reichard's colleague, Dr. Bush, has received some sand paintings Newcomb sent to him. She writes,

> *If they are there I will send him another "statement"—because I need*
> *the money—My brother has had a nervous breakdown and right*
> *in the midst of frantic collecting—I have to stop and take him to a*
> *sanatorium in Calif[ornia]—so every penny has to do the work of*
> *two just now. (28 September 1932)*

Newcomb complains at another point that "funds seem to vanish into thin air" (n.d.). Such requests activate a script of financially motivated data collection, casting Newcomb, again, as a needy recipient of the resources that Reichard—located more advantageously through her institutional affiliation—is able to provide.

At other moments, however, Newcomb's discussions of payment shift this relationship, instead affirming her status as a professional who merits compensation for her skills and expertise. In response to a check from Reichard that is "$10 above par," Newcomb explains that this extra payment will "apply on [Reichard's] next two" sand painting reproductions (15 April 1932). Although she has mentioned her financial struggles to Reichard, Newcomb here reestablishes that their relationship is not one of charity, but rather a matter of straightforward accounting. Newcomb further asserts her professional status by explaining that she has "adopted a standard rate for orders that include sets or graphs. $25.00 each—with description and section of the myth that explains the sketch. $20.00 without any explanation" (15 April 1932). In this way, her discussion of finances inserts her relationship with Reichard into a different cultural script, one that reasserts her standing as a researcher who merits compensation for her expertise. Such assertions attempt to reidentify Newcomb as an expert, one with the power to set a price on her special, skillful services.

Newcomb's efforts to secure publication for her research further shift the ethos she negotiates relative to Reichard. Newcomb seeks Reichard's advice on her attempts to publish—positioning herself as a learner rather than an accomplished scholar—yet also demonstrates her familiarity with the terms of value in academic communities by pursuing publication that would solidify her status and, potentially, secure further rewards among academic networks. For instance, Newcomb thanks Reichard for returning a manuscript to her with "helpful criticism" (14 November 1935) and goes on to say—in the resigned tone of a student to a mentor:

> *Yes I know that I do have a bad habit of using the word clan for family*
> *or kind of folks I am speaking about. I suppose the thing will come*
> *back [from an editor] all full of notes for changes. (14 November 1935)*

She reports on another manuscript's rejection with similar resignation, writing:

> *My article that I sent to the National Geographic was returned—*
> *without thanks—with the advice to send it to the Bureau of Eth-*
> *nology—ahem!! Guess I am simply a* <u>dud</u> *on the writing end of*
> *it—because I know the pictures were O.K. Oh! Well!! I am having the*
> *fun of collecting even though I never get any "fame" for so doing. (10*
> *November 1932)*

Such moments when Newcomb appears to embrace "collecting" itself as sufficient compensation remain in tension with instances when Newcomb overtly attempts to establish an ethos as an independent researcher. In other letters, Newcomb outlines her plans for publications, saying, for example, that she wants to start on a book to include "some very clever folklore . . . some that I know has never been published" (n.d.). She also discusses her interest in securing future publication rights through copyrighting her reproductions of sand paintings, noting that she "might be wise to get a few copyrights—Not that I was not willing to have it published but others might get the same idea, and there wouldn't be a thing I could do about it" (n.d.). In contrast to moments when Newcomb scripts herself as a subordinate, student, or amateur data collector, in many other letters she casts herself as an independent researcher, one who bears her own expertise, who approaches her work with intellectual curiosity and responsibility, and who has authority to judge the quality of others' research. In these ways, Newcomb shifts her status relative to Reichard, negotiating an ethos textually that complicates the relation of subordination she sometimes assumes.

Newcomb's claims to expertise are made repeatedly in letters in which she relates anthropological information to Reichard under the mantle of her own authority. She frequently explains ceremonial information to Reichard and offers her interpretations of texts and images. She asserts, for instance, that

> *one can always tell whether a medicine man is beyond the oth-*
> *ers or not. There is only one way of getting these ceremonies and*
> *sand-paintings and that is—one medicine-man at a time—No two*
> *even though they sing the same chant, have the same medicines or*
> *the same type of changes, in their pictures. (8 April [no year])*

She writes with confidence about her own interpretive choices, not as a writer seeking guidance but as a researcher who has worked out an intellectual problem to her own satisfaction, as when she explains to Reichard that other

medicine men . . . may have a slightly different version as no two
sections paint their pictures just the same, but I think that the differ-
ences will not be so great but that a few notes will cover it. That is the
way I have been doing when I find that there are two opinions about
the details of a picture. (5 April 1932)

She speaks often with a ready authority, explaining, for example, that "There
are two varieties of that particular picture—one with humps on their backs
and striped masks—the other with straight figures—brown masks with buffalo horns at the sides" (28 September 1932). She unapologetically points out
when Reichard's own explanations have been unclear, as when she writes,

You did not tell how their heads pointed—that picture can be made
with a center and the heads pointing each direction or it can be
made with all heads to the east, which gives the snake people length
adding power*—I have it both ways—I think yours must be this last.*
(10 November 1932)

She even at times contests Reichard's interpretations of ceremonial images;
for instance, she claims, "Well! I have just re-read your letter and that is not a
buffalo painting at all. How strange!!! It is one that our Nahtoie chanters use
on the last day some times" (28 September 1932). Her underlining suggests
emphatic confidence, and brooks no disagreement with her assessment of the
image Reichard has sent her. These textual markers position Reichard and
Newcomb within a different cultural script—that of colleagues consulting
with each other, sharing status through their shared engagement with the
intellectual problems that employ their expertise.

Newcomb also positions herself as someone compelled to research by her
own intellectual curiosity—rather than an informant who is merely gathering
data for pay. She conveys her excitement about research repeatedly, as when
she describes the sand paintings she is working on as "simply gorgeous" and
predicts that she is "going to work my fingers off getting them on to the paper—Two were so different that I nearly passed out with joy" (28 September
1932). She conveys a similar enthusiasm for varieties of sand painting that
appear to deviate in significant (if subtle) ways from the forms with which
she is already familiar, explaining, for example, that although she "already
had 41 sketches" of paintings from a particular series of chant, she has just
encountered "an older type—a whacker!!—when the corn was painted with
twelve ears instead of two" (22 January 1932). Even when she is engaging in

work at Reichard's behest, she represents herself as someone who relishes an intellectual puzzle, as when she explains confidently that she

> *shall work them all out eventually. Wherever the arrangement is*
> *obscure, I shall have a conference of my four Nahtoie-medicine-men*
> *friends and get each point settled as we go along—and wherever there*
> *are two interpretations, I shall make them both ways—so that between*
> *us we can get some idea of the old and the new!! (22 January 1932)*[8]

In these instances, Newcomb shifts the ground through which she negotiates her ethos, positioning herself as "busy and happy," glad to be doing "the thing I enjoy" (18 October 1937).

In these and other passages, Newcomb accomplishes this shift not only by conveying enthusiasm for her work, but also by highlighting her intellectual investment in the research questions and interpretive possibilities that her sand painting work opens up. For instance, she describes her work on a particular sketch as "the most 'artistic' yet," and remarks that certain sketches she is making for Reichard are "a little different than the ones I have—just enough to make it interesting sketching them" (15 April 1932). Newcomb elaborates on the detailed differences among paintings in the current series, and muses that she is "wondering just what the significance of that change may be—and in the next one, the heads point in different directions—and there must be a reason for that" (15 April 1932). She speculates further that the distinct quality of this painting "gives a new slant to snake power in sand paintings" (15 April 1932). In another instance, Newcomb shifts quickly from expressing her enthusiasm to conveying quite strongly her *intellectual* involvement in the research she is undertaking, declaring:

> *Yes! Indeed I will be very glad to do a series of sketches for the U.—*
> *and I do hope there is somewhere in existence—old manuscript*
> *describing ceremonies and sand-paintings by medicine men when*
> *the Catholics first came to St. Michaels—I am so anxious to know*
> *what the general trend is—if they are elaborating—simplifying—or*
> *combining. And as no one has ever made a real study of it I have no*
> *material upon which to work! Excepting Mathews and Stevenson.*
> *(22 January 1932)*

Newcomb here positions herself clearly in the role of an academic—not a gatherer of data for others' use, nor a student seeking mentorship, but a scholar who is "anxious to know what the general trend is" over time, and both frustrated and excited by the significant gaps that persist in prior academic work.

Newcomb also asserts an intellectual partnership with Reichard by identifying herself as a scholar whose primary responsibility is toward the production of knowledge. She writes of the necessity of being prepared to participate in an unusual upcoming chant, determined not "to miss a trick anywhere—we may never see it again" (18 October 1937). She positions herself as extremely conscientious about accuracy, writing, for example, that she is "anxious to go over to the other side of the reservation this summer . . . to see Hosteen Ghonnie," because although she has "finished [reproducing] his paintings as good as I can," enough time has elapsed that is has been "too long a period to trust my memory for every-thing. So I want him to check them over and see what I have left out" (8 April [no year]). In other passages she expresses her dedication to sand painting research despite domestic responsibilities, social obligations, and even the physical strains of "spending all my time sitting at the table 'drawing.' Three hours a day is my schedule and that does not hurt my eyes or my 'blood-pressure'" (15 April 1932). Such expressions of responsibility toward her *work*—rather than toward Reichard as a financial or intellectual patron—cast Newcomb according to a different cultural script, one in which the researcher pursues her object of study so carefully and so obsessively that she forgets to attend to her own health.

Newcomb further positions herself as an authority relative to established, published scholars. About Father Berard Haile, an early anthropologist who wrote about Navajo religion, Newcomb writes,

> *Fr. Berard certainly did mix up his characters most remarkably. If he knew what I think of his myths he probably wouldn't care for me either. I never had such a headache as when I tried to make sense out of his Anadje Myth—it seems as though he has missed the point of every incident—and I happened to know that tale—and the whys and where-fores—so that it was extremely exasperating to read. (10 November 1932)*

She evaluates Clyde Kluckhohn and Leland Wyman—both well-published and well-respected professionals—with similar severity, writing,

> *I don't think much (not anything at all) of Clyde Kluckhohn as an ethnologist—and not any too much of Wyman. But perhaps that is because I have very little use for the younger medicine-men who will*

mix up anything they happen to see or hear just in order to hold a
ceremony and get the money. (14 November 1936)

This evaluation is not merely personal, but based in her own expertise, from which she generates specific criticisms of their research, writing that

some of those that Kluckhohn lists as separate ceremonies are just
minor sings that may be included in the Nahtoie if certain circum-
stances arise that require it. No medicine man sings all his songs, or
performs all of his ritual at any one ceremony. This makes a great
deal of confusion in getting a cut-and-dried list. (14 November 1936)

She is critical of the published work of amateur researchers as well, finding one popular writer's work so derivative that she "wonder[s] that [the writer] could find a publisher who would take it" (n.d.). Newcomb's ethos, negotiated throughout this correspondence, ultimately shows both flexibility and rhetorical dexterity, as she variously assumes a subordinate position relative to her more powerfully located collaborator and, at other times, contests that subordination through assertions of her own authority, expertise, and intellectual independence.

Reframing Identifications: Ethos in Coauthored Publication

Newcomb's shifting identifications are significantly reframed in the coauthored publication that resulted from their collaboration. Although Reichard and Newcomb share authorship of their 1937 publication, *Sandpaintings of the Navajo Shooting Chant*, and although the title page identifies the book as "by Franc J. Newcomb with text by Gladys A. Reichard," in fact the ethos generated in this text reestablishes a significant imbalance between these coauthors. The shifting roles Newcomb used to position herself throughout their collaboration are smoothed away in the published text, in which Reichard reframes Newcomb's status, diminishing some and emphasizing other identifications. Reichard's role, in her words, "as the writer of the text" provides her with the opportunity to recast their shared ethos in ways that distinctly diminish Newcomb's independence, authority, and intellectual involvement in the research process and that reallocate authority primarily to Reichard.

The imbalance of ethos established in this published text highlights the significance of the concept of *presence* that rhetorical scholar Lisa Shaver has articulated. As Shaver reminds us, it is precisely because "ethos involves a negotiation between a speaker/writer and audience" (66) that presence is a significant dimension of ethos—physical presence in specific sites and spaces, as well as textual presence, as Newcomb's *absence* from a speaking position demonstrates. In the pages of *Sandpaintings of the Navajo Shooting Chant*, Newcomb's textual presence is diminished in several ways. For instance, although the preface carries both authors' names and uses the plural pronoun "we," at no further point is Newcomb included as a speaker; the entirety of the subsequent text positions Reichard as speaker who *refers* to Newcomb. This would not on its own preclude Newcomb from sharing in the ethos established textually, but combined with other textual features, this diminished textual presence has the effect of relegating Newcomb to the role of artist—a significant role, but one less encompassing than Newcomb assumes in her correspondence with Reichard.

Reichard further constrains Newcomb's presence in *Sandpaintings* by supplying terms of identification for Newcomb that undermine her status. When Reichard first introduces Newcomb in the body of the text, she identifies Newcomb as "a trader's wife" (3), establishing the primacy of *that* identification over others that Newcomb has, in her correspondence, asserted for herself. Furthermore, Reichard thanks Newcomb in the opening acknowledgements in ways that cast Newcomb in a distinctly secondary role. Reichard praises her "collaborator and friend" Franc J. Newcomb

> for understanding my needs and placing at my disposal every facility within her power, for her uncomplaining, even uplifting companionship in uncomfortable as well as in unpleasant circumstances, and for her hearty cooperation in making the sandpainting collection and this book possible. (viii)

These terms of praise are primarily personal rather than intellectual, and they are markedly gendered, ultimately mitigating the sense of intellectual partnership that Newcomb's letters strove for.

Reichard further assigns authority to herself through textual choices that highlight her own academic, independent status. For instance, even in thanking Newcomb for her assistance, Reichard assumes a privilege to speak independently that is not granted to Newcomb; in deciding "as the writer of the text . . . to add a personal word of thanks to that which we both feel" (viii), Reichard establishes her priority as primary speaker. Furthermore, although the preface represents the two as coauthors who speak collectively, even this shared textual space makes clear that Reichard has been the recipient of research funds establishing her stature as a scholar. Here the writers thank the Southwest Society for "from time to time . . . [making] it possible for *the writer of the text* to study Navajo ceremony" (vii, emphasis added), and "the Council for Research in the Social Sciences [which] also participated in the work, for much of the material on ceremony was gathered *when she was learning to weave*" (vii, emphasis added). In the body of the text, Reichard speaks individually, something Newcomb never does. Such practices significantly minimize Newcomb's presence and augment Reichard's authority as the actual author of this text.

Reichard's ethos is further augmented through narrative choices that establish her work in relation to an academic tradition and that frame Newcomb's work within Reichard's own research. In the opening chapter, Reichard narrates at length an anthropological tradition of research into Navajo chants and locates her own research in this tradition. She identifies Washington Mathews's 1887 Report of the Bureau of Ethnology as "the first account of a Navajo chant" (1), links his study with subsequent anthropological studies that demonstrate contemporary research interests in Navajo religious expression, and then inserts her research into this academic sequence, explaining that it was "with the intention of discovering the manner in which the Navajo regard their most engrossing activity, religion, that the writer began in 1930 the attempt to master some of the more intricate and less apparent phases of Navajo culture" (1). Outlining the intellectual problems that became clear to her over "seven years" of "studying and interpreting . . . upon every possible occasion" (2) and the chants she witnessed during "the five summers" (2) she spent living with the family of the chanter Miguelito, Reichard establishes clearly both the academic tradition grounding her research and the long fieldwork experience that authorizes her expertise on Navajo religious life.

Subsequent to establishing this tradition for her own research, Reichard writes,

> Some two years after I began my work on ritual I learned that Franc Johnson Newcomb, a trader's wife living at Newcomb . . . had become so interested in Navajo sandpaintings that she was making a collection of them and developing a technique for recording. (3)

In contrast to the academic tradition grounding Reichard's research, she asserts that Newcomb's interest "grew out of an appreciation of art, a natural ability to get along with Indians, and a sense of almost appalling futility at the realization that here was a field untouched by, practically unknown to, artist or scientist" (3). Newcomb, unlike Reichard, is prompted by "only her personal urge" (3). This narrative frames Newcomb's research in time as subsequent to Reichard's and further positions Newcomb's work in relation to a nonacademic tradition, in contrast to Reichard's, which proceeds from academic study. This same narrative also positions Newcomb as a user of Reichard's research, arguing that Reichard's work enabled Newcomb's rather than the other way around. Reichard writes that after she had "put the myth [of the Shooting Chant] into a form which could be read by Whites," Newcomb was able, "armed with [Reichard's translation] which has many descriptions of sandpaintings," to complete her reproductions of the branches and variations of the sand paintings that accompany the Shooting Chant, resulting in this lavishly illustrated book (3).

Ultimately, these textual reallocations of authority cause *Sandpaintings of the Navajo Shooting Chant* to yield greater rewards of ethos for Reichard than for Newcomb. Reichard is figured textually as the writer, an established researcher, and one who merits institutional funding and invests significant resources of time and labor into her intellectual work. Newcomb, in contrast, is figured textually as Reichard's friend, companion, and assistant, a trader's wife; her skill in accurately reproducing sand paintings makes her useful to researchers like Reichard, but her own investments of time, intellect, expertise, and material resources are minimized.

Resisting Collaboration: Marshaling Ethos for Single Authorship

The imbalance of ethos established in Newcomb and Reichard's published text had cumulative consequences, extending into and shaping a future collaboration that Newcomb proposed but Reichard successfully resisted. Instead, Reichard marshaled her greater resources for ethos and transformed this subsequent project into a single-authored publication of her own, forestalling Newcomb's opportunity to garner the publication she hoped for.

The collaborative project Newcomb proposed to Reichard in the late summer of 1938 was initiated by Minnie Harvey Huckel, wealthy daughter of Fred Harvey, whose Fred Harvey Company was influential in cultivating and capitalizing on widespread interest in Southwestern tourism and in Indian arts and crafts in the early twentieth century. Minnie Huckel's husband, John Huckel, amassed a significant collection of reproductions of Navajo sand paintings in the mid-1920s. After her husband's death, Mrs. Huckel sought to arrange for the collection's publication and contacted Franc Newcomb to propose that Newcomb and Reichard should together write the text that would accompany the paintings.

Conveying this proposal to Reichard, Newcomb seems to have assumed Reichard's interest in further collaboration, opening with "Hurray!! and Hurray!! We are going to help with the assembling of material and publishing another Sand-painting book" (n.d.). Newcomb lays out a plan in which Huckel and another collaborator write a preface covering the history of the collection, after which

> comes you, to give it an ethnological standing—as much space as you need—Then comes the myth . . . and the sand-paintings with descriptions. Then I have a chapter on the Symbols of the various paintings, and then there are the notes which you and I will see fit to use for explanation. (n.d.)

Although Newcomb solicits Reichard's suggestions for other ways to organize the publication, she assumes Reichard will share her enthusiasm for a further collaboration.

Although Reichard's direct response to Newcomb's letter is not extant, Newcomb's subsequent letters suggest that Reichard's reaction to the proposal was less enthusiastic than Newcomb anticipated. Newcomb backs almost apologetically away from the outline she proposed, explaining,

> I didn't see any place for me to do anything about the book unless I wrote a little on color symbolism and character of sand-paintings, to be put in the back some place. . . . If you do not think my chapter would add anything of value to the book it could simply be left out— after all it is not my material and all I know about it is from doing some that were similar. (25 October 1938)

Newcomb continues to express intellectual interest in the project—proposing, for instance, that emphasizing the Bead Chant would fill a significant research gap—yet she reassumes a subordinate status, telling Reichard, "You asked just what I wanted you to do about it—in four words—'Take charge of it'—tell me what to do and I will follow on to the best of my ability" (25 October 1938). Newcomb's role diminishes further as she repositions herself not as a collaborator but as a conduit between Reichard and Huckel, charged with the task of inducing Reichard to participate. Newcomb explains that Mrs. Huckel "asked me if I thought you would take charge of the script and I told her that I would write and ask you" (7 November 1938). She attempts to secure Reichard's involvement by assuring her that "this is not going to be difficult material to work with, as so much of it is in good shape to begin with" (7 November 1938). Nevertheless, Newcomb persists in planning a role for herself in this collaboration, describing a timeline that "gives us several months to prepare the script and send it in" (7 November 1938).

Reichard, in contrast, has greater success in converting her prior ethos into further academic and financial rewards. Letters between Reichard, Huckel, and Herman Schweizer, Huckel's agent, attenuate Newcomb's involvement as Reichard "takes charge" of the publication as its sole author. Reichard explicitly stipulates to Huckel and Schweizer that her involvement depends upon Newcomb's *non*involvement. She writes to Huckel that her "one condition" is that she "would not undertake the writing unless I could do all of it" (n.d.), and explains to Schweizer that

> the work will be sufficiently complicated with Mrs. Huckel in Kansas City, and me in New York without having a third author in Albuquerque. I also told her [Newcomb] that I should be glad if you would leave me out entirely and have her do it. She then said she would drop out, urging me to do the writing if Mrs. Huckel agrees to the arrangement. (30 November 1938)

Although Reichard claims that she will "not feel the least bit offended if [Huckel] gets someone else to write the text" (30 November 1938), her letter makes clear her desire to assume authorship. She describes in detail her own outline for the book, insists that she could easily travel to Kansas City to consult with Huckel over the next two months, and enthusiastically recounts a sing she has just returned from

> which was the form you have in your paintings and record, the most complete form of the Shooting Chant. The paintings were the most beautiful I have ever seen, and I secured understanding of them and the Chant which I had never had before. (30 November 1938)

Through these negotiations, Reichard not only secures sole authorship of a publication based on an extensive sand painting collection, but translates her status into financial compensation as well—a fee of a thousand dollars for three months of work on the project, compensation that far exceeds the payment Newcomb was able to command for her intellectual work. Reichard's prior publications and her affiliation with powerful institutions like Columbia University signify resources she can capitalize on for ethos—while

Newcomb's lack of such standing contributes to the ease with which her role in this project was attenuated and then eliminated entirely.

Franc Newcomb and Gladys Reichard's collaborations in the 1930s underscore both the complexity of ethos negotiations and the significant stakes that attend collaborative work for women writers. Although Newcomb was sensitive to the distinctions between working *with* and working *for* another, and although she endeavored to position herself as an intellectual who undertook research through her own motivations and investments, other dimensions of her rhetorical situation prevented her from establishing such an ethos in the pages of their coauthored book. Structural inequalities between coauthors could be somewhat mitigated in their correspondence, but were reinforced in published work in ways that diminished rather than improved Newcomb's further opportunities to translate her rhetorical performances into additional symbolic and material rewards. As this case has shown, ethos is neither an isolated nor an innocent practice; instead, it remains only partially within a writer's control, deeply inflected by the structures of power that shape human relationships.

Notes

1. Although I use "Navajo" as the designation used by Newcomb and Reichard in their correspondence and publications, *Diné*, which means "The People," is the term preferred by many contemporary members of this group.

2. Specific healers or medicine men would typically learn one or two full chants, and certain chants fell in and out of popularity among practitioners. Reichard notes that of the fifty-six individual sand paintings recorded by Newcomb in relation to the Shooting Chant, the book reproduces forty-four of these. See Newcomb and Reichard 1–17.

3. See Latour and Woolgar; Moody; Myers.

4. Anthropologists' recognition of the necessity of establishing ethical relationships with members of the communities they study has led many to rearticulate relationships between anthropologists and Others over the past several decades. See especially Behar; Crapanzano.

5. On Mead and Benedict's collaboration, see Banner; on broader networks of women in anthropology, see Applegarth.

6. For a few examples of this extensive discussion, see in particular Cotera; Deloria; Wolfe.

7. Newcomb inscribes throughout her correspondence a remarkable attention to the varied material costs of research—noting, for example, the time required

for domestic labor that prevents her from undertaking her research work and even the cost of postage and packing cases for sending her paintings to Reichard (Newcomb to Reichard, undated letter from Gallup).

8. As a white woman, Newcomb gained access to Navajo sand paintings only through further ethos negotiations in her collaborative partnership with Hosteen Klah, the Navajo leader who permitted Newcomb to witness and reproduce his paintings. Records of *their* partnership are not available, and treatment of the power disparities shaping their collaboration lies beyond the scope of this essay.

Works Cited

Applegarth, Risa. "Field Guides: Women Writing Anthropology." *Women and Rhetoric between the Wars.* Ed. Ann George, Elizabeth Weiser, and Janet Zepernick. Carbondale: Southern Illinois UP, 2013. 193–208.

Banner, Lois W. *Intertwined Lives: Margaret Mead, Ruth Benedict, and Their Circle.* New York: Knopf, 2003.

Behar, Ruth. *The Vulnerable Observer: Anthropology That Breaks Your Heart.* Boston: Beacon, 1996.

Cotera, María Eugenia. *Native Speakers: Ella Deloria, Zora Neale Hurston, Jovita Gonzalez, and the Poetics of Culture.* Austin: U of Texas P, 2008.

Crapanzano, Vincent. *Tuhami: Portrait of a Moroccan.* Chicago: U of Chicago P, 1980.

Deloria, Vine, Jr. *Custer Died for Your Sins.* 1969. Norman: U of Oklahoma P, 1988.

Fontana, Bernard. Rev. of *Hosteen Klah: Navajo Medicine Man and Sandpainter,* by Franc J. Newcomb. *American Anthropologist* 67.2 (Apr. 1965): 567–68.

Hyde, Michael J. "Rhetorically, We Dwell." *The Ethos of Rhetoric.* Ed. Michael J. Hyde. Columbia: U of South Carolina P, 2004. xiii–xxviii.

Latour, Bruno, and Steve Woolgar. *Laboratory Life: The Construction of Scientific Facts.* Princeton, NJ: Princeton UP, 1979.

Moody, James. "The Structure of a Social Science Collaboration Network: Disciplinary Cohesion from 1963 to 1999." *American Sociological Review* 69.2 (2004): 213–38.

Myers, Greg. "Politeness and Certainty: The Language of Collaboration in an AI Project." *Social Studies of Science* 21.1 (1991): 37–73.

Newcomb, Frances. Correspondence. Gladys Reichard Collection. MS-22. Museum of Northern Arizona, Flagstaff.

Newcomb, Franc J., and Gladys A. Reichard. *Sandpaintings of the Navajo Shooting Chant.* New York: J. J. Augustin, 1937.

Reichard, Gladys. Correspondence. Gladys Reichard Collection. MS-22. Museum of Northern Arizona, Flagstaff.

Reynolds, Nedra. "Ethos as Location: New Sites for Understanding Discursive Authority." *Rhetoric Review* 11.2 (1993): 325–38.

Shaver, Lisa. "'No Cross, No Crown': An Ethos of Presence in Margaret Prior's *Walks of Usefulness.*" *College English* 75.1 (2012): 61–78.

Sharer, Wendy. "Genre Work: Expertise and Advocacy in the Early Bulletins of the U.S. Women's Bureau." *Rhetoric Society Quarterly* 33.1 (2003): 5–32.

Wolfe, Patrick. *Settler Colonialism and the Transformation of Anthropology: The Politics and Poetics of an Ethnographic Event.* London: Cassell, 1999.

11. Creating Contemplative Spaces

Ethos as Presence and the Rhetorics of Yoga

Christy I. Wenger

To frame her 2008 book *The Activist WPA*, Linda Adler-Kassner describes the importance of the breath in hatha yoga not only as it benefits the individual but also as it highlights her connection to others.

> "Hearing everyone else's breath," [our yoga teacher] said, "reminds us that we practice in a community—we don't practice alone." Instead, we're a group. If we need help with poses we can look around us at fellow practitioners to see what they're doing. It also reminds us to focus on the here and now—to be in *this* moment, in this time and space. Not two minutes ago, not in the future—now, now, and now. Together, here, now. Together, here, and now are three ideas that run throughout this book. (vii)

If we typically understand breathing as a fundamentally individual practice, Adler-Kassner emphasizes how her breath mingles with that of her fellow yogis, solidifying a sense of community in her class. Adler-Kassner's alignment of the individual with the community in her opening reflection on yoga presents *The Activist WPA*'s message as one about how personal experiences can inform strategic social practices, of how activism can and does start at the local level from where both writing program administrators (WPAs) and yogis often work. Yoga teaches that "our breath is our own, yes. But when we hear the breath of others and develop our practice in concert with others, that practice changes in ways we don't always anticipate" (Adler-Kassner vii). In other words, we may come to presence through the recognition of our breath as our own in a deeply and personally embodied way, but we also recognize the sameness of our experience in others (here, testified to by the sounds of mutual and reciprocal breathing): community is key. Our bodies lead us to connection; difference and change is inevitable, but so is identification.[1] In recognizing ourselves, we recognize others.

In these ways, Adler-Kassner ties her agency, voice, and rhetorical presence to her embodied presence as a communicative body[2]—both as a yogi and as an activist WPA. While WPAing is not the focus of this chapter,[3] I'd like to use Adler-Kassner's example as well as my own experiences as a yogi and feminist writing teacher to argue for a feminist-contemplative version of *ethos* as "presence," or the "space we include" (Iyengar 203). Presence takes into account how our available means of persuasion always includes our bodies. Contemplative rootedness in the present complicates easy relations between presence and essence, a difference we might press given the latter's persistent thorniness for body-minded feminists. Because presence places more weight on our identifications than our identities as rhetors, it shifts focus from our narrative identities to our coalitional collaborations—or, to our relational negotiations as opposed to our static identity markers. My chapter, then, seeks to complicate the relationship between ethos and the writing body so that we might claim a more body-minded concept of ethos than either classical or contemporary feminist versions, one secured by the ways we *take up* space, utilizing metaphors of fullness not emptiness. These metaphors draw upon the "primordial" meaning of ethos as dwelling place (Hyde xiii) and stress the "locatability" of ethos, as discussed in this collection's introduction.

In what follows, I will examine how presence, as understood within the contemplative traditions of yoga, brought into the fold of feminist composition theory and approached through theories of ethos as dwelling, is predicated on the fullness of bodies as they self-consciously negotiate language and material space without being reduced to either. A contemplative understanding of presence, I argue, is less embedded in the tropes of the theoretical body and forwards instead a lived, moment-to-moment understanding of materiality, complementary to understandings of the mindful yogi within contemplative philosophy. In this chapter, contemplative philosophy will be represented by what is arguably the most influential school of modern postural yoga, Iyengar yoga.[4] Seeing ethos as presence, I will argue, allows us to approach a writer's rhetorical authority as singularly embodied even as it is also located via her interaction or "dwelling with" other material and social bodies. In other words, presence implicates the individual body in an ethics of dwelling while demanding that she also responsibly respond to the ways bodily boundaries are constantly shifting. This makes both individual agency as well as collective action possible and desirable. For feminist activism, both are necessary.

Western Embodied Spaces

Like Michael Hyde, who aligns ethos with dwelling places (xiii), Nedra Reynolds urges us to embrace spatial metaphors of ethos and to see "writers' identities as well as their associations with writing and writing instruction [as] constructed by space and the spatial" (*Geographies* 335–36). Doing so allows us to appreciate how compositionists have operated within what Reynolds calls a "border mentality" (*Geographies* 6), which draws our attention more to crossing boundaries than to the places and spaces constructed by those boundaries in which we might dwell. As such, a border mentality has led us to entrenched forms of exclusion, according to Reynolds (*Geographies* 6). Here, I heed this author's advice like so many in this collection but examine the limitations of tying our feminist definitions of ethos to Western conceptions of space. Instead, I suggest we rethink concepts of women's ethos and writing spaces through the Eastern contemplative rhetoric of yoga. Such a rethinking can help us see how our border mentality has largely excluded the body as an inhabitable material space and can help us accordingly reimagine the ways we inhabit ethos materially and spatially, not just metaphorically. This reimagining will ultimately lead me to reconsiderations of Reynolds's heuristic of dwelling viewed through non-Western understandings of movement and mindfulness.

Western conceptions of space tend to see the body as a border that needs crossing, a barrier between understanding and shared experience. This border mentality is reinforced every time we ask our students to avoid using the personal pronoun *I* in their writing, insinuating that arguments can be made with objective distance from the biasing body of the observer. The hope that Massive Open Online Courses (MOOCs) and online courses will somehow equalize the playing field for students also courts this kind of disembodied logic. Beyond our classrooms, Linda Flower shows how this logic works in our field's literature. Because different bodies accrue different experiences, bodies themselves can be blamed when collaborative dialogue fails us, according to Flower. Using Andre, "an African American inner-city teenager with no apparent credentials" (43) as an example, Flower notes that because of the distance created by our bodies, while we often "hop[e] for a collaboratively constructed understanding, we instead encounter an unarticulated chasm. For behind the words we use in common lie strikingly different life experiences that instantiate a concept (such as 'police-enforced') with different flesh and blood realities" (38). That is, Flower recounts a city meeting on the subject of city curfews for teens where Andre claims a rhetorical space of authority warranted by his experiences as a teenager who has both studied and followed the curfew policies in question by his community. Andre solidifies his ethos through his daily life experiences, of which he is an expert, even though this young man is not privy to more conventional means of establishing credibility. But because it is connected to his body, Flower notes that "the source of [Andre's] ethos lies outside" (44) the boundaries of the rhetorical tradition, historically represented by a *polis* of homogeneous bodies and not the kind of contact zone that Andre inhabits.

While powerful here, the body becomes a barrier to shared understanding. Situated knowledge, which is as much a product of the body as it is of the mind, becomes a "submerged iceberg" (Flower 42) floating in and threatening the waters of successful negotiation. For Flower, if danger lies in our materiality, promise lies in problem-solving dialogue to "talk across [embodied] difference" (40). Not surprisingly, Flower equates activism with coming to voice (45). Despite the barriers the body presents for dialogue, Flower's notion of situated knowledge ironically validates the everyday authority and personal experience of individuals who might lack conventional means of developing a voice that carries ethos.

While we must be careful not to reify the body, we nonetheless need a connected picture of ethos and embodied knowing that sees the body as an epistemic origin and doesn't ask us to validate materiality only to discredit the body's own connective functions. Without such a model, we cannot account for Adler-Kassner's claim that the seemingly individual and distancing act of breathing is actually a means of building connections and coalitions between individuals. Neither can we account for a rhetorical tradition that defines rhetoric as a "bodily art: an art learned, practiced, and performed by and with the body as well as the mind" (144), according to Debra Hawhee's historical work to uncover the connection between Sophistic rhetorical training and athletic training. In other words, we cannot account for an embodied ethos as presence, the way we take up space, and as establishing rhetorical authority responsibly based on connection while remaining cognizant of difference. This is precisely where a contemplative viewpoint leads us.

A more contemplative picture of situated knowledge comes from feminist Donna Haraway. While Haraway is not typically seen as offering a contemplative viewpoint, her interest in non-Western spirituality and the nonhuman environmental surround brings much of her theory into dialogue with contemplative philosophy and the ecological thinking that guides women's creation of new ethē. The energy of this connection between the feminist, the ecological, and the contemplative is what I'd like to take from her theory as I move toward an understanding of ethos as presence. Haraway defines situated knowledge as "partial, locatable, critical knowledges sustaining the possibility of webs of connection" (191). The knower's location in a sociomaterial context gives rise to what she knows, but rather than limiting connection, locatedness "sustains" it, according to Haraway—a notable divergence from Flower. Rhetorical authority is authorized by the body and manifested through coalitions of connection organized around affinity, not identity. Here, the body is the lynchpin for connection: because the embodied "knowing self is partial . . . [it is] *therefore* able to join with another, to see together without claiming to be another" (193). This connection via partiality is based on our embodiment so that all our views are "view[s] from a body" (195). And as Haraway's choice to ground the body's agency in its viewpoint suggests, Haraway gives precedence to sight where Flower instead privileges voice in her conception of situated knowledge. Haraway reclaims vision, in part, because she is committed to changing the rhetorics of science where ways of seeing have been emptied of their mediations, their connections to embodied beings, in order to make them "objective."

Within this understanding of situated knowledge, feminist objectivity becomes responsibly limited and tied to an environment and a body and the notion of an omniscient observer is shattered. With vision thusly recast, observation becomes a type of conversation between subjects and subjects as well as between subjects and objects, insisting on the agency of both subjects and objects of study. Not only does this theorizing problematize the default scientific position of disembodied objectivity, it also denies that the object of study is simply removed and passive. Contemplatively, Haraway's observation is reflected in the mantra of yogic integration and living in balance with nature. A yogic emphasis on a vegetarian diet or environmentalism, for example, recognizes that as manifestations of nature ourselves, we must

241

approach our world in conversation, as an agent and not a resource to be appropriated. This inclusive orientation is explicitly feminist.

Concepts of situated knowledge are crucial to feminist definitions of ethos because, historically, women have been excluded from positions that guaranteed the construction of credible, rhetorical space. If we are not "good m[e]n skilled in speaking" (Quintilian 12.1.1), we are "excluded from the polis, hence decentered, 'disoriginated,' deinstitutionalized" (Miller 6). The Western conception of bodies as barriers has impacted feminist attempts to claim rhetorical authority—in attempting to assert our rhetorical authority, do we dismiss the very same body that was the reason for this primary exclusion? For feminists then, claiming ethos is a political act that exceeds the pragmatic choice made by a rhetor to persuade an audience by constructing a credible character, as in Aristotle's classical legacy, and also exceeds the inherent morality of a rhetor, as in a Platonic model. Rhetorical authority is otherwise guaranteed, according to feminist rhetoricians like Reynolds, by situated knowledge.[5]

Situated knowledge draws our attention to the negotiations bodies make when audiences and speakers interact and when rhetorical authority and agency are in question. In an effort to explore the cultural politics of how agency is constructed and how women have been systematically excluded from traditional spaces of rhetorical authority, many feminists now see ethos as a "sticky" amorphous web that forms between but never within bodies—akin to Sara Ahmed's understanding of emotion. Ahmed argues that emotions do not exist within a body but rather move between bodies: "emotions are not 'in' either the individual or the social, but produce the very surfaces and boundaries that allow the individual and the social to be delineated" (10). If emotion is not found in either social or individual bodies alone, it is best to see emotion in terms of circulation, a "transference of affect" where objects, such as bodies, become "sticky," according to Ahmed (91). Reminding us of the overlap between the *pisteis*, Reynolds, in a move parallel to Ahmed, locates ethos in the "betweens," a concept outlined in this collection's introduction as the shifting intersections between individual bodies and texts. Quoting Karen Burke LeFevre, Reynolds positions ethos *between* bodies rather than *within* them so as to stress the communal nature of its construction and the ways it moves amid audiences and rhetors (*Ethos* 333).

Locating ethos in the "betweens" means that feminist writers earn rhetorical authority by explicitly naming their multiple and shifting locations. Representing this view, Reynolds notes that "writers construct and establish *ethos* when they say explicitly 'where they are coming from'" (*Ethos* 332). Naming guarantees negotiated agency, the only kind of agency we can reasonably claim. Johanna Schmertz therefore advocates for a tactical and self-conscious use of ethos that recognizes how naming creates identity, what she calls a "pragmatics of naming" (88). Schmertz's pragmatics recognizes the ways naming draws boundaries and excludes: "In naming my politics of location, I displace the structures from which I have emerged. I create *empty* spaces, and new places, from which others may speak" (Schmertz 89, my emphasis).

While this process of naming has helpfully drawn our attention to situatedness, I argue that it has often equated this term with the discursive spaces of language, "empty spaces," and not the fuller, material spaces of the writing body from which we act. If we are always "between" bodies, we are never "within" them. Currently, our feminist definitions of ethos limit our ability to claim the spaces writing bodies "include." But, we need to claim these spaces for the "present, here, now" promise of Adler-Kassner's formulations; we need to claim them for a feminist activism that sees the body as a source for constructing mindful argument in public spaces. Problematically, our current definitions forward a view of situated knowledge more in line with Flower's Western model, wherein the body is a barrier, than Haraway's, where the body is a generative connector, as it is also within Eastern traditions.

We can advance Haraway's formulations and make them even more applicable to the spaces and places of writing studies, then, if we join them with the practices and philosophies from Eastern contemplative traditions such as yoga. Yogis experience their bodies as connectors, as my own practice, many studies, and my students' testimony confirm. In one study, a yoga student noted that yoga develops social responsibility despite the ostensive focus on the self.

> You think that doing yoga would make you more self-centered. You are focusing on yourself more. But by doing that I become more open, more conscious of what's going on around me and more sensitive to people who are near me. (Kipnis 120)

Responsible action toward others thus starts with the self. Or, as Sarah,[6] an advanced writing student in my "Zen of Writing" class (where we marry the writing process with contemplative practices like yoga) recently put it in her blog, "Practicing yoga throughout my day helps me understand others as much as myself." It is the way contemplative presence teaches us receptivity to others, by providing awareness of our bodies in time and space, asserting the importance of dwelling within them, that I explore in the next section.

Contemplative Space and Ethos as Presence

Feminists have continued to write about the need to find alternative spaces to inhabit, according to Gillian Rose in *Feminism and Geography*, because of the persistent cultural and geographical boundaries that have metaphorically and practically limited women's movement (155–59). New concepts of rhetorical space and ethos can provide not only new conceptual maps of our environments and our bodies, what Rose calls "unexplored conceptual territories" (155–56), but they can also give us a new set of practices to occupy. In this section, I'm most interested in an alternative view of rhetorical space that privileges neither voice nor sight—valuations that have tended to reify difference and limit agency in our notions of ethos—but instead the fullness of our felt, embodied experience. What would it mean to our rhetorical theories to claim the individual body as a primary place of dwelling?

Conceptually, feminist rhetorical theories of ethos have grappled with how to both claim a body and to recognize that our relationships with others shape our construction of self. This has led to understandings of ethos as being constructed *between* bodies and never *within* them, as I explored in the last section. Yoga deals with this predicament of ethos by seeing it as stemming from a body that by its very materiality is relational; this means that ethos both exists within bodies, guaranteed by their material presence, *and* between bodies, existing in the interactions between a speaker and an audience. The choice to see ethos as either marking a central self or highlighting a social reality is a false one. Discussions of feminist standpoint theories and situated knowledge currently hinge on the exclusion of the center from the circumference. But yoga sees these as continuous. Not only can we and must we claim "our center," but in doing so, we find a world of others. In his postmodern study of yoga and Buddhist philosophy, George Kalamaras notes that

> paradoxically, the yogi, through various meditative practices, withdraws consciousness from the periphery of the body in ways which heighten the inner sensorium; in total intimacy with a "center" of awareness, then, the advanced mediator's consciousness expands to embrace the immensity of the universe, moving beyond all awareness of limitation, psychological borders, or psychic "circumference." (9)

Kalamaras's summary reminds us that the doubling back of center and circumference is integral to a contemplative spatial heuristics of dwelling. And similarly, Adler-Kassner's example shows that connection with the community and individuation can happen simultaneously without diminishing either.

My own practice of yoga confirms such double dwelling. In a recent yoga class, my teacher, Diana, asked us to spread our hands out in front of us. She suggested that we first concentrate on our fingers, to see the bones and shape of the flesh, noting also the space our hands took up in the room. To see our hands was to recognize the solidity of our bodies and the ways they enabled our practice. This move was similar to our standard practice of locating our centers before moving into active *asana* or postures, usually accomplished through the deep breathing of *ujjayi* or another practice of *pranayama*, or breath control, at the start of class. But, rather than stopping with this immediate view, my teacher then asked us to shift our focus to the space between our fingers. Diana invited us to see how the space between enabled us to comprehend our fingers' circumference and to appreciate them as ten entities. The space between provided us the felt sense of our fingers by connecting them in its fullness and joining all of our hands in the room together—but we could only appreciate this complementary space when we were also tuned in to the presence of our hands themselves.

My example shows how yogis practice *asana*, physical postures, *pranayama*, breathing, and *dhyana*, meditation, to develop the felt space of the self, which, in turn, connects them to others. If this integration seems like an impossibility, it is because our heuristics tend to needlessly divorce center and circumference. Yoga refuses to separate the individual body from other material beings and refuses the resulting disconnect that occurs when bodies are seen as borders. "Paradoxically, looking within has a comparable unifying effect as visiting space does for astronauts," since looking within brings awareness that "inside the microcosm of the individual exists the macrocosm of the universe" (Iyengar 203). In my example, Diana is teaching us to see our bodies both as integral to our agency and individual practice but also as part of a larger, shared material space. We must both recognize our fingers themselves and the space between; to see just one image is to see only partially in this contemplative landscape. Through such teaching, yoga claims something closer to what feminists interested in cultural geography, like Reynolds, have labeled "thirdspace"—following Edward Soja.

Thirdspace is a conception of geography where things and thoughts are equal (Mauk 212), or where the temporal and the spatial are joined and mapped on a matrix where space is always bound by a trialectics as it is lived, perceived, and conceived (Reynolds *Geographies* 16). In its simplicity, yoga takes the idea of a trialectics in a more radical, spatial direction by seeing all matter, including that which makes up bodies and minds, as connected and indivisible. In yoga, this continuous concept is called *prakarti*. Prakarti highlights the lack of division between body and mind and between self and other: "The physical body is not something separate from our mind and soul" (Iyengar 5). Because we are connected by virtue of prakarti, the materiality of all things, as we explore even our own bodies, we are exploring nature itself and pursuing a connection to others (Iyengar 22). In other words, as we explore our bodies, we unfold to the world. And it is only by claiming the presence of the individual body that this process can occur.

Unexpectedly, recognizing our commonality with others by virtue of our shared materiality and existence allows us to respect difference without reifying it: "We too are part of nature, therefore constantly changing, so we are always looking at nature from a different viewpoint. We are a little piece of continual change looking at an infinite quantity of continual change" (Iyengar 7). And while we have a core, a center, we are always connected materially to others, which presumes that while we are connected we are not diminished by the connection. This is because the yogi must take note of the "space we *include*, the space within, for it is largely that which gives true life and beauty to the *asana*" (Iyengar 203). To say that we remain undiminished or that we maintain a core is not the same as claiming inviolable presence. The contemplative theories of yoga reject the Western binary of self/other for an intersubjective approach that is reflected in the common greeting used at both the start and end of practice, "Namaste." This Sanskrit greeting can be translated as,

> I honor the place in you in which the entire universe dwells. I honor the place in you which is of love, of truth, of light, and of peace. When you are in that place in you, and I am in that place in me, we are one. (Tourda and McCullough 124)

Through the translation of "Namaste," we can see how yoga understands that a turn to the self is simply not, as Western logic might have it, a turn from the other; rather, because of our interconnection, as we turn inward and grow aware of our fullness, we recognize our oneness with the rest of the material world. If we understand asana to include any practice of movement (physical or rhetorical) completed with mindfulness—a practice commonly understood by practitioners as "living our yoga"—then a version of contemplative presence built on the theories of yoga provides feminist rhetors an alternative space to inhabit, one that does not deny the role of the body in the delivery, embodiment, and construction of ethos. This alternative rhetorical space guaranteed by presence aligns activism with awareness of our connection to others so that the lived body becomes central to our public ethos.

Dwelling in Our Bodies: Extension and Expansion

If our feminist conceptions of ethos are to engage the ways the writer's lived body shapes her rhetorical authority and agency, we need traditions to claim these fuller material spaces. In what remains of this chapter, I examine how the spatial heuristics that govern the theory and practice of yoga change the ways we understand the borders of the self and, therein, how we "dwell" within our bodies. I borrow this term from Reynolds whose ideas illustrate most vividly for me the feminist potential of the theory of ethos as dwelling. Building upon Heidegger's theory, Reynolds says that dwellings are "a set of practices as well as a sense of place" and that "learning to dwell . . . means paying attention to place, not just the borders that surround it, and building thirdspaces" (*Geographies* 140; 142–43). Yet, while Reynolds argues for the embodiment of geography and calls upon Adrienne Rich to highlight how the body is implicated in our sense of space, she concedes that bodies become borders, more notable for the attention they mark between self and other than as dwelling places in themselves. Reynolds claims, "bodies occupy a space between self and other, [so] they 'catch' and hold the imprints or layers that create one's habitus" (*Geographies* 144). Because Reynolds argues that "bodies occupy a space between self and other," she can't acknowledge the body itself as a primary place for dwelling. But this is exactly where contemplative practice leads us.

Reconceived through the spatial heuristics of yoga, the individual body becomes a generative place of dwelling, and ethos becomes contingent upon the ways we claim presence within this body. Dwelling contemplatively, in other words, becomes a radical way of practicing mindfulness in rhetorical spaces. Reynolds claims that learning to dwell helps us to see how "geography constructs difference" (*Geographies* 143); the same can be said of understanding dwelling through contemplative presence. Understanding ethos as presence consequently opens up potential negotiations for a body-based agency that invites attention to difference and intention in writing and writing instruction. Furthermore, dwelling seen through a contemplative lens also emphasizes sameness and connection. To examine these negotiations, I explore the ways contemplative presence requires us to take up space mindfully through the dual actions of "extension," a movement of rooting within our bodies, and "expansion," or a shifting toward the community (Iyengar 33–34). But, first, I turn to the ways these acts are applications of mindfulness.

As important for our rhetorical theories as our classroom practices is the notion that presence can be taught. In both rhetoric and yoga, we come to presence through the practice of mindfulness. Mindfulness is moment-to-moment awareness taught by contemplative traditions like yoga, where each "thought, feeling, or sensation that arises in the attentional field is acknowledged and accepted as it is" (Bishop et al. 232). Rather than overidentifying with or immediately reacting to thoughts and feelings as they play out in the moment, the practitioner of mindfulness creates a critical distance, a space, that allows for eventual, intentional response as opposed to automatic, unthinking, and habitual reaction (Bishop et al. 232). Theories that tie ethos to dwelling often stress the habitual nature of communal existence (Hyde xvi; Reynolds 8), but ethos as presence illustrates that our habituating processes are not always mindful of the present and may not always lead us to make responsible, deliberate responses to others. When we expect critique from our partner, for instance, we may react defensively whether or not it is warranted; our expectations, built on habit, can prevent us from listening in the present moment—making us prone to rehashing the same arguments over and over. The space introduced by mindfulness requires us to instead acknowledge and examine any biases we might bring to the rhetorical situation. Cultivating present-centered mindfulness translates into a feminist deliberative practice that is more responsive to the bodies present at the moment of a rhetorical act than to our preconceptions of these bodies prior to the rhetorical moment. Of course, the closer we are to the present and the more responsive our listening, the greater our chance at successful negotiation and persuasion.

Because mindfulness is regulation of the here and now, *this* moment, it is always situated in a particular body. And because it asks us to interrupt our ruminative thoughts about experience to focus on experience itself, inhibiting "secondary elaborative processing of the thoughts, feelings and sensations that arise in the stream of consciousness" (Bishop et al. 233), it involves a direct experience of and respect for embodied events. The very act of turning off rumination (or at least putting our resources toward that noble goal) increases our capacity for attending to the present because our attentional range is limited when focused on both rumination and processing (Schneider and Shiffin 1977; qtd. in Bishop et al. 233). Quite literally, by shutting off our ruminations, or at least short-circuiting them, research shows that we can devote more brain space to the present, allowing us to actively and consciously inhabit it. We tacitly know this in our own field of writing studies, which is why we promote freewriting as a way to ease writing anxiety, often caused by ruminating, which leads to circular pathways of thinking that actually impede invention, connection, and creativity.

Our ability to bring mindfulness to the rhetorical situation we face impacts the ways our ethos is projected and embodied. Simply, as we cultivate a present-centered ethos, we change our and others' experience of ourselves. In his definitive book on yoga philosophy, *Light on Life*, Iyengar targets two complementary skills necessary for the development of presence through the practice of asanas or poses: "extension," attending to our inner space, and "expansion," reaching out toward others and the unknown beyond us. Both acts are situated within a personal body but teach this body simultaneously to be inner- and outer-directed. Extension and expansion are interrelated actions because to reach out and create new space, you must first understand your own locatedness, must be aware of your center. Extension is attention to our immediate space, focusing on being *in* a unique body. Actions of extension include centering oneself through reflection and developing awareness of one's thoughts and feelings. Extension asks us to marry the thinking and feeling gestures that permeate the doing of a pose and is practiced attentively when both means of expression are balanced: wherein the "sensitive awareness of the body and the intelligence of the brain and heart... [meet together] in harmony" (Iyengar 29). In these married actions, we are reminded that "the borders between the *pisteis* of ethos and pathos are not discrete; they are permeable" (Fleckenstein 333).[7]

While vision isn't unimportant here, it does get dethroned from its typical position of authority, since yoga recognizes the limitations of sight. Increasing presence through awareness "is different from seeing with your normal two eyes. Instead you are feeling; you are sensing the position of your body" (Iyengar 29). Full-body awareness can indeed be more powerful than sight because it exchanges the receptivity of two outward-looking eyes for the sensations of the entire sensitive body which folds in on itself (through extension) as well as out toward the world (through expansion). When practicing warrior III (fig. 11.1), for instance, I cannot see the leg I lift behind me as my body leans forward and I balance on my other leg; nor can I always see if my outstretched arms are parallel to the floor—if I try to look, I lose my balance. Instead, I must learn through repeated practice to feel the positioning of my leg behind me and to use my felt presence as a guide for how to maneuver

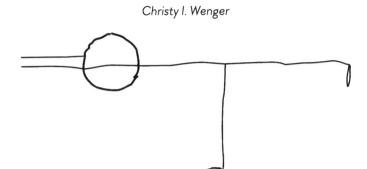

Figure 11.1. Warrior III.

my body in space. To find balance, I need to be aware of the sensations of the pose, the emotions the pose calls up, and the ways my intellect processes this bodily input and language captures and shapes it. Acts of extension therefore root us in the personal body, helping us understand our immediate material-semiotic placement and provide a path toward self-determination, but they are not to be completed alone.

Expansion complements extension because it reaches beyond the self's perceived center. The body unfolds and energy flows outward. Actions of expansion include the experience of creating spaces in new directions: opening the inner body and expanding to the experience of the external. Using a concrete example of expansion to show how it works together with extension to promote awareness and increase presence, Iyengar states,

> When most people stretch, they simply stretch *to* the point they are trying to reach, but they forget to extend and expand from where they are. When you expand and extend, you are not only stretching *to*, you are also stretching *from*. Try holding out your arm at your side and stretch it. Did your whole chest move with it? Now try to stay centered and extend out your arm to your fingertips . . . Did you notice the space you created and the way in which you stretched from your core? (33–34).

I invite my reader to try this exercise. The space created through this stretching is the space for new ideas and transgressed boundaries. We experience our limits differently when we expand; for when we only extend, we may feel limited by the length of our grasp. But when we also expand, we recognize that we can stretch out much further than we first thought, and we create new openness. As this simple exercise shows, we actually create more space by being aware of our bodies and centered in them as opposed to simply reaching out with no thought as to the embodied origin of that movement.

In warrior III, expansion encourages me to reach my leg out from the center of my body, but extension reminds me to ground the stretch in the resistance I create by pressing my tailbone into my pelvis instead of reaching my arms out as far forward as possible. A lesson I relearn each time I practice is that mindlessly reaching out without conscious extension will push too much weight on the ball of my planted foot and not enough on my heel, making me tip forward. Without a balanced sense of self, I cannot reach toward the unknown. Instead, I must feel my arms create space against the resisting pull of my leg in the opposite direction as if I were pinching a rubber band with two fingers and attending to those fingers as much as the feeling of pulling the rubber band in the opposite direction. This pose makes me understand the importance of feeling centered in my hips and middle body so that I can reach beyond my center without losing myself for the sake of the movement itself; it's a conscious, intentional action. Attentive form makes this pose a freeing experience at the same time as a rooted one, dependent on the stability of my standing leg as if it were a tree trunk sinking roots into the earth—an imaginative visualization I often use. Literally and metaphorically, this kind of movement increases presence at the same time that it demands we remain accountable to the limits of our flesh.

Extension and expansion translate into feminist rhetorical acts as they shift our experience of ourselves and others and lead to both personal and systemic change. Gwen Gorzelsky has recently argued that the contemplative practices advocated by Zen teacher Thich Nhat Hanh are best understood as literacy acts that shape the self and our response to others because they "provide a conceptual framework for interpreting one's individual experience and one's relation to larger systems" (406). The same can be said of the contemplative practices of yoga. In other words, yoga teaches us to dwell consciously in our bodies in such ways that will not only allow us to shift understandings of our experiential knowledge—asking us to resee it through the conceptual framework of extension, expansion, and presence in the moment—but also to align these experiences with a community of others. This rewriting of our experience of embodiment translates into a deliberative rhetorical practice that positions ethos as presence, focused less on habit and more on mindfulness. As Gorzelsky argues of Hanh's practices, yoga teaches "practitioners to reorient their responses to their own subjectively grounded perceptions and to their emotional and behavioral habits . . . [enabling] them to reconstruct those habits" (407). The acts of extension validate experiential knowledge in the deliberative process, as it shapes our participation in social systems. We first "stretch from" our bodies and experiences. But, unlike other theories, approaching dwelling contemplatively means that we also expand, "stretch to," or move beyond habitual response. This stretching to allows us to identify and alter, as necessary, behavioral and cognitive patterns that may reify differences between ourselves and others and instead move toward more consciously mindful and deliberate responses that stress our connection to and affinities with others.

In her analysis of the coalitional politics of speaking about homosexuality on campus, Zan Meyer Gonçalves argues that student rhetors need "sponsoring institutions" that enable them to link private discourses and needs with public aims, focusing on her campus's Speaker's Bureau, an open forum for students dedicated to this issue, as such an institution. Gonçalves's argument resonates here and can be applied more widely, without resting on institutional initiatives like the Speaker's Bureau; after all, not all campuses are so lucky to have such rhetorical forums in place. Within feminist theories of ethos as presence, the rhetor's own body becomes a "sponsoring institution" if she only learns to dwell within it mindfully, to practice the self-reflexivity of extension and the other-directedness of expansion. In turn, activism becomes answerable to lived bodies in public spaces. This feminist deliberative practice can be applied to our classrooms. To teach students in our courses to claim their own bodies as sponsoring institutions, we must both invite them to inhabit discourses and their bodies via presence.

One way we can do this is by training our students to use pranayama as a rhetorical tool and to integrate it into their writing processes. In my advanced writing class this semester, my students and I worked with basic pranayama and breathing-based meditations, which asked students to follow their in- and out-breaths to find presence as writers. Laura, one of my advanced writing students, wrote in her blog that our practice of pranayama slowly helped her to stay present during the act of writing. She noted as the semester neared its end, "After meditating and breathing, I find it easier and easier to really put aside other thoughts and concentrate." She claimed that her practice of yoga made her a more responsible and deliberate writer: "[My practice] lengthens the discovery phase [of writing] for me, and helps me when reading multiple sources and absorbing lots of information while looking for a narrative thread that would pull much of it together." Laura credited her success to the attention she has begun to pay to her body while writing, what she calls a "thereness" that impacts her writing, testifying that Laura has claimed her body as a sponsoring institution. By teaching our students to use contemplative practices like yoga, we are guiding them to develop an ethos of presence and to dwell within their own bodies to create a responsible rhetorical space from which mindful arguments can emerge.

This is a space of connection, according to her classmate, Allison:

> I feel like many people, myself included in the beginning, sort of sometimes see mindfulness as a lonely and solitary practice. Granted, it is physically and emotionally solitary, sometimes, [but] it actually is not a lonesome experience, but, instead, a very powerful one that connects us.

Allison came to these conclusions by reflecting on her experiences of breathing and meditating with our class. Allison began to see her body as sponsoring and validating her rhetorical acts, largely because she paired these acts with the contemplative practices of extension and expansion. If "inhalation engulfs the whole body, expanding from center to periphery" (Iyengar 75–76), then extension occurs in turn: "During exhalation, the tide recedes, drawing back toward the center" (Iyengar 75–76). This coupling is astutely and simply related by Allison's peer, Dennis, who ends our class,

> most happy with my understanding that we are always a breath away from understanding our situations and our friends better—it just takes listening and a little mindfulness. This understanding has made me a better writer and person I think.

Responsible dwelling therefore requires intentional movement.

Dennis serves as a reminder that even when we attempt to sever ethos from the writing body in our theories, students are often aware of the ways their bodies are involved in their writing and speaking. In other words, giving our students deliberative means to claim their bodies as sponsoring institutions is both liberating and powerful. To Dennis, increasing presence in his writing makes him not only a more skilled rhetor, important to his creative writing major, but a better person who lives more intentionally. He links rhetorical responsibility and presence because both acts emerge now from his center—a real and rhetorical space he skillfully accessed through our practice of yoga throughout the semester. And, for him, such rhetorical responsibility is more about the ways he can identify with his audiences—listen to them and respond effectively—than habitual responses. Approaching ethos as presence becomes a transformative way for students to respect the functions of their communicative bodies as rhetors and to see how those bodies connect them to others when tuned to the present moment. As Dennis and his classmate testify, we are often only a "breath away" from understanding and, therein, responsible action.

Notes

1. This contemplative understanding of identification as a process of recognizing our interconnectedness stands in contrast to a Burkeian view where we communicate with others in order to overcome our inherent separateness from them: "Identification is affirmed with earnestness precisely because there is division. Identification is compensatory to division" (*Rhetoric of Motives* 22).

2. Adler-Kassner's alignment of her ethos as a writing teacher and administrator with the rhetorical authority guaranteed her body through yoga is reminiscent of Mary Rose O'Reilley's central theme of "radical presence" in her exploration of contemplative practice, specifically Buddhist meditation and Quaker spirituality, in *Radical Presence: Teaching as Contemplative Practice* (1998).

3. Though, of course, as a writing program administrator, this is a material position from which I always write.

4. Elizabeth De Michelis's *A History of Modern Yoga* notes that not only is Iyengar yoga the most influential and widely practiced school of modern hatha yoga worldwide, but its teachings are also integrated and upheld within many other modern styles of yoga. It is its popularity and widespread network of both theory and practice that makes Iyengar an ideal representation of the significance of contemplative theory and yoga practice in my research. In successive references, I will simply use the term *yoga*, but look most frequently to the practice and theories of Iyengar to make my argument.

5. Important to my project is that feminists have already attempted to move beyond the seeming either/or choice of viewing ethos as character or as habit. We have instead attempted to find a middle ground; however, in doing so, we've often found ourselves "somewhere between" as James Baumlin notes, which is the space of "a discourse whose language is in part one's own but in equal part a possession of one's time and culture" (xxii). Here, I question the "between" that only claims the empty spaces of language.

6. All student names have been changed to protect privacy. Student reflections come from a course blog students were required to post to weekly, reflecting on their integrated practice of yoga and writing in my advanced composition course. Permissions are IRB approved.

7. That feeling demonstrates the folding back or doubleness of our embodied selves has also been theorized by philosopher Merleau-Ponty. Calling this the "double sensation" of feeling, he has said:

> Between feeling (the dimension of subjectivity) and being felt (the dimension of objectivity) . . . is a gulf spanned by the indeterminate and reversible phenomenon of the being touched of the touching, the crossing over of what is touching to what is touched . . . In the double

sensation my right hand is capable of touching my left hand as if the latter were an object. But in this case, unlike an object, my left hand has the double sensation of being both the object and the subject of the touch. (qtd. in Grosz 100)

Works Cited

Adler-Kassner, Linda. *The Activist WPA: Changing Stories about Writing and Writers*. Logan: Utah State UP, 2008. Print.

Ahmed, Sara. *Cultural Politics of Emotion*. New York: Routledge, 2004. Print.

Baime, Michael. "This Is Your Brain on Mindfulness." *Shambhala Sun* July 2011: 44–49. Print.

Baumlin, James S. "Introduction: Positioning Ethos in Historical and Contemporary Theory." *Ethos: New Essays in Rhetorical and Critical Theory*. Ed. James S. Baumlin and Tita French Baumlin. Dallas: Southern Methodist UP, 1994. xi–xxxi. Print.

Bishop, Scott, Mark Lau, Shauna Shapiro, Linda Carlson, Nicole D. Anderson, James Carmody, Zindel V. Segal, Susan Abbey, Michael Speca, Drew Velting, and Gerald Devins. "Mindfulness: A Proposed Operational Definition." *Clinical Psychology: Science and Practice*. 11.3 (Autumn 2004), 230–41. Print.

Burke, Kenneth. *A Rhetoric of Motives*. Berkeley: U of California P, 1969. Print.

Fleckenstein, Kristie S. "Cybernetics, Ethos, and Ethics: The Plight of the Bread-and-Butter—Fly." *JAC* 25.2 (2005): 323–46. Print.

Flower, Linda. "Talking across Difference: Intercultural Rhetoric and the Search for Situated Knowledge." *College Composition and Communication*. 55.1 (Sept. 2003): 38–68. Print.

Gonçalves, Zan Meyer. *Sexuality and the Politics of Ethos in the Writing Classroom*. Carbondale: Southern Illinois UP, 2005.

Gorzelsky, Gwen. "Experiential Knowledge: How Literacy Practices Seek to Mediate Personal and Systemic Change." *College English*. 75.4 (Mar. 2013): 398–419. Print.

Grosz, Elizabeth. *Volatile Bodies: Toward a Corporeal Feminism*. Bloomington: Indiana UP, 1994. Print.

Haraway, Donna J. "Situated Knowledges: The Science Question in Feminism and the Privilege of Partial Perspective." *Simians, Cyborgs, and Women: The Reinvention of Nature*. New York: Routledge, 1991. 183–202. Print.

Hawhee, Debra. "Bodily Pedagogies: Rhetoric, Athletics, and the Sophists' Three Rs." *College English* 65.2 (Nov. 2002): 142–62. Print.

Iyengar, B. K. S. *Light on Life: The Yoga Journey to Wholeness, Inner Peace and Ultimate Freedom*. New York: Rodale, 2005. Print.

Kalamaras, George. "The Center and Circumference of Silence: Yoga, Poststructuralism, and the Rhetoric of Paradox." *International Journal of Hindu Studies.* 1.1 (Apr. 1997), 3–18.

Kipnis, Andrew. "Yogic Meditation and Social Responsibility." *Buddhist-Christian Studies* 14.1 (1994): 111–25. Print.

Mauk, Johnathon. "Location, Location, Location: The 'Real' (E)states of Being, Writing, and Thinking in Composition." *Relations, Locations, Positions: Composition Theory for Writing Teachers.* Ed. Peter Vandenberg, Sue Hum, and Jennifer Clary-Lemon. Urbana: NCTE, 2006. 198–225. Print.

Miller, Nancy K. "Changing the Subject: Authorship, Writing, and the Reader." *Coming to Terms.* Ed. Elizabeth Weed. New York: Routledge, 1989. 3–16. Print.

O'Reilley, Mary Rose. *Radical Presence: Teaching as Contemplative Practice.* Portsmouth, NH: Boynton/Cook, 1998. Print.

Quintilian. *The Institutio Oratoria of Quintilian.* Trans. H. E. Butler. 4 vols. Loeb Classical Library. Cambridge, MA: Harvard UP, 1920–22. Print.

Reynolds, Nedra. "Ethos as Location: New Sites for Understanding Discursive Authority." *Rhetoric Review* 11.2 (Spring 1993): 325–38. Print.

———. *Geographies of Writing: Inhabiting Places and Encountering Difference.* Carbondale: Southern Illinois UP, 2004. Print.

Rose, Gillian. *Feminism and Geography: The Limits of Geographical Knowledge.* Minneapolis: University of Minnesota Press, 1993. Print.

Schmertz, Johanna. "Constructing Essences: Ethos and the Postmodern Subject." *Rhetoric Review.* 18.1 (Autumn 1999): 82–91. Print.

Tourda, Wayne F., and Vincent D. McCullough. *Harmony with the Movement of the Universe: A Collection of Writings on Aikido and Yoga.* 4th ed. New York: McGraw Hill, 2009. Print.

"Zen of Writing" Advanced Composition student blogs from 2012–13 study. Shepherd University, Shepherdstown, WV. Institutional Review Board (IRB) approved.

12. Conocimiento as a Path to Ethos

Gloria Anzaldúa's Networked Rhetoric

Kendall Leon and Stacey Pigg

R hetorical theory has recently emphasized vocabulary that can help researchers and practitioners account for the breakdown of the autonomous individual rhetorical agent. From assemblages to rhizomes and from networks to ambience, theoretical symbols that describe the distribution and enmeshing of rhetorical capacity and agency across people, institutions, ideologies, and objects have become crucial for emerging rhetorical production and criticism.[1] In this essay, we join the ongoing theoretical work by offering a model for rhetorical authority and its development that builds explicitly from related rhetorics articulated by women of color. Specifically, we look to Gloria E. Anzaldúa's concept of conocimiento[2] in "now let us shift" in the 2002 edited collection, *this bridge we call home: radical visions for transformation*. We argue that Anzaldúa's enacted practice of knowing grounds rhetorical action in strategic connectivity with (and disconnection from) different environments, people, and discourses. While recent scholarship has stressed Anzaldúa's role in advocating for hybrid languages and genres, as a theorist of rhetorical connectivity, Anzaldúa offers feminist rhetoricians a path: a linked, relational set of stances that can productively inform rhetorical designs.

By positioning Anzaldua's theory to participate in broader discussions about distributed agency, we highlight the importance of listening to longstanding contributions from women of color as rhetoricians move forward with dynamic, ecological approaches to theorizing rhetorical production. Although we only have space to develop a single potential contribution in this chapter, we have each continually returned to insights from Chicana theory as foundations for grounding engagement efforts that work within existing environments without reducing potential agency or denying the impact of material and discursive worlds. One aspect of Chicana rhetoric that provides a model for acting outside of this schism can be articulated through the Nahuatl concept of difrasismo in which two terms are coupled together in relation to create a new term. As a trope, difrasismo operates through affinities made between disparate parts. This practice has been realized in Chicana theory textually. For example, theorists have placed different languages and discursive practices beside and in between each other (Calafell), have disrupted subjectivities based on *chromos* (Emma Pérez; Gaspar de Alba), have connected materiality and lived experience as the development of critical consciousness (Moraga), and have used coupling as methodological apparatus (Laura Pérez; Dicochea). In the chapter that follows, we draw on this and other features of the broad field that we describe here as Chicana theory to build a bridge with feminist, Greco-Roman reframings of rhetorical ethos.

In the following paragraphs, we first discuss two challenges that accompany theories of women's ethos as positioned or located. In response, we suggest that conocimiento offers a model of feminist ethos that is not only positioned within particular environments but also networked across multiple, shifting spaces and stages. Following a description of conocimiento, we draw on Anzaldúa's language to illustrate this seven-stage movement as a methodology of dwelling across a networked feminist symbolic. As performed in her essay, these *topoi* not only illustrate rhetorical positionings but also rhetorical movements, demonstrating a nonlinear path across multiple rhetorical stances ranging (in our shorthand) from *rupture* and *detours* to *composing* and *networking*. We conclude the essay by analyzing conocimiento against the backdrop of feminist rhetorics of positionality and indeed against Anzaldúa's own "positioned" uptake in rhetoric and composition. Through this analysis, we argue that listening carefully to this painful, evolving process of connection can provide a means for negotiating historical problems of hyperlocation, in which feminist and other nondominant positions are framed as static, disconnected, or narrowly relevant.

Taking Positions and Being Positioned

Before explicating how conocimiento can make a contribution to rhetorical theory, we should describe some theoretical challenges that make it a timely and useful conceptual tool. Like Rebecca Jones, Nancy Myers, and Kathleen J. Ryan in this collection's introduction, we believe that feminist rhetorical scholarship's moves to decenter ethos from normative embodiments are also important for rhetorical theory's broader efforts to decenter the autonomous rhetor. In particular, feminist rhetoricians analyzing ethos have highlighted complex ethical and communal dimensions involved in building and performing credibility (Reynolds and Jarratt, Killingsworth, Heilker and Yergeau, Leon, Pittman). Adopting what Jones, Myers, and Ryan identify as *ecological ethē* invites us to consider ethos as constructed, relational or communal, and agentive. Furthermore, tracing the etymological scholarship on ethos and ēthos brings to light how relationships between values, community, and location contribute to the construction of feminist ethē (Ryan, Myers, and Jones). Within this framework, moving ethos away from internalized character need not mean stripping agency; rather, authority emerges as embedded in relationships and connected to acts of "owning" one's positionality and credibility. As Nedra Reynolds and Susan Jarratt describe, rather than claiming a normative credibility potentially built on sexist assumptions about authority, a woman's position can be "an ethical political tool ... a way of claiming and taking responsibility for our positions in the world, for the ways we see, for the places from which we speak" (52). This claiming and naming of self and others has led to an important focus on the active voice of credibility, in which feminist action and advocacy through acts of ongoing "naming" and identification redraw what is possible for rhetorical situations (Schmertz).

We contribute to the collection's conversations about ecologically positioned ethos by addressing two potential challenges with this concept. First, aligning ethos with location requires that women address the flip side of positioning: that actively voicing and naming one's commitments means simultaneously being positioned by others. Indeed, women whose bodies do not fall in line with normative credibility may find themselves already "positioned" outside attempts to voice particular stances. Material conditions and embodiments are read and interpreted by those around us, even outside discursive techniques we employ to name and give meaning to our positions. Second and relatedly, understanding ethos as located can be reductive if we understand "locations" as static spatial containers. Because we (and ecologies more broadly) evolve and change over time, women's ethos both moves and is multiply located. We need rhetorical vocabulary to help account for dynamic networks of ethos without overstabilizing locations from which we invent. In the remainder of the chapter, we define and take up these challenges by addressing how Chicana theory can provide vocabulary for understanding women's ethos not only as located or positioned but also interconnected across different relationships with people, spirit, and objects like land. We then move to reflect on how Anzaldúa's performance of conocimiento in "now let us shift" presents a series of networked symbolic dwelling places and a performance engaging with others and the world that resists the objectification that accompanies "owning" nondominant positions.

Understanding Networked Ethos through Conocimiento

As we have foreshadowed, Chicana theorists share with feminist rhetoricians a focus on theorizing locations from which identities, positions, and authority might be invented.[3] Although we will not have space in this chapter to explicate Chicana theories fully, Emma Pérez's concept of decolonial imaginary, Chela Sandoval's theory of differential or oppositional consciousness, and Anzaldúa's mestiza consciousness have in common that they name material and conceptual locations from which oppressed women invent from outside topoi that maintain dominant ideologies. Theorizing "third space" for rhetoric studies, Adela C. Licona brings together these approaches to describe a dwelling space for invention that is "an interstitial space of intersection and overlap, ambiguity and contradiction, that materializes a subversion to either/or ways of being and reproducing knowledge" (11). Both material and metaphorical in her conception, third spaces are "relational space[s] of contestation" but also of "shared understanding and meaning making" (Licona 13). Third spaces, then, have been traced both as material/textual sites (like physical borders or particular genres of writing like zines in Licona's example), as well as dispositional locations individuals or groups can inhabit—often resulting from sustained oppression.

Rhetoric and composition scholarship has drawn on mestiza consciousness to theorize a range of writing and rhetoric activities (Dolmage; Ede, Glenn, and Lunsford; Flower; Lunsford). For instance, scholarship has analyzed how Anzaldúa's mixed genre and language use indicates and performs mestiza consciousness (Dolmage; Enoch; Ritchie and Boardman) and has made use of the "border" and "borderlands" both to analyze material places and as a metaphor for locations marked by contestation, difference, struggle, or "alternative discourse" (Kyburz; Min-Zhan Lu; Trimbur). Though understanding mestiza consciousness as a discursive position has opened many generative conversations, locating this consciousness as a "position" can also have a stabilizing effect that downplays the dynamic experience of living this space in the everyday. Instead of describing compositions or authority as emerging from one position, Anzaldúa's theory describes many. Alongside static or even intersectional locations, her theory emphasizes bridges—pathways that connect places and people. Of course, this dynamic and multiple sense of positioning and the long process of interconnecting that Anzaldúa lays out for developing and performing it are also difficult to represent and describe (see Wallace for one reading of Anzaldúa's multiple stances as a pathway of development).

Introducing Conocimiento as Knowledge/Skill

The name that Anzaldúa assigns to the knowledge or knowing associated with mestiza consciousness across her writings is "conocimiento," a word "derived from . . . a Latin verb meaning 'to know' and is the Spanish word for [both] knowledge and skill" ("now let us," 577). As both knowledge and skill (we associate the Greek terms in our heads, but will work with the Latin), conocimiento is contextual and situated. It is a way of knowing but also of acting in situations that continually change, thereby altering who we are and can be. A closer examination of conocimiento can illustrate the dynamism of mestiza consciousness, as well as its intense networked connection to multiple objects, people, and symbols. While we hope to build a path between conocimiento and feminist reframings of Greek ethos, presenting a close examination of conocimiento is a daunting task. This theory is not built on rational or linear assumptions about what it means to know.

In order to describe some challenges of applying conocimiento as a theoretical model, we wish to briefly relate a story from our own prior experience. Several years ago we designed and carried out a research project analyzing how graduate students' digital writing and professionalization intersect (Leon and Pigg). When designing our study, we relied on Anzaldúa's theory while making decisions about how to focus our study's data collection and analysis. We drew on Anzaldúa's conception of writing as an embodied process that involves affect, perception, and connectivity as a means for sensing connections across domains of literate practice often assumed to be separate (i.e., personal, academic, and professional). This move allowed us to understand, for instance, how graduate students might visit particular online sites to work through complex academic ideas, develop professional identities, critique racist narratives, and maintain personal relationships all at once. Where writing in community blogs or keeping an activist library archive might seem "off-topic" with respect to students' lives as academic professionals, listening for how these rituals shaped personal and professional development helped us understand them as meaningful to both.

While deeply influenced by Anzaldúa's theory, we initially struggled to explain why and how her ideas had been so important. As we moved forward and reflected, we have learned two things that we now see as noteworthy for discussions of ethos as located or positioned. First, we found that this theory was not easily transported, cited, summarized, or imported into methodology sections or framing for literature reviews. No single passage clearly mapped onto our data analysis or collection, and no schema succinctly captured the methodological stance we had taken. While "locating" what we gained from Chicana rhetoric in a static way would make it easier to articulate, conocimiento was difficult to position into argumentative structures typically valued by the academy. Second, we sensed that it seemed out of place to rely on the work of this queer, Chicana, decolonial theorist in a research report that did not focus explicitly on race, sexuality, or gender. As we discussed in the prior section, nondominant forms of authority can easily become so located—so objectified—that we fail to apprehend their broader contributions. It is tempting to fall into a reductive conception of ethos's location, rendering the authority of women of color relevant only to static, controlled places. Thus, though central to our way of thinking, *Borderlands/La Frontera* did not appear in the works cited list of our research article.

Conocimiento as a Nonhierarchical Collaborative Performance

As we have already begun to discuss, conocimiento suggests authority that is positioned but also distributed across multiple interconnected dwelling spaces, positions, or sites that emerge from changing experiences, interactions, and relationships among writers, audiences, and the social and material environments that unite them. Reflecting on the shared cultural space and moment of which conocimiento is borne, Anzaldúa states:

We are experiencing a personal, global identity crisis in a disintegrating social order that possesses little heart and functions to oppress people by organizing them in hierarchies of commerce and power—a collusion of government, transnational industry, business, and the military all linked by a pragmatic technology and science voracious for money and control. This system and its hierarchies impact people's lives in concrete and devastating ways and justify a sliding scale of human worth to keep humankind divided. (541)[4]

Resisting forms of division and hierarchy (i.e., the separation of mind and body or "heart" and logic; divisions of labor and categorizations of knowledge) is key to what conocimiento enables. On the one hand, this idea that knowing builds bridges and resists divisions could be described as a key thematic content of "now let us shift." Anzaldúa describes conocimiento as a wisdom that emerges not from individual intention or authority but from an emergent understanding of how institutions, individuals, and groups are linked and how individual action relates to social action. This sense of interconnectedness emerges through a growing self-awareness about how one is positioned in relationship to broad social, political, and material context. Anzaldúa writes, "Through creative engagements, you embed your experiences in a larger frame of reference, connecting your personal struggle with those of other beings on the planet, and with struggles of the Earth itself" (542).

Explicating conocimiento, however, is more complicated than extracting key points like "interconnection" that could be transported out of context. This is because Anzaldúa's chapter is not presented through an argument built on traditional forms of authority but instead calls for interconnected engagement between writer and audience. In her interview with Andrea Lunsford, Anzaldúa highlighted that she intended to break from traditional notions of meaning making, prevalent both in the academy and in the public/ social imaginary. Tracing "rules" of invention and delivery of logical knowledge building back to Greco-Roman argumentation, Anzaldúa insisted that she was "trying to present another way of ordering and composing, another rhetoric" (253). Because Anzaldúa's explanation of conocimiento does not originate from a personal telos, individual purpose, or the good intentions of a strong moral authority, understanding what it means requires more than simply accepting the writer's authority, memorizing her key themes, or even applying them to one's life. Where a reader habituated to Aristotelian compositions might expect Anzaldúa's appeals to be presented in a deductive linear organization with a thesis or goal statement clearly stating those claims, Anzaldúan rhetoric means entering into a circular process of listening and parsing connections among interconnected stances, experiences, and symbols. It means building a bridge between oneself and those objects. In other words, we stress that the nonlinear approach that Anzaldúa takes to writing about conocimiento is a clue to how we might rethink ethos as constructed between individuals and elements of their environments and histories.

We highlight this complexity because Anzaldúa presents the path to con-ocimiento in "now let us shift" as seven stages (suggesting a progression) *and* spaces (suggesting positions or stances from which one might speak). We understand Anzaldúa's slippage between stages and spaces as central to the unique form of authority described in the essay, reflecting both methodological and cultural frameworks. Because the symbolic terrain represents both stages and spaces, an individual continually develops while moving across it, while also being situated within the different ecologies that result from the networks of discourse and material she encounters. Like the Coatlicue figure that Anzaldúa uses when symbolizing how dualisms of life (like destruction and creation) can be synthesized, we suggest that the use of stage *and* space enacts a both/and of positioning and movement. Drawing on difrasismo, we read her use of stage/space to reflect one crucial both/and of a networked ethos.

As Anzaldúa explains, the stages

> symbolize los siete "ojos de luz" or seven chakras of the energetic, dream-body, spirit body (counterpart of the physical body), the seven planes of reality, the four stages of the alchemical process (negredo, albedo, citrin-itas, and rubedo), and the four elements: air, fire, water, and earth. (545)

Each stage/space involves telling at least one story (and often many stories) of past experience and presenting one key mythological symbol (and often many symbols) that processes the experience. Anzaldúa positions these symbolic dwelling places to reclaim female spiritual symbols demonized because of their incessant search for knowledge. Xochiquetzal, the "Mexican indigenous deity" who "ascends to the upperworld to seek knowledge from 'el arbol sagrado,'" and Eve who "snatches the fruit (the treasure of forbidden knowl-edge) from the serpent's mouth and 'invents' consciousness" both ground cultural narratives that negatively position women's paths to understanding (143). While the stories that begin each stage arise from an individual, they extend outward to discuss how one relates to her environment. In another example of difrasismo, these stories and actions are both personal and so-cial—particularly when the audience or reader of the essay is understood not as a passive observer but instead as a participant in the story called on to respond, relate, understand, or simply bear witness. Anzaldúa's personal stories are never simply personal. Through this circular pattern of movement through story, symbol, and the feminist reclamation of women and deities, Anzaldúa introduces her reader to a number of interconnected generative dwelling places that are linked in a process of becoming. We might think of those locations through a shorthand language: dislocating, suspending, claiming, remembering, composing, connecting, and networking.

We have developed this shorthand in an attempt to build bridges between the stories and symbols of this theory and Greco-Roman rhetorical feminism. It reflects our own positions and those that we have inherited through dis-ciplinary training. While Anzaldúa separates these spaces, and we've given them a name in order to identify them within our writing, we stress that these stages resist being divided and hierarchized. (Press us, and we'll tell you about the multiple times we have tried and failed.) Instead, each stage encompasses parts of others, and the whole of the pathway to knowing takes the shape of something like a spiraling trajectory (or "zigzagging" as she describes on p. 545) that passes repeatedly through key "moments" along a circular pathway, each moment recalling other past movements in something like a spiral of spirals. Thus, the stages are not linear steps (not that any process ever is) but instead dispositions-in-place that are inhabited and materialized in a process of thinking and acting that is long, unfolding, painful, both inward and outwardly focused, and recursive. Conocimiento involves complex emo-tions, responding to situations beyond one's control, and finding peace and perspective in the midst of personal and communal conflict.

The Seven Stages of Conocimiento

In the following paragraphs, we describe the seven rhetorical spaces on the pathway to conocimiento, focusing on a key experience and a central symbol.[5] We do not present these stages/spaces as coherent practices in order to stay as true as possible to the essay's logic, which resists generalizing or rendering any location static. These symbols represent an alternative *topos* that con-structs authority from which to invent in opposition to thinking that divides thought from emotion, spirituality, or experience. Taken together, the process of inhabited linked places combines cultivating cultural/critical awareness, actively composing responses, paying attention to the possibilities enacted, and seeking out and building alliances with others who work outside binaries.

Stage One: el arrebato . . . rupture, fragmentation
. . . an ending, a beginning (dislocating)

> You're strolling downtown. Suddenly the sidewalk buckles and rises before you. Bricks fly through the air. Your thigh muscles tense to run, but shock holds you in check. Dust rains down all around you, dimming your sight, clogging your nostrils, coating your throat. In front of you the second story of a building caves into the ground floor . . . (542).

Anzaldúa begins the process with the earth, la tierra, and with losing the ground beneath us[6] or our placement. In this stage, there is a simultaneous loss of self, place, and safety. The metaphor for this stage is the earthquake that uplifts us, while throwing our relationship to the world off balance. We lose our footing, as who we are and where we thought we were is ruptured. We are dislocated. Anzaldúa introduces us to Coyolxauhqui, the dismembered moon goddess to symbolize the split of the "body/mind/spirit/soul" (546).

When we experience violence and oppression, we develop a heightened sense of awareness: the kind that is materialized in hair that stands up when you enter a dangerous situation. Anzaldúa labels this "la facultad," or the "the capacity to see in surface phenomena the meaning of deeper realities to see the deep structure below the surface" (*Borderlands* 60). La facultad is a perceptiveness that allows us to quickly see beneath the surface of what appears benign and ever present. La facultad operates outside of our consciousness, outside of language and logos, and instead, in feelings, images, and senses. La facultad emerges when we are forced away from the comfort of home, which can lull us into dullness or complacency. The "susto," the shock, rattles us into awareness.

Stage Two: neplanta . . . torn between ways (suspending)

> There's only one other Chicana in your PhD program at UT Austin, Texas, a state heavily populated with Chicanos, and you're never in the same class. The professors dislike the practice of putting yourself into the texts, insisting your papers are too subjective. They frown on your unorthodox perspectives and ways of thinking . . . Bereft of your former frame of reference, leaving home has cast you adrift in the liminal space

between home and school. In class you feel you're on a rack, body prone across the equator between the diverse notions and nations that comprise you . . . (548)

Anzaldúa begins the second stage with the experience of feeling out of place in every place, of being in between two differing and competing spaces and worldviews of her home and school. Anzaldúa labels this in-between space "Nepantla," which comes from the "Nahuatl word meaning tierra entre medio" (preface, *This Bridge We Call Home*). The in-between place allows us to see from different perspectives as both a participant and a distanced observer (549).

In the transition to this positioning, we become a double-faced woman, "una cara in her profile and the other looking ahead" (549). As the symbol for this step, the double-faced woman operates through suspension, testing competing theories and experiences of the world we inhabit against one another, not to achieve compatibility but rather a full awareness in which everything that has been split (mind/body; everyday and the sacred; material and spiritual) exists alongside each other. Eventually, Anzaldúa writes, a new identity will emerge.

Stage Three: the Coatlicue state . . . desconocimiento and the cost of knowing (claiming)

You're furious with your body for limiting your artistic activities, for its slow crawl toward the grave. You're infuriated with yourself for not living up to your expectations. . . . Guilt and bitterness gnaw your insides and, blocked by your own grand expectations, you're unable to function. You double over. Clinging to the rail you look down. Con tus otros ojos you see the black hole of anger sucking you into the abode of the shadow. Que desgracia. (550)

How does one react at "the reality of having a disease that could cost you your feet, your eyes, your creativity . . . the life of the writer you've worked so hard to build?" (450). Anzaldúa opens her discussion of the third stage by narrating a moment three weeks after being formally diagnosed with diabetes.

The "Coatlicue state" is the symbol of the "hellish third phase of your journey." Coatlicue, the Aztec "Mother of Gods," "depicts the contradictory" and "the fusion of opposites" (*Borderlands* 69). Coatlicue represents more than duality: as the "Goddess of birth and death," depicted with a head of rattlesnakes, eagle claws, and necklace of hearts and open hands, she "gives and takes away life; she is the incarnation of cosmic processes" (*Borderlands* 68). As the "prelude to a crossing," (*Borderlands* 70), the Coatlicue state describes another central paradox of learning and becoming: moving closer to knowing means embracing moments of despair, desconocimiento, and failure. As we define and position ourselves, we often hide failures. However, Anzaldúa asks us to experience and reflect on the unthinkable, as the "knowledge that exposes your fears can also remove them" (53). Claiming the negative and painful is a necessary step toward transformation: "our greatest disappointments and painful experiences—if we make meanings out of them—can lead us toward becoming more of who we are" (*Borderlands* 68).

*Stage Four: the call . . . el compromiso . . . the
crossing and conversion (remembering)*

> It feels like you are giving birth to a huge stone. Something pops out, you fall back onto the mattress in blessed relief. Is this what it feels like to die? Cool and light as a feather you float near the ceiling looking down at your body spread-eagle on the bed. (555)

Anzaldúa invokes the fourth stage in the path to conocimiento by relaying an out-of-body feeling following a moment that mimics both giving birth and experiencing death. Removed from the constraints of perspective that had been previously imposed, Anzaldúa describes reentering the body feeling "not contained by your race, class, gender, or sexual identity" in such a spirit that breaks the "mind/body, matter/spirit dichotomy" (555).

The *naguala*, the Mesoamerican shapeshifter with the ability to take animal form, is the first dominant symbol of the fourth stage. Answering the call of the moon and Coyolxauhqui, we invite the alternative perspective of "el jaguar, tu doble" and then "re-member . . . experiences in a new arrangement" (556) and in turn "reshape [our] present" (556). Doing so is not only an act of self-identification, but of learning how we can contribute to local communities. The naguala now represents our ability to find a "core passion, which will reveal a sense of purpose" that connects us to the world around us (557). Anzaldúa explores this through the metaphor of the bridge: crossing the bridge initiates change but is also an act of converting oneself by building connection: "Recognizing the preciousness of the earth, the sanctity of every human being on the planet, the ultimate unity and interdependence of all things" (558).

Stage Five: putting Coyolxauhqui together . . . new personal and collective "stories" (composing)

> Returning from the land of the dead, you wake up in the hospital bed minus your ovaries and uterus. Scattered around you en pedazos is the old story's corpse with its perceptions of who you used to be. (558)

Anzaldúa opens the fifth stage by describing the feeling of waking up after a surgery that radically reframed her body and identity. One's former self and body unrecognizable, this stage involves abandoning the desire for a return to the past in favor of a new composition, one that revises "the scripts of your various identities" such that one might "use these new narratives to intervene in the cultures' existing dehumanizing stories" (559). Through loss and dismemberment, "you shed your former bodymind and its outworn story like a snake its skin" (559), creating new narratives that "embod[y] alternative potentials" (559).

As evidenced here, the final phases of "now let us shift" consider acts of making (story, narrative, self) to be productive responses to being aware that reality is constructed. In the fifth stage, reassembling what has previously been fragmented is described as the beginning of productive action. As in her other works, Anzaldúa refers to this creative process as "putting Coyolxauhqui back together," again invoking the Aztec story of the moon goddess daughter of Coatlicue who was dismembered by her brother, Huitzilopochtli. The stage involves resisting easy relationships between individual and collective. It emerges from the deep pain of losing what has previously connected oneself to a collective identity while producing the possibility of forging connections in new ways. Writing stories that narrate "shifts of consciousness as they play out in your daily activities," connects to collective experience and recreates a "group/cultural story" (560). The most powerful new compositions, Anzaldúa argues, question dominant narratives and rework ideas like progress and manifest destiny. This process of making new stories is the end, not the stories themselves. To create new stories, we must resist the idea that we will eventually get it right, that somehow we will create the permanent story, "not carved in stone but drawn on sand and subject to shifting winds" (578).

Stage Six: the blow-up . . . a clash of realities (connecting)

> You fly in from another speaking gig on the East Coast, arriving at the feminist academic conference late. Hayas un desmadre. A racist

incident has unleashed flames of anger held in check for decades. In postures of defiance, enraged women of color protest their exclusion from the women's organization decision-making processes; "white" middle-class women stand, arms crossed, refusing to alter its policies. When they continue conducting business as usual las mujeres de colores walk out. (563)

Anzaldúa begins this stage by conveying a moment at a feminist conference in which tensions between women of color and white feminists were high. Narrating the moment, she explains how white feminists refuse to acknowledge their own relationship to racism at the same time that women of color "fall into the trap of claiming moral higher ground" leading to an impasse (565). The bridge that was a dominant metaphor to describe the acts of making central to this space now "buckles under the weight of these feminist factions" (567).

Facing this dissonance and collapse head on, Anzaldúa describes drawing on connectivity to address binaries and disconnections that come from these challenges. When alliances collapse, Anzaldúa reintroduces the *nepantlera*, who looks across boundaries "from both sides of the divide" and forges dialogue. In moments like this, we must "know [our] work lies in positioning [ourselves]—exposed and raw—in the crack between these worlds, and in revealing current categories as unworkable" (567). Listening across difference to all sides of the debate, "las nepantleras attempt to see through the other's situation to her underlying unconscious desire" (567). This means "accepting doubts and ambiguity" not with the end of convincing another to change her mind, but to "reframe the conflict and shift the point of view" (567). This act of connecting requires a new form of vision and sensation:

> *When perpetual conflict erodes a sense of connectedness and wholeness* la nepantlera calls on the "connectionist" faculty to show the deep common ground and interwoven kinship among all things and people. This faculty, one of less structured thoughts, less rigid categorizations, and thinner boundaries, allows us to picture—via reverie, dreaming, and artistic creativity—similarities instead of solid divisions. (567–68, italics added)

Nepantleras offer rituals for setting aside past experiences and ways of being that prevent us from hearing and connecting with others as whole beings (569), which includes "spiritual techniques (mindfulness, openness, receptivity) along with activist practices" that remind us of our relatedness (568).

Stage Seven: shifting realities . . . acting out the
vision or spiritual activism (networking)

> You're three years old and standing by the kitchen table staring at the
> bright orange globe. You can almost taste its sweet tartness. You'll die
> if you don't have it. You reach for it but your arms are too short. Body
> quivering, you stretch again, willing yourself to reach the fruit. Your arms
> elongate until your small hands clasp the orange. You sense you're more
> than one body—each superimposed on the other like sheaths of corn . .
> . . The ability to recognize and endow meaning to everyday experience
> (spirituality) furthers the ability to shift and transform (68).

The culmination of the path to conocimiento is a vast interconnectedness
that is itself a rhetorical space. Anzaldúa introduces this stage by reflecting
on a moment as a child, seeing the "bright orange globe" of an orange (connected, presumably, to the tree she referenced earlier) and willing her arms to
lengthen to grasp the object of her desire. In her reach, she realizes that her
arm and body have become multiple and simultaneously located. Through
this image of desire, contemplation, and shifting, she launches into the sev-
enth stage as a spiritual activism that involves a constant shift of recognition
with others, sensing positions through what she calls a "move to a roundtable"
(570). Identified again as the position of "la naguala," this "knowing/knower"
is distinct from ego-driven positioning: it involves seeing from the perspective
of the other (a material object or a person) while knowing that one can act; it
is in this sense rhetorical. Although Anzaldúa highlights that individuals are
foundational to this work, their authority only emerges when they displace
their egos, engage their connection to others, and thus "la naguala and the
object observed merge" (569).

Importantly, Anzaldúa highlights that this form of connecting will not
always be successful. She notes that "it doesn't work with things that are
insurmountable, or with all people at all times" and its impacts may be slow.
She stresses that it takes others to make change: "it works with las nepantleras,
boundary-crossers, thresholders who initiate others in rites of passage, ac-
tivistas who, from a listening, receptive, spiritual stance, rise to their own
visions and shift into acting them out, haciendo mundo nuevo (introducing
change)" (571). Here the position or space she introduces is a bridge of fire,
"Las nepantleras walk through fire on many bridges . . . by turning the flames
into a radiance of awareness that orients, guides, and supports those who

cannot cross on their own" (571). It is within this space that we can articulate a "discourse of signs, images, feelings, words" that articulates experience for a moment, but that is not an isolated point of view, but instead an interconnected web of meaning. This connectivity comes also from avoiding the "rush of continual doing" (572) that disallows the reflection, contemplation, and spirituality that ultimately are central to creating group purpose. It is a completely different sense of how we construct authority or character with/in relationship to a community: the work of continually seeking alliance and knowing that the work lies in the "constant transition, the most unsafe of all spaces" (574).

From Locating to Interconnecting Rhetorical Contributions from Women of Color

In the concluding passages after introducing each stage, Anzaldúa offers another experience/symbol/image "as a ritual . . . prayer . . . blessing . . . for transformation" (574). Near the mouth of the ocean, the ritual involves drawing a circle in the sand as a symbol of connectivity. Anzaldúa moves then to face each direction; each position correlates with an element and experience. The circle is completed, and we look downward, "honoring those whose backs served as bridges" (576), and then look upward, praying that our love will "inspire others to act" (576).

This concluding ritual enacted through movement along cardinal points shifts us to our reading of how theoretical contributions from Anzaldúa and other women of color are located with respect to broader conversations in rhetorical scholarship. As we look through texts that have honored her as a bridge, Anzaldúa's applicability to the concerns of rhetoric and composition has often been located *unilaterally* rather than multidirectionally, positioned rather than networked. Her theory is often understood as relevant to a narrow range of rhetorical practices and bodies. Analyzing Anzaldúa's uptake in rhetoric and composition (and Anzaldúa's own subsequent shock at the field's enthusiasm), Wendy Hesford and Eileen Schell write, "Anzaldúa's canonical location is emblematic of the field's modernist tendencies, namely how we continue to privilege the postcolonial writer, over the study of the transnational and postcolonial rhetorical practices" (461). The irony, they note, is that theoretical scholarship in rhetoric and composition often canonizes an individual writer but does not "redefine the field's terrain and its objects of study" in relationship to the thinking of that theorist (462). While Hesford and Schell analyze this as a problem for transnational praxis, we might reframe their concern as a problem of ethos. Their insight that the authority arising from nonnormative positions tends to be located and associated with their bodies rather than the theories, praxis, or practice they describe presents a challenge for theories of ethos as location. When a writer's authority is positioned as inextricably bound to her embodiment, the ideas and engagement she describes can be positioned as applicable only to people with bodies like hers. While scholars like Yvonne Yarbro-Bejarano have written at length about the problems of applying Anzaldúa's work in contexts that write out its materialities (such as using the "border" as a metaphor rather than a material location), there is also a danger in hyperlocating her theory: rendering it relevant only to bodies most like her own or abstracting only narrow principles while minimizing more holistic lessons.

Again, feminists of color have theorized this problem. As Chela Sandoval has argued,

> US third world feminist criticism (which is a set of theoretical and methodological strategies) is often misrecognized and underanalyzed by readers when it is translated as a demographic constituency (women of color only) and not as a theoretical and methodological approach in its own right. (171)

Building on Sandoval, to position Anzaldúa as a representative of a particular community or group (i.e., Chicana, indigenous, queer, multilingual) and assume that her contribution lies in her ability to represent the experience of that group is to rely on a static sense of authority and knowledge that is untrue to the networked, dynamic potential waiting to be realized in her theory. Anzaldúa's writing continually challenges readers to accept and complete the bridge for which her writing lays foundation, and the "positions" or dwelling places that theory develops are multiple, dense, and resist reduction.

Relatedly, to read Anzaldúa's theory as only about individual consciousness raising and the connection between embodiment and voice is, again, to reduce her theoretical impact by grounding it in a static sense of authority. "How to Tame a Wild Tongue," from *Borderlands/La Frontera*, read in its historical context, is situated in a particular moment of "identity crisis" in critical theory.[7] As these problems were debated in rhetoric and composition, the field increasingly recognized that writers mirrored their social locations in rhetorical, linguistic, and stylistic choices. The multiple languages of "How to Tame a Wild Tongue" and, indeed, Anzaldúa's personal narrative, are read in her text and in her body as important for claims about hybrid texts of all mediums and for arguments about language diversity (see for example Canagarajah). Analyses of Anzaldúa's writing helped support this emerging understanding that writing could both consciously represent identity and bring one toward a more critical consciousness of how she has been conditioned by social and material context. However, to end an analysis of Anzaldúa's writing here is to treat it as reflecting—and not refracting—reality. In other words, to position Anzaldúa's work as a "stylistic and linguistic argument for a special voice that expresses identity" makes the dwelling place of her authority static rather than lived, located rather than networked (Flower 129).

While this way of building on Anzaldúa's work is accurate and has been generative, Anzaldúa's writing is also decidedly methodological, action-based, and public-oriented; in other words, it is rhetorical. When read from the perspective of a networked rather than static sense of authority, Anzaldúa's theory offers multiple, interconnected places to stand that can become the foundation for action, including for research (as we have described in relationship to our own past empirical scholarship) and teaching (which we hope to discuss in future scholarship) and that push us to recognize the ways positions continually change in relationship to material and social contexts. Specifically, Anzaldúa articulates, demonstrates, and operationalizes an embodied composing process of dwelling in commonplaces that invent new forms of connection. Furthermore, while Anzaldúa's epistemological invention happens through writing, the products of composing are understood to be objects that have futures beyond their immediate impact. Anzaldúa writes,

> My "stories" are acts encapsulated in time, "enacted" every time they are spoken aloud or read silently. I like to think of them as performances and not as inert and "dead" objects (as the aesthetics of Western culture think of art works). (67)

"now let us shift" opens by describing the text as *una ofrenda* to the reader consisting of interwoven "signs, images, feelings, words" (540). Anzaldúa's offerings are interconnected dwelling places on a path toward a knowledge that is both imbued with and that produces what many feminist rhetoricians value in our scholarship: connectivity, relationality, materiality. Anzaldúa's process presents a path of pathways, a journey of journeys. Though we can learn from looking separately at each of the rhetorical spaces, it is their sum that "transform[s] perceptions" and therefore "conditions of life" (540). Enacting Anzaldúa's theory of making and composing a version of the world is painful, arduous, and dangerous. We want to reiterate the slow, undulating nature of this path. Reading Anzaldúa's essay as it is written is an invitation to a process of becoming that is not only about developing as an individual rhetor, but also about interconnecting, grounding, and collectively transforming. now let us shift.

Notes

1. The work on networked transnational feminism by scholars like Dingo, for instance, brings a lens that we have found particularly compelling (p. 8–15).

2. We intentionally elected to not italicize the words with Spanish and indigenous origins to normalize their usage.

3. Writing classified as Chicana theory (or falling within the purview of Chicana studies) is diverse; many people define Chicana theory or studies through looking solely at the identification of the writer, which is not always accurate. We want to be careful, then, to avoid assuming complete agreement or stability within this body of work.

4. From this point forward in the chapter, all citations come from Anzaldúa's "now let us shift" unless otherwise noted.

5. We have adopted Anzaldúa's own naming for each stage as a way to give readers a better sense of the essay and of Anzaldúa's narrative techniques. We have coupled Anzaldúa's title for the stage with our shorthand in parenthesis to emphasize the movement for each stage (see endnote 3).

6. Throughout "now let us shift," Anzaldúa writes from a both/and perspective of first person and second person. The first person is invoked through the retelling of personal experience while simultaneously being written with the use of "you." This both/and perspective places the reader alongside/with Anzaldúa experientially. In our recapitulation of the stages, we have elected to adopt a both/and perspective as well: we discuss Anzaldúa in the third person when describing her techniques or the logos of her essay, while invoking "we" to locate ourselves as readers alongside you as audiences to the essay.

7. In her book *Visible Identities*, Linda Martín Alcoff responds to the critics of identity politics who perceive identity as a barrier to alliance, as a push to conformism, or as a "political problem." Theorists (and public intellectuals) argue that identity and acknowledging difference cannot lead to change because it *necessarily* ends up causing fragmentation. Alcoff argues instead "the *refusal* to acknowledge the importance of the differences in our identities has led to distrust, miscommunication, and thus, disunity" (6). In place of a denial of identity, Alcoff offers "a sustained defense of identity as an epistemically salient and ontologically real entity" (5). See also Moya for an articulation of identity as a vehicle through which we learn about the world we live in, and how to then act in the world.

Works Cited

Alcoff, Linda Martín. *Visible Identities: Race, Gender, and the Self.* Oxford: Oxford UP, 2006. Print.

Anzaldúa, Gloria E. *Borderlands/La Frontera: The New Mestiza.* San Francisco: Spinsters/Aunt Lute Book Company, 1987. Print.

———."now let us shift . . . the path of conocimiento . . . inner work, public acts." *this bridge we call home: radical visions for transformation.* Ed. Gloria E. Anzaldúa and AnaLouise Keating. New York: Routledge, 2002. 540–78. Print.

———."Putting Coyolxauhqui Together: A Creative Process." *How We Work.* Ed. Marla Morris, Mary Aswell Doll, and William F. Pinar. New York: Peter Lang, 1999. 241–61. Print.

———."Toward a Mestiza Rhetoric." Interview with Andrea Lunsford. *Interviews/ Entrevistas.* Ed. AnaLouise Keating. New York: Routledge, 2000. 251–80. Print.

Calafell, Bernadette Marie. "Pro(re-)claiming Loss: A Performative Pilgrimage in Search of Malintzin Tenepal." *Text and Performance Quarterly* 25 (2005): 45–58. Print.

Canagarajah, A. Suresh. "The Place of World Englishes in Composition: Pluralization Continued." *College Composition and Communication* 57.4 (2006): 586–619. Print.

Dicochea, Perlita R. "Environmental Justice on the Mexico-U.S. Border: Toward a Borderlands Methodology." *Chicana/Latina Education in Everyday Life.* Ed. Dolores Delgado Bernal, Alejandra C. Elenes, Francisca E. Godinez, and Sofia Villenas. Albany: State U of New York P, 2006. 231–43. Print.

Dingo, Rebecca. *Networking Arguments: Rhetoric, Transnational Feminism, and Public Policy Writing.* Pittsburgh: U of Pittsburgh P, 2012. Print.

Dolmage, Jay. "Metis, Mêtis, Mestiza, Medusa: Rhetorical Bodies across Rhetorical Traditions." *Rhetoric Review* 28.1 (2009): 1–28. Print.

Ede, Lisa, Cheryl Glenn, and Andrea Lunsford. "Border Crossings: Intersections of Rhetoric and Feminism." *Rhetorica: A Journal of the History of Rhetoric* 13.4 (Autumn 1995): 401–41. Print.

Enoch, Jessica. "Para La Mujer: Defining a Chicana Feminist Rhetoric at the Turn of the Century." *College English.* 67.1 (Sept. 2004): 20–37. Print.

Flower, Linda. *Community Literacy and the Rhetoric of Public Engagement.* Carbondale: Southern Illinois UP, 2008. Print.

Gaspar de Alba, Alicia. *La Llorana on the Longfellow Bridge: Poetry y Otras Movidas.* Houston: Arte Público, 2003. Print.

Heilker, Paul, and Melanie Yergeau. "Autism and Rhetoric." *College English* 73.5 (May 2011): 485–97. Print.

Hesford, Wendy S., and Eileen E. Schell. "Introduction: Configurations of Trans-nationality: Locating Feminist Rhetorics." *College English* 70.5 (May 2008): 461–70. Print.

Jarratt, Susan C., and Nedra Reynolds. "The Splitting Image: Contemporary Feminisms and the Ethics of *ethos.*" *Ethos: New Essays in Rhetorical and Critical Theory.* Ed. James S. Baumlin and Tita French Baumlin. Dallas: Southern Methodist UP, 1994. 37–63. Print.

Killingsworth, Jimmie M. "Rhetorical Appeals: A Revision." *Rhetoric Review* 24.3 (2005): 249–63. Print.

Kyburz, Bonnie Lenore. "Meaning Finds a Way: Chaos (Theory) and Composition." *College English* 66.5 (May 2004): 503–23. Print.

Leon, Kendall. "*La Hermandad* and Chicanas Organizing: The Community Rhetoric of the *Comisión Femenil Mexicana Nacional,*" *Community Literacy Journal* 7.2 (Spring 2013): 1–20. Print.

Leon, Kendall, and Stacey Pigg. "Graduate Students Professionalizing in Digital Time/Space: A View from 'Down Below.'" *Computers and Composition* 28 (2011): 3–13. Print.

Licona, Adela C. *Zines in Third Space: Radical Cooperation and Borderlands Rhetoric.* Albany: State U of New York P, 2012. Print.

Lu, Min-Zhan. "Professing Multiculturalism: The Politics of Style in the Contact Zone." *College Composition and Communication* 45.4 (Dec. 1994): 442–58. Print.

Lunsford, Andrea. "Toward a Mestiza Rhetoric: Gloria Anzaldúa on Composition and Postcoloniality." *JAC: A Journal of Composition Theory* 18.1 (1998): 1–28. Print.

Moraga, Cherríe. "La Güera." *This Bridge Called My Back: Writings by Radical Women of Color.* Ed. Cherríe Moraga and Gloria Anzaldúa. 3rd ed. Berkeley, CA: Third Woman, 2002. 24–33. Print.

Moya, Paula. *Learning from Experience: Minority Identities, Multicultural Struggles.* Berkeley: U of California P, 2002. Print.

Pérez, Emma. *The Decolonial Imaginary: Writing Chicanas into History.* Bloomington: Indiana UP, 1999. Print.

Pittman, Corretta. "Black Women Writers and the Trouble with Ethos: Harriet Jacobs, Billie Holiday, and Sister Souljah." *Rhetoric Society Quarterly* 37 (2007): 43–70. Print.

Pérez, Emma. *The Decolonial Imaginary: Writing Chicanas into History.* Bloomington: Indiana UP, 1999. Print.

Pérez, Laura. *Chicana Art: The Politics of Spiritual and Aesthetic Altarities.* Durham, NC: Duke UP, 2007. Print.

Ritchie, Joy, and Kathleen Boardman. "Feminism in Composition: Inclusion, Metonymy, and Disruption." *College Composition and Communication* 50.4 (1999): 585–606. Print.

Sandoval, Chela. *Methodology of the Oppressed.* Minneapolis: U of Minnesota P, 2000. Print.

Schmertz, Johanna. "Constructing Essences: Ethos and the Postmodern Subject of Feminism." *Rhetoric Review* 18.1 (Autumn 1999): 82–91. Print.

Trimbur, John. "Linguistic Memory and the Politics of U.S. English." *College English* 68.6 (July 2006): 575–88. Print.

Yarbro-Bejarano, Yvonne. "Gloria Anzaldua's *Borderlands/La Frontera*: Cultural Studies, 'Difference,' and the Non-Unitary Subject." *Cultural Critique* 28 (1994): 5–28. Print.

Wallace, David L. "Alternative Rhetoric and Morality: Writing from the Margins." *College Composition and Communication* 61.2 (2009): 18–39. Print.

Afterwords
Contributors
Index

Afterwords

Twenty years ago, Andrea Lunsford claimed that the scholars' words and women's rhetorics in *Reclaiming Rhetorica: Women in the Rhetorical Tradition* were "a portent of things to come" (319). That collection of sixteen original chapters concluded with the writers' reflections on past, present, and future issues and research questions about women's rhetorics. Here, we echo that practice from *Reclaiming Rhetorica* as a means of enacting the kind of feminist ecological ethē we theorize. Chapter writers responded to four questions tied to this collection's argument and the future of feminist rhetorical studies, and we title this section "Afterwords," rather than "Afterword," to highlight this collaboration. We offer these afterwords with the hope of forwarding and igniting new and nuanced directions for teaching and studying ethos and deploying feminist ecological habits of mind as we engage new questions.

Kathleen J. Ryan, Nancy Myers, and Rebecca Jones

Implications of a Feminist Ecological Subject for Ethos Construction

This collection has advocated for analyzing how feminist ethē develop in close relationship with the world and the objects, technologies, cultural values, and other people who reside in it. This sense of ethos is ecological because it forces us to decenter the human subject and revisit its interconnected relationship with other materials. One implication for thinking this way is that we should also understand theorists' authority as constructed in relation to their place in cultural and material ecologies. That is to say, theories cycle through moments of prominence and then intermittently fade into the periphery as the material and social contexts around them shift. There are moments when ideas that have been there all along suddenly resonate in new ways, leading us to feel as if we've discovered something. Sometimes, perhaps even often, these gems existed all along, but what has changed is that we have become attuned to them.

We raise this discussion because the current scholarly moment in rhetoric studies seems to call for theories, metaphors, and lenses for thinking that can help us reconsider the relationship among human and nonhuman agents, as well as the role of materiality and affiliations in rhetorical action. It is our hope that our contribution to this collection will remind readers that Chicana theorizing as it emerged and was enacted has *always* been ecological, material, and relational. However, rhetoric studies may not yet be broadly attuned to understanding the possibilities that Chicana feminism offers for understanding materiality and connectivity. At the same time, we think that Chicana theory has implications for helping us complicate how ecological metaphors direct our gaze. One danger of ecological thinking is that it can be read as naturalizing interconnections, such that they appear to have naturally evolved rather than to have been actively constructed. We shift because we are shifted and because we shift ourselves. *Kendall Leon and Stacey Pigg*

I particularly appreciate how the collection interrogates and retheorizes, both implicitly and explicitly, normative, outmoded notions of ethos that are not particularly germane to our contemporary situation. Indeed, as the editors elucidate, considerations of ethos should be responsive to the contexts and oppressions within which all humans are compelled to function, yet for too long such considerations have been beyond the realm of conceivability or articulation in rhetorical studies or—worse—silenced or marginalized. This collection compels readers to consider that our positioning in a transnational world—one that is situated at a political, moral, and ecological crossroads—requires a worldview that presumes difference and fluidity, contemplates the implications of oppression, and understands that knowing, acting, and decision making produce consequences not only for ourselves, but also for others. The editors make this shift meaningful and palpable through their careful retheorizing of ethos.

Valerie Palmer-Mehta

On Feminist Ecological Habits of Mind and Pedagogy

While I have enjoyed the opportunity to consider the multiple ethē that women construct and negotiate throughout their rhetorical enterprises, I have been struck by the power of what is called in the introduction an "ecological habit of mind." It seems that ecological ethē as a concept emerges from that very ecological habit of mind; concomitantly, approaching ethos as ecological requires a similar habit of mind on the part of the rhetor. That is, deliberate negotiation of (and among) multiple ethē emerges from an awareness of the existence of those ethē as rhetorical resources. Thus, *ecological ethē* becomes an important component not only of how we "do" rhetoric but also how we teach rhetoric. Discovering the ways in which women deploy multiple ethē to interrupt, advocate, and relate constitutes only a starting point, albeit an absolutely essential one. Encouraging such deployment in a generation of girls growing up in a culture that continues to subject them to violence, marginalization, and economic deprivation requires a new way of teaching ethē as well as a new way of conceptualizing or performing it.

Kristie S. Fleckenstein

Exploring the rhetorics of yoga has sparked my interest in the spatial dynamics of this contemplative practice—how it both teaches a process and an ethics of moving bodies—and how these dynamics connect to classical concepts like "ethos," especially since this term has recently been approached as place-based dwelling. In essence, the collection has helped me to bridge feminist pedagogy to feminist rhetorics. Given that our current academic culture still values rhetorical work over pedagogical work in many cases, this bridging is essential not only for my work as a feminist scholar but also to strengthen the connection between theory and application and to illuminate their synergy. As I move forward, I'd like to continue to explore what alternative concepts yoga may provide feminist rhetors and to bridge these rhetorical concepts to the pedagogical questions that originally inspired my research.

Christy I. Wenger

This collection demonstrates how ecological, interactional models of rhetoric look in action. Once we understand how individuals are putting these theories to work, we can figure out how to fold these approaches into our instruction so that we can condition our undergraduates to conceive of their responsibility as speaker and audience in different ways. We can learn from these examples how to direct our graduate students' understanding of the evolution of rhetorical theory as informed by feminism, pragmatism, ecological studies, environmentalism, and more. This collection demonstrates how these broader philosophical movements direct our basic understanding of communication and meaning-making. *Mary Beth Pennington*

In the end, I hope my students feel called to imagine new possibilities for their writing and their lives by deconstructing more conventional notions of ethos and building a more ecologically and politically layered ethē—one conscious of its own making, its own time, its own failures and possibilities. In a time of common core and state standards, the future of education itself in this country is dependent on helping our students resist, extend beyond, and imagine out of the systemic and masculinist ways of thinking that shape their notions of self, text, and world. *Stacey Waite*

Hopes for This Collection's Contribution

In "Global Turns and Cautions in Rhetoric and Composition" (*PMLA* 2006), I claimed that as rhetorical scholarship reorients itself toward an examination of the global that it will increasingly need to pursue interdisciplinary and collaborative work. I argued then and believe even more strongly now that the "global turn" in rhetorical studies requires that we forge newly imagined geographies and methodologies for the field, and yet that we also remain apprehensive about idealistic notions of global civil society and attentive to the challenges of interdisciplinary work. Correspondingly, my contribution to this edited collection argues for an understanding of feminist ethos as an interdisciplinary analytic, as a method that broadens our understanding of the sociopolitical and legal consequences, mobilization, and translation of women's human rights discourses. *Wendy S. Hesford*

I hope this collection contributes to a radical and comprehensive reconsideration of the traditional, androcentric, heteronormative foundations of western rhetoric, which, despite copious efforts by some contemporary scholars, continue to serve as the foundation of much of our rhetorical thinking and practice. *Valerie Palmer-Mehta*

As I came to develop a more sophisticated understanding of Zitkala-Ša's ability—as a rhetor, as a writer, as an artist, as an advocate, and as a woman—to move strategically between subject positions, I also struggled as a scholar with appropriate and effective ways to convey Zitkala-Ša's individualized identity—her subjectivity, her ethos, her constructed essences—to contemporary audiences. Even as my research confirmed, for me, that rhetorical power and agency resides within multiplicity, I struggled with repeated requests from advisors, editors, and readers who insisted that I name my "subject" and construct her "subjectivity" as a singular entity with one stable, fixed form of identity.

Certainly as the editors of this collection note in their thoughtful introduction, agency is always contingent, and the strategic employment of rhetorical agency includes recognizing that individuals are often constrained by social conventions and "assigned" subject positions. Existing academic and textual conventions also require named subjects and defined subjectivities. At a minimum, perhaps my research on Zitkala-Ša's legacy as a political advocate will continue to trouble and challenge traditional notions of naming, the subject, and subjectivity as fixed and singular concepts, particularly for marginalized or doubly marginalized rhetors. It is my hope that feminist rhetorical studies will continue to adopt and critically examine habits of mind that are multifaceted and certainly more ecologically focused.

Paige A. Conley

I hope this work serves as an invitation to welcome a broader range of contributors to rhetorical scholarship and at the same time to expand the kinds of figures we choose to examine. I think feminist studies often omit female subjects who don't fit a certain mold. The scope of feminist/women's studies ought to be more inclusive. *Lynée Lewis Gaillet*

New Visions, Directions, and Questions

It's been interesting for me to work on a project that speaks to a vision of "women's rhetorics" when my gender is a somewhat amorphous and ambiguous one that may or may not be considered "woman." Importantly, however, thinking of myself in these terms reminds me that those of us who occupy those "counterpublic" positions do, as Michael Warner suggests, "intuitively understand relations of power" and that feminist and queer visions of our world learn more from staying close to one another in those messy and overlapping ways we already are. Audre Lorde often spoke in speeches and in essays about the insidiousness of a "divide and conquer" politics whereby feminists (or any group trying to work for change) spend a large amount of time arguing among themselves rather than working together. So this project reminds me of the ways that feminist and queer undertakings are joined, even as we can notice (and hopefully celebrate) their differences.

But I do think creating spaces for queer and feminist intersections (at conferences, in journals, in institutions, and in politics) is something we need to work at again and again in order to keep the connections lively, rich, and mutually informing. To many, of course, the connections seem obvious, but I often find myself seeing the words "feminist" and "queer" circulating in different circles of study. The closer and more explicitly we can bring these notions to one another, the more our ethē can be informed by the contradictory, unstable, and shifting ideas of the future itself.   *Stacey Waite*

The editors remind us that "we live in one world," a world that contains the hopeful feminist ethē outlined here but also the persistent cultural belief that women's voices and experiences matter less than men's. I want to push this idea even further. As we move forward to investigate transformative feminist rhetorical concepts and theories, I hope we will continue to look across cultures for new ideas. We live in one globalized world, after all. The challenge of this cross-cultural reach is not leaving the context and philosophical import of the ideas we may borrow and reshape as we use them for feminist work in the West. I'm constantly resisting the notion that embracing the body from a contemplative stance means accepting radical individualism or essentialism. This kind of oppositional thinking characterizes Western ideology, not so easily Eastern philosophy. It may be thorny to take on cross-cultural and transnational thinking and maintain openness to the new worldviews this exposes, but it may be one of the most valuable lessons of a feminist ecological epistemology. It's also a process that I would argue can be aided by a hefty dose of applied mindfulness.   *Christy I. Wenger*

What might we discover if we "borrow" concepts from ecology to further investigate the nature of ecological ethē? Let me offer three examples. First, what might we discover about ethē if we consider homeostasis: how—or do—women negotiate multiple ethē to maintain a "steady state," or a sense of an identity that, if not singular or discrete, at least possesses a contingent unity? Along the same lines, how do multiple contingent ethē become reified within a culture's gender ideology and presented implicitly as the available means of persuasion especially as manifested in the continuing dominance of a male-female gender binary?

Second, what insights into ecological ethē might we derive from the emergence of "resilience thinking" in ecological studies? If current theorizing in environmental studies emphasizes resilience—the ability of a natural system to maintain its health within certain thresholds or parameters—to what degree, then, might resilience be an important component of ecological ethē? What constitutes the parameters of an ethos-system? What forces push that system beyond its thresholds? Or what forces alter the nature of the thresholds in such a way that the system's identity is transformed?

Finally, what about the failures of ecological systems? If multiple ethē constitute an ecological system comprised of interrelating components that gain identity through those interrelationships, then how might decisions made at one level threaten the identity or health of the system as a whole? I am reminded here of a story that Gregory Bateson recounts in *Angels Fear* in which the Native American Church was under siege for its use of peyote in a key ceremony. Sol Tax, an anthropologist, offered to film the ceremony to demonstrate the religious significance of the peyote. After much discussion, however, the members declined the offer, explaining that, by so doing, they would sacrifice the integrity of the religion as a means to save the religion whose very purpose was to foster integrity.   *Kristie S. Fleckenstein*

Work Cited

Lunsford, Andrea A., ed. *Reclaiming Rhetorica: Women in the Rhetorical Tradition.* Pittsburgh: U of Pittsburgh P, 1995. Print.

Contributors

Editors

Rebecca Jones is a University of Chattanooga Foundation associate professor of rhetoric and composition at the University of Tennessee–Chattanooga. She has published articles on protest, activist rhetorics, and argumentation studies in *Enculturation; Composition Studies; Writing on the Edge* (reprinted in Parlor Press's *Best of the Independent Rhetoric and Composition Journals, 2013*), and the collection *Activism and Rhetoric: Theories and Contexts for Political Engagement.*

Nancy Myers, an associate professor of English at the University of North Carolina–Greensboro, served as president of the Coalition of Women Scholars in the History of Rhetoric and Composition from 2010 to 2012. Her feminist publications include essays in *Political Women: Language and Leadership; Rhetoric, History, and Women's Oratorical Education; Rhetoric: Concord and Controversy*; and *Silence and Listening as Rhetorical Arts.*

Kathleen J. Ryan is an assistant professor of rhetoric and writing at Montana State University. She is a coauthor of *GenAdmin: Theorizing WPA Identities in the Twenty-First Century,* and she coedited *Walking and Talking Feminist Rhetorics: Landmark Essays and Controversies* with Lindal Buchanan. Her current research examines intersections between feminist rhetorical studies and ecological feminism.

Chapter Contributors

Risa Applegarth is an associate professor of English at the University of North Carolina at Greensboro. Her research on gender and genre has appeared in *College Composition and Communication, Rhetoric Society Quarterly*, and *College English* as well as in her book *Rhetoric in American Anthropology: Gender, Genre, and Science* (Pittsburgh 2014). Her current research examines children's rhetorical agency and activism.

Sean Barnette, an associate professor in the Department of English and Foreign Languages at Lander University in Greenwood, South Carolina, teaches writing, rhetoric, and linguistics courses. His main scholarly interests include first-year writing pedagogy and theories of hospitality, material rhetoric, and religion.

Paige A. Conley is a full-time member of the English faculty at Milwaukee Area Technical College in Wisconsin, where she teaches courses in writing and literature. Her scholarly interests include developmental writing, composition theory and pedagogy, civic engagement, public activism, and early twentieth-century histories of rhetoric and composition.

Beth Daniell recently retired from the English department at Kennesaw State University, where she taught writing, rhetorical theory, literacy theory, and research methods. She is the author of *A Communion of Friendship* and a coeditor of *Women and Literacy* and *Renovating Rhetoric in Christian Tradition*. She has written on literacy, rhetoric, and pedagogy for a number of journals and collections.

Kristie S. Fleckenstein is a professor of English at Florida State University. She is the recipient of the 2005 CCCC Outstanding Book Award for *Embodied Literacies: Imageword and a Poetics of Teaching* and of the 2009 W. Ross Winterowd Award for *Vision, Rhetoric, and Social Action in the Composition Classroom*.

Lynée Lewis Gaillet is a professor and chair of the English department at Georgia State University. She is the editor of *Scottish Rhetoric and Its Influence, Stories of Mentoring*, and *The Present State of Scholarship in the History of Rhetoric*; and the coauthor of *Scholarly Publication in a Changing Academic Landscape* and *Primary Writing and Research: People, Places, and Spaces*.

Letizia Guglielmo is an associate professor of English at Kennesaw State University. Her research focuses on feminist rhetoric and pedagogy, gender and pop culture, and the intersections of feminist action and digital communication. She is the coauthor of *Scholarly Publication in a Changing Academic Landscape*, the editor of and a contributor to *MTV and Teen Pregnancy*, and the coeditor of *Contingent Faculty Publishing in Community*.

Wendy S. Hesford is a professor of English at the Ohio State University. She is the author of *Framing Identities: Autobiography and the Politics of*

Pedagogy and *Spectacular Rhetorics: Human Rights Visions, Recognitions, Feminisms*, and the winner of the 2012 Rhetoric Society of America Book Award. She has published essays and reviews in a range of journals and co-edited two collections with Wendy Kozol.

Kendall Leon is an assistant professor of rhetoric and composition and the director of technical and professional writing at Portland State University. Her current research project examines the relationship between identity and the practices of community organizations. She is also completing an empirical study on the impact of service-learning pedagogies on the rhetorical learning of composition students and instructors.

Valerie Palmer-Mehta is an associate professor in the Department of Communication and Journalism at Oakland University. Her research, which explores the intersection of rhetorical studies and gender studies, can be found in such journals and edited collections as: *Communication, Culture, and Critique*; *Text and Performance Quarterly*; *Women's Studies in Communication*; and *Mediated Moms: Contemporary Challenges to Motherhood*.

Mary Beth Pennington is a lecturer in the English department at Old Dominion University in Norfolk, Virginia, where she teaches courses in introductory and advanced writing, as well as literature, and has served as interim director of composition. Her research interests include the rhetorical identity of Appalachians, activist rhetorics, and intersections of literature and rhetoric.

Stacey Pigg is an assistant professor of scientific and technical communication at North Carolina State University, where she teaches courses in professional communication, rhetorical theory, and digital writing. Her research analyzes the impact of mobile and networked writing technologies and has appeared in journals such as *College Composition and Communication, Rhetoric Society Quarterly, Technical Communication Quarterly*, and *Written Communication*.

Stacey Waite is an assistant professor of English at the University of Nebraska–Lincoln and has published essays most recently in *Writing on the Edge* and *College Composition and Communication*. She is a coeditor of *Ways of Reading: An Anthology of Writers*. Waite has published four collections of poems, including *Choke, Love Poem to Androgyny, the lake has no saint*, and *Butch Geography*.

Christy I. Wenger is an assistant professor of rhetoric and composition and English at Shepherd University in Shepherdstown, West Virginia, where she serves as the director of writing and rhetoric. She is the author of *Yoga Minds, Writing Bodies: Contemplative Writing Pedagogy*, and her articles appear in *English Teaching: Practice and Critique; JAEPL;* and *WPA: Writing Program Administration*.

Index

Page numbers in italics indicate illustrations.

Studies in Rhetorics and Feminisms

Studies in Rhetorics and Feminisms seeks to address the interdisciplinarity that rhetorics and feminisms represent. Rhetorical and feminist scholars want to connect rhetorical inquiry with contemporary academic and social concerns, exploring rhetoric's relevance to current issues of opportunity and diversity. This interdisciplinarity has already begun to transform the rhetorical tradition as we have known it (upper-class, agonistic, public, and male) into regendered, inclusionary rhetorics (democratic, dialogic, collaborative, cultural, and private). Our intellectual advancements depend on such ongoing transformation.

Rhetoric, whether ancient, contemporary, or futuristic, always inscribes the relation of language and power at a particular moment, indicating who may speak, who may listen, and what can be said. The only way we can displace the traditional rhetoric of masculine-only, public performance is to replace it with rhetorics that are recognized as being better suited to our present needs. We must understand more fully the rhetorics of the non-Western tradition, of women, of a variety of cultural and ethnic groups. Therefore, Studies in Rhetorics and Feminisms espouses a theoretical position of openness and expansion, a place for rhetorics to grow and thrive in a symbiotic relationship with all that feminisms have to offer, particularly when these two fields intersect with philosophical, sociological, religious, psychological, pedagogical, and literary issues.

The series seeks scholarly works that both examine and extend rhetoric, works that span the sexes, disciplines, cultures, ethnicities, and sociocultural practices as they intersect with the rhetorical tradition. After all, the recent resurgence of rhetorical studies has been not so much a discovery of new rhetorics as a recognition of existing rhetorical activities and practices, of our newfound ability and willingness to listen to previously untold stories.

The series editors seek both high-quality traditional and cutting-edge scholarly work that extends the significant relationship between rhetoric and feminism within various genres, cultural contexts, historical periods, methodologies, theoretical positions, and methods of delivery (e.g., film and hypertext to elocution and preaching).

Queries and submissions:
Professor Cheryl Glenn, Editor
    E-mail: cjg6@psu.edu
Professor Shirley Wilson Logan, Editor
    E-mail: slogan@umd.edu

Studies in Rhetorics and Feminisms
Department of English
142 South Burrowes Bldg.
Penn State University
University Park, PA 16802-6200